STUDIA PATRISTICA

VOL. LXXIII

© Peeters Publishers — Louvain — Belgium 2014

All rights reserved, including the right to translate or to
reproduce this book or parts thereof in any form.

D/2014/0602/99
ISBN: 978-90-429-3154-1

A catalogue record for this book is available from the Library of Congress.

Printed in Belgium by Peeters, Leuven

STUDIA PATRISTICA

VOL. LXXIII

Including papers presented at the Conference on
Early Christian Iconography,
held in Pécs, Hungary

Edited by
A. BRENT and M. VINZENT

PEETERS

LEUVEN – PARIS – WALPOLE, MA

2014

Table of Contents

Preface

The early Christian excavations at the necropolis in Pécs (Sopianae), and its sixteen monuments, that began in the 17th century, with new additional finds more recently, have brought to light a most significant European site for researchers in various disciplines. Though acknowledged and supported by UNESCO as a world heritage site (in AD 2000), a cursory literary search soon reveals that Sopianae remains neglected by many art historians, ancient historians, archaeologists, patristic scholars, classicists, and social scientists. Yet in the early Christian centuries, a soil rich in Roman artefacts, a large burial ground was gradually developed and adapted that has left us with an amazing treasure, especially for the history of the beginnings of Christianity in the Valeria Province, one of the four sub-provinces of Pannonia. As we will discover on the following pages, we have now, as a precious, shared European inheritance, one of the most didactic, but also sustainable, subterranean archaeological parks to explore.

The present volume is a collaboration between major Hungarian scholars, including leading colleagues from Pécs and other places, and the researchers who lead the British Academy funded project at King's College London on 'Early Christian Iconography – beyond Dölger,' in the years 2010-2012. Part of the remit of the project was to look into the ambiguous nature of early Christian symbols and iconographies, and to reflect critically on the methodologies that we employ in their investigation. Hence, this volume does not only introduce the reader into the iconographical world of Sopianae, but, as Olivér Gábor shows in his contribution ('Early Christian Buildings in the Northern Cemetery of Sopianae'), the examination of nearly 30 buildings raise questions such as: 'What kind of Christianity do we encounter in Pécs' archaeological site?' and: 'What kind of rituals may they have celebrated in this cemetery?' But we have also benefited from the history of the excavation at Pécs, and we publish an expert outline of the contemporary archaeological site, written by Zsolt Visy, the eminent Hungarian archaeologist who led the excavations there ('The Paradise in the Early Christian cemetery of Sopianae').

The contribution of Gaetano S. Bevelacqua ('Observations on Christian Epigraphy in Pannonia') has broadened our view through his considerable insights into the wider social-setting of Christianity in Pannonia. And two further contributions on iconographies of Roman Catacombs, paralleling the phenomenon of catacomb murals in the capital with those at Sopianae, establish that this provincial city clearly displays art reminiscent of what had occurred over a hundred years earlier at Rome, but what nevertheless had developed its own, unique individual features. Fabienne Jourdan ('The Orphic Singer in Clement of Alexandria and in the Roman Catacombs') establishes not only a comparison between the literary and the iconographic early Christian representation of

Orpheus, but also traces the motif of the Golden Age as a transformation that is more than the product of simple influence. Eileen Rubery ('From Catacomb to Sanctuary: The Orant figure and the cults of the Mother of God and S. Agnes in early Christian Rome, with special reference to Gold Glass') highlights that female figures in the orant pose in Gold Glass are not, as one may have commonly expected, dominated by portraits of Mary, the Mother of God, but rather representations of S. Agnes that can be found three or four times more often. And Luise Marion Frenkel ('Some theological considerations on the visual representation of the 'Suffering on the Cross' in the first half of the fifth century') broadens the topic of the Orant figure, by looking at the cross and its iconography that spans from Egypt to Rome.

In accordance with the aims of the British Academy funded project, we have included contributions on methodological questions. Levente Nagy has complemented the historical review with his contribution ('Zoltán Kádár and the Early Christian Iconography of Roman Pannonia'). György Heidl ('Remarks on the Iconography in the 'Peter-Paul' [No. 1] Burial Chamber of Sopianae') has taken up the thorny interpretation of the logic and structure of the Biblical scenes appearing on the walls of the Peter-Paul Burial Chamber. His suggestions show the fragile nature of such interpretations in the specialist disagreement about the identification of some of the scenes. Péter Csigi ('Deliberate Ambiguities in Early Christian Wall Paintings in Sopianae') shows that not only can those scenes be read in different ways, but it is arguable that they were originally designed to admit multiple interpretations. Additionally, Krisztina Hudák ('Technical Observations on the Paintings in the St. Peter and Paul [No. 1] Burial Chamber in Sopianae') demonstrates the valuable contribution of methods of modern archaeologists to our reading and interpreting such murals. Istvan M. Bugár ('Theology on Images: Some Observations on the Murals in the Peter and Paul Burial Chamber of Pécs') highlights that even if the first centuries of Christianity reveal an absence, to a large extent, of a theology *of* images, burial places were loci in which 'consciously and emphatically' the production of visual art was influenced by theological considerations. Allen Brent ('Methodological Perspectives in the Interpretation of Early Christian artefacts') together with Markus Vinzent ('Conquest or Shared Backcloth – On the Power of Tradition') critically review the history of methodologies. Brent develops in particular a Wittgensteinian approach as the basis of an interpretative model whereby culture is not reified into classes, regions and religions or along ethnical lines, but where shared meanings are sought. Disagreements and agreements 'in opinion' are understood as requiring fundamentally shared meaning as a conceptual backcloth to a 'language game,' that requires for its playing a prior 'agreement in form of life'. Vinzent develops further his conclusion that more than the written words, the non-verbal, iconographic languages need open and differentiated models that encompass both vertically in time and horizontally in socio-geography a breath of people's exchanges that defy binary options such as pagan/christian, hellenistic/non-hellenistic, jewish/christian, low-class/high-class, literate/illiterate and alike.

This publication could not have been produced without the generosity, hospitality and enthusiasm of our colleagues in Pécs, especially the constant support of György Heidl. Special thanks we owe to Dr. György Udvardy, the Bishop of Pécs, and for his valued reflections in his moving address, and of Attila Üveges, the director of the World Heritage Center in Pécs, and his assistant Lola Kálóczi, who assisted greatly in organizing the Conference, and who magnificently lead our exploration of the sites *in situ*. Last, but not least, we would like to thank for his organisational skills and logistical support Péter Csigi, a PhD student at King's College London and member of the British Academy project, whose critical, initial influence began our fruitful, scholarly exchange.

Allen BRENT – Markus VINZENT,
King's College London

Abbreviations

AA.SS	see ASS.
AAWG.PH	Abhandlungen der Akademie der Wissenschaften in Göttingen Philologisch-historische Klasse, Göttingen.
AB	Analecta Bollandiana, Brussels.
AC	Antike und Christentum, ed. F.J. Dölger, Münster.
ACL	Antiquité classique, Louvain.
ACO	Acta conciliorum oecumenicorum, ed. E. Schwartz, Berlin.
ACW	Ancient Christian Writers, ed. J. Quasten and J.C. Plumpe, Westminster (Md.)/London.
AHDLMA	Archives d'histoire doctrinale et littéraire du moyen âge, Paris.
AJAH	American Journal of Ancient History, Cambridge, Mass.
AJP	American Journal of Philology, Baltimore.
AKK	Archiv für katholisches Kirchenrecht, Mainz.
AKPAW	Abhandlungen der königlichen Preußischen Akademie der Wissenschaften, Berlin.
ALMA	Archivum Latinitatis Medii Aevi (Bulletin du Cange), Paris/Brussels.
ALW	Archiv für Liturgiewissenschaft, Regensburg.
AnalBoll	Analecta Bollandiana, Brussels.
ANCL	Ante-Nicene Christian Library, Edinburgh.
ANF	Ante-Nicene Fathers, Buffalo/New York.
ANRW	Aufstieg und Niedergang der römischen Welt, ed H. Temporini *et al.*, Berlin.
AnSt	Anatolian Studies, London.
AnThA	Année théologique augustinienne, Paris.
APOT	Apocrypha and Pseudepigrapha of the Old Testament in English, ed. R.E. Charles, Oxford.
AR	Archivum Romanicum, Florence.
ARW	Archiv für Religionswissenschaft, Berlin/Leipzig.
ASS	Acta Sanctorum, ed. the Bollandists, Brussels.
AThANT	Abhandlungen zur Theologie des Alten und Neuen Testaments, Zürich.
Aug	Augustinianum, Rome.
AugSt	Augustinian Studies, Villanova (USA).
AW	Athanasius Werke, ed. H.-G. Opitz *et al.*, Berlin.
AZ	Archäologische Zeitung, Berlin.
BA	Bibliothèque augustinienne, Paris.
BAC	Biblioteca de Autores Cristianos, Madrid.
BASOR	Bulletin of the American Schools of Oriental Research, New Haven, Conn.
BDAG	A Greek-English Lexicon of the New Testament and Other Early Christian Literature, 3rd edn F.W. Danker, Chicago.
BEHE	Bibliothèque de l'École des Hautes Études, Paris.
BETL	Bibliotheca Ephemeridum Theologicarum Lovaniensium, Louvain.
BGL	Benediktinisches Geistesleben, St. Ottilien.
BHG	Bibliotheca Hagiographica Graeca, Brussels.
BHL	Bibliotheca Hagiographica Latina Antiquae et Mediae Aetatis, Brussels.

BHO	Bibliotheca Hagiographica Orientalis, Brussels.
BHTh	Beiträge zur historischen Theologie, Tübingen.
BJ	Bursians Jahresbericht über die Fortschritte der klassischen Altertums-wissenschaft, Leipzig.
BJRULM	Bulletin of the John Rylands Library, Manchester.
BKV	Bibliothek der Kirchenväter, ed. F.X. Reithmayr and V. Thalhofer, Kempten.
BKV2	Bibliothek der Kirchenväter, ed. O. Bardenhewer, Th. Schermann, and C. Weyman, Kempten/Munich.
BKV3	Bibliothek der Kirchenväter. Zweite Reihe, ed. O. Bardenhewer, J. Zellinger, and J. Martin, Munich.
BLE	Bulletin de littérature ecclésiastique, Toulouse.
BoJ	Bonner Jahrbücher, Bonn.
BS	Bibliotheca sacra, London.
BSL	Bolletino di studi latini, Naples.
BWAT	Beiträge zur Wissenschaft vom Alten Testament, Leipzig/Stuttgart.
Byz	Byzantion, Leuven.
BZ	Byzantinische Zeitschrift, Leipzig.
BZNW	Beihefte zur Zeitschrift für die neutestamentliche Wissenschaft, Berlin.
CAr	Cahiers Archéologique, Paris.
CBQ	Catholic Biblical Quarterly, Washington.
CChr.CM	Corpus Christianorum, Continuatio Mediaevalis, Turnhout/Paris.
CChr.SA	Corpus Christianorum, Series Apocryphorum, Turnhout/Paris.
CChr.SG	Corpus Christianorum, Series Graeca, Turnhout/Paris.
CChr.SL	Corpus Christianorum, Series Latina, Turnhout/Paris.
CH	Church History, Chicago.
CIL	Corpus Inscriptionum Latinarum, Berlin.
CP(h)	Classical Philology, Chicago.
CPG	Clavis Patrum Graecorum, ed. M. Geerard, vols. I-VI, Turnhout.
CPL	Clavis Patrum Latinorum (SE 3), ed. E. Dekkers and A. Gaar, Turnhout.
CQ	Classical Quarterly, London/Oxford.
CR	The Classical Review, London/Oxford.
CSCO	Corpus Scriptorum Christianorum Orientalium, Louvain.
	Aeth = Scriptores Aethiopici
	Ar = Scriptores Arabici
	Arm = Scriptores Armeniaci
	Copt = Scriptores Coptici
	Iber = Scriptores Iberici
	Syr = Scriptores Syri
	Subs = Subsidia
CSEL	Corpus Scriptorum Ecclesiasticorum Latinorum, Vienna.
CSHB	Corpus Scriptorum Historiae Byzantinae, Bonn.
CTh	Collectanea Theologica, Lvov.
CUF	Collection des Universités de France publiée sous le patronage de l'Association Guillaume Budé, Paris.
CW	Catholic World, New York.
DAC	Dictionary of the Apostolic Church, ed. J. Hastings, Edinburgh.

DACL	see DAL
DAL	Dictionnaire d'archéologie chrétienne et de liturgie, ed. F. Cabrol, H. Leclercq, Paris.
DB	Dictionnaire de la Bible, Paris.
DBS	Dictionnaire de la Bible, Supplément, Paris.
DCB	Dictionary of Christian Biography, Literature, Sects, and Doctrines, ed. W. Smith and H. Wace, 4 vols, London.
DHGE	Dictionnaire d'histoire et de géographie ecclésiastique, ed. A. Baudrillart, Paris.
Did	Didaskalia, Lisbon.
DOP	Dumbarton Oaks Papers, Cambridge, Mass., subsequently Washington, D.C.
DOS	Dumbarton Oaks Studies, Cambridge, Mass., subsequently Washington, D.C.
DR	Downside Review, Stratton on the Fosse, Bath.
DS	H.J. Denzinger and A. Schönmetzer, ed., Enchiridion Symbolorum, Barcelona/Freiburg i.B./Rome.
DSp	Dictionnaire de Spiritualité, ed. M. Viller, S.J., and others, Paris.
DTC	Dictionnaire de théologie catholique, ed. A. Vacant, E. Mangenot, and E. Amann, Paris.
EA	Études augustiniennes, Paris.
ECatt	Enciclopedia Cattolica, Rome.
ECQ	Eastern Churches Quarterly, Ramsgate.
EE	Estudios eclesiasticos, Madrid.
EECh	Encyclopedia of the Early Church, ed. A. Di Berardino, Cambridge.
EKK	Evangelisch-Katholischer Kommentar zum Neuen Testament, Neukirchen.
EH	Enchiridion Fontium Historiae Ecclesiasticae Antiquae, ed. Ueding-Kirch, 6th ed., Barcelona.
EO	Échos d'Orient, Paris.
EtByz	Études Byzantines, Paris.
ETL	Ephemerides Theologicae Lovanienses, Louvain.
EWNT	Exegetisches Wörterbuch zum NT, ed. H.R. Balz *et al.*, Stuttgart.
ExpT	The Expository Times, Edinburgh.
FC	The Fathers of the Church, New York.
FGH	Fragmente der griechischen Historiker, Berlin.
FKDG	Forschungen zur Kirchen- und Dogmengeschichte, Göttingen.
FRL	Forschungen zur Religion und Literatur des Alten und Neuen Testaments, Göttingen.
FS	Festschrift.
FThSt	Freiburger theologische Studien, Freiburg i.B.
FTS	Frankfurter theologische Studien, Frankfurt a.M.
FZThPh	Freiburger Zeitschrift für Theologie und Philosophie, Freiburg/Switzerland.
GCS	Die griechischen christlichen Schriftsteller, Leipzig/Berlin.
GDV	Geschichtsschreiber der deutschen Vorzeit, Stuttgart.
GLNT	Grande Lessico del Nuovo Testamento, Genoa.
GNO	Gregorii Nysseni Opera, Leiden.

GRBS	Greek, Roman and Byzantine Studies, Cambridge, Mass.
GWV	Geschichte in Wissenschaft und Unterricht, Offenburg.
HbNT	Handbuch zum Neuen Testament. Tübingen.
HDR	Harvard Dissertations in Religion, Missoula.
HJG	Historisches Jahrbuch der Görresgesellschaft, successively Munich, Cologne and Munich/Freiburg i.B.
HKG	Handbuch der Kirchengeschichte, Tübingen.
HNT	Handbuch zum Neuen Testament, Tübingen.
HO	Handbuch der Orientalistik, Leiden.
HSCP	Harvard Studies in Classical Philology, Cambridge, Mass.
HTR	Harvard Theological Review, Cambridge, Mass.
HTS	Harvard Theological Studies, Cambridge, Mass.
HZ	Historische Zeitschrift, Munich/Berlin.
ICC	The International Critical Commentary of the Holy Scriptures of the Old and New Testaments, Edinburgh.
ILCV	Inscriptiones Latinae Christianae Veteres, ed. E. Diehl, Berlin.
ILS	Inscriptiones Latinae Selectae, ed. H. Dessau, Berlin.
J(b)AC	Jahrbuch für Antike und Christentum, Münster.
JBL	Journal of Biblical Literature, Philadelphia, Pa., then various places.
JdI	Jahrbuch des Deutschen Archäologischen Instituts, Berlin.
JECS	Journal of Early Christian Studies, Baltimore.
JEH	The Journal of Ecclesiastical History, London.
JJS	Journal of Jewish Studies, London.
JLH	Jahrbuch für Liturgik und Hymnologie, Kassel.
JPTh	Jahrbücher für protestantische Theologie, Leipzig/Freiburg i.B.
JQR	Jewish Quarterly Review, Philadelphia.
JRS	Journal of Roman Studies, London.
JSJ	Journal for the Study of Judaism in the Persian, Hellenistic and Roman Period, Leiden.
JSOR	Journal of the Society of Oriental Research, Chicago.
JTS	Journal of Theological Studies, Oxford.
KAV	Kommentar zu den apostolischen Vätern, Göttingen.
KeTh	Kerk en Theologie, 's Gravenhage.
KJ(b)	Kirchliches Jahrbuch für die evangelische Kirche in Deutschland, Gütersloh.
LCL	The Loeb Classical Library, London/Cambridge, Mass.
LNPF	A Select Library of Nicene and Post-Nicene Fathers of the Christian Church, ed. P. Schaff and H. Wace, Buffalo/New York.
L(O)F	Library of Fathers of the Holy Catholic Church, Oxford.
LSJ	H.G. Liddell and R. Scott, A Greek-English Lexicon, new (9th) edn H.S. Jones, Oxford.
LThK	Lexikon für Theologie und Kirche, Freiburg i.B.
MA	Moyen-Âge, Brussels.
MAMA	Monumenta Asiae Minoris Antiqua, London.
Mansi	J.D. Mansi, Sacrorum conciliorum nova et amplissima collectio, Florence, 1759-1798. Reprint and continuation: Paris/Leipzig, 1901-1927.
MBTh	Münsterische Beiträge zur Theologie, Münster.

MCom	Miscelanea Comillas, Comillas/Santander.
MGH	Monumenta germaniae historica. Hanover/Berlin.
ML	Mediaevalia Lovaniensia, Louvain.
MPG	See PG.
MSR	Mélanges de science religieuse, Lille.
MThZ	Münchener theologische Zeitschrift, Munich.
Mus	Le Muséon, Louvain.
NGWG	Nachrichten der Gesellschaft der Wissenschaften zu Göttingen.
NH(M)S	Nag Hammadi (and Manichaean) Studies, Leiden.
NovTest	Novum Testamentum, Leiden.
NPNF	See LNPF.
NRSV	New Revised Standard Version.
NRTh	Nouvelle Revue Théologique, Tournai/Louvain/Paris.
NTA	Neutestamentliche Abhandlungen, Münster.
NT.S	Novum Testamentum Supplements, Leiden.
NTS	New Testament Studies, Cambridge/Washington.
OBO	Orbis biblicus et orientalis, Freiburg, Switz.
OCA	Orientalia Christiana Analecta, Rome.
OCP	Orientalia Christiana Periodica, Rome.
OECS	Oxford Early Christian Studies, Oxford.
OLA	Orientalia Lovaniensia Analecta, Louvain.
OLP	Orientalia Lovaniensia Periodica, Louvain.
Or	Orientalia. Commentarii editi a Pontificio Instituto Biblico, Rome.
OrChr	Oriens Christianus, Leipzig, then Wiesbaden.
OrSyr	L'Orient Syrien, Paris.
PG	Migne, Patrologia, series graeca.
PGL	A Patristic Greek Lexicon, ed. G.L. Lampe, Oxford.
PL	Migne, Patrologia, series latina.
PLRE	The Prosopography of the Later Roman Empire, ed. A.H.M. Jones *et al.*, Cambridge.
PLS	Migne, Patrologia, series latina. Supplementum ed. A. Hamman.
PO	Patrologia Orientalis, Paris.
PRE	Paulys Realenzyklopädie der classischen Alterthumswissenschaft, Stuttgart.
PS	Patrologia Syriaca, Paris.
PTA	Papyrologische Texte und Abhandlungen, Bonn.
PThR	Princeton Theological Review, Princeton.
PTS	Patristische Texte und Studien, Berlin.
PW	Paulys Realencyclopädie der classischen Altertumswissenschaft, ed. G. Wissowa, Stuttgart.
QLP	Questions liturgiques et paroissiales, Louvain.
QuLi	Questions liturgiques, Louvain
RAC	Rivista di Archeologia Cristiana, Rome.
RACh	Reallexikon für Antike und Christentum, Stuttgart.
RAM	Revue d'ascétique et de mystique, Paris.
RAug	Recherches Augustiniennes, Paris.
RBen	Revue Bénédictine, Maredsous.
RB(ibl)	Revue biblique, Paris.

RE	Realencyklopädie für protestantische Theologie und Kirche, founded by J.J. Herzog, 3e ed. A. Hauck, Leipzig.
REA(ug)	Revue des études Augustiniennes, Paris.
REB	Revue des études byzantines, Paris.
RED	Rerum ecclesiasticarum documenta, Rome.
RÉL	Revue des études latines, Paris.
REG	Revue des études grecques, Paris.
RevSR	Revue des sciences religieuses, Strasbourg.
RevThom	Revue thomiste, Toulouse.
RFIC	Rivista di filologia e d'istruzione classica, Turin.
RGG	Religion in Geschichte und Gegenwart, ed. Gunkel-Zscharnack, Tübingen
RHE	Revue d'histoire ecclésiastique, Louvain.
RhMus	Rheinisches Museum für Philologie, Bonn.
RHR	Revue de l'histoire des religions, Paris.
RHT	Revue d'Histoire des Textes, Paris.
RMAL	Revue du Moyen-Âge Latin, Paris.
ROC	Revue de l'Orient chrétien, Paris.
RPh	Revue de philologie, Paris.
RQ	Römische Quartalschrift, Freiburg i.B.
RQH	Revue des questions historiques, Paris.
RSLR	Rivista di storia e letteratura religiosa, Florence.
RSPT, RSPh	Revue des sciences philosophiques et théologiques, Paris.
RSR	Recherches de science religieuse, Paris.
RTAM	Recherches de théologie ancienne et médiévale, Louvain.
RthL	Revue théologique de Louvain, Louvain.
RTM	Rivista di teologia morale, Bologna.
Sal	Salesianum, Roma.
SBA	Schweizerische Beiträge zur Altertumswissenschaft, Basel.
SBS	Stuttgarter Bibelstudien, Stuttgart.
ScEc	Sciences ecclésiastiques, Bruges.
SCh, SC	Sources chrétiennes, Paris.
SD	Studies and Documents, ed. K. Lake and S. Lake. London/Philadelphia.
SE	Sacris Erudiri, Bruges.
SDHI	Studia et documenta historiae et iuris, Roma.
SH	Subsidia Hagiographica, Brussels.
SHA	Scriptores Historiae Augustae.
SJMS	Speculum. Journal of Mediaeval Studies, Cambridge, Mass.
SM	Studien und Mitteilungen zur Geschichte des Benediktinerordens und seiner Zweige, Munich.
SO	Symbolae Osloenses, Oslo.
SP	Studia Patristica, successively Berlin, Kalamazoo, Leuven.
SPM	Stromata Patristica et Mediaevalia, ed. C. Mohrman and J. Quasten, Utrecht.
SQ	Sammlung ausgewählter Quellenschriften zur Kirchen- und Dogmengeschichte, Tübingen.
SQAW	Schriften und Quellen der Alten Welt, Berlin.
SSL	Spicilegium Sacrum Lovaniense, Louvain.

StudMed	Studi Medievali, Turin.
SVigChr	Supplements to Vigiliae Christianae, Leiden.
SVF	Stoicorum Veterum Fragmenta, ed. J. von Arnim, Leipzig.
TDNT	Theological Dictionary of the New Testament, Grand Rapids, Mich.
TE	Teologia espiritual, Valencia.
ThGl	Theologie und Glaube, Paderborn.
ThJ	Theologische Jahrbücher, Leipzig.
ThLZ	Theologische Literaturzeitung, Leipzig.
ThPh	Theologie und Philosophie, Freiburg i.B.
ThQ	Theologische Quartalschrift, Tübingen.
ThR	Theologische Rundschau, Tübingen.
ThWAT	Theologisches Wörterbuch zum Alten Testament, Stuttgart.
ThWNT	Theologisches Wörterbuch zum Neuen Testament, Stuttgart.
ThZ	Theologische Zeitschrift, Basel.
TLG	Thesaurus Linguae Graecae.
TP	Transactions and Proceedings of the American Philological Association, Lancaster, Pa.
TRE	Theologische Realenzyklopädie, Berlin.
TS	Theological Studies, New York and various places; now Washington, D.C.
TThZ	Trierer theologische Zeitschrift, Trier.
TU	Texte und Untersuchungen, Leipzig/Berlin.
USQR	Union Seminary Quarterly Review, New York.
VC	Vigiliae Christianae, Amsterdam.
VetChr	Vetera Christianorum, Bari (Italy).
VT	Vetus Testamentum, Leiden.
WBC	Word Biblical Commentary, Waco.
WUNT	Wissenschaftliche Untersuchungen zum Neuen Testament, Tübingen.
WZKM	Wiener Zeitschrift für die Kunde des Morgenlandes, Vienna.
YUP	Yale University Press, New Haven.
ZAC	Zeitschrift für Antikes Christentum, Berlin.
ZAM	Zeitschrift für Aszese und Mystik, Innsbruck, then Würzburg.
ZAW	Zeitschrift für die alttestamentliche Wissenschaft, Giessen, then Berlin.
ZDPV	Zeitschrift des Deutschen Palästina-Vereins, Leipzig.
ZKG	Zeitschrift für Kirchengeschichte, Gotha, then Stuttgart.
ZKTh	Zeitschrift für katholische Theologie, Vienna.
ZNW	Zeitschrift für die neutestamentliche Wissenschaft und die Kunde der älteren Kirche, Giessen, then Berlin.
ZRG	Zeitschrift für Rechtsgeschichte, Weimar.
ZThK	Zeitschrift für Theologie und Kirche, Tübingen.

Methodological Perspectives in the Interpretation of Early Christian Artefacts

Allen BRENT, King's College London, UK

ABSTRACT

This article seeks to examine a number of selected examples of iconography drawn mainly from the Roman cemetery of Ss Petrus and Marcellinus and the Vatican Museo Pio Cristiano in order to create an interpretative context for the iconography of Pécs (Soprianae) in Hungary. The creation of such a context does not rest only on features of style that indicate a common artistic tradition with Rome at the time of the production of these images. Rather we need as part of an interpretive model Wittgenstein's concept of a 'language game', involving both disagreement and and agreement 'in opinion' as well as a contrastingly 'agreement in form of life.' We need a model in terms of which we can establish a pattern between images drawn from a number of areas that constitute a non-verbal, iconographic language game.

Theodor Klauser applied a strict empiricist methodology in the interpretation of early Christian art. In this respect his approach seemed to be rigorous. But his rigor was the rigor of someone who saw an individual looking at an individual artifact and asking what impression would have been made upon the individual viewer. My problem is the problem with empiricism in general: it regards the problem of knowledge as the problem of how an individual subject achieves a veridical picture of the world: it fails to grasp the social character of claims to knowledge that arise from a discourse shared in common between human beings in assessing in community whether the meaning and truth of verbal propositions or the meaning of non-verbal art and artifacts.

Let us take Klauser's examination of the recurrent images of the Good Shepherd on sarcophagi from the second to the fourth centuries, classifying them as 'explicitly Pagan', as 'biblical motifs' (15), and 'neutral motifs' (88).[1] Klauser claimed for example that we have no right to classify the statue of Apollo as shepherd as a figure also of Christ: its original location is unknown. The figure has a long, pre Christian history in a purely pagan culture. We have in the Museo Pio Christiano, still classified as part of Wilpert's 'crypto Christian' collection, the sarcophagus of the Three Good Shepherds (Plate 27). Wilpert

---

[1] See the catalogue in Theodore Klauser, 'Studien zur Entstehungsgeschichte der christlichen Kunst I', *JbAC* 1 (1958), 20-51; 46-51.

Studia Patristica LXXIII, 1-38.
© Peeters Publishers, 2014.

had originally interpreted the three shepherds as an image of the centrally, bearded Christ, flanked on the right and left by un-bearded Peter and Paul. Klauser was to oppose such an interpretation with a rigorous empiricist methodology that demanded recognition only for what could be safely inferred from what was registered on the sense organs of an individual viewer as they viewed an object.[2]

Any Christian interpretation of the figures on the Three Good Shepherds sarcophagus was unsafe on such an empiricist criterion. Depictions of a shepherd god such as Hermes were too general, with a long, Pagan history: they could not therefore be allowed to be identified as Christ the Good Shepherd.

But let us see what methodology was implied in Klauser's assessment here. When we look at the Three Good Shepherds sarcophagus, we cannot register any unambiguous Christian elements, so we exclude any Christian significance for this artifact on the part of any, third or fourth century viewer. Thus we ignore the fact that meaningful viewing is not an individual activity on the part of one person, but is in fact an interpersonal activity involving a community of persons sharing a common, non verbal and iconic language game in terms of their agreement to see what they see in terms of shared concepts and categories.

We have come to place what is Pagan and what is Christian in distinct categories, and meaning in Pagan is quite distinct from meaning in Christian discourse. We might concede that there is no individual 'Christian mind' or individual 'Pagan mind' consisting of the sum total of sense impressions made upon the mind of a single individual. We might look instead for a universe of meaning inhabited by a 'Pagan' whether as viewer and producer of an artifact and pronounce this 'Pagan' as though 'Paganism' and 'Christianity' existed in culturally uncontaminated forms. But our implicit and unexamined assumption in so arguing is that Pagan discourse and Christian discourse operated according to the distinctive logic of each, producing two world-views logically insulated from each other. Thus Paganism and Christianity are two alternative social constructions of reality, the inhabitants of one constellation of meaning finding the other alien and incomprehensible. Thus even if we concede that the viewer of the Three Good Shepherds sarcophagus shared a common iconographic discourse, we are often too confident that those participants saw the iconography in purely Pagan terms.

But to proceed thus is to produce two quite artificial, post Enlightenment constructs, Paganism and Christianity. I call them 'artificial' because they do not correspond to what we can conclude from actual examples of discourses and the way that they function, whether the discourse is verbal, or iconographic and non-verbal, in Early Christian and Pagan society.

Let us look at two examples, one verbal and one iconographic that each in its own way will help us to expose our implicit assumptions about culturally insulated discourses and demonstrate the artificiality of such assumptions.

---

[2] Th. Klauser, 'Studien', I.1 (1958), Tafel 4a.

The general impression created by a Tertullian, or by a Cyprian recounting to Donatus his conversion experience is that Christian and Pagan discourse are quite separate constructions of reality so that to inhabit one is to find the other totally incomprehensible. Tertullian may ask 'What has Athens to do with Jerusalem' as though he possessed a divine revelation described in concepts and categories that were culturally uncontaminated and came from some Platonic world of timeless ideation. Cyprian might talk of the light shed on him from above immediately following his baptism in which he forgot his old Pagan world of his rhetor's formation and left his old world behind. But Tertullian's and Cyprian's Stoicism remained and informed their conception of Christian theology. Cyprian's Christian eschatology was formulated and argued in terms of Stoic metaphysics, as I have shown, as much as his view of Church Order in terms of Roman constitutional theory.[3] One world-view has not completely replaced another as if it could suffer no contamination in the process of change. The process of conversion is far subtler than that.

If this is the case with a construction of reality expressed verbally, my argument is that it is equally the case with non-verbal, iconographic discourse. Klauser has in his interpretation of early Christian artifacts behaved as if there was a formal difference here. My argument is that though the Christ Apollo statuette or the three Good Shepherds' sarcophagus may have come to us from an eighteenth century Cardinal's collection without pedigree, or indeed from the rubble that infilled the ruined cemetery of St. Calistus, with no account of original level or position in the Catacomb, nevertheless it is testimony to a discourse that is neither Pagan nor Christian but forms the backcloth to the social life and conceptual interaction of Graeco Roman society of the third and fourth centuries.

Finney, I believe, shared Klauser's false assumption when he proposed his view of Early Christian iconography as the product of a process of expurgation of pagan details from images that could then be seen as purely Christian.[4] We have a number of seals impressed upon clay oil lamps from the second century onwards that prefigure a shepherd figure, and these in isolation we might conclude, following Klauser, were Pagan and not Christian. But we have the famous Wulff 1244 engraving by Bellori in 1691 preserving the original form of the seal for a second century lamp with which Finney was clearly familiar.[5] Here we find the figure of the Shepherd central, where it is an image of Christ carrying the lost sheep on his shoulders amongst his flock, which clusters around him on his return. Why is it an image of Christ?

Well presumably because we have an image of Jonah and the Ketos on the left and on the right, another of him asleep under the Gourd, so familiar from early Christian art. But above his head we have the seven signs of the Zodiac

---

[3] Allen Brent, *Cyprian and Roman Carthage* (Cambridge, 2010), 91-116.
[4] Paul Corbet Finney, *The Invisible God* (Oxford, 1994), 110-5.
[5] P.C. Finney, *Invisible God* (1994), 119.

and on the right Caelus spreading out the heavens, and on the left Sol, the sun god. There is no process of expurgation here where only Pagan symbols that were able to be given Christian meanings in an expurgated form are allowed to remain. Rather we are in the presence of a non-verbal, iconographic discourse in which these different images of the divine can interact with one another in the form of a picture.

When therefore the shepherd image appears on its own, it should, I submit, be regarded as part of that collective, shared discourse and not separated from it. The existence of that discourse to which Wulff 1244 bears witness is a discourse that forms the collective backcloth shared by individuals who had either produced or viewed those lamps on which the figure of the shepherd appeared in isolation.

This situation is similar in the case of the iconography of the three Good Shepherds' sarcophagus (Plate 27). Whether here, or in Wulff 1244, the images were not alien to a Christian worldview with different and incommunicable sets of meanings. There was no individual meaning describable in terms of sense data registered on the sensory organs of an individual viewer but rather collective meanings that arose from participation in a language game. There was no one individual meaning of the artifact that arose from the interaction of subject viewer to it as an object in isolation. We need therefore an account of meaning in iconography that takes account of that interpersonal backcloth of a shared language game. Some viewers might make more definitive moves in the language game than others but such moves are potentially available to all who share such a common backcloth.

My argument is that these images of the shepherd, of Sol and Caelus and the Zodiak, of Jonah and the Ketos stand in close relationship with each other, and share a family resemblance, whether Pagan or Christian. They are not unrelated juxtapositions but form into a logical pattern in non-verbal, iconographic discourse. And it is this discourse that it is my intention to explore and articulate in my discussion of the Early Christian site in Pécs, Hungary.

I propose now, therefore, to re-examine a current interpretation of two mausolea at Sopianae in Panonia (Pécs, Hungary) excavated under the present day cathedral.[6] I will show how, as expressions of an iconographic language game, they are not to be interpreted as isolated phenomena but as non-verbal, iconographic statements that arise from a language game that is played in common with related artefacts in Roman catacombs.

1. The Peter and Paul and Wine Jug Burial Chambers

Let us begin therefore with the painted burial chamber known as the 'Peter and Paul' Burial Vault,[7] first discovered in 1780 but further excavated and restored

[6] Ferenc Fülep, Sopianae: *The History of Pécs during the Roman Era and the Problem of the Continuity of the Late Roman Population*, Archaeologia Hungarica a consilio archaeologorum academiae scientarum Hungaricae Redacta L (Budapest, 1984), Chapter 4.
[7] F. Fülep, *Sopianae* (1984), 36: I, 1780.

in 1939, and to the painted, 'Wine Jug' burial chamber, also excavated and restored at these dates.[8]

I will argue that the iconography of the 'Wine Jug' burial chamber has been viewed in a one-dimensional way that parallels in some respects Klauser's empiricist approach. Gerke, for example, followed by Fülep, interprets the wine jug depicted in the niche set into the back wall as a Eucharistic symbol.

Plate 1. Wine Jug Burial Chamber (Gerke: Fig. 31).

The circumference of the niche is decorated with a large red vine that enters the half circle of the lunette so as to curl around the wine jug with fruit and leaves hanging over it.[9]

The large vine is set in a paradisiacal scene that links its iconography with that of the Peter and Paul burial chamber (Mausoleum I):

Plate 2. (Pécs Brocchure).

Plate 3. (Fülep: Plate XII).

---

[8] F. Fülep, *Sopianae* (1984), 42: II.

[9] Friedrich Gerke, 'Wandermalereien in Pécs', in *Neue Beiträge zur Kunstgeschichte des 1 Jahrtausends*, Forschungen zur Kunstgeschichte und Christlichen Archäologie (Baden-Baden, 1952), 115-57, 122; F. Fülep, *Sopianae* (1984), 45.

Here in the barrel-vaulted ceiling, natural foliage entwines around the four medallions containing images of four persons, who may be the four evangelists, or martyrs whose relics were originally buried there (Plate 2). The medallions are framed with rich vine tendrils heavy with fruit. There are two peacocks and two doves on each side of two bouquets of flowers in the centre of the panel at whose centre in turn is a Christogram.[10]

Plate 4. (Pécs Brocchure).   Plate 5. (Fülep: Plate XIII).

The monogram of Christ in the lunette towards which point the right hands' of Peter and Paul has six green flower stars set between its letters. There are red roses, lilies, and other flowers surrounding them (Plate 3).[11]

The paradisiacal theme extends to the entrance itself where the same nature theme, characterised by thick vine tendrils, decorates the archway.

Plate 6. (Fülep: Plate XI).   Plate 7. (Gerke: Fig. 32).

And it is here that we come to a thematic similarity between I (Peter and Paul Burial Chamber) and II (The Wine Jug Burial Vault). At the entrance set

[10] F. Fülep, *Sopianae* (1984), 38-9.
[11] *Ibid.* 36.

into the wall immediately opposite the Lunette with the Wine Jar (Plate 24), and with its vines and grapes extending into the Niche around the jar itself, we have a paradisiacal theme that is to continue throughout the two sides (the barrel vault in this case has been destroyed so we do not know how this was decorated). To the right and left of the entrance, there is criss-cross grid pattern that seems to represent a garden fence, and this continues from the right and left of the entrance along the right and left, longitudinal walls. There are stereotyped depictions of flowers set into the fence pattern both right and left of the entrance arch in the form of arrows (Plates 7, 12 and 13). Along the two longtitudinal walls the garden-fence motif gives way to two marble slabs set adjacent to the far wall and the lunette with the vines and wine cup. One slab (Plate 8), on the left, consists wholly of geometric lines, with a central triangle with half-circles connected to each other.

Plate 8. (Gerke: Fig. 33).

The other, on the right (Plate 9), consists of two oblongs, one set into another, with five half circles along both longest edges, with a single half circle at each end.

Plate 9. (Gerke: Fig. 34).

How are we to interpret this iconography?

Gerke, with great perspicacity, saw that the significance of the iconography of the grid work at the entrance represented a simple park gate constructed of bamboo and of wood through which one entered into the park landscape within.[12] The effect therefore upon the viewer is of entrance into a garden of paradise. The creation of this 'sacredly designated, inner space (*als heilig gekennzeichneten Innenraum*)' expresses the Christian hope for the life everlasting in which the deceased in the sarcophagus shares due to the Eucharistic symbol of the Wine Jar surrounded by grapes in so central a position.

The fence encloses us with the deceased and his sarcophagus in the garden of Paradise enjoying the heavenly banquet, the marriage supper of the Lamb. We are involved here in a mystery, and the iconography expresses a 'mystical relation (*eine geheime Verbindung*)' between the various scenes.[13] Gerke does not comment on the meaning of the geometrical figures on the encrusted marble slabs (Plates 8 and 9), nor on the stylized flowers represented as arrows (Plate 13). Presumably they are to be understood as part of the general ambience as mystical symbols whose meaning cannot be determined?

It is here that we reach the limitations of Gerke's account in the terms within which his discussion proceeds. His interpretation is, I shall now argue, a sanitized and expurgated one, made possible by his unreflective and anachronistic adoption of a twenty-first century discourse in which the wine jug and the paradisiacal scene can be given a purely Eucharistic and eschatological significance. We shall need to seek to reconstruct the fourth and fifth century, non-verbal, iconographic discourse whose meaning derives from common pagan and early Christian elements that are not mutually exclusive but interact with one another in a shared web of meaning.

Our inference can be made within an empiricist framework of a one-for-one relationship between object and viewer. The sense impressions made upon an individual observer in the Pécs site can be compared with similar sense impressions made upon the viewer in other sites such as, in the case of the lattice fence motif, in the catacombs of the Jordani, of Pamphilius, in the Domus Petri in San Sebastiano, in the Oceanus Crypt in Callistus, etc.[14] The vine tendril decoration can be by such observations connected with that found in the burial-chamber at Nis, or in wall painting at grave 7, as in the church of Santa Sophia also in Sophia in Bulgaria.[15] But inferences within such an individualist, empiricist framework are not the only ones to be made in this discussion.

In interpreting what those who built and used tombs I and II meant by the iconography that was employed by their constructors, and appreciated by those

[12] F. Gerke, 'Wandermalereien' (1954), 116-7.
[13] *Ibid.* 121.
[14] *Ibid.* 124-9.
[15] F. Fülep, *Sopianae* (1984), 45.

who used these sites, we need to recover and to reconstruct the symbolic universe of meaning in terms of which the contemporary social owners of these sites understood individual images and artefacts. Instead of — or rather perhaps supplementary to — our interpretation in terms of a 'symbolic universe of meaning' on a social construction of reality model, we might speak instead of the later Wittgenstein seeing meaning and objectivity as arising socially from a language game in which disagreement in opinion requires a prior and collective agreement, an agreement in form of life.

Regarding such a language game the logic of which moves the dialogue between those who collectively participate in it I propose further to invoke a Chomskyan view of meaning. In studying the linguistic behaviour, or I would add the non-verbal iconographic behaviour of social groups in antiquity, in pursuing what they mean by the concepts and categories that they invoke, we cannot rely on examining behaviourally and simply actual articulation of meaning by a particular individual. We must look not simply at actual individual conceptual performances in verbal and in non-verbal, conceptual language, but rather what the playing of the language game with others shows that the individual has competence to perform.

Chomsky wished to look for this competence to perform whether or not the competence was ever actualized as due to an innate rule structure possessed biologically by the human species. I am not concerned with issues of the genetic or biological basis of linguistic behaviour. Nevertheless, whatever its roots, I wish to explore Chomsky's insight in how in fact human discourse proceeds and develops meanings and new meaning. Human languages are characterised by rule structures that make all kinds of new applications of concepts as human discourse proceeds between individuals. No one individual is ever able due to the shortness of human existence and the unlimited possibilities created by the underlying logic of human discourse to perform all that the logic of the discourse makes it possible for him to perform.

Indeed, for someone to 'know what he means' in a linguistic performance, he must in a sense know what he does not mean. Behaviourism, as Chomsky well realised, cannot capture this feature of a human speech-act. Meaning is not simply a general and consistent behavioural response to a visual stimulus. It is the conscious assertion of meaning x rather than meaning y or z: the assertion of x therefore implies knowledge of what it would have meant to assert y or z. Agreements or disagreements in opinion, in Wittgenstein's classical statement, imply a prior agreement, an agreement in form of life. In other words it is a shared conceptual background that govern the logic of disagreeing as well as the logic of agreeing.

How can we therefore recover and construct the general conceptual, non-verbal, iconographic background in terms of which the iconography of Pécs tombs I and II mean what they do?

Firstly we must begin with suspicion about describing anachronistically the scene of paradise at whose centre is the Jug and whose background is the park fence and vine tendrils. We must assert other features witnessed by the iconography of tombs I and II in similar backgrounds in other places. There are some iconographical conceptual performances here that imply competences that are found actualized in other sites, as we shall see. Those features are 'pagan' and reflective of a shared conceptual background with third and fourth century Christianity in which a logic of synthesis and mutual understanding rather than of exclusion and contradiction is operative.

If we are to concede a Eucharistic interpretation of the themes of the garden of paradise, the vine tendrils and the image of the jar, then we would have to concede that the images are very amorphous and ambiguous as Eucharistic images. They are ambiguous because their very imprecision means that they can easily take the form of a *refrigerium*, a refreshment meal for the dead which has, nevertheless, as we shall see, as common home in Graeco-Roman paganism as it has in early Christianity. It is important however, following the insights of the later Wittgenstein, not to consider such ambiguity so much as a communicative weakness but rather as one of communicative strength.

Wittgenstein characterised a certain kind of ambiguity, in terms of our discussion a kind of conceptual, iconographical amorphism, as 'family resemblance'. Ambiguity in certain concepts at the foundation of certain forms of discourse did not bring communication to an end, did not lead each party to claim that the other had 'missed the point', did not stop further explanation by its failure to define clearly and exhaustively certain fundamental points of view. In fact, as Bambrough pointed out, if we were to have a clear picture in the form of an exhaustive definition of many universal terms, the logic of human languages would become unoperable.

Suppose that we gave a child, or the child himself constructed, a picture of a table, clear, its features exhaustively defined, so that its difference with all other objects was clear and all other objects were non-tables. If we did this with all or even most universal terms, then the logic of our language would cease to function. Tables come in all sorts of shapes, sizes and colours, made of a variety of materials, there are round tables, square tables, oblong tables, blue, red and green tables, wood tables and marble tables, tables with four legs, three, and no legs at all, etc. If language proceeded by applying exhaustive definition, it could not be used to explore the world: exhaustive definition in regards to fundamental concepts would not further communication in exploring the world but rather bring all such communication to an end. It is the very conceptual vagueness of the concept of a 'table', its amorphous ambiguity that is its communicative strength: the conceptual vagueness enables new particulars to be incorporated into known schemes.[16]

---

[16] Marcia Yudkin, 'On Quine's contretemps of translation', *Mind* 88 (1979), 93-6; Renfrew Bamborough, 'Universals and family resemblances', in G. Pitcher (ed.), *Wittgenstein* (London, 1968), 186-204; Allen Brent, *Ignatius of Antioch and the Second Sophistic*, Studien und Texte zu Antike und Christentum 36 (Tübingen, 2006), chapter 1.

Wittgenstein characterised the mental process by which we performed such an incorporation of particulars into known schemes as the detection of 'family resemblance'. A particular example does not have to have all the features of an exhaustive definition of the traits of a given family in order to be included within the general category of 'members of family x'. Furthermore there is not one, 'essential' feature that all members must have in common. They must however be linked in a pattern of 'family-resemblance'.

In the Churchill family, using Bambrough's example, x may have the Churchill eyebrows (i) and the Churchill nose (ii), y may have the Churchill scowl (iii) and the Churchill forehead (iv) but neither eyebrows (i) nor nose (ii), and z may have the Churchill eyebrows (i) but not the nose (ii), but have the scowl (iii) but not the forehead (iv). Thus x (with features (i)-(ii)) and y (with features (iii)-(iv)) have no features in common but are members of the Churchill family because z links them by sharing features (i) with x and feature (iii) with y. We are playing a language game in which we detect and agree on family-resemblances on the basis of open-ended concepts lacking exhaustive definition. Our agreement and disagreement in opinion requires a conceptual backcloth with fundamental concepts having a particular kind of vagueness and ambiguity that enables new particulars to be incorporated into known schemes.

Early Christian or Pagan Art produces countless examples similarly of non-verbal, iconographical images the imprecision and ambiguity of which enabled the Pagan-Christian dialogue to proceed. Such images point to a shared conceptual backcloth to Pagan and Christian dialogue in which disagreement in opinion implied a prior agreement, an agreement in a form of life. As examples I propose such figures as Hermes-Shepherd-Christ, Christ-Orpheus, the Ketos-Hippocamp of the Jonah cycle, Jonah-Endymion, Jonah-Ariadne, etc. But this agreement in a form of life extends also to the ambiguities of family-resemblance between scenes such as those of Paradise, with the heavenly Eucharist-Refrigerium, with the Eucharist celebrated for the faithful-departed and the cult of the dead celebrated with drink offerings in which their souls participated.

We have already noted one connection between tombs I and II in terms of the floral, paradisiacal motif in the depictions of vine tendrils that decorate the arch of tomb II and the vault of tomb I. This shared, iconographical discourse is sustained by the architectural context in which it is depicted. Both tombs have barrel vaults characteristic of a pagan Heroon.[17] A pertinent example may be found in the excavated site at Kalydon, and the reconstructed plan of the excavators, in which there was an above ground edifice, leading down to the tomb itself, and in which there was a space for cultic meals to the dead adjoining a pagan chapel.[18]

---

[17] F. Gerke, 'Wandermalereien' (1952), 115-7; Einar Dyggve, Frederick Poulsen, and Konstantinos Rhomaios, *Das Heroon von Kalydon* (Kobenhavn, 1934).
[18] E. Dyggve *et al.*, *Heroon* (1934), chapter 7, tafel V and VI.

Both I and II had ground level chapels built above the below ground burial chamber,[19] and would have been the site for Christian *refrigeria* meals, particularly if saints were buried there to whom votive prayers were to be offered, as the evidence is that they were at *Ss Petrus et Paulus ad Catacombas*, as we shall shortly see.[20]

Plate 10. (Pécs Brocchure).   Plate 11. (Pécs Brocchure).

Are there, we may now ask, any tighter links with *refrigeria* meals in Roman burial practices to be drawn such that the central image of the Jug with grapes and vines surrounded it could be given closer definition in terms of these features as much as with Eucharistic features?

We now need to ask how the iconographic discourse in which those who constructed these tombs contained logical possibilities that were not actualized here, but were actualized elsewhere, or, in Chomsky's terms, what further performances did that discourse make them competent to perform however few of such performances they in fact actualized?[21]

2. Ss Petrus et Paulus ad Catacombas: Refrigeria and Paradisiacal scenes

The paradise scene with its garden-fence motif (Plates 12 and 13) derives its meaning from a discourse, a language-game which the constructors of these tombs shared with, or played with, those Roman artists who decorated *Ss Petrus*

---

[19] F. Fülep, *Sopianae* (1984), 44.

[20] Einar Dyggve, *History of Salonitan Christianity*, Instituttet for sammelignende Kulturforskning, Ser. A, XXI (Oslo, 1951), Chapter V.

[21] For an explanation of the Chomskyan terms used in my discussion here, see Noam Chomsky, *New Horizons in the Study of Language and Mind* (Cambridge, 2000) and A. Brent, *Ignatius and the Second Sophistic* (2006), 8-16, 321-6.

et Paulus ad Catacombas. The garden-fence motif is found in the villa built over the in-filled tombs of Clodius Hermes, the Innocentiores, and the Axe in the clay pits there around AD 239.

Plate 12. (Gerke: Fig. 34).

Plate 13. (Gerke: Fig. 35).

The fence scene was in the bottom panel of a wall whose top panel was decorated with fragments on which in graffiti letters votive prayers were found (Plate 14). The wall itself was behind *the triclinium* bench where *referigeria* meals were eaten as some votive prayers written in graffiti letters testify.

Plate 14. (Styger Tav. V): Ss Petrus et Paulus ad catacombas.

It was here within the exact boundaries of the in-filled mausolea of the villa that a portico was erected above it and faced a courtyard placed at a lower level. Here a flight of steps led down to a water tank hewn from a rock. On the east side of the portico along its rear wall ran a masonry bench with a small fountain at its north end. This bench indicated that it was part of a structure identified as a Triclia or dining hall, in which the group that had constructed this building prepared and ate *refrigeria* meals in commemoration of the apostles Peter and Paul. The rear wall behind the bench was decorated with graffiti with votive prayers to these two saints and apostles, and in which the garden fence motif is visibly present.[22] We find here the famous:

PAVLE ED PETRE PETITE
PRO VICTORE[23]

Here we have clear reference to votive prayers to Paul and Peter but we also have many references to votive offerings in the form of *refrigeria* meals, for example:

PETRO ET PAVLO
TOMIVS COELIVS
REFRIGERIVM FECI[24]

Or,

AT PAVLV[M]
ET PET[RVM]
REFRI[GERAVI][25]
DALMATIVS
BOTVM IS PROMISIT
REFRIGERIVM[26]

Thus the garden fence motif of the paradisiacal scene in tomb II at Pécs is more than a pleasant picture adopted from the work book of a *pictorius* that had arrived at Pécs from Rome amongst his fellow craftsmen and which simply looked pleasant and was adopted in isolation. We have seen how in *Ss Petrus et Paulus ad Catacombas* images of the fenced garden of paradise were associated in the graffiti with *refrigeria* meals in which the living joined with the two

[22] Paul Styger, 'Il Monumento Apostolico della Via Appia', *Dissertazioni della Pontificia Accademia Romana di Archeologia*, Serie II, Tomo XIII (1918), 3-115.
[23] *Ibid.* 58 and Tav. I.
[24] *Ibid.* 59 and Tav. II.
[25] *Ibid.* 61 and Tav. XXII.
[26] *Ibid.* 62 and Tav. IV.

saints in the eternal world of the life to come. The imagery of the paradisiacal garden did not stand alone but was associated in the non-verbal, iconographic discourse in the context of which a narrative with developing meanings was unfolding.

But if these images and their interrelationship were part of the shared, iconographic discourse in which groups at Rome participated with the group that built the tombs at Pécs, what indications do we have that the common images are not simply piecemeal and arbitrary selections from the repertoire offered in a *pictorius'* workbook? How, in Chomskyan terms, can we be sure that specific banquet-*refrigeria* images were implicit in the logic of the discourse in which both shared, that the discourse enabled those at Pécs to have competence to perform more than they actually performed?

3. Libation apertures (piscinae) and Heroon architecture

The Pécs' mausolea adopted a barrel vault architecture reminiscent of a Heroon. Furthermore the structure of an above ground cult area leading by a staircase to a lower ground tomb may give clues to the conducting there of a banquet-*refrigerium*. But such clues are, within an empiricist model, insufficient to establish the existence of the presence of potentially dynamic concepts seeking to become actualized through their interaction in an iconographic language-game. But let us look, therefore, in the light of our preferred, Wittgensteinian model, at the marble slabs inscribed with what Gerke regarded as 'the mystery filled symbolism of this grave painting.'[27] It was as such that he regarded, as we have seen, the two marble slabs (fig. 33 and 34) as geometrical ornamentation.

But if we look more closely at both, and in particular the more fully preserved right hand slab on the right long wall we can see that the imagery is not purely abstract and geometrical. The depiction (in Plate 9) is of a flat sarcophagus lid inset with five half circles of three concentric lines on the two sides of the bevelled *mensa*, with two single line concentric circles one at either of the shorter ends. These resemble cup shaped objects incised into sarcophagi for receiving drink offerings in *refrigeria* rites for the dead.

In the funerary architecture of the pagan Heroon, as Gyggve pointed out, 'detached sarcophagi in the open air in a cemetery may for instance have incised, bowl-shaped depressions in various places... at burials under the level of the earth the usual top stone may be supplied with bowl-shaped depressions.'[28]

---

[27] F. Gerke, 'Wandermalereien' (1952), 117: '... die geheimnisvolle Symbolik dieser Gruft-malerei'.

[28] E. Dyggve, *Salonitan Christianity* (1951), 106.

Plate 15. (Dyggve V32).   Plate 16. (Dyggve V22).

Dyggve gives examples of grave-*tesellae* that are square with a round, flat basin that are called *piscinae* in Salona, which is the usual term for a baptismal font. Sometimes, as these examples show, *piscinae* are perforated and sometimes not (Plate 16). Found sometimes in thin, polished marble, they are placed on a grave plate or are raised on legs like an altar-*mensa* over the grave. Evidence of supporting legs of wood or of bronze suggest some were portable.[29]

In the representation on the slab along the right hand long wall of tomb II, whether it is of a grave plate or of the table of an altar-*mensa*, we see symbolic depictions at each shorter end of the representation of a *piscina*, not depicted fully circular due to its fitting into a bevelled *mensa*-slab or grave plate (Plate 9). The reason that they are perforated when they are is to receive a wine libation as part of a *refrigerium* meal honouring the dead. I would suggest also that the corresponding marble slab facing it (Plate 8), although partly obliterated, also suggests a sarcophagus slab, in this case pointed rather than flat, like that in another of Dyggve's examples (Plate 17).

Plate 17. (Dyggve V23).   Plate 18 (Dyggve V25).

---

[29] E. Dyggve, *Salonitan Christianity* (1951), 107.

Here too the pointed sarcophagus slab over a Christian grave has at its left hand corner and at its narrow end perforations for drink-offerings. In Dyggve's other example, a slab with two perforated *piscinae* (Plate 18) lies over pagan graves for two adults and three children.[30] *Refrigeria* rites are common to what we regard as both Paganism and Christianity. We are not far removed here from the benches in the *triclia ad Catacombas* where votive prayers were offered to Peter and Paul with benches for a communal meal, and with the graffiti expressing those prayers inscribed on a wall with a paradisiacal scene of a fenced garden, like that of the scene at the entrance to Tomb II at Pécs. Nor are we far removed from the *triclinium* scene depicted, as we shall see, in Ss Petrus and Marcellinus, in which the space immediately at the bottom of the lunette is decorated with half cup-like images set alternatively in an upright and in a turned down position (Plate 21) in a pattern evocative of the piscina imagery that we witnessed in Plate 9.

A *tesella* was originally a cube shaped brick used as a burial cover for a grave. Dyggve mentions four Diocletian common soldier martyr graves at Salona erected originally in the open air with a large *tesella* that served as a sacrificial table, with benches on three sides for celebrations of a *refrigerium*. Such was the arrangement for dining at the *Triclia* in *Ss Petrus and Paulus ad Catacombas*, as we have indicated. A half-century later saw the erection of a burial basilica in honour of these martyrs over this structure with the floor now at the level of the *tessella* so that the benches were now buried and disused, but the *tessella* itself remained.[31]

Furthermore, the *piscinae* with perforations for drink offerings show that the iconography was not merely an expurgated version adapted to the developing cult of the saints. We have other, early Christian examples to which Dölger drew attention.[32]

Plate 19. Dölger, Antike und Christentum Bd. II, taf. 6.1 and 2.

---

[30] *Ibid.* 106.

[31] *Ibid.* 102-3.

[32] Franz Joseph Dölger, 'Darstellung einer Totenspende mit Fisch auf einer christlichen Grabverschlussplatte aus der Katakombe Pietro e Marcellino in Rom', *Antike und Christentum: Kultur- und Religionsgeschichtliche Studien* II (Münster in Westfalen, 1930), 81-99, 90, note 36.

Justa's husband was clearly a Christian, as indicated by the Constantinian monogram depicted on the left and the right of the *piscinae* (Plate 19). Furthermore, his dedication to his dead wife also indicates her Christianity, with its address to someone who is 'most holy and most worthy (SANCTISSIMAE ET DIGNISSIMAE).'[33] But the five, drilled holes are apertures into which drink offerings for or to the dead could be poured. Dölger compared this grave plate with the Pagan parallel (in 6.2) in which Caecilius Fuscus has a dedication around a *piscinae* with the formula *D(iis)M(anibus)*.[34]

Those *piscinae* on Christian tombs clearly indicate unambiguously *refrigeria* rites and connect the symbolism of Pécs tomb II (Gerke: Fig. 34) with both paradisiacal scenes and with the votive prayers at the *Triclia* in *Ss Petrus et Paulus ad Catacombas*. A pattern is emerging that links in a chain as one image connects with another over various sites set at a geographical distance. But also we find representations similar in form to such *piscinae* in connection with banquet scenes in the well-documented case of those of the cemetery of Ss Petrus and Marcellinus.

4. Ss Petrus and Marcellinus: the paradisiacal banquet

Here, set into wall 2 of the Cubiculum of the two Agapi (Deckers Nr 78, wall 2), we find a lunette with a banquet scene.

Plate 20. (Deckers Taf. 64.a).

Plate 21. (Deckers Taf. 63).

---

[33] Di Stefano (1995) 43 b.9, Paries 32 (pars dextra) *Monumenta vetera Christianorum* X.
[34] From 'Samlung H. Wollman.'

Here, we find under a *loculus* a lunette in which we have depicted a banquet scene. We have a round table with three legs whose ends are formed as animal feet. The table is set with a yellow table cloth with hems on which a round, silver coloured plate is laid with a whitish fish. A youthful servant, with short, brown hair comes from the left towards the table (Plate 20). We have the piscina motif (Plate 21) that I indicated also at Pécs (Plate 9).

On the right a young woman is depicted holding in her left hand a delicate little pitcher of clear glass, and in her raised right hand a cone shaped glass cup. Behind the table and the two persons serving lays a curved shaped cushion. Behind the cushion we can see the upper bodies of five men. All are wearing a white tunic with long, narrow sleeves, the neckline of which is edged with a black border. The five men have each different features as they turn to each other from which we conclude that they are not formal and stereotypical figures but depictions of actual participants in a banquet. On the white background between the heads of the five men and the servant girl we have inscribed in black letters IRENE.

There are a number of similar scenes in Petrus and Marcellinus in a number of further vaults. It would be difficult to see these scene in terms of a Eucharist, since there is no president, the fish is unaccompanied by loaves, and any relation to the Feeding of the Five Thousand is precluded by the depiction of the five men as individuals and not as stereotyped symbols of figures in a scene from the Gospels. IRENE has been associated with εἰρήνη as a Eucharistic theme, but parallels with other such banquet scenes suggest rather that IRENE is a personification of an abstract quality in the form of the servant girl on the right (Plate 22). We can see this more clearly on wall 3, which has an arcosolium with a similar meal scene that stands almost opposite its counterpart in wall 2 (Plate 23).

Plate 22. Deckers Taf. 64.b).

Above the head of the servant girl on the right is inscribed AGAPE MISCE ('Agape, mix [the wine]'. In the juxtaposition of the scenes opposite each other

on walls 2 and 3 the two figures of Irene and Agape are brought together as in
other such frescoes.

Plate 23. (Wilpert 157.1).

Here we find again in black letters over against a white background the inscription, on the left: IRENE DA CALDA (Irene, provide warm [food] and on the
right: AGAPE MISCE MI(hi) ('Agape mix for me [the wine].[35] Agape and Irene
are clearly counterparts to each other in such a scene.

Furthermore we have a connecting image here with the Pécs iconography
(Plates 24 and 25).

Plate 24. (Tomb II: Gerke Fig. 31).   Plate 25. (Closeup: Wilpert 157.1).

---

[35] Arcosolium I, chamber 11. See also Dölger ΙΧΘΥΣ IV (1927), taf. 262.1; Jastrzebowska
(1979), 'Iconographie des banquets', XVII.9. For close-ups of these see Deckers Farbtafel 12.a
and b, and cat. nr. 39. For commentary see Wilpert 435; Dölger ΙΧΘΥΣ V (1943), 492-3.

Clearly the jar along with the cup and fish cooking on the barbecue were standard features of Agape and Irene's *refrigerium* meal. Thus we find emerging a common discourse shared by an artistic community that stretched from Fourth Century Panonia to Rome in this period. Cultural distance is not always, as I have emphasised elsewhere, the equivalent of geographical distance. The detection of a common discourse whose images interact dynamically with each other in the construction of a symbolic universe of meaning reveals connections that geographical distance or simply isolated and fragmented performances of a larger set of linguistic competences might otherwise lead us to deny.

The scene, only partially expressed in particular instances, is of the paradise of the world to come set within a fenced garden, in which the four seasons are experienced in eternal succession bringing harvest and labour, joy and rest. A banquet is celebrated with a fish and a jar of wine in which the living join with the faithful departed but in a *refrigerium* meal quite distinct from the Eucharist since no hierarchically ordained president is required for such a rite. Nevertheless in the private organisation of such a meal a president, a Tricliniarch does emerge (Plate 39).

On wall 3 of the crypt of the Tricliniarch, we find a near square picture located underneath two childrens' *loculi*. It is unclear whether the figure is sitting on a stone block or on a chair. He appears to be presiding over a *refrigerium* evidenced by similarities with other such scenes in which a table with a fish appears (nr 45). Similarly in the cubiculum of the two Agapi (Plate 23), we witnessed a *refrigerium* scene with a single figure who appeared presidential in terms of the meal.[36]

In the arcosolium of Sabina (Plate 26), we have depicted a figure holding a wine jar in her right and a cup in her left hand.

Plate 26. (Deckers Taf. 55 a).

The four figures depicted reclining at the meal in front of the tripod with its fish are looking in her direction, one with his right hand outstretched in her

[36] Deckers nr. 78.

direction. The figure herself (Plate 26) resembles that with an inscriptional identification as Irene or as Agape in other depictions of a *refrigerium*-meal scene that we have examined (Plates 23 [Irene] and Plate 22 [Agape]). Behind the servant girl is a metal container whose lid has a handle in the form of a flying bird, at the vessel's bottom are located two knobs in the form of cats' paws. SABINA MISCE is in brown colours depicted on a white background.[37]

Here we have Sabina playing the role in the *refrigerium* meal that Irene and Agape played in other scenes. How are we to explain Sabina's relationship to these other, abstract figures? I would suggest firstly that Irene and Agape are Christianized equivalents of Psyche and Amore in other paradisiacal scenes where their figures occur. One example, that Klauser insisted was 'Pagan', is the three Good Shepherd sarcophagus in the Museo Pio Cristiano, as we mentioned at the beginning and to certain features of which we can now return.

5. The Three Good Shepherds Sarcophagus: Amor and Psyche

Here we find a vintage scene with the *genii* of the seasons with their appropriate activities emerging from the vine tendrils.

Plate 27. Three Good Shepherds Sarcophagus (Museo Pio Cristiano).

For Klauser the interpretation of this scene and the explanation for its use in a funerary context was simply that the deceased had been owner of a vineyard and his life was simply expressed in symbols 'von der bukolischen Gedankenwelt.'[38] It was an individualistic interpretation expressing the impression left upon the sense organs of an individual following an individual's confrontation

---

[37] Deckers nr. 75; Jastrzebowska, 'Iconographie des banquets' (1979), 23, fig. 7.
[38] See above, footnote 3.

with a work of art. But we have emphasized that participation in a social backcloth implies participation in a language game, albeit an iconographic and non-verbal one, and that such a language game has its own dynamic logic continuing to realize new possible meanings in addition to those that have been actualized.

The depiction of the vineyard scene on this sarcophagus is not simply the suggestion of a workshop *pictorius* about how to commemorate the life of an individual owner of a vineyard. Rather it connects with a collective narrative about hope for the life hereafter expressed in terms of a supernatural foliage in a paradisiacal nature scene, a collective narrative that includes as we have seen the iconography of the garden fence and the vine jar with the votive prayers in the *refrigeria* at *Ss Petrus et Paulus ad Catacombas* and the figures feasting in a barbecue scene in frescoes in *Ss Petrus et Marcellinus*. The appearance of the *genii* of the seasons was not an empirical experience for visitors to vineyards even if the pedestals on which the three shepherds are standing indicate that they are depictions of statues that stood in such vineyards. The statues are icons that point beyond themselves to the transcendent message of the iconography: those *genii* locate the scene in a transcendent world of the eternal cycle of nature in the paradise of the world to come.

With those *genii* and also set into the vine tendrils of the paradisiacal scene are the figures of Amor and Psyche also resting in their branches (Plate 28).

Plate 28. (Closeup of Plate 27).

Thus we come to these new additions to the paradisiacal iconography, new actualizations of what the discourse potentially contains in the inner working out of its logic. The figures of Amor and Psyche appear in the foliage of the sarcophagus of the three Good Shepherds, as we have seen, and are here part

of the paradisiacal banquet in which the visitors to Mausoleum II at Pécs join
in as they enter the iconography of the enclosed garden, or in which the figures
in the *refrigerium* in the *Ss Petrus et Marcellinus* banquet-scenes are also
participants, with Agape and Irene standing for Amor and Psyche.

Apuleius, in recounting the story of Amor (Ἔρως) and Psyche, is aware that
their story is an allegory of the soul seeking divine love.[39] The last and final
task that the vengeful Venus gets Psyche to perform is to bring back a day's
supply of the beauty of Proserpina, goddess of the underworld. Psyche is aware
that this meant that she would have to die but she was allowed as the result of a
message from the tower from which she was about to throw herself to enter the
underworld whilst still alive, carrying two pieces of bread and two coins with
which to appease Cerberus and Charon both at the entrance and at the exit to the
underworld. She succeeded in her quest and obtained the box from Proserpina,
but proceeded to open it, despite what she had been commanded, with the result
that she was overpowered by a fatal sleep.[40] This was the result of her seeking
to make herself more beautiful so as to regain Amor's (Cupid's) love. But Amor
come to her aid in his love for her and wakes her, and with Juppiter's consent,
marries her. Juppiter makes her Venus' equal by giving her immortality.[41]

Like the myth of Demeter and her daughter Persephone, whom she delivers
from her capture and abduction to the underworld by Pluto, god of the dead,
the myth appears in a funerary context as an allegory of the soul seeking escape
from death and obtaining immortality. Set in a paradisiacal scene such as that
of the three Good Shepherds, Amor and Psyche become allegories of the soul
finding immortality in the garden of Paradise.

Such a transcendent theme with such iconography is repeated on the sides
of the sarcophagus of Junius Bassus, and those features are repeated and woven
into the scenes on the front panel of the pillars on each side of Christ ascended
and supported by Caelus. Here we once more find exemplified the conceptual
and iconographic backcloth, the form of life that makes disagreement as well
as agreement possible as a human discourse dynamically develops.

6. Junius Bassus: Paradisical scenes with Scriptural narratives

The newly baptised Roman Prefect, head and leader of the senate, and *vir claris-
simus* was undoubtedly a Christian, as the notice of his death (August 25th, 359)
on the upper edge of his sarcophagus makes clear.[42] The scene on the front

---

[39] Apuleius, *Metamorphoses*, 4.28-6.24.
[40] Apuleius, *Metamorphoses*, 6.20-21.
[41] Apuleius, *Metamorphoses*, 6.23-24.
[42] Elizabeth Struthers Malbon, *The Iconography of the Sarcophagus of Junius Bassus: Neofitus
iit ad deum* (Princeton, 1990), 3-4.

panel of the sarcophagus consists mainly of Biblical scenes, with Christ enthroned in heaven representing the central upper section.

But on the left and right hand side panels we have a Paradisiacal scene reminiscent of the Three Good Shepherds' sarcophagus (Plates 27 and 28).

Plate 29. Genii of the Seasons (3).   Plate 30. Four seasons.

Here we have the eternal cycle of the years with the divine activity of the *genii* imaging an eternal Paradise (Plate 29). At the lower panel of the left hand side we may have at the extreme right a representation of Amor who gives a bird to Psyche as an indication of his winged form, and Psyche with her bowl of bitter water (Plate 30).

It is impossible to dismiss the 'Pagan' iconography of the two side panels as merely the conventional product of a Pagan workshop that had no significance for Junius Bassus' family. The reason against such a 'conventionalist' interpretation is that the two side panels and their iconography are not conceptually isolated and insulated from the 'Christian' panels on the front of the sarcophagus. We are not here confronted by two, alternative social constructions of reality each nihilating the rival claims of the other by explaining away the construction of the other in their own terms.[43] Rather the iconographic themes of the side-panels interweave themselves into the non-verbal, iconographic discourse of the front panel with its Biblical themes.

The images of the *genii* of the four seasons and the foilage in which they appear are found on the two pillars each side of Christ enthroned in the heavens (Plates 31 and 32).

---

[43] As might be argued using the perspective of Peter L. Berger and Thomas Luckmann, *The Social Construction of Reality. A Treatise in the Sociology of Knowledge* (Harmondsworth and New York, 1979), 122-46.

Plate 31.

Plate 32.

   The 'Pagan' iconographic discourse of the soul achieving immortality in the Paradisiacal garden from the two sides continues into the 'Christian' front of the sarcophagus, both Christian and Pagan themes achieving their coherence in a common discourse and forming part of a shared conceptual backcloth or 'form of life.' It is not simply the *genii* of the four seasons admist the vine tendrils of the pillars that make the situation plain. Under the feet of the exalted Christ is Caelus, god of the heavens, supporting him (Plate 33). Caelus cannot be regarded, alongside the two pillars, as merely conventional: they have become part of the Christian message of the family of Junius Bassus.

Plate 33.

   So far the other feature of the Paradisiacal garden, witnessed at Pécs, at *Ss Petrus et Marcellinus*, and at *Ss Petrus et Paulus ad Catacombas* seem to be absent, namely the *refrigerium* meal, a theme conceptually present in the discourse in its Chomskyan competence to express what it may not actually express in any one instance. But that such a meaning was available to those who constructed the Paradisiacal scene on the sides and on the pillars depicted in the front can be seen from the fragmented remains of the sarcophagus lid (Plate 34).

Plate 34.

Here on the right we see the remains of a mask of Luna, with, in the centre, those of a three legged table for a *refrigerium* meal, with fish, double basket bottle, and remains of female instrument player, couch, child and dog.[44]

Having shown a clearly 'Christian' discourse in which the figure of the ascended Christ is interwoven with the Paradisiacal garden and its *refrigerium* meal, let us now turn to the figures of Agape and Irene and Amor and Psyche in the *refrigerium* scenes in *SS Petrus et Marcellinus* (Plates 20, 22 and 23).

7. Agape and Irene in SS Petrus et Marcellinus

Because the figure of Sabina is found fulfilling a similar role to these figures (Plate 23 and 43) and since Sabina is an actual figure, they have been identified as real persons, either of the deceased or of servants of the deceased.[45] The problem with such a reading is two-fold:

(i) The repeated occurrence of these names against stereotypical figures in *refrigerium* scenes, and
(ii) The repeated occurrence of Agape and Irene together shows an association of these names that is hardly accidental: an Agape or an Irene might recur separately as an individual, real person, but not jointly, unless in the case of twins.[46]

---

[44] Malbon, *Junius Bassus*, Plate 40 and p.

[45] G.B. De Rossi, 'Escavazioni nel cimitero dei Ss. Pietro e Marcellino sulla Via Labicana', BAC (1882), 11-130: p. 126; C.M. Kaufmann, *Die sepulcralen Jenseitsdenkmäler der Antike und des Urchristentums* (Mainz 1900), 199; Dölger ΙΧΘΥΣ V (1943), 498-9: 'Sind die Trinksitten der Antike hier auf unserem Bilde so genau der Wirklichkeit entsprechend dargestellt, so sieht man nicht ein, warum auf einmal die zwei Frauen, die beim Gelage angeredet werden, keine wirklichen Personen, sondern nur Personifikationen darstellen sollen'. He goes on to site examples of names of Agape and Irene on epitaphs, 499-500.

[46] *Inscriptiones Sanctae Sedis I, Index Inscriptionum Musei Vaticani 1, Ambulacrum Iulianum sive "Galleria Lapidaria"*, ed. Ivan Di Stefano Manzella (In Civitate Vaticana, 1995), 135 (citing *Digest* [Modestinus] 40.4.44, where Irene is one of the names of three slaves given their freedom on condition that they light a lamp every month on his grave and conduct a *refrigerium* meal.

There is, I suggest, furthermore, a connection between the 'Christian' qualities of Εἰρήνη (Peace) and Ἀγάπη (Love) and associated 'Pagan' terms Amor (Ἔρως) and Psyche (Ψυχή). The significance of the myth was of the soul through love finding finally peace when Psyche finally escapes a world of hostility created by the jealousy of Venus and through Cupid's (Amor's) love attains the immortality which finally ends that hostility. In the continuing dialogue between Paganism and Christianity, disagreement in opinion is made possible once more by prior agreement, an agreement in a form of life. The open-ended character of general concepts, the 'family-resemblance' rather than identification by an exhaustive list of particular features, makes once again the conceptual transition possible.

As part of the interpersonal conceptual backcloth, non-verbal concepts are able to include new instances within a known scheme because of a logical quality of ambiguity in which family resemblances are detected rather than one exhaustively defined concept compared with another. Those non-verbal concepts are sufficiently open-ended and amorphous, as part of a shared backcloth or form of life, and enable the Christian to fill the conceptual spaces with icons of Agape and Irene, but the Pagan with icons of Amor and Psyche.

But how are we to interpret precisely the role of Agape and Irene in the *refrigerium* banquet. Are they, finally, metaphorical abstractions or allegorical figures or personifications if they are not real individuals, whether deceased or servants of the deceased? We need to dispense at this point with the categories that have arisen in contemporary discourse subsequent to the European Enlightenment. I would suggest that there is an ontological significance in the figures of Irene and Agape, of Psyche and Amor that defy classification in such categories.

It is clear that the Dionysius-Ariadne motif is characteristic of female graves but the Selene-Endymion motif of male graves. In these cases, it is not so much that the myth is an allegory of the soul being awakened from the slumber of death by divine acts, but that, if you like, sacramentally, the departed becomes Endymion or Ariadne as they awake to immortality. Similarly with the myth of Amor and Psyche as may be observed in the following sarcophagus scene:

Plate 35. (Dölger, ΙΧΘΥΣ [1922] III 53).

Two central figures sit on a sofa whose side arms are shaped in the form of a dolphin.[47] Note that the female on the right has butterfly wings so that she is clearly identified as Psyche. Amor (or Cupid) on the right is depicted with birds' wings. Between them both flies a winged Genius, offering to them in his closed hands a dove that is the symbol of the goddess Venus.

Note that here as in the Christian *refrigerium* meals that we have so far considered, stands a three legged table whose legs are moulded in the shape of lions' paws. On the left of the couch on a high-backed, patchwork chair is a female lute-player, behind whom is a servant girl with a pitcher in her left hand (the right is broken off). Behind her stands a male servant with fruit. On the right half of the panel stands a lyre-player, with his head disproportionately turning. Then there is next a youthful lad with a garland of flowers. The peacock between the feet of the two last figures sets the scene with the meal in the realm of the eternal and transcendent.

The two figures represent the husband and wife there buried within in mutual embrace having achieved immortality, and engaged reclining in the heavenly banquet that begins here on earth as loved ones gather for the *refrigerium* with their departed loved ones. This was the case with the *refrigerium* as one entered Sabina's tomb and where, in the depiction of the meal, she as the departed one commemorated was shown responding to the request of the dinners to mix the wine and bring this to them (Plate 23 and 43). But it was also the case with those other examples where the names of the deceased were replaced with Agape and Irene, as Christianized counterparts to the images of Amor and Psyche representing the deceased on the British Museum sarcophagus.

The two figures of Irene and Agape and their significance has not always been well grasped. There has been a tendency to try to identify them with actual persons, or simply as servants. Jastrzebowska is the most recent example of the latter, where the figures standing at either end of the couch are simply described as 'servants.'[48] But the figures are wearing body length dalmatics, with *clavi* or embellished strips, sometimes with circular roundels (*orbiculi*). Such decoration, added to tunics and cloaks, became usual in the later empire after Diocletian's reforms for non-military government officials. But they are evidenced from Commodus' reign onwards, and characterize figures generally in catacomb art.[49]

[47] Dölger, ΙΧΘΥΣ V (1943), 394-402.

[48] Johannes Georg Deckers, Hans Reinhard Seeliger, and Gabriele Mietke, *Die Katakombe 'Santi Marcellino e Pietro', Repertorium der Malereien*, Roma Sotterranea Cristiana per cure del Pontificio Istituto di Archeologia Cristiana VI (Münster, 1987) Textband and Tafelband; E. Jastrzebowska, 'Les scenes de banquet dans les peintures et sculptures chrétiennes des IIIe at IVe siècles,' *Recherches Augustiniennes* 14 (1979), 3-9, 24, XIV: Tricliniarch: 'a chaque extremité du *stibadium* se trouve une servante debout...' which he repeats consistently, p. 19 IX fig. 4 (for 'Irene'), p. 22 XII, fig. 7 = Deckers Taf. 55 a (for 'Sabina misce'), p. 21 XI fig. 5 (for 'miscemi Irene').

[49] See, Dio Cassius, LXXII.17.2; SHA, *Com.* 8.8; *Heliog.* 26.2; *Pertinax* 8.2; Isidore, *Or.* XIX.22.9 which describes them as white with purple stripes.

But servants did not so dress. We have the example from the *arcosolium* of
Vibia (Plate 36), Rome of a figure of servant in short *tunica*, two servants with
flowers both of whom appear similarly to have short *tunicae*.

Plate 36. (Dölger IV 264.4).

These figures stand in stark contrast to the depiction of Vibia coming through
the archway and entering into the banquet set in the Elysian fields.[50]

The depiction of servants in short *tunicae* can also be seen in another example, in the right hand section of sarcophagus lid, lacking a surviving inscription,
discovered in a pagan burial area in the vicinity of S. Sebastiano (Plate 37).

Plate 37. (Dölger V 311.2).

The left hand section has a scene that depicts a meal, which, in view of the
overhanging canopy, is perhaps in a marquee. On the left stands a large jug
with a handle on a three-legged stool, that connects the presupposed iconographic discourse with that of the Vibia grave and its Elysium banquet (Plate 36).
A servant with a jug in his right hand moves towards a group of five diners,
who are reclining on a couch. Of a second servant only the head can be seen

---

[50] Dölger V, p. 442; See also drawing in Jastrzebowska (1979), p. 38 XXV fig. 12.

in the background. On the far right a servant stands with a flat plate on which there is a fish. This figure can be none other than a servant, and is identified by the shortness of his *tunica*.

But the *refrigerium* scenes of *Ss Petrus et Marcellinus* depict the several examples of standing figures designated as Agape and Irene or the one of Sabina wearing long tunicae decorated clearly with *clavi*. Furthermore, as we have said, those figures are stereotypical: they do not therefore appear to describe as in the case of Vibia the individual deceased persons. Let us look at a comparison of these figures:

Plate 38. Pomponius Leto
(From Wilpert 157.1).[51]

Plate 39. Tricliniarch
(Wilpert 159.2)[52]

Plate 40.

Plate 41.

Tricliniarch (Wilpert 133.2).[53]

[51] For another photograph, see Deckers, taf 24b, commentary nr. 29.
[52] Deckers, Fbtaf 21.
[53] For another photographic view, see Deckers, taf. 30b Fbtaf 20, commentary nr. 45.

Plate 42. Arcosolium: Crypt of Gaudenzia
(Wilpert 157.2).[54]

Plate 43. Sabina
(Deckers Fbtaf. 55a).

Plate 44. Irene
(from Deckers Fbtaf. 57b).

Plate 45. Agape
(from Deckers Fbtaf. 57b).

In the example from the crypt of Gaudentia (Plate 42), we have behind the figure of the woman standing on the right a seated banqueter above whose head appears the inscription IREN[E] MISCE, thus presumably addressing the woman with the raised cup as Irene who is to mix the wine for them that they are eager to drink. The woman is clearly no servant: her tunic is full length and decorated with *clavi* and *orbiculi*, and a similar point would hold for the other images as well. As we can see in catacomb iconography as in old Christian mosaics, an ungirdled figure with a tunic reaching right under the knees with wide sleeves covering the elbows, white stripes with two red ones, running from the shoulders to the hem, is a typical depiction of a dalmatic. Under the dalmatic was worn a long, narrow, tunic with long arms.

[54] For another photograph, see Deckers, taf. 33c, commentary nr. 47.

Furthermore, in common with the other depictions, she has on the crown of her head her hair woven into a plat. Indeed, whether the figure is of Irene or of Agape (or indeed of Sabina), both are distinguished with such a style of hair decoration.

Plate 46. (Wilpert, 157.2).

The damage to the lower part of the lunette has almost obliterated the figure that stands opposite to Irene with cup raised in her extended right arm (Plate 39). But the original figure now missing is able to be identified from the inscription above the head of the seated diner on the left of the circle that reads: AGAPE P[OR]GE CALDA, or 'Agape, provide warm food.' (Plate 46)

Dölger was convinced that 'Agape' and 'Irene' were usual and indeed popular names for sisters and this would explain the replication of what is a commemoration of actual individuals there buried.[55] But his evidence comes from epitaphs, and the marking of figures in a fresco painting is hardly equivalent and would be a unique and unusual way of making reference to the particular deceased buried in a tomb. Furthermore, the depictions are too stereotypical to be able to stand for one particular individual who happened to have the same name as another individual so depicted (Plates 40 and 42). Rather I have suggested that these are metaphysical figures, the immortalized departed come to conduct and celebrate the *refrigerium* meal with those still in this world. The departed have assumed their form and shape, like a deceased woman appearing like Ariadne as she finds union with the Dionysiac divine life in all its eternal vitality, or like a deceased man taking the form of Endymion as he is awakened from everlasting sleep by the caresses of Selene. Or, much closer to the comparison of a likeness that results in metaphysical absorption, like a married couple who are equated with Amor and Psyche, and with their enactment of a love stronger than death. We should remember here the metaphysical principle

[55] Dölger V, 498-9.

of Hellenistic philosophy that coming to resemble is a process of being transformed ontologically into that which one has come to resemble. Here in the
iconography the deceased are depicted in the form of the divine beings with
who they are in process of assimilation.

Let us summarise where our account has now taken us in our interpretation
of the iconography of the sites that we have examined in this article. We have
rejected a model of understanding art in terms of an artefact that is a sole
depository of meaning confronted by an individual viewer seeking with partial
or complete success to discern the meaning thus embedded in a single artefact.
Meaning arises out of what Wittgenstein described as a shared 'form of life'
and with it a shared discourse whose underlying conceptual structure licensed
both agreements and disagreements in opinion. Dialogue between human
beings was made possible, as was the translatablity of human languages that
this required, because those languages possessed a certain kind of conceptual
vagueness that is a 'family resemblance' between differing concepts enabling
new data to be incorporated into known schemes. We transferred this model
from human beings sharing in a verbal discourse to human beings engaging
in a non-verbal, iconographic discourse in producing and appreciating iconic
artifacts.

Thus the Jar set into the paradisiacal landscape enclosed by the garden fence
is an image or set of images emanating from a conceptual discourse whose
central concepts are characterised by a vagueness that Wittgenstein described
as 'family-resemblance.' This conceptual vagueness enabled new instances to
be classified into known schemes and thus made possible a meaningful dialogue between classical Paganism and Early Christianity. We find ourselves
asking whether the Jar surrounded by the vine tendrils represents the wine of
the Eucharist in the heavenly banquet continued eternally in the paradise of the
world to come within its fenced garden. Or do the representations of what look
like *piscinae* on the seemingly geometrical shapes on the marble slabs mean
that it is not a Eucharist but a *refrigerium* that is being depicted?

We need to cease searching for an account of what impression was going on
in an individual's head or what an individual artist intended to convey but has
failed unambiguously to convey. That search was based upon a false, empiricist
epistemology that blinded us to the dynamic logic of a collective discourse
whose conceptual vagueness enables new possibilities implicit in the language
game to be actualized in new ways.

We saw how the logical potentiality of the iconography at Pécs was actualized in the frescoes of *Ss Petrus et Marcellinus*, in what we must regard as a
shared constellation of meaning common to both these places, as well as *Ss Petrus
et Paulus ad Catacombas* and the Via Latina cemetery. The meaning actualized
at one site is nevertheless present potentially in that of another site whose artefacts configure into a shared constellation of meaning.

We therefore see emerging a common, non-verbal, symbolic discourse of art and iconography unfolding that is a shared discourse, with its own logic, enabling new discoveries to be incorporated into known schemes. Part of the web of meanings are explict and part implicit. As we argued, individuals who share in a human language game only ever partially actualize what the logic of their language contains potentially: human beings only perform part of what the logic of their language makes them competent to perform. But we are dealing with a non-verbal, iconographic language game with logical interrelationships between different parts of its web of meaning.

This point is an important one since often an empiricist methodology such as Klauser espoused has often lead to breaking up such a web of meaning without consciously realizing that this was the case. By individualizing a reaction to an early Christian or Pagan artefact, we have often fragmentalized the language game that is being played out. We list a number of images such as for example Jonah or the Good Shepherd and we envisage a consultation between the client and the *pictorius* as he opens a book of designs that he shows him how individual frescoes or symbols cut in stone, in a burial vault that he is to construct, might look. And we hypothesize, if we are Finney, a kind of arbitrary selection of images by an individual that is no more than the result of an impression being made upon a particular individual by the image.

We have argued that this was not the case with the imagery at Pécs. Neither the Paradisiacal scene, nor its enclosing fence, nor the fresco of the vase painted prominently were fragmented and isolated artefacts the product of an arbitrary collection of individual sense impressions.

There are certain points of relationship, following Klauser, which can be detected on the model of an individual observer recording isolated sense-impressions of what he had seen and making an inference of what relationship held between the two objects observed. And such iconographical links have been drawn between Pécs, Mausolea I and II with similar features and styles in Roman Catacombs, in particular *Ss Petrus et Marcellinus*, and the Via Latina/ Via Dino Compagni site.[56]

But Chomsky's criticisms of an empiricist or behaviourist approach to language is pertinent to our proposal for a new understanding of the interpretation of the non-verbal language of Early Christian art and iconography. Chomsky criticized a view of language learning that implied that a child learned concepts by a systematic labelling of objects in which he/she repeated an adult's label when their response was suitably reinforced with approving reward. Chomsky pointed out that we do not as children learn our first language in the way that a systematic language course teaches us a second language never as successfully as we learned our first.

---

[56] Antonio Ferrua, *The Unknown Catacomb. A Unique Discovery of Early Christian Art* (New Lanark, 1991).

Children experience empirically spasmodic and often degenerate examples of adult speech, accidentally and fortuitously: adults do not open a textbook with a chapter headed *Im Garten* and then proceed to rehearse all the words and phrases that enable a garden to be comprehensively described in German, and likewise *Im Wohnzimmer*, *Im Flughafen*, *Im Sportplatz*, etc, systematically constructing a picture of the world in German.

Children simply pick up isolated and fragmented examples of adult speech without such a structured and comprehensive learning program. From these isolated and fragmentary examples they construct complex sentences and this activity points to a pre-existent syntactic and semantic structure with which a human child is pre-programmed, Chomsky believed, genetically. Without such a pre-progamming, a child could not learn a human language from the fragmented and degenerate forms of adult speech available to him.

My account does not rest on the debate about the genetic foundations of such linguistic structures. It rests rather on Wittgenstein's concept of a language game in which agreement in opinion requires prior agreement in a form of life by whatever means that fundamental agreement has taken place. Applied specifically to the historical understanding of both written and iconographic data, it would explain what happens in two areas of historical study.

The first example may be found in how an epigraphist works on fragments of inscriptions found on stone and other materials. Often epigraphs and epitaphs are dug out of the earth in a fragmented and ruined condition, with gaps in the words and lines, and with many of the words obliterated. How does the epigraphist supply the missing words or lines, or reconstruct those that are damaged beyond scant recognition? What he does can hardly be explained solely in terms of seeking comparable words and lines in less damaged examples, though this he will no doubt do. Part of his method in filling the gaps and repairing the words is his ability to play the language game by thinking his way into the form of life and its logic. Some of his acts of recognition of lines and words in other artefacts moreover are not a case of registering exact equivalence but rather of detecting family-resemblance as we have described it.

The process in which the epigraphist is engaged is not that of an individual recording sense data on his sensory organs. If he were, then much of the data would remain ill defined and without restoration. An epigraphist is more like a child exposed to ill formed words and concepts picked up haphazardly and arbitrarily on which he imposes an intelligible, syntactical and semantic form.

If that explains how in fact the methodology of an epigraphist proceeds, then indeed, I submit, it ought to be used to explain more fruitfully than would otherwise be possible how both the interpreter and indeed for that matter the creator of an artistic or iconographic product proceeds. Whether in Pécs Hungary or in *Ss Petrus et Marcellinus* or San Sebastiano or St. Callistus the individual, random and often ill-formed artefacts that we encounter have meaning because they presuppose a collective language game being played in and between these sites by those who originally created them. Some possibilities granted by the logic of the game are realized but others remain potentially there, with the playing of the language game implying a competence to perform what will not actually always be performed. Some images in some sites are not identical with those of others, yet a logical, though non-verbal logic enables them to be associated within a shared discourse in a pattern of family-resemblance.

With the aid of such a model, we were able to retell the story shared by such sites as that of Pécs with that of *Ss Petrus et Marcellinus*, San Sebastiano, and St. Callistus differently from what their partially formed condition would otherwise have allowed. In the light of such a model we did not simply regard such iconography as inert and unrelated fragments of art, related only through individual visual elements, but as part of a discourse in which interaction powered by an underlying logic is dynamic.

We find here reason to be critical of Finney's hypothesized account of the encounter between the Pagan *officinator* (proprietor [*dominus*] or manager), *pictorius* (painter) of the *officina* (workshop) such as those of Annius Serapidorus, Florentius, or Saeculus and their Christian clients.[57] The character of the interaction between the Pagan painters and proprietors of the workshop and their Christian clients was not the meeting of two rival constructions of reality, as though they were mutually exclusive culturally insulated domains, with individual images being allowed by them in accordance with their ability to expurgate them and produce an *interpretatio Christiana* that the Pagan workshop staff would have found alien. Such individual images selected on such a principle would have related to each other in a quite arbitrary fashion and been quite static and inert, the isolated fragments drawn from a discourse and its logic that were otherwise to be ignored.

Wittgenstein grasped that the character of human dialogue in such a negotiation was not like that. Wittgenstein's theory of language games in relation to underlying forms of life have given us a more plausible model with the power to explain precisely what was taking place in this Pagan-Christian non-verbal, iconographic interaction. The Wine jar of Mausoleum II, set into the scene of a fenced garden of Paradise, presupposed a discourse in which those present within the fenced space entered the eternal world and enjoyed the *refrigerium* feast with their departed loved ones. Though such an explicit gathering for a *refrigerium* may not have been represented iconographically in what has survived as decorations, nevertheless the existence of such imagery is present potentially in the discourse, as indicated by the geometrical patterns evocative of the *piscinae* found actually elsewhere in bowl-like structures with orifices to receive libation wine.

There is a certain conceptual vagueness about these geometrical shapes to which Wittgenstein gave the name of 'family-resemblance' to indicate not their

---

[57] P.C. Finney, *Invisible God* (1994), 152-4.

weakness but their conceptual strength that enabled classifications of new particulars to be included in known schemes. There were Pagan as well as Christian examples with the result that one conceptualization flowed easily over into the other because the conceptual language of both, iconographic and not verbal, exhibited this open-ended quality that defied making exhaustive definitions. Potentially in the iconographic discourse of Mausoleum II there existed figures not expressed there of present and departed banqueters, a potentiality in the discourse that is realised on the part of those *pictorii* and *officinatores* of the frescoes of *Ss Petrus et Marcellinus*, with their actual depictions of such figures. The paradisiacal scene with its fencing, in Pécs Mausoleum II, was depicted on a wall that contained no votive prayers as that of *Ss Petrus et Paulus ad Catacombas*. But that such prayers were part of the logic of the iconographic discourse in which the scene was expressed has become quite clear.

Early Christian Buildings in the Northern Cemetery of Sopianae

Olivér GÁBOR, Pécs, Hungary

ABSTRACT

To date we have known more than 30 buildings from the cemetery. Of these buildings the most important ones are presented in this paper. The main questions are dealt with: When? Who? What kind of Christians? What kind of rituals did the Christians keep in the cemetery?

Some answers can be given accurately and some are speculative.

I. The cemetery[1] buildings and their religion

The cemetery situated on the southern foothills of the Mecsek Mountains and to the North of Sopianae. By law, the cemetery was established outside the walls.[2] (Fig. 1) The stream-valleys defined the line of the roads that crossed the cemetery. It was a horizontal/*sub divo* cemetery, not a catacomb. The latest and the farthest part from the city was the north-western corner of the cemetery. It became a Christian grave-district with numerous buildings, some of which had wall-paintings. However, the grouped placement of Christian graves was traditional according to the custom of *depositio ad sanctos*. To date we have known more than 30 buildings from the cemetery. The main cult observed in the cemetery was tomb-centric Christian, and there are only traces of relic-centric or saint-centric cult. I would like to show some of the buildings, concentrating on the most current questions raised in connection with each, as well as on their religious role belonging to.

Burial chamber No. V[3] (Fig. 2)
The octagonal burial chamber is the first building to present. It was the most important one, because a martyrial grave-monument is located in it. The most recent trend in research is to deny the possibility of the exact definition of the

---

[1] Ferenc Fülep, 'Sopianae', *Archaeologia Hungarica* 50 (1984), 36-267.
[2] Aristoteles, Ἀθηναίων πολιτεία 50,2; *Leges Duodecim Tabularum* X/1; *Hebr.* 13:12.
[3] Gábor Kárpáti, 'A pécsi V. számú sírkamra', *Műemlékvédelem* 46 (2002), 142-4.

Studia Patristica LXXIII, 39-57.

places of ancient martyr-shrines.[4] This concept, in turn, makes us feel even the possibility of the presence of martyr graves in a cemetery impossible. However, the 4th century trend was in fact to accumulate martyrial places.[5] I have some arguments to prove the existence of a *martyrium* in Sopianae.

- There is an Imperial style octagonal grave monument[6] on the highest point in the provincial town's cemetery.
- There were at least two windows to light the interior and a door open (for the visitors?). (Fig. 3) The worn threshold proves that the chamber was often visited that was extraordinary in the case of a burial chamber in this cemetery.
- The visitors could walk around in the chamber passing before the grave, as suggested by the central plan of the building.
- Only a single grave was placed within the chamber, therefore it was not a burial chamber for a family.
- The tomb was short – like an *ossarium* for relics? (The stone pillow on its bottom shows the place for the skull).
- The pedestals next to the tomb served as places for gifts and oil (Fig. 4).[7] No other burial chamber had a pedestal in Sopianae, thus these might rather be connected to the visitors than to the burial ceremony.
- Made either by the builders or the visitors, there are early Christian symbols on the plaster of the chamber (*e.g.* Christogram) (Fig. 5).[8]

---

[4] Friedrich W. Deichmann, 'Märtyrerbasilika, Martyrion, Memoria und Altargrab', *Mitteilungen des Deutschen Archaeologischen Instituts, Roemische Abteilung* 77 (1970), 144-69; Wolfgang Schmidt, 'Spätantike Gräberfelder in den Nordprovinzen des Römischen Reiches und das Aufkommen christlichen Bestattungsbrauchtums', *Saalburg Jahrbuch* 50 (2000), 213-440.

[5] *E.g.* Eunapios of Sardeis 472; Prudentius, *Peristephanon;* Damasi *Epigrammata, etc.*

[6] The central plan with circular or octogonal layout of the mausoleums owned by emperors are the earlier examples. Rome: Mausolea of Romulus-Maxentius, Augustus, Hadrianus, Constantina, Helena, *etc.* Mediolanum: Mausoleum of Maximianus. Saloniki: Mausoleum of Galerius. Spalato: Mausoleum of Diocletianus.

Götz Waurick, 'Untersuchungen zur Lage der römischen Kaisergräber in der Zeit von Augustus bis Constantin', *Jahrbuch des Römisch-Germanischen Zentralmuseums Mainz* 20 (1973), 107-46, 121; James S. Curl, *A Celebration of Death* (London, 1993), 52-61; Tóth Endre, 'Az alsóhetényi 4. századi erőd és temető kutatása 1981-1986' (Vorbericht über die Ausgrabung der Festung und des Gräberfeldes von Alsóhetény), *Archeologiai Értesítő* 114-5 (1987-1988), 20-60, 48-9; W. Schmidt, 'Spätantike Gräberfelder in den Nordprovinzen des Römischen Reiches und das Aufkommen christlichen Bestattungsbrauchtums' (2000), 290.

[7] Tertullianus, *Apologeticus pro Christianis* 13,7; Augustinus, *De civitate Dei* VIII 27; Rodolfo Lanciani, *Pagan and Christian Rome* (Boston and New York, 1892), 218.

[8] The pagan or Christian graffities were not unusual in the late Antique cemeteries. There are lot of example of Christian scratchings on plaster in the catacombs of Rome, in Trier, nay in England. Above the suspected house of Peter in Capernaum, there was found a fifth century octogonal building and its plaster also scratched by visitors. See Andrea Binsfeld, 'In Konstantins Namen', *Archäologie in Deutschland* 5 (2006), 38-9, 39; Charles Thomas, *Christianity in Roman Britain* (London, 1985), 89; Tibor Grüll, 'Mit keresitek a holtak között az élőt?', *Hetek* 43/III (1999), 57-9.

- The monument was later reconstructed by early Christians with respect to the tomb.
- The No. I burial chamber was fitted closely between chambers No. V and IV, as it were in the case of the *depositio ad sanctos*.[9] There were also some graves built close to the No. V burial chamber.
- The lack of human bones suggests a conscious *translation*,[10] because in the other burial chambers of cemetery the skeletons were scattered, but not removed.
- And finally, Sopianae town was very much dependent on Rome.[11] Its Christianity was influenced by Ambrosius of Mediolanum, who personally

[9] This tradition originated from the opinion of the church teaching that all the Christians will be close to the saints on the last day, see Augustinus, *De cura gerenda pro mortuis*, 4. 6; Peter Brown, *A szentkultusz kialakulása és szerepe a latin kereszténységben* (Budapest, 1993), 58. Julian the Apostate felt real antipathy towards this custom (Iulianus, *Contra Galilaeos*, 335 C. 339 E), however Hieronymus found it entirely right (*Contra Vigilantium* VI 359a). Despite the warning of *Isaias* (65:4) the burial of the dead close to a martyr's tomb became a tradition in the 4th century North-African Donatist church. In Rome, the prelude to this tradition was a habit of matrons. They collected the martyrs' bodies into their private cemeteries and they were buried next to them. The body of Maximilia was taken to Carthago by Pompeiana, who had herself buried next to her and close to the tomb of St. Cyprian (*Acta Maximiliani*, 3,4). Veneranda was placed behind a martyr shrine and Julia Florentia (a little baby) was also buried near another saint, see P. Brown, *A szentkultusz kialakulása és szerepe a latin kereszténységben* (1993), 57, 84, 95. The popes that reigned between St. Linus (64/67-76/79) and St. Victor (189-199) were laid together at the same place close to the tomb of Peter. In the 2nd half of 4th century in Rome Proiecta (relation of Damasus) was buried near the saints, and Anicia Faltonia was placed in the St. Peter basilica. Cynegius was laid next to St. Felix in Nola, and Celsus (son of Paul of Nola) was also buried next to the saints in Barcelona, see Paulinus, *Carm.* 31. 109-10; P. Brown, *A szentkultusz kialakulása és szerepe a latin kereszténységben* (1993), 50. Collected inscriptions on the tradition of the *depositio ad sanctos*: Orazio Marucchi and Hubert Vecchierello, *Manual of Christian Archeology* (New Jersey, 1935), 218-9. The most significant example of martyr cult was when a great cemetery or a 'city' was built around the shrine, like in the case of the 5th century Martyropolis/Abu Minas/Menas near Alexandria, see Christpoher Haas, 'Alexandria and the Mareotis Region', in Thomas S. Burns and John W. Eadie (eds), *Urban Centers and Rural Contexts in Late Antiquity* (Michigan, 2001), 47-62, 54 or of the 6th century Martinopolis/vicus Christianorum in Gallia, see Bailey K. Young, 'Autun and the Civitas Aeduorum: Maintaining and Transforming a Regional Identity in Late Antiquity', in T.S. Burns and J.W. Eadie (eds), *Urban Centers and Rural Contexts in Late Antiquity* (2001), 25-46, 34. In Pannonia the *depositio ad sanctos* is known in case of the Sineros-chapel in Sirmium. In Salona (close to Pannonia) Aesclepia had a family mausoleum constructed next to the tomb of Anastasius, see Ejnar Dyggve, *History of Salonitan Christianity* (Oslo, 1951), 78.

[10] A great deal of *translatio* and moving the relics *intra muros* was necessary in Rome because of the barbarian attacks. The relics of martyrs were brought to Italy and the Balkans from Pannonia at the latest in the first half of the 5th century. It is possible that the reclosed, empty tombs near the Late Roman fortress at Alsóhetény, Hungary are indicative of the *translation*, see Endre Tóth, 'Das Christentum in Pannonien bis zum 7. Jahrhundert nach den archäologischen Zeugnissen', in E. Boshof and H. Wolff (eds), *Das Christentum im bayerischen Raum* (Köln, Weimar and Wien, 1994), 241-72, 251.

[11] In the 3rd-4th centuries Sopianae became a walled capital city of the *provincia* Valeria by the grace of emperors. The best analogies to the wallpaintings of the burial chambers in Pécs are known from the catacombs of Rome *etc.*

defeated the pannonian Arianism.[12] He was the first to make a *translatio* in the western part of the empire in AD 386.[13] Moreover, he favoured the octagonal shape in Christian architecture.[14] The construction of the burial chamber No. V. as a *martyrium* could be connected to his local activity[15] (but, sadly we do not know who was buried there).

Burial chamber No. I (Peter and Paul) (Fig. 6. and Fig. 7)

The first early Christian burial chamber was found in the 18th century[16] and has been visitable ever since. This is the best known burial chamber. It has paintings. As I mentioned, this crypt was built very close to the previously mentioned *martyrium*. It is also imaginable that there were other relics behind the niche of this crypt, in a *fenestella* that could be reached from the overground building with brandea-ribbons hanged by the believers from above.[17] The entrance of the burial chamber was walled up and the staircase was backfilled with earth. The overbuilding was therefore constructed to serve both as a monument and as a place of memorial ceremonies.[18] This was the case with the family crypts.

---

[12] It happend during the Synod of Aquileia in AD 381. Anemius, bishop of Sirmium, signed the orthodox decree of the Synod in the name of all Pannonian Christians (*Gesta conc. Aquil.* 76).

[13] Ambrosius built a basilica for the relics of martyr twins (Protasius and Gervasius - Ambrosius, *Epistulae* 77). According to Levente Nagy AD 386 was the exact date for the *terminus post quem* since which a *translatio* was possible in Pannonia, too, see Levente Nagy, *Pannóniai városok, mártírok, ereklyék* (Pécs, 2012), 97.

[14] Ambrosius baptised St. Augustin in the octogonal baptistery of Milan which was excavated in 1961.

[15] More details on Ambrosius' activity in Pannonia in L. Nagy, *Pannóniai városok, mártírok, ereklyék* (2012), 181.

[16] Josephus Koller, 'Prolegomena', in *Historiam Episcopatus Quinqueecclesiarum* (Posonii, 1804); F. Fülep, *Sopianae* (1984), 36-41.

[17] The brandea-ribbons were hung down into the tomb of St. Peter and so got blessed. Emperor Justinianus received only one of these brandeae instead of the relic of St. Peter. For the objects to be hung by ribbons, there were three little niches in the cover of the window that led to the *confessio* of St. Paul (*fenestella confessionis*). These objects became blessed at the rate of their depth of hanging (*prima-, secunda-* and *tertia cataracta*), see Edgár Artner, *A keresztény ókor régiségei* (Budapest, 1958), 25. Remains of a *fenestella confessionis* are also known from the trichora in the Callixtus catacomb, see Umberto M. Fasola, 'Le ricerche di archeologia cristiana a Roma fuori le mura', in *Actes du XIᵉ Congrès International d'Archéologie Chrétienne'* I-III (Roma and Vatican, 1989), 2127-76, 2153-55. The best example is the mausoleum of Anastasius in Salona, Marusinac I. burial chamber, see Emilio Marin, *Starokršćanska Salona* (Zagreb, 1988), 111. 120, where relics were also placed in the apse of the burial chamber.

[18] From the end of the 4th century the destination of the *cella memoriae* as a monument became more important, and its use as a feast-hall declined. The originally pagan yearly rite was more and more symbolic. The overground building of No. XIX burial chamber is a good example. It was too small for a cemetery-feast and it did not have a real entrance, therefore it was a monument and not a *triclinium*.

Burial chamber No. II (Pitcher)[19] (Fig. 8)

This is one of the oldest buildings in the Christian part of the cemetery. There is not even a single definitely Christian symbol on the painted wall of the crypt, and the overground-building's rectangular layout shows a classical shape without apse. However, this building was constructed in the Christian part of the cemetery and its paintings include a painted fence pattern that can be seen in other crypts with Christogram. That is why this burial chamber should be defined as Christian.

Burial chamber No. XVI (communal)[20] (Fig. 9)

In this crypt not all the burial places were filled with tombs. Some places remained empty, thereby suggesting that burial *collegia* existed also under Christianity till the end of the Roman age of Sopianae.

Cemetery buildings No. XXXI[21] (Fig. 10) and XXXVI[22] (cellae trichorae)

The type of three-apsidal construction was first used as audience hall or feast room in late roman palaces.[23] Soon after polyapsidal plans were used to construct cemetery buildings to house ritual feasting places or burial chambers mainly by Christians. In the Sopianae cemetery the tombs were only placed underground. Therefore the overground Cella trichora2 (XXXVI) cannot be considered as burial chamber. At the same time there was a separated crypt-level under it. The Cella trichora1 (XXXI) was a half-lifted down building, therefor it should be defined as a burial chamber.

Cemetery building No. XXXII (Cella Septichora)[24] (Fig. 11)

It was the largest of the known buildings in the cemetery. Never completed by Romans, because the province was given up in the 430s. We can only guess about its function. The Cella Septichora was located in the early Christian part of the cemetery, so it seems to be related to the Christian funeral ceremonies. Its lower part was constructed underground like a burial chamber. There was a great central octagonal hall that was appropriate for an assembly. Considering these characteristics of the building, the six side-apses could have been burial places and the central hall with the eastern apse was intended to serve as a Christian ceremonial place.

---

[19] Gyula Gosztonyi, 'A pécsi II. számú ókeresztény festett sírkamra és sírkápolna' (Die bemalte altchristliche Grabkammer und Grabkapelle no. II.), *Archeologiai Értesítő* 69 (1942), 196-206; F. Fülep, *Sopianae* (1984), 42-6.

[20] *Ibid.* 79-81.

[21] *Ibid.* 51-3.

[22] Zsolt Tóth, 'Régészeti kutatások a Rózsakertben 2010-2011', in *Pécsi Szemle, tél* (Pécs, 2011), 2-13.

[23] Barbara Polci, 'Some Aspects of Transformation of the Roman Domus between Late Antique and the Early Middle Ages', in L. Lavan and W. Bowden (eds), *Theory and Practice in Late Antique Archeology* (Leiden and Boston, 2003), 79-109, 81-2, 90.

[24] F. Fülep, *Sopianae* (1984), 57-9; Visy 2007A.

Burial chamber No. XXXIII (Mausoleum)[25] (Fig. 12)
This burial chamber was built for one person. He was not an earlier martyr but he died contemporarily, because his sarcophagus was not completed. There was a great overground building too. We might conclude that it was also a cemetery building of the Christian church with hall for an assembly. Later, other sarcophagi and bodies were put into the crypt, just like in the case of the custom of *depositio ad episcopi*? - this is a question.

Cemetery building No. XIII[26] (Fig. 13)
Originally it was a simple *mensa* for funeral banquets with a grave underneath.[27] Later a building was constructed here, and the *mensa* became its apse. We don't know exactly whether or not this new building was Christian. But we think, that all the late reconstruction works in this part of the cemetery were undertaken by Christians. These Christians probably kept some elements of the pagan funeral rites and the *mensa* was not a *subsellium* of presbyters.

II. The dating of the buildings (Fig. 14)

The next question is when were the buildings constructed, or *Quando*? The short answer: The cemetery was used from the 1st and 2nd centuries[28] up to the first half of 5th century. The Christian buildings can be dated to the second half of 4th and first decades of the 5th century (up to the arrival of Attila). During this short period of usage of the buildings there were *spoliae*/reconstructions, too.

III. What was the nationality of the buried?

On the one hand, Sopianae was a Roman town with Romanized citizens of local origin and also from all over the Empire. On the other hand, there is information, based on literary sources (Amm. Marc., *Rerum Gestarum Libri* XXVIII 1,5), about the barbarian Carpi settled by the Romans in the vicinity in the 3th century.

---

[25] Ferenc Fülep, 'A pécsi későrómai ókeresztény mauzóleum feltárásáról' (The excavation of the Late – Roman – old Christian Mausoleum in Pécs), *A Janus Pannonius Múzeum Évkönyve* 32 1987 (1988), 31-44.

[26] F. Fülep, *Sopianae* (1984), 99-107.

[27] There are many examples for *mensae* used in cemeteries by Christians, *e.g.* in Tipasa, see W. Schmidt, 'Spätantike Gräberfelder in den Nordprovinzen des Römischen Reiches und das Aufkommen christlichen Bestattungsbrauchtums' (2000), 315; Salona, Sirmium, see Noël Duval, 'Mensae funeraries de Sirmium et de Salone', *Vjesnik za Arheologiju i Historiju Dalmatinsku* 77 (1984), 187-226; L. Nagy, *Pannóniai városok, mártírok, ereklyék* (2012), 51-2, *etc.*

[28] To prove the 1st century use of the cemetery, we only have gravestones found in secondary position, see Ferenc Fülep and Alice Burger, *Pécs római kori kőemlékei*, Dunántúli Dolgozatok 7 (Pécs, 1974), 3.

Thirdly, there was a bucket in a grave, indicating German infiltration into the city from the North. Fourthly, there was a 'catacomb' grave in another cemetery of Sopianae.[29] This burial type was used by Iranian peoples. Lastly, the inhumations with fetal position show servants or slaves of unidentifiable origin.

IV. What kind of christians lived here?

The power of Arianism in Pannonia in the 4th century is well known, due to the historical background and the literary sources. The Arian Paulus was a hypothetical bishop here.[30] The other main branch of Christianity was Roman orthodoxy (Nicaean-Constantinople creed, *fides catholica*). It became the main stream in Pannonia after 380s, because of the personal actions taken by Ambrosius bishop of Mediolanum. In the burial chamber I the pictures of Peter and Paul as saints of Rome show the victory of Roman orthodoxy.[31]

V. What kind of rituals did the Christians keep in the cemetery?

Originally most of the deceased of the pagans were cremated and buried with numerous grave goods. It slowly changed to inhumation from the 2nd century and the number of cremation graves dropped dramatically by the 4th century. Initially, the orientation of inhumation graves was varied. Later the orientation changed to W-E and there quantity of grave goods decreased. Pagans had two types of ceremony. The first one was kept with a banquet during the funeral. The other was the yearly commemoration also in the cemetery. They prepared the meal next to the grave and symbolically ate and drank with the dead. The pagan cemeteries were controlled by the *pontifex*[32] and the *collegia*.[33] The

---

[29] A catacomb grave in itself is not a catacomb cemetery. A pit was dug and on its bottom-level a niche was built to hide the body from the robbers. The catacomb grave-type originated in the prehistoric times of the Eastern European plain (steppe). This type of burial appeared during the period between the 4th and 6th centuries AD in the Carpatian Basin, introduced by an immigrated Iranian nation – perhaps by the Sadagares, see Iordanes who wrote about them in *Getica* under 265 and 272-73, see Zsolt Visy, 'The roman frontiers and the barbarians', in *Limes XIX. – Proceedings of the XIX*th *International Congress of Roman Frontier Studies* (Pécs, 2003), 213-20, 214-6.

[30] Tibor Nagy, *A pannoniai kereszténység története a római védőrendszer összeomlásáig – (Die Geschichte des Christentums in Pannonien bis zu dem Zusamennbruch des römischen Grenzenschutzes)*, Dissertationes Pannonicae Ser. II no. 12 (Budapest, 1939), 210, 217.

[31] Krisztina Hudák and Levente Nagy, *A Fine and Private Place* (Pécs, 2005), 36.

[32] R. Lanciani, *Pagan and Christian Rome* (1892), 307-8.

[33] There have been cemeterial *collegii* at least from the time of Septimius Severus onwards. Their members were collected mainly from the lower strata of society, because the wealthy families could have their own parcels. The *collegii* regulated the use of the membership fees, arranged the funerals and the banquets. Those who breached the regulations were punished, see O. Marucchi and H. Vecchierello, *Manual of Christian Archeology* (1935), 41-3, 91-2, 159, 239.

ceremonies were usually organized by the family rites[34] and were only rarely supported by the state.

The Christians inhumated their dead from the beginning. The W-E orientation, *i.e.* facing towards the Paradise (Mesopotamia) from where the return of Christ was expected.[35] Initially the Christians continued the earlier pagan cemetery-rites, and only changed them gradually. For example, they seldom put *obuli*[36] and other grave goods into the graves. The Christian families kept the feasts at funerals and also at the yearly commemorations, but the meals became more symbolic, without cooking in the cemetery. The funeral procession was not a show and caricature of the dead any more from the 2nd part of the 4th century. It became an event of sorrow and joy at once, because they believed that the faithful dead would reach Heaven and eventually be reborn.[37] The deceased would symbolically take part in the banquet but became passive and more separated in the pictures. The overground buildings above the family burial chambers were built for intimate[38] symbolic banquets and as monuments. The Christian cemeteries were controlled by the church[39] and by funeral *collegia*. The simple funerals were family events and these remained half-pagan rites as yet in the 4th century.

---

[34] Éric Rebillard, *Religion et sépulture. L'Église, les vivants et les morts dans l'Antiquité tradive*, Civilisations et Sociétés 115 (Paris, 2003).

[35] Adalbert G. Hamman, *Így éltek az első keresztények* (Budapest, 1987), 183.

[36] Volker Zedelius, 'Obolos oder Signum Christi?', in *Spurenlese – Beiträge zur Geschichte des Xantener Raumes* (Köln, 1989), 175-8.

[37] The concept of early Christians was not simply about after-life. They believed in Heaven and Resurrection simultaneously. Of course the idea of eternal life meant after-life and Resurrection at once also for Jews, see Tibor Grüll, *A kövek kiáltanak* (Veszprém, 2009), 100. Gabriel showed the preview of the Apocalypse of the New Testament to *Daniel* (*Dan.* 8:16-27). It seems, that the longing for rebirth in relation to Doomsday or to the empire of Jesus (*Rev.* 20:3) was strongest in the 1st century AD (millenarism/khiliasm). Yet in the 2nd century the coming of the Apocalypse was believed by Justin and Irenaeus, althought the exact date of it was unknown (*Matth.* 25:13). Subsequently, as a result that the Doomsday obviously did not occur, this belief changed to desire for Heaven/Paradise and at the same time the waiting for Resurrection became sporadic (*e.g.* on the inscription of Damasus; O. Marucchi and H. Vecchierello, *Manual of Christian Archeology* (1935), 163. Only the followers of Marcion denied entirely the possibility of the resurrection of the flesh (Tert., *Adv. Marc.* I 14).

[38] Intimacy was very important for the Christians. Approaching a Christian altar or mensa was forbidden for pagans. Even the catechumens were left out of the Eucharists. After the times of the Apostles the Christian assemblies were not kept *sub Divo* anymore, with the exception of the North-African area (Carthage, Cherchell) and the *mensae* at the cemeteries, see A.G. Hamman, *Így éltek az első keresztények* (1987), 185, 193. Because of the continental climate in Pannonia it was practical to cover the cemeterial *mensae*, too.

[39] Before the 4th century the Christians paid taxes for their cemeteries (Tert., *Apol.* 39). Cyprian scolded the *episcopi* who took part in pagan *collegii* (*Epistula* 67,6). In the 3rd century several catacombs were ruled by the church under the Roman bishops Zephyrinus and Callixtus. Pope Fabianus parceled the cemeteries and ordered them under the rule of *diaconi*. Pope Dionysios prescribed rules for cemeteries. In the end, burying in pagan cemeteries was forbidden for Christians by the 9th canon of the Laodikeian synod (343-381).

Christians had a different relation to the corpse and bones of martyrs. Their distancing with the dead disappeared. Following the tradition of pope Damasus and bishop Ambrosius, the Christians of Sopianae opened and visited the martyr-tombs, touched and collected their bones and buried their dead near them. The tombs and memorial buildings of martyrs and bishops were maintained by the church in the end of 4th century. The Christians rarely kept *eucharistia* or agape in the cemetery,[40] but it was the beginning of Christian pilgrimage. The greatest buildings in the cemetery of Sopianae belonged to the church too (*e.g.* Cella Septichora, No V. burial chamber and Early Christian Mausoleum).

In summary:
The northern cemetery of Sopianae dates to the 1st to the 5th centuries AD (however, the buildings date to the 2nd half of the 4th century and the first decades of the 5th century). It was a horizontal (*sub divo*) cemetery with Christian parts. The Christian graves and tombs show transitional rites from paganism to Christianity. Finally, the cemetery became a territory controlled by the church, but at the same time the vast majority of graves, buildings and most funeral rites remained private. In the end of this era the most important new Christian improvements, features and rites were introduced by the church: *e.g.* the most significant buildings in the cemetery, orientation of this buildings, control of the new custom of *depositio ad sanctos*, and organization of visits at the martyr-tombs.

---

[40] From early times the Christians celebrated Eucharist on the anniversary of the dead (*Acta Ioannis* 72. Tert., *De corona* 3; *Didasc.* XXVI 22,2-3). There is one reference to a Eucharistic assembly kept in a catacomb (*Acta Ioannis* 46,85), and pope Felix I (269-274) ordered masses to be celebrated at the tombs of martyrs in Rome (*missa ad corpus*), see László Vanyó, *Az ókeresztény művészet szimbólumai* (Budapest, 1988), 44, 47. Dated to the 2nd half of the 4th century, there is an inscription in a tomb of the Priscilla-catacomb which says that three men (Florentinus, Fortunatus and Felix) stood before the chalice (*ad calicem*), according to *Matth.* 20:22; *Mark* 10:38, see L. Vanyó, *Az ókeresztény művészet szimbólumai* (1988), 63. On the anniversary day of his dead wife, senator Pammachius fed the poor at the tomb of St. Peter (Paulinus, *Ep* 13. 15), see P. Brown, *A szentkultusz kialakulása és szerepe a latin kereszténységben* (1993), 59. According to inscriptions the Christians kept common banquets at the tombs to pray for the souls of the dead, see O. Marucchi and H. Vecchierello, *Manual of Christian Archeology* (1935), 223-4. It would be evident to find a connection between the cemeterial banquet, the agape and the Eucharist. Initially, there was real connection between the agape and the Eucharist outside of cemeteries: Plinius wrote of two kinds of Christian assemblies, one of which was a common meal (*Epist. ad Traian.*, X 97). Christians said Eucharistic prayers after the agape. Later, in the 2nd century, the agape lost ground to the Eucharist. Justin also wrote about the detachment of these two rites (1*Apol.* 66). According to Ignatius of Antioch, the agape was the higher ranking event, because during this rite the presence of the bishop was necessary (*IgnSmyrn.* 8), see O. Marucchi and H. Vecchierello, *Manual of Christian Archeology* (1935), 288, 376.

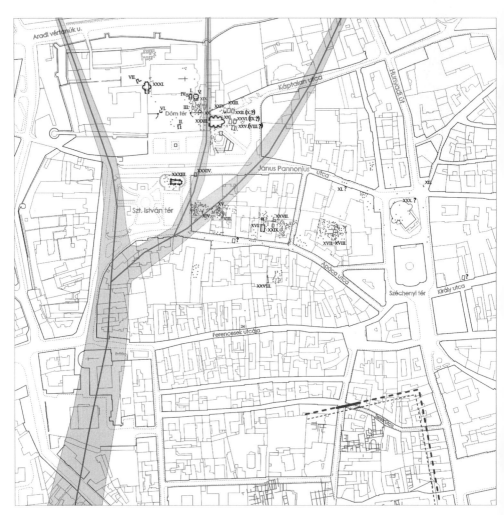

Fig. 1. The cemetery North to Sopianae, and its stream-valleys
(O. Gábor – J. Kraft – K. Szijártó).

Fig. 2. The No. V burial chamber (photo: O. Gábor).

Fig. 3. Window of the No. V burial chamber (photo: O. Gábor).

Fig. 4. The pedestals right to the arcosolium in the No. V burial chamber
(photo: O. Gábor).

Fig. 5. Christogram on the plaster in the No. V burial chamber
(photo: O. Gábor).

Fig. 6. A drawing showing the No. I burial chamber in the beginning of the 20th century (Dörre Tivadar).

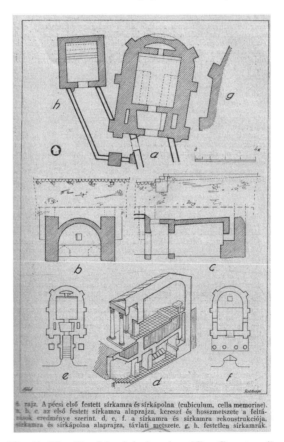

Fig. 7. The No. I burial chamber (Gy. Gosztonyi).

Fig. 8. Model of the No. II burial chamber (A. Fetter).

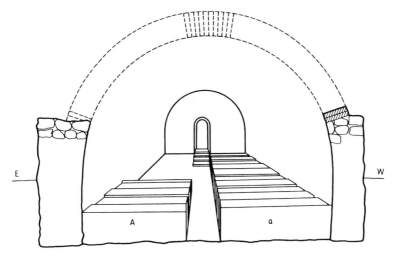

Fig. 24.a. The reconstruction of burial-chamber G/4 from the N

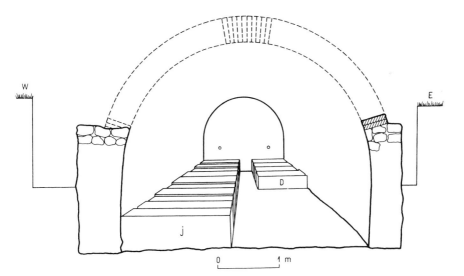

Fig. 24.b. The reconstruction of burial-chamber G/4 from the S

Fig. 9. The No. XVI burial chamber (F. Fülep).

Fig. 10. Model of the Cella trichora1 (A. Fetter).

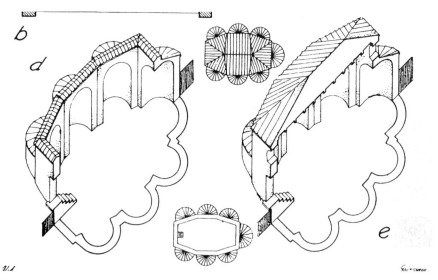

Fig. 11. The Cella septichora (Gy. Gosztonyi).

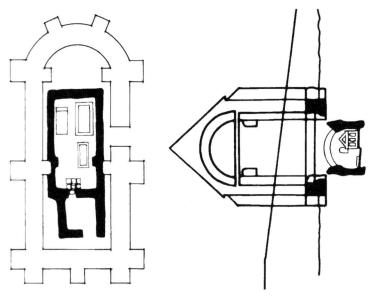

A kápolna alatt, attól szerkezetileg függetlenül, de egyidőben épült a kisebb méretű sírkamra. A festett oldalfalú sírkamra dongaboltozata beszakadt állapotban került elő. A falfestmények a helyiség északi falán találhatók: egy-egy keretezett mezőben a bűnbeesés és Dániel próféta az oroszlánok vermében. E két, viszonylag jó állapotban fennmaradt figurális festményen kívül a többi falon növényi díszek, krisztogram és egy erősen megrongálódott ülő férfialak képe látható. Eredetileg a dongaboltozatos mennyezet is festett volt.

Az ókeresztény mauzóleum alaprajza és metszete
Ground plan and cross-section of the Early Christian mausoleum

Fig. 12. The Early Christian Mausoleum of Pécs (F. Fülep).

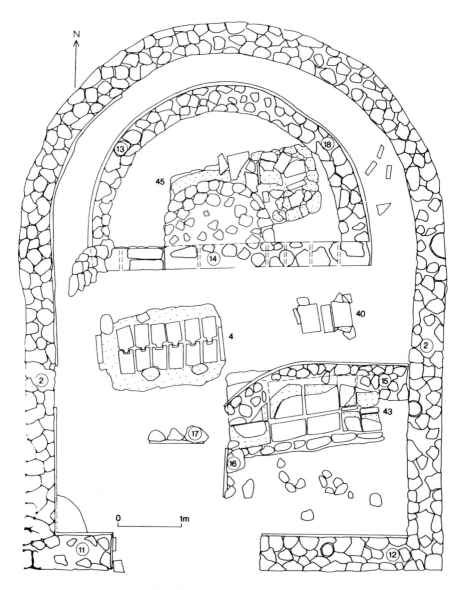

Fig. 51. The ground plan of burial-chamber XIII

Fig. 13. The No. XIII burial chamber (F. Fülep).

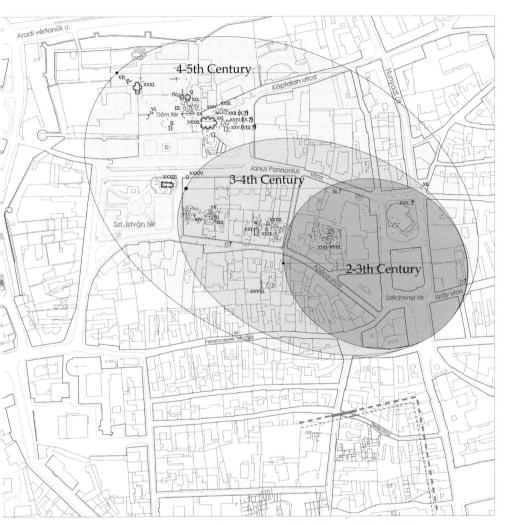

Fig. 14. The chronology of the cemetery (O. Gábor – K. Szijártó).

The Paradise in the Early Christian Cemetery of Sopianae

Zsolt VISY, Pécs, Hungary

ABSTRACT

Sopianae was the civil centre of the province Valeria in the 4th century, and also the most important base of the Christianity north of the river Drava. The most intact *hypogaeum* was found in its late Roman – early Christian cemetery north of the town in the late 18th century. As it could be proved that its entrance had been blocked by stone slabs and also the entrance shaft of the crypt had been filled with earth after the deceased had been put into the crypt, and later no one entered the grave chamber, it is evident that all decorations and paintings on the walls served the other world happiness of the deceased and represented the paradise. Similarly some other old Christian graves in the cemeteries of Sopianae built from stone slabs or bricks had been plastered in the inner side and sometimes decorated with a painted Christogram. These graves represent the same idea and point out the strong Christian belief in the resurrection.

The history of Sopianae in the first three centuries is not totally clear. Only the excavations in the previous decades shed some light on the earlier phases of the settlement. It could be proved that in the 1st-2nd centuries a native vicus was in the place, and only the Severan era brought a municipal development. At the time of the tetrarchy Sopianae should have been a significant town, if Diocletian chose it for the civil centre of the new province Valeria. The town lived and flourished in the 4th century, at least up to the first years of the fifth (Fig. 1). In the last about 30 years the town declined. At first its higher society, later numerous civilians left for Italy. The evacuation was so strong that no signs of continuity can be found.[1]

The prosperous evolution of Sopianae and the strengthening of Christianity in the region took place at the same time. It is then no surprise at all that this town became one of the most important Christian centres north of the Drava. It can be supposed that the clerks in the provincial administration were in their majority Christians who contributed a lot to this process. They were the owners of the elegant houses in the town and of the villas in the surrounding slopes of the Mecsek hill. Such houses could be partly unearthed in Sopianae (Fig. 2)

---

[1] Gábor Kárpáti, 'The Roman Settlement of Sopianae', *Situla* 42 (2004), 279-87; Zsolt Visy, 'Pécs a római korban (Pécs in the Roman Age)', in *id.* (ed.), *Pécs története* I (The history of the town Pécs I) (Pécs, 2013), 93-152.

Studia Patristica LXXIII, 59-73.
© Peeters Publishers, 2014.

Fig. 1. Sopianae in the modern town of Pécs (Zs. Visy).

Fig. 2. A late Roman house partly reconstructed in the southeast part
of Sopianae. Photo of Zs. Visy.

Fig. 3. The bronze plate of a casket with biblical scenes from a late Roman villa
at Bakonya. Photo of Zs. Visy.

and more villas could be identified outside of the town. In the villa at Kővágószőlős remains of a *cella memoriae* with a crypt beneath it have been
excavated,[2] and not far from it, south of Bakonya, some bronze plates of a
casket were found, decorated with biblical scenes[3] (Fig. 3). Most of the Christians of Sopianae were buried in the big cemetery on the north side of the
Roman town. As O. Gábor pointed out, this cemetery was enlarged more times
to the west.[4] The bulk of the grave chapels and burial buildings were built in
the north western sector of the cemetery.[5] Both from this topographic order and
the archaeological evaluation of the finds could be concluded that they belong
to the second half of the fourth century, up to the beginning of the fifth.

---

[2] Alice Sz. Burger, 'The Roman Villa and Mausoleum at Kővágószőlős', *Janus Pannonius
Múzeum Évkönyve* 30-1 (1985-1986; Pécs, 1987), 65-228.

[3] Zsolt Visy, in Ferenc Fazekas, Olivér Gábor, Levente Nagy, Zsolt Visy, *Sopianae and Valeria
in the Late Roman Age – Early Christianity* (Pécs, 2010), 38.

[4] Olivér Gábor, 'Sopianae ókeresztény egyháza(i) (Old Christian church(es) of Pécs)', *JPMÉ* 2
(2005-2007 [2008]), 109, fig. 4.

[5] Zsolt Visy, 'Cella septichora. Előzetes beszámoló a Szent István téren, az ókeresztény temető
területén folytatott régészeti kutatásokról (Cella septichora. Preliminary report about the archaeological investigations in the St. Stephan square in the territory of the Old Christian cemetery)',
Pécsi Szemle IX/1 (2006), 3-13; *id.*, 'Von Sopianae bis Fünfkirchen: Neuere Untersuchungen
im frühchristlichen Gräberfeld von Sopianae', in P. Herz, P. Schmied, O. Stoll (eds), *Zwischen
Region und Reich. Das Gebiet der oberen Donau im Imperium Romanum* (Berlin, 2010), 77-90;
Zsolt Tóth, 'Hány sírkamrát rejt a föld Sopianae északi temetőjében? (How many grave buildings
are hidden in the earth in the north cemetery of Sopianae?)', *Pécsi Szemle* XV/1 (2012), 2-15.

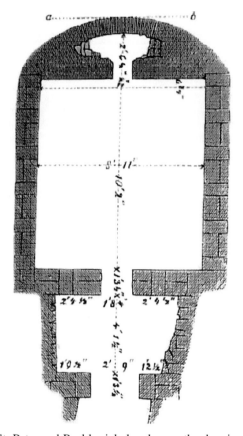

Fig. 4. The St. Peter and Paul burial chamber on the drawing of J. Koller.

The investigation of the burial buildings and the cemetery of Sopianae goes back to the 18th century. The first and up to now most intact painted *hypogaeum* (crypt) was found in 1782 and soon published by József Koller[6] (Fig. 4). It has a small narthex and a burial chamber. Its entrance is on the south side, and there was only one grave on the northern side. The West-East orientation allowed putting the corpse with his head to the west, looking to the East, according to the general orientation in the 4th century, and applied almost without exception by the Christians. This grave building has been subject of numerous scientific investigations and it is the base also for the present study.

---

[6] József Koller, *Prolegomena in historiam episcopatus Quinqueecclesiarum* (Posonii, 1804), 25-6.

The building consists of two parts, the *hypogaeum* and the *cella memoriae* (grave chapel). It could be observed that the foundation level of the *cella memoriae* lies about 1 m above the floor level of the crypt, also the survived two pillars from the four ones in front of the building have the same fundament level.[7] Another observation could be made on the basis of the drawing and description of Koller. He mentioned that the door of the crypt was blocked by broad stones, and outside this door two stone groups were depicted by him in both side. The right meaning of this situation could be solved only some years ago. The two stone groups supported the earthen walls of the entrance shaft, and the door had to be blocked because this shaft was filled with earth after the burial.[8]

Opposite to the entrance a little niche is to be seen, but exceptionally its rear wall is missing. It could be interpreted as a *fenestella*. Behind it there is a semicircular niche. It was automatically formed by the straight wall of the grave chamber and the apse wall of the *cella memoriae* which goes here down to the same level as the other wall. However, the hole was not filled, and because no other remains of the burial chapel than the fundaments survived, one cannot decide, whether this *loculus* (?) was open from the upper level or not. This knowledge could help to decide whether this burial chapel served also for relics. It is also to be mentioned that three biblical scenes were depicted on both sides of the crypt. They belong to the group of salvation compositions which corroborates the possibility that the grave chamber could contain also martyr relics as it was put forward by K. Hudák.[9]

The Christianity spread out in the first centuries AD also in the European provinces, and became strong enough also in Pannonia to be able to give martyrs at the turn of the fourth century. The belief in Pannonia was determined after the Nicaean synod step by step by the Arianism. This heresy was taken over by the majority of the population of the Balkan provinces, and its centres were Sirmium and Mursa. The Arianism was favoured by Constantius II, and the orthodoxy could overcome it only at the beginning of the eighties of the fourth century as Ambrose, bishop of Mediolanum, and the pope Damasus (364-388) drove out this heresy from the Christianity forever.[10] The victory of the orthodoxy brought some changes in the Christian doctrine in Pannonia, but also in the art of the region. It has been pointed out that Christ as *verus deus*

---

[7] Zsolt Visy, 'Recent data on the Structure of the Early Christian Burial Buildings in Pécs', *Acta Classica Universitatis Scientiarum Debreceniensis* 43 (2007), 137-55.

[8] Zs. Visy, 'Recent data' (2007), 144-6.

[9] See the detailed discussion in Krisztina Hudák, 'The Iconographical Program of the Wall-paintings in the Saint Peter and Paul Burial Chamber of Sopianae (Pécs)', *Mitt. Christl. Arch.* 15 (2009), 64-70.

[10] Tibor Nagy, *Die Geschichte des Christentums in Pannonien bis zu dem Zusammenbruch des römischen Grenzschutzes*, Diss.Pann. II.12 (Budapest, 1939).

and *victorious salvator* was put in the centre and the significance of the apostles Petrus and Paulus as saint martyrs of Rom grow intensively.[11]

Sopianae was situated near to the Arian centres, and surely went under their influence. The orthodox reaction had to bring some modifications also in the archaeological material. Such changes could be found in the representation of the two apostles Petrus and Paulus in the burial chamber Nr. I,[12] and also the ivy leaves in the Jonah-cycle instead of those of the gourd-tree suggest the same, as it was pointed out by György Heidl. The change was due to the new translation of the Bible by Jerome and his commentary in 389/390–392, where the ivy leaves first appeared. The consequence could be drawn that the burial chamber was built and painted about at the end of the fourth century.[13]

However, it is only one thing, though very important, regarding the religious connections and the dating of the grave chamber. It is also important that the whole pictorial program of it is tightly connected to the paradise, to the heavenly home of martyrs by the side of Christ. This thesis has been treated many times, at latest by Krisztina Hudák, Levente Nagy and Zsolt Magyar.[14] In the centre, above the open niche a Christogram is to be seen, on its both sides Saint Peter and Saint Paul, waving with their hands towards the Christogram. It is worth to refer to the closest parallel of the scene in the crypt 3 of the catacomb SS. Marcellino e Pietro in Rome, but also the painting in a *hypogaeum* of Naissos (Nis) is very similar. All the three and some others like a painting of a burial chamber in Thessaloniki emphasise the growing importance of Rome and can refer to the victory of the orthodoxy.[15]

In the centre of the painting of the vault a Christogram was painted and round it four medallions with male busts (Fig. 5). In the rear flowers and birds represent the Paradise. One of the questions is who are the four persons in the medallions? According to the widely spread interpretation the deceased persons

[11] K. Hudák, 'Iconographical Program' (2009), 71-5; Levente Nagy, *Pannóniai városok, mártírok, ereklyék*, Thesaurus historiae ecclesiasticae in Universitate Quinquecclesiensi 1 (Pécs, 2012), 96-7.

[12] K. Hudák, 'Iconographical Program' (2009), 61-3.

[13] György Heidl, 'A pécsi 1. számú sírkamra Jónás-freskója és Szt. Jeromos Jónás-kommentárja (The fresco of Burial Chamber no. 1. in Sopianae and the commentary of St. Jerome about the book of Jonah)', *Katekhón* 2 (2005), 221-35; K. Hudák, 'Iconographical Program' (2009), 63-4.

[14] Krisztina Hudák and Levente Nagy, *Megfestett mennyország. Barangolás a pécsi ókeresztény temetőben / A Fine and Private Place. Discovering the Early Christian Cemetery of Sopianae*, Örökségi Füzetek 4 (Pécs, 2005), 31-47; Zsolt Magyar, 'The World of Late Antique Sopianae: Artistic Connections and Scholarly Problems', in Miša Rakocija (ed.), *Niš and Byzantium. Seventh Symposium Niš, 2008. The Collections of Scientific Works VII* (Niš, 2009), 110-1; K. Hudák, 'Iconographical Program' (2009).

[15] Zoltán Kádár, 'Pannónia ókeresztény emlékeinek ikonográfiája (L'iconografia dei monumenti paleocristiani della Pannonia)', *Regnum* 3 (1938/1939), 62, exceptionally 6-7; K. Hudák, 'Iconographical Program' (2009), 51.

Fig. 5. The dove of the St. Peter and Paul burial chamber. Photo of A. Török.

buried in the crypt are represented in the four *imagines clipeatae*,[16] but it is impossible, because there was only one grave in the crypt, and there are no remains or any information by Koller that more graves could have been placed in it. Other scholars believed that the *loculus* had been made for relics, and the *imagines clipeatae* represent martyrs.[17] In a newer study Krisztina Hudák rejects the idea about depicting of the deceased persons, and also the possibility that they could be cosmic symbols, and raises the hypothesis that the four men could be the *quattuor sancti coronati*.[18] L. Nagy is on the same meaning, but emphasises that because off the presence of the *fenestella* and the *loculus* the interpretation as a martyr shrine cannot been excluded, even if other data for it or a funerary basilica built in a nearby place could not be found.[19]

The hypothesis of bringing relics of the four Pannonian martyrs from Rome – in the reality not those of them but those of four soldier martyrs – to Sopianae and putting them in the mysterious niche is attractive. The four portrays could

---

[16] At first it was accepted also by K. Hudák and L. Nagy, see K. Hudák and L. Nagy, *Meg-festett mennyország* (2005), 46.

[17] Einar Dyggve, 'Das Mausoleum in Pécs', *Pannonia Könyvtár* (1935), 1-3, 67-75; Z. Kádár, 'Pannónia' (1938/1939), 8.

[18] K. Hudák, 'Iconographical Program' (2009), 70.

[19] L. Nagy, *Pannóniai városok* (2012), 176-9.

support the idea, but one has to be very cautious with this interpretation. However, in a way also the construction of the painting of the vault allow it, because it proves that all the four are in the Paradise by the side of Christ. Although the men of different age but in similar white dress with red stripes represent surely heavenly persons, their identification with the four sculptors is not compulsory. Lots of similar portrays in medallions were prepared in profane and religious context on all kinds of objects, like brooches, spoons or sarcophagi. Silver plates with portraits of the sons of Constantine as *imagines clipeatae* can be mentioned as well. The Animal ewer of the Seuso treasure was decorated with 10 portraits on the lid (Fig. 6-7). While evaluating the young man portraits on a silver plate of the Kaiseraugst treasure M. Guggisberg stated, that such portraits are general happiness allegories both in the imperial and private art.[20] Annelie Kaufmann-Heinimann emphasised the role of the Constantine dynasty and dated these portraits between the first quarter of the fourth and the beginning of the 5th century.[21] The number of the persons represented in a painting or on an object is quite different, but they are in the most cases four in number. Taking into account all these possible interpretations I think that the ambition of any exact identification as martyrs or family-members of the persons represented in the medallions in the Peter and Paul grave chamber can be put aside, because the four young men round the Christ's monogram and amongst trees and birds of a garden represent the joy and happiness in the paradise.[22] It can be added that according to the Christian belief this joy and happiness can be ascribed first of all to martyrs after their heavenly birth, and so their general identification as martyrs is the most plausible possibility. To be able to identify them with the *quattuor sancti coronati* an independent new source should be found. This new source could be only the funerary basilica which should have been built to the memory and honour of the martyrs in a nearby place.[23] The only place where it could stand is the terrace of the medieval cathedral, but here, in its crypt, no remains of a Roman building have been found.[24]

---

[20] Martin A. Guggisberg, 'Schlussbetrachtungen', in Martin Guggisberg with Annemarie Kaufmann-Heinimann (eds), *Der spätrömische Silberschatz von Kaiseraugst. Die neuen Funde. Silber im Spannungsfeld von Geschichte, Politik und Gesellschaft der Spätantike*, Forschungen in Augst, Bd. 34 (Augst, 2003), 285-91.

[21] Annemarie Kaufmann-Heinimann, 'Decennalienplatte des Constans', in Martin Guggisberg with Annemarie Kaufmann-Heinimann (eds), *Der spätrömische Silberschatz von Kaiseraugst* (2003), 145-50.

[22] Zsolt Visy, 'Contributions to the archaeology of the Seuso Treasure (Lecture given in the Society of Antiquaries of London, 14.02.2008; *Spec. nova* 21-2 [2013], 221-44), see http://www.sal.org.uk/newsandevents/folder.2010-01-13.6340317245/, note 76.

[23] Pasquale Testini, *Archeologia cristiana* (Bari, 1980), 126-7.

[24] It was supposed by Gyula Gosztonyi, *A pécsi ókeresztény temető* (Pécs, s.a. [1943]), 139; similarily Zsolt Visy, 'Adatok Sopianae ókeresztény leletegyüttesének értékeléséhez', *Örökségi Füzetek* 2 (Pécs, 2004), 117-23, 120-2, although now I do not believe that the channel which runs along the north side of the cathedral (Ferenc Fülep, *Sopianae*, Archaeologia Hungarica 50,

Fig. 6. The upper part of the Animal Ewer of the
Seuso treasure. Photo of the Hungarian TV2.

Fig. 7. Two busts from the lid of the Animal Ewer of the Seuso treasure.
Photo of Bennett – Mango.

   Although this identification is uncertain, the program of the paintings is
surely the representation of the Paradise. It is evident but the question should
be answered, for whom? The scholarly research revealed that the context of
the representation reflects the newest tendencies of the Christian religion. One
could think that not without any propagandistic intention. The question is who
could see these paintings? Being a grave in a cemetery, being a crypt of a
person one could think that perhaps the relatives and other acquainted people
of the dead person who could do so. It was believed earlier, but it is not the
case. The *hypogaea*/crypts served only as containers of the corpses. Living
people entered the crypts only during the funeral ceremony as the body was
put in the sarcophagus.[25] Thereafter the crypt was closed and the burial feast
and the later memorial banquets were held outside, in the *cella memoriae* built
above the crypt. It is similar to the situation in the common cemetery. The
corpse was put in a coffin and placed deep in the earth, and above on the
surface memorial banquets could be held. The same is to be imagined for the
burial buildings of more persons. The mausoleum in Alsóhetény was full
with sarcophagi,[26] and also the burial building G/4 in the Apáca Street in Pécs.[27]
It can be only supposed that the deep in the earth built *cella septichora* was
planned to serve in the same way, but as it was not finished and no graves were
placed in it we can not reveal the exact situation. It is, however, important that
the floor of all crypts and burial buildings built for one or more persons were
deepened in the earth as in the case of the simple graves. Their floor level can
measure sometimes also 3-4 meters under the surface.[28] The only exception in
Sopianae was probably the burial chapel XIII in the Apáca Street. It was not
deepened under the surface, and at least in its second phase it could serve as a
cella memoriae.[29]
   The deceased's area was strictly separated from that of the livings. Nobody
entered the crypts except during a newer funeral. It could be observed in almost
all burial chambers that also in the smallest crypt later another grave was
placed. Although the space in the burial chamber nr. I could have given enough
places for one or two more graves, it cannot be decided, because no data had
been noticed in the original description. It could be, however, proved also in
this case, that the entrance of the crypt was blocked and the passage filled with
earth. This kind of closing the crypts could be observed in three more burial

---

[Budapest, 1984], 23-4) would be of Roman origin. To the lack of Roman remains under the
cathedral see Gábor Kárpáti, 'Janus Pannonius sírja', *JPMÉ* 2 (2005-2007 [2008]), 123-4.
   [25] Zs. Visy, 'Recent data' (2007), 146.
   [26] Endre Tóth, 'Az alsóhetényi 4. századi erőd és temető kutatása, 1981-1986. Eredmények és
vitás kérdések', *Archaeologiai Értesítő* 114-5 (1987-1988), 22-61.
   [27] F. Fülep, *Sopianae* (1984), 76-81.
   [28] That is why the ideas are erroneous which interpret some burial buildings like a baptistery
or a medieval church. No baptistery or church was built with a floor 2-3 m under the surface.
   [29] F. Fülep, *Sopianae* (1984), 99-101.

chambers, and the same situation can be supposed in the earlier excavated burial chambers, too, where the entrance section cannot be investigated any more.[30]

The coffin was the last home of the deceased. It was generally put in the earth but placed in a crypt, if the family was wealthy enough and had a higher social reputation. The crypt belonged to the deceased; it was built and decorated for him (or for her).[31] It can be assumed as well that these burial buildings were planned and built by themselves during their life.

The house like form of lots of brick graves and sarcophagi are in this respect the same as the house like form of the burial chambers. Both were built under the surface in an area which belonged to the other world. Both could be plastered and painted, and in the cemetery of Pécs lots of late Roman, from stone or brick built graves are known which were plastered and sometimes painted in the inner side. The interior walls of the tombs in the 8 Apáca Street were coated with lime mortar,[32] the inside of the grave L/45 in the apse of the burial chamber nr. XIII was covered by a pink layer of mortar.[33] The interior side of many other built graves were covered with plaster in the Apáca Street and in the yard of the gymnasium[34] (Fig. 8-9). It is the same in a simple form as the plastering and painting of the crypts. Sometimes the inner plastering and painting of the graves was made also in a crypt as in the grave chamber XX (Fig. 10). The interior of this grave which was secondarily placed on the northern side of the crypt was at first covered with mortar, and after painted with red stripes in form of the so called fence of the Paradise. There is a Christogram in the triangle above the head of the corpse (Fig. 11). A similar case could be observed in the tombs G/1-2 in the Apáca Street[35] (Fig. 12). In the cemetery in the Székesfehérvár Street 12 from the 21 brick graves were plastered in the inner side.[36] It is to be emphasised that the grave chamber was coated only by mortar and then whitened. The Christogram within a grave refers clearly to the fact that all decorations were planned and offered to the holy existence of the deceased in the other world.

Yes, a Christogram inside in a grave speaks clearer for the better interpretation of this funerary custom than the grave chambers. The closed and for nobody accessible area within a grave proves that all things and decorations belong

[30] Zs. Visy, 'Recent data' (2007), 137-55.

[31] *Ibid.* 146: '… the crypt belongs to the realm of the dead. Hence the images of the frescoes are all connected to their salvation.'

[32] F. Fülep, *Sopianae* (1984), 76.

[33] *Ibid.* 104.

[34] Among others the graves 13, 36, 74, 75, 77, and 102 in the Apáca Street, the graves 25 and 39 in the yard of the gymnasium and in other late Roman graves in Sopianae. I owe my gratitude to Olivér Gábor for these data.

[35] F. Fülep, *Sopianae* (1984), 76.

[36] I thank Zsuzsa Katona Győr for this information.

Fig. 8. An inner plastered brick grave in the north
cemetery of Sopianae. Photo of O. Gábor.

Fig. 9. An inner plastered grave in the north cemetery of Sopianae.
Photo of O. Gábor.

Fig. 10. The crypt of the burial building XX in Sopianae. Photo of Zs. Visy.

exclusively to the dead person. If it is so, also the crypt must be interpreted similarly. In this respect the grave and the crypt represent the same thing: both areas belong to the dead person. They have nothing to do with the living world; they belong to the other world, to the paradise. If biblical scenes were painted, they represent the paradise only for the dead person, not for everybody. These representations have no propagandistic aim; they do not want to be a painted bible. They want to represent the paradise to the deceased as it was imagined in the actual time. If a slight change took place in it like at the end of the fourth century it had to be represented at once in the funeral art.

One last note. The presence of a jug and beaker in the Christian graves has been interpreted differently. On the basis of their representation in the niche of the burial chamber no. II some scholars thought that they are characteristic for the Christian graves, they can be interpreted as indicators of the Christianity in the cemeteries. It has been put forward, too, that they could hold the Eucharist. However, other scholars pointed out that it had been a general and earlier practice in the Roman cemeteries which was taken over by the Christians. They concluded that the jug and the beaker are to be excluded from the œuvre of the Christian finds. However, this conclusion is not compulsory. It is clear that the

Fig. 11. The plastered inner wall of the eastern built grave in the crypt
of the burial building XX in Sopianae. Photo of Zs. Visy.

Fig. 12. The plastered inner walls of the built graves G1-2 in Sopianae.
Photo of A. Török.

Christians took over this – and other – practices from the non-Christians, but they gave them another meaning. If they put jug and beaker in their graves, also this finds have to be interpreted in the context of the new belief. If they changed the graves into a little paradise, also the finds of the graves should be interpreted similarly. The real role of the jug and beaker in the Christian graves should be searched in this context.

Observations on Christian Epigraphy in Pannonia

Gaetano S. Bevelacqua, Rome and London

ABSTRACT

We do not have a critical corpus of the Christian inscriptions found in Pannonia. Those who undertake an analytic study of the epigraphic testimonials of this province have to face the fact that they are published in diverse corpora, quite often accompanied by an inadequate commentary. This paper, in seeking to present some remarks on the Christian epigraphy of Pannonia, will highlight the noteworthy elements in the formulae of this group of inscriptions and will propose both new reflections and suggestions.

It will begin with the presentation of the corpora and publications that contain the texts, in order to detect their provenance, the dating (including some considerations about the methodological approach used to date them) and the decoration (traditional elements and explicit *signa Christi*). Then will consider the onomastics in detail (the name system underwent great changes in Late antiquity), the biometric data (including a small-scale analysis of mortality rate by age group), the persistence of the tradition (*e.g.*, the dedication to the *Di Manes* in the inscription of *Aurelia Iustina*) and the evolution of Latin and Greek (including details of the linguistic phenomena attested in the documentation). Eventually the peculiar lexicon of the Christians will be presented: the use of the term *fidelis* to indicate that the deceased was baptized (referred both to adults and children); the purchase of the tombs and the topographical indication of *ad sanctos* burial places; the dedication of *tituli* and *memoriae* (and other terms that indicate the burials: *locus, arca, sepulcrum*); the notion of death as 'departing' or 'ending life'; the use of identifying and locative formulae such as: *hic (re)quiescit, depositus/depositio + illius, hic iacet, hic positus*; the presence of foreigners, travellers and immigrants in Pannonia; the activities and professions carried out by the deceased while still alive (including who held prestigious roles in public administration and military); members of ecclesiastical hierarchy; wishes and prayers addressed to the deceased. We will add only brief mentions and allusions that will allow one to understand several of the little-known aspects or daily events of the early Christian communities of Pannonia.

1. The Christian inscriptions from Pannonia are undoubtedly a conspicuous group of documents of great importance in diverse aspects.

While we wait for scholars to undertake an analytic and thorough study or a *corpus* of all the Christian inscriptions, which could autoptically examine all the known testimonials, analyzing them exhaustively, in this article, I would like to put forward several considerations and make some observations, based most of all on the most recent acquisitions, but also on the known epigraphic material of the greatest significance. Without claiming to do it comprehensively, I wish to highlight some noteworthy elements in the formulae of this group of inscriptions.

The most substantial collections of Christian texts are the ones published in the third volume of the *Corpus Inscriptionum Latinarum* (CIL)[1] – followed and, quite often revised, by Diehl in his *Inscriptiones Latinae Christianae Veteres* (ILCV)[2] –, in the volumes of the *Dissertationes Musei Nationalis Labacensis* (ILJ),[3] *Die römischen Inschriften Ungarns* (RIU)[4] and *Corpus Inscriptionum Graecarum Pannonicarum* (CIGP);[5] several other texts, the most recent findings and new readings of old epigraphs are published in diverse works and journals, which are accompanied by an 'apparatus' that supplies a brief critical commentary.[6]

Despite the fact that Pannonia was one of the most significant regions of the *orbis Christianus antiquus* in the 4th century, the epigraphic findings do not reflect the same importance of Christianity in it.[7]

---

[1] *Corpus Inscriptionum Latinarum* (CIL) (Berolini, 1863-). CIL III, 3551, 3986, 3991, 3996 (= ILCV 1449), 3996a (= 1686), 4002-4005, 4219 (ILCV *add.*, 352), 6446 (=10238)-6449, 10231-10240, 10251-10252, 11206 (?), 13382, 14340²⁻⁷, 15136², 15181² (= ILCV 3659).

[2] E. Diehl, *Inscriptiones Latinae Christianae Veteres* (Berlin, 1925-1930; Dublin-Zürich, ²1961, ³1970).

[3] Anna and Jaro Šašel, *Inscriptiones Latinae quae in Iugoslavia inter annos MCMXL et MCMLX repertae et editae sunt*, Situla 5 (Ljubljana, 1963), 283; *id.*, *Inscriptiones Latinae quae in Iugoslavia inter annos MCMII et MCMLX repertae et editae sunt*, Situla 25 (Ljubljana, 1986), 3021-3055, 3057-3068, 3071, 3073-3079, 3081-3089.

[4] Làszlò Barkòczi – Andràs Mòcsy, *Die römischen Inschriften Ungarns*, vol. 1 (Amsterdam, 1972), 75-86, 122, 128; Làszlò Barkòczi – Andràs Mòcsy, *Die römischen Inschriften Ungarns*, vol. 2 (Amsterdam, 1976), 632, 633, 634.

[5] Péter Kovács, *Corpus Inscriptionum Graecarum Pannonicarum* (CIGP) (Debrecen, 2001), cat. nos. 132-8, 208-9.

[6] J. Brunšmid, *Vjesnik Hrvatskoga arheološkoga društva, nova serija* (VHAD), 10 (Zagreb, 1908-1909), 224, no. 366; V. Hoffiller and B. Saria (eds), *Antike Inschriften aus Jugoslawien* (AIJ), *1, Noricum und Pannonia Superior* (Zagreb, 1938), 576; N. Duval, 'Sirmium, 'Ville imperial' ou "Capitale"?', in *XXVI Corso di cultura sull'arte ravennate e bizantina* (Ravenna, 1979), 53-90, esp. 83-4 for the inscription; AE 1986 (Paris), 601; 602 (= CIL III, 10204); *id.*, 1996 (Paris), 1256; Dragoslav Srejović (ed.), *Roman Imperial towns and palaces in Serbia* (Belgrade, 1993), 349, no. 156; Branka Migotti, *Evidence for Christianity in Roman Southern Pannonia* (*Northern Croatia*). *A Catalogue of Finds and Sites*, BAR International series (Oxford, 1997), 51, II. c. 7a – d; P. Zsidi, *Frühchristliche Denkmäler in Aquincum* (Budapest, 2000), 52, no. 6; Branka Migotti, Mario Šlaus, Zdenka Dukat, Ljubica Perinić (eds), *Accede ad Certissiam* (Zagreb, 1998), no. 204; Péter Kovács, *Tituli Romani in Hungaria reperti: Supplementum* (TRH) (Budapest – Bonn, 2005), 26.

[7] For the history and archaeology of Pannonia in Late Antiquity the literature is extensive: A. Mócsy, *Pannonia and Upper Moesia. A History of the Middle Danube Provinces of the Roman Empire* (London, 1974), esp. 297-406 and its select bibliography, 407-19; D. Gaspar, *Christianity in Roman Pannonia. An Evaluation of Early Christian Finds and Sites from Hungary* (Oxford, 2002); E. Tóth, 'Late Antique imperial palace in Savaria', in *Acta Antiqua Archaeologica Academiae Scientiarum Hungaricae* 25 (Budapest, 1973); *id.*, 'Das Christentum in Pannonien bis zum 7. Jahrhundert nach den archäologischen Zeugnissen', in E. Boshof and H. Wolff (eds), *Das*

According to Pèter Kovàcs, the number of Christian inscriptions (Table 1) is 139[8] (although P. Kovàcs does not include CIL III, 4219 in this group, I think it should be regarded as a Christian inscription; consequently, in this paper, it will be numbered among the other ones. In addition it must be noticed that the text in CIL III, 10240 is the same as in AE 1986, 602 and that the two entries are not referring to two different inscriptions[9]): 128 are in Latin (92% of all the inscriptions), 9 in Greek (7%) and 2 are bilingual (1%).

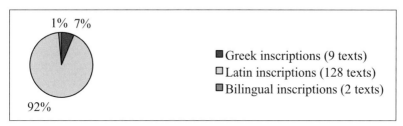

Table 1. Number and percentage of Christian inscriptions from Pannonia
(Latin, Greek and bilingual).

2. P. Kovács, one of the best and keenest current experts in epigraphy of Pannonia – who is likely to have seen most of the epigraphic materials – notes that almost all the Pannonian Christian inscriptions are funerary and a great number of them inscribed on marble slabs.[10] They were found almost exclusively in the

---

Christentum im bairischen Raum. Von den Anfängen bis ins 11. Jahrhundert (Wien, 1994), 242-74; Z. Kádár, 'Lineamenti dell'arte romana della Pannonia nell'epoca dell'antichità tarda e paleocristiana', in *XVI Corso di cultura sull'arte ravennate e bizantina* (Ravenna, 1969), 177-9; Roderic L. Mullen, *The Expansion of Christianity. A Gazetteer of its First Three Centuries* (Leiden and Boston, 2004), 178-83; Lucreţiu Mihailescu-Bîrliba, Valentin Piftor, Răzvan Cozma, *L'espérance de vie, la structure d'âge et la mortalité en Pannonie (Ier-IIIe s. ap. J.C.)* (Iaşi, 2007); Craig H. Caldwell III, 'The Balkans' in Scott. F. Johnson (ed.), *The Oxford Handbook of Late Antiquity* (Oxford and New York, 2012), 92-115. For the history of Christianity in Pannonia, the influence of its bishops and the significance of its martyrs see J. Zeiller, *Les origines chrétiennes dans les provinces danubiennes de l'Empire romain* (Roma, 1967); Neil B. McLynn, *Ambrose of Milan. Church and Court in a Christian Capital* (Los Angeles and London, 1994); H. Leclercq, 'Illyricum', *DACL* 7, 1, cols. 99-104, 114; *id.*, 'Pannonie', *DACL* 13, 1, cols. 1046-1063 (which records also many Christian inscriptions); M. Pavan, 'Romanesimo, Cristianesimo e immigrazioni nei territori pannonici', in *Romanobarbarica: contributi allo studio dei rapporti culturali tra mondo latino e mondo barbarico* 9 (Roma, 1986-1987), 161-228; T. Nagy, *A pannoniai* (Budapest, 1939); B. Migotti, *Evidence for Christianity* (1997); A. Alföldi, *Tracce del Cristianesimo nell'epoca delle grandi migrazioni in Ungheria* (Roma, 1938); B. Migotti, M. Šlaus, Z. Dukat, L. Perinić (eds), *Accede ad Certissiam* (1998).

[8] P. Kovács, 'Christian Epigraphy in Pannonia', in *Thiasos. Festschrift für Erwin Pochmarski zum 65. Geburtstag herausgegeben* (Wien, 2008), 495-501, 495. Three inscriptions are reused (RIU 632-34).

[9] On the opposite see P. Kovács, 'Christian Epigraphy in Pannonia' (2008), 495.

[10] P. Kovács, 'Christian Epigraphy in Pannonia' (2008), 498.

biggest urban centres (which probably were also bishopric seats), most of the time placed obviously along the *limes* (Table 2). Most of the inscriptions come from *Sirmium*, present-day Sremska Mitrovica in Serbia (98 inscriptions; the nine above-mentioned Christian inscriptions in Greek come from here), 15 from *Savaria* (modern Szombathely, in Hungary), 7 from both *Certissia-Murs(i)a* (now Štrbinci(?)-Osijek, Croatia) and *Cibalae* (now Vinkovci, Croatia), 6 from *Siscia* (modern Sisak/Sissek, Croatia), 3 from both *Aquincum* and *Brigetio* (modern Budapest and Komárom/Szőny respectively, Hungary), only 1 from *Carnuntum* (which now covers the municipality Petronell-*Carnuntum* and Bad Deutsch-Altenburg in Austria). The two bilingual inscriptions were found in *Savaria* and *Aquincum*.

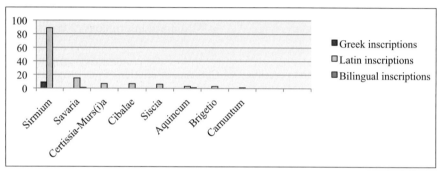

Table 2. Distribution of Christian inscriptions in Pannonia.

The dating of these epigraphs merits a preliminary note. Christian inscriptions from Pannonia are generally dated between the 4[th] and the 5[th]/6[th] centuries (the tombstone of *Fl(avia) Cal[v]ena*[11] (Fig. 1) is even dated no later than 'the second half of the 3[rd] century and the first half of the 4[th]'[12]), not only on the strength of their find spot or the form of the gravestones (including frame, ornament, etc.), but also on the basis of both their formulae and palaeographical elements.

Broadly speaking, despite the limits that belong to this methodological approach, the above-mentioned chronology is correct. However further reflections should be taken into account with some precautions. Early Christian cemeteries (according to the scholarly statement, all dating from the 4th century onwards),

---

[11] CIL III, 13382; ILCV, 8028; T. Nagy, 'Un monument méconnu du christianisme d'Aquincum', in *Archaeologiai Értesitő, Series III*, Vols. 5-6 (Budapest, 1944-45), 266-82, for the inscription esp. 274 tables XCI, 2 and XCII, 2; AE 1947, 38; TRH 252; CIGP, cat. no. 102; P. Kovács and Á. Szabó, *Tituli Aquincenses: Tituli Sepulcrales et alii Budapestini reperti*, vol. 2 (Budapest, 2010), no. 947.

[12] P. Kovács, 'Christianity and the Greek Language in Pannonia', in *Acta Antiqua Academiae Scientiarum Hungaricae* 43 (Budapest, 2003), 1-2, 120.

are attested for *Sopianae* and *Naissus*,[13] *Aquincum*[14], *Certissia*[15], *Savaria*[16] and, *naturally, for Sirmium.*[17] *Early Christian cemeteries at Sirmium* were excavated in the nineteenth century with little care, unfortunately without using a rigorous method that could allow us to use the excavation data – data which normally are of inestimable value, especially when the subterranean chambers and the *sub divo* cemeteries are only partially or no longer visible –, both for historical and scientific purposes.

Since the vast majority of these inscriptions come presumably either from such extemporaneous excavations or coincidental and sporadic findings, as a general rule, it is not possible to easily distinguish the inscriptions of the 4th century from the ones of the 5th on the strength of textual elements or other clues, even though sometimes one can be inclined to consider some tombstones dating later than others. Except for several recurring expressions, the texts do not adhere to stereotyped schemes and a further examination does not show such evolution of formulae that one can discern – with the exception of several particular cases – the most recent inscriptions. Also the linguistic analysis is not of great help, for those inscriptions that can be regarded as the most ancient ones, bear several corrupted forms, solecisms and 'volgarismi', which generally characterize, in other centres and regions, the *tituli* of the 5th-6th centuries.

Furthermore, we must bear in mind that several Christian inscriptions reveal very close ties with the formulae of the traditional epigraphic praxis, distinguishing themselves from these sometimes only by slight – and not always certain – indications. Not infrequently, the formulae are still neutral; only the

---

[13] They are excluded from this research because, thus far, no Christian inscriptions have come to light in these two important centres, beside several painted Christological monograms in both the towns and a wall graffito in *Sopianae*, see F. Fülep, 'Ujabb kutatások a pécsi késörómai temetőben', in German 'Neuere Forschungen im spätrömischen Gräberfeld von Pécs (Fünfkirchen)', in *Archaeologiai Értesítő* 89 (Budapest, 1962), 44, fig. 21.

[14] For its Christian cemetery dating back to the 4th century see András Mócsy, *Pannonia and Upper Moesia* (1974), 313, 333-34; J. Fritz, 'The Way of Life', in A. Lengyel and G.T.B. Radan (eds), *The Archaeology of Roman Pannonia* (Lexington and Budapest, 1980), 161-75; K. Póczy, 'Pannonian Cities', in A. Lengyel and G.T.B. Radan (eds), *The Archaeology of Roman Pannonia* (1980), 239-74; Richard J.A. Talbert (ed.), *Barrington Atlas of the Greek and Roman World* (Princeton and Oxford, 2000), map 20.

[15] For the two cross-shaped grave vaults identified as Christian because of their peculiar shape and dated from 320 or later see B. Migotti, *Evidence for Christianity* (1997), 37-8; R.J.A. Talbert (ed.), *Barrington Atlas* (2000), map 20.

[16] K. Póczy, 'Pannonian Cities' (1980), 266 (Póczy notes a Christian cemetery dating to some time in the 4th century); Hubert Jedin, Kenneth Scott Latourette and Jochen Martin (eds), *Atlas zur Kirchengeschichte*, 3rd edition (Freiburg, 1987), 4; R.J.A. Talbert (ed.), *Barrington Atlas* (2000), map 20.

[17] For the archaeological remains of an early Christian cemetery at *Sirmium* see András Mócsy, 'Pannonia', in *RA Suppl.* 9 (Stuttgart, 1962), cols. 516-776; A. Mócsy, *Pannonia and Upper Moesia* (1974), 326-27; J. Fritz, 'The Way of Life' (1980), 170; for *Sirmium* in general: J. Zeiller, *Les origines chrétiennes* (1967), 79-88; H. Jedin, K.S. Latourette and J. Martin (eds), *Atlas* (1987), 5; R.J.A. Talbert (ed.), *Barrington Atlas* (2000), map 21.

provenance of the inscription or just the *signa Christi* testifies in favour of them being Christian.

There are no dated inscriptions, except two Greek ones:

I) a funerary document[18] that mentions in the first five lines the Eastern consuls' iteration that permits to date it back to the consulate of the Emperor *Flavius Iulius Constantius Augustus*, consul for the fifth time, and *Flavius Claudius Constantius Caesar*, consul for the first time. The Macedonian calendar is used to indicate the name of the month (Ξανδικός = March). This is the year 352 A.D.:

ὑπατείᾳ τῶν δεσπότων | ἡμῶν Φλαυ(ίου) Ἰουλ(ίου) Κωνσταντίο | υ ἀνικήτου Σεβαστοῦ τὸ ε΄ καὶ Φλαυ(ίου) | Κωνσταντίου ἐπιφανεστάτου | Κέσαρος μηνὸς Ξανδικοῦ δκ΄.

II) an inscribed tile that represents the latest Christian epigraph[19] from Pannonia (Fig. 2), which can be roughly dated to 579-582, before the Avars sieged and destroyed the city of *Sirmium*. It is worthy of attention in many respects, not least for the fact that it shows how the influence of the Greek language became more and more important in the 6th century, when the province of Pannonia belonged to the Eastern Roman empire between 527 and 582.

A fragmentary Latin inscription[20] bears the mention of an *indictio* – *indic*] *tion(e) V* –, which could be from any of the years in a 15-year cycle. Given the fact that the cycles were not numbered, other information is needed to identify the specific year, which remains uncertain.

3. The marble slabs bear a simple 'neutral' decoration (*hedera distinguens, uva, palmula* and *columba*), whereas others bear explicit *signa Christi*: christograms (about 20 times, rarely within a clypeus, with and without the apocalyptical letters α and ω; it always appears as a symbol, the so-called *chrismon*, never as *compendium scripturae*), staurograms, maybe the *crux decussata* with I and X interwoven together standing for Ἰησοῦς Χριστός (it may have occurred once,[21] however the low resolution of the picture and the lacking of an autoptic study of the slab do not allow one to resolve the issue), a cross.

Among the inscriptions, that of *Victorinus* (Fig. 3), dedicated to his wife *Felicissima*, is remarkable, since it bears two peculiar monograms:

---

[18] Th. Mommsen, in *Bullettino dell'Instituto della Corrispondenza Archeologica – Bulletin de l'Institut de Correspondance Archeologique* (BICA) (Roma, 1868), 143, no. 2; ILJ 3021; CIGP, cat. no.129.

[19] J. Brunšmid, 'Eine griechische Ziegelinschrift aus Sirmium', in *Eranos Vindobonensis* (Wien, 1893), 331-3; *Supplementum Epigraphicum Graecum* (SEG), 39 (Amsterdam, 1989), 1096; CIGP, cat. no. 138.

[20] ILJ 3064.

[21] See note 11.

I) one is composed of a X surrounded by Greek letters (the two oblique strokes, crossing each other, create four spaces which contain α and ω to the left and to the right respectively, π and ρ above and below respectively). No previous scholar has given any explanation about it. Assuming that what was recorded about this inscription in CIL III, 3996a was accurate, I wonder whether the π and ρ, in place of the usual vertical stroke of the P, might be an abbreviation for the *nomen sacrum* Π(ατή)ρ (in reference to the two eternal persons of Trinity – see *Apoc.* 1, 8; 21, 6; 22, 13 –; to my knowledge, this would be an *unicum* yet, since in Christian epigraphy α and ω are always and only attributed to Christ[22]), or just one of the Greek prepositions + the name of Christ (as expressing the wish for the deceased to stay in the presence of Christ, who is *alpha* and *omega*).

II) the other one is a X with a P inserted in one of its oblique stroke, with the eschatological letters α and ω on either side. It could be either a bad staurogram or a christogram/*crux decussata* without the vertical stroke[23].

4. With regard to onomastics, which has been partially studied in the past, it can be pointed out that also in Pannonia the name system underwent great changes. The *praenomen* has almost totally disappeared and has been replaced by the *cognomen* (*praenomina* exceptionally appear only in CIL III, 10238 and in the rare polyonymy of RIU 76, where also the inversion of the order of the names can be observed). The use of *duo nomina*, which had already become evident in many classical inscriptions, is noticeably frequent in the documentation. However the *nomina* are in a minority, the name form being the one composed of a single, sometimes double, *cognomen* – the few cases of a name composed of two juxtaposed *cognomina* will be presented and properly commented on in the notes – or a *nomen* used as a *cognomen*, whose extensive use testifies the lessening of the importance of the *nomen* in Late Antiquity. Furthermore the *cognomen* of the *Flavii* or *Aurelii* and *Iulii* is so frequent in those centuries, that some inscriptions bear those names abbreviated like a sort of *praenomen*. This makes it possible not to regard those names as real *gentilicia* anymore.[24] Among the more or less rare names, the newly coined names with the suffix *-anus/-ianus*, *-icinus/-a*, *-ius* emerge.

---

[22] See, for example, A. Ferrua, *La polemica antiariana nei monumenti paleocristiani* (Città del Vaticano, 1991), 48.

[23] See F. Usiello, 'Appendice', in D. Mazzoleni, 'Origine e cronologia dei monogrammi: riflessi nelle iscrizioni dei Musei Vaticani', in I. Di Stefano Manzella (ed.), *Le iscrizioni dei cristiani in Vaticano. Materiali e contributi per una mostra epigrafica* (Città del Vaticano, 1997), 168-9, figs. 14, 17, 20-3, 25.

[24] See *Inscriptiones Christianae Italiae* (ICI) (Bari, 1985-), 12, LXXV; G. Lettich, *Le iscrizioni sepolcrali tardoantiche di Concordia* (Trieste, 1983), 38-9; M. Sannazzaro, 'Attestazioni di militari e militaria a Milano', in M. Buora (ed.), *Miles Romanus dal Po al Danubio nel Tardoantico* (Pordenone, 2002), 72; Kajava, in A.E. Felle, 'I reperti epigrafici del complesso di s. Ilario ad bivium presso Valmontone (Roma)', *Vetera Christianorum* 38 (2001), 247-85, 254.

The sole German name recorded is *Otgarius* or *R]otgarius*,[25] whereas it has already been noticed that many of the earliest Christians in the region had Greek names.[26]

Among the *cognomina* one can find: *Artemidora*,[27] *Dionisia*,[28] *Herculanus*[29] and *Iovinus*[30] (which are mythological and traditional theophoric names. The reused inscription of *Dionisia* has been ambiguously passed on; to become aware of how this equivocal text tradition actually refers to the same inscription, read the bibliographical references I suggest in the note); Ἰωάννα,[31]

---

[25] CIL III, 6449; VHAD, 10, (1908-1909), 238-9, no. 388. See also P. Kovács, 'Christianity and the Greek Language in Pannonia' (2003), 119, notes and references.

[26] A. Mócsy, *Pannonia and Upper Moesia* (1974), 259.

[27] CIL III, 10233; ILCV 2181. See also *Onomasticon provinciarum Europae Latinarum, composuit et correxit* B. Lőrincz, I² (Budapest, 2005), *Appendix*, 340. The name *Artemidora* – which, besides our inscription, recurs only in another Christian inscription from *Ostia*: CIL XIV, 1886; ILCV 3203; AE 2000, 250 – is known almost exclusively from classical inscriptions: CIL III, 13739; CIL VI, 1458, 1772 (= CIL XI, *155 a); 3383, 5930, 8533, 10849, 15474, 15730 (= CIL I, 1282), 26498, 38470; CIL X, 2623; CIL XIV, 479, 2330; H. Thylander, *Inscriptions du Port d'Ostie* (Lund, 1951-1952), A 189. See also: *Onomasticon provinciarum Europae Latinarum* I² (2005), 177.

[28] RIU 632; AE 1977, 624; Josef Ceška and Radislav Hošek (eds), *Inscriptiones Pannoniae Superioris in Slovacia Transdanubiana asservatae* (Brno, 1967), no. 43; Harl Friederike and Lőrincz Barnabás (eds), *Führer zum römischen Lapidarium in Bastion VI der Festung Komárno. Forschungsgesellschaft Wiener Stadtarchäologie* (Komárno, 2002), no. 48. The name is known from both classical inscriptions (CIL V, 08735a; CIL VI, 10246, 13765, 25787, 38808; CIL VIII, 3326, 4349, 15500 (= 26436); CIL IX, 3222, 4476; CIL XI, 3418, 4726, 7175; P. Kovács and Á. Szabó, *Tituli Aquincenses* (2010), 534), and Christian ones, see *Inscriptiones Christianae Urbis Romae septimo saeculo antiquiores* (ICUR), *colligere coepit I. B. De Rossi, compleverunt et ediderunt* A. Silvagni, A. Ferrua, D. Mazzoleni, C. Carletti, I-X (Romae, 1922-92), I, 3007; ICUR III, 6651; ICUR V, 12934a, 13786n; ICUR VII, 18656, 18779; ICUR VIII, 22416, 23323; see also *Onomasticon provinciarum Europae Latinarum, composuit et correxit* B. Lőrincz, II (Wien, 1999), 101 and *Appendix*, 216.

[29] CIL III, 3551; ILCV 435, 2395, 3476; CLE 440; AE 1947, 38; P. Kovács and Á. Szabó, *Tituli Aquincenses*, vol. 1 (Budapest, 2009), no. 799. The name is widely attested in various regions; in Pannonia it appears three more times in classical inscriptions. See also *Onomasticon provinciarum Europae Latinarum* II (1999), 178.

[30] CIL III, 10239. The name occurs quite regularly in various regions and in Pannonia appears in less than a dozen of inscriptions.

[31] VHAD 8, (1905), 102, no. 188; Vladislav Popović, Edward L. Ochsenschlager (eds), *Sirmium: Archaeological investigations in Syrmian Pannonia* I (Belgrade, 1971), 90, 110; CIGP, cat. no. 135. The name frequently appears in Latin Christian inscriptions (CIL II, 266; CIL III, 9551; CIL V, 5429; CIL VI, 41340, 41420c (= CIL VI, 8566, ICUR II, 4184, ILCV 110); CIL VIII, 1169; CIL XI, 2174, 2465; CIL XIII, 87, 173-74, 195, 201, 323; ICUR I, 1031, 3249; ICUR II, 5751; ICUR VIII, 20813; G. Sotgiu, *Iscrizioni latine della Sardegna* (Padova, 1961), 11, 362) and less frequently in the Greek ones, both in Christian and Jewish epigraphs: *Inscriptiones Graecae* (IG), X: *Inscriptiones Epiri, Macedoniae, Thraciae, Scythiae. Pars II, fasc. 1*: *Inscriptiones Thessalonicae et vicinae*, Charles Edson (ed.) (Berlin, 1972), no. 403 (= Denis Feissel, *Recueil des inscriptions chrétiennes de Macédoine du IIIᵉ au VIᵉ siècle* in *Bulletin de correspondance hellénique. Supplément* 8 [Paris, 1983], no. 135); Evaristo Breccia, *Iscrizioni greche e latine. Service des Antiquités de l'Égypte. Catalogue géneral des antiquités égyptiennes du Musée*

Paulus,[32] *Petrus*,[33] *Petro*]*nilla* (?)[34] (most of the time derived from the books of the Bible), *Sabatia*[35] (a Christian 'date name'), *Timotheus*[36] (a Christian theophoric name), *Laurentia*/*-anus* (?)[37] and *Martoria*[38] (the former name related to the martyr *Laurentius*, the latter one to martyrdom in general), *Stercorinus*[39] and *Proiectus*[40] (the former is a 'diminutive' of the predominant, and

d'Alexandrie (Cairo, 1911), no. 253 (= Walther Judeich, in Carl Humann, Conrad Cichorius, Walther Judeich, and Franz Winter, *Altertümer von Hierapolis* [Berlin, 1898], IV, no. 22); Jean-Baptiste Frey, *Corpus Inscriptionum Iudaicarum, 2. Asie-Afrique* (Roma, 1952), no. 1429. See also *Onomasticon provinciarum Europae Latinarum* II (1999), *Appendix*, 223.

[32] CIL III, 4217; ILCV 1376; RIU 76; T. Endre, *Lapidarium Savariense* (Savaria, 2011), 142. For the occurrence of the name in classical and Christian inscriptions respectively, see the long list in: *Onomasticon provinciarum Europae Latinarum, composuit et correxit* B. Lőrincz, III (Wien, 2000), 130 and *Appendix*, 180.

[33] Dragoslav Srejović (ed.), *Roman Imperial towns* (1993), 349, no. 156. For obvious reasons the name is very popular: *Onomasticon provinciarum Europae Latinarum* III (2000), 136 and *Appendix*, 180.

[34] CIL III, 14340[4]; ILCV 3530. The name probably appears one more time in Pannonia (ILJ 351) and is particularly attested in Rome: ICUR I, 943; CIL VI, 13367 (= ICUR III, 8456 = ILCV 1995); ICUR V, 13606; ICUR VIII, 20734; A. Ferrua, *Tavole lusorie scritte* in *Epigraphica*, 10 (Milano, 1948), 42.

[35] CIL III, 4185; ILCV 296; F. Bücheler and E. Lommatzsch, *Carmina Latina Epigraphica* (CLE) (Leipzig, 1930), 578; A. Mócsy and T. Szentléleky (eds), *Die römischen Steindenkmäler von Savaria* (Amsterdam and Budapest, 1971), 117, no. 161; RIU 80; P. Cugusi and M. Teresa Sblendorio Cugusi, *Studi sui carmi epigrafici. Carmina Latina Epigraphica Pannonica* (CLE-Pann) (Bologna, 2007), 25; T. Endre, *Lapidarium Savariense* (2011), 145; AE 1984, 722. For the occurrence of the name see I. Kajanto, *The Latin Cognomina* (Roma, 1982), 62, 135; ILCV III, 140; *Onomasticon provinciarum Europae Latinarum, composuit et correxit* B. Lőrincz, IV (Wien, 2002), 39 and *Appendix*, 34.

[36] VHAD, 10, (1908-9), 192, no. 401; ILJ 3031 (the name appears two times in the same epigraph). The name *Thimotheus* is widely attested in diverse regions of the *orbis Christianus antiquus*. See *Onomasticon provinciarum Europae Latinarum* IV (2002), *Appendix*, 198.

[37] M. Milin, 'An Exorcist on an Epitaph from Sirmium', in *Starinar* 47 (1996), 245-7; AE 1996, 1256. The names *Laurentia* and *Laurentianus* appear very often; see *Onomasticon provinciarum Europae Latinarum* IV (2002), *Appendix*, 174 and *Onomasticon provinciarum Europae Latinarum* III (2000), 21 respectively.

[38] ILJ 0283; Ž. Demo (ed.), *Od nepobjedivog sunca do sunca pravde. Rano kršćanstvo u kontinentalnjo Hrvatskoj/From the invincible sun to the sun of justice* (Zagreb, 1994), 98, no. 96; B. Migotti, 'Sol Iustitiae Christus est. (Origines) Odrazi solarne kristologije na ranoskršćanskoj gradi iz sjeverne Hrvatske (Izvorni znanstveni rad)', *Diadora* 16/17 (1994/1995), 279-80; B. Migotti, *Evidence for Christianity* (1997), 45-6; AE 1997, 1270. The name *Martoria* appears only in one other epigraph, see J. Vives, *Incripciones cristianas de la España romana y visigoda* (Barcelona, 1969), 189; G. Alföldi, *Die Römischen Inschriften von Tarraco* (Berlin, 1975), 944; AE 1938, 25; the variants *Marturia*/*Martyria* are more frequent and well attested (*Martyria*, in particular, at Rome). See also *Onomasticon provinciarum Europae Latinarum* III (2000), *Appendix*, 177.

[39] TRH 26; T. Endre, *Lapidarium Savariense* (2011), 151. The anthroponym in all probability is an *unicum*; also the female form *St(e)rcorina* recurs only once in CIL III, 2739 (= CIL III, 9748). See *Onomasticon provinciarum Europae Latinarum* IV (2002), 95.

[40] CIL III, 11206a-c; ILCV *add.*, 1856a; E. Vorbeck, *Militärinschriften aus Carnuntum* (Wien, [2]1980), 299. The name occurs only here in the inscriptions from Pannonia. These *nomina humilitatis*, if they were all really such, have probably lost their original meaning and ended up

84   G.S. BEVELACQUA

more frequent, name *Stercorius*, which along with the latter, is one of the so-called *'nomina humilitatis'*[41]; *Syneros*,[42] the martyr who is most likely recorded in three diverse inscriptions. The other names are: *Am[a]ntius* [43] (one of the new *cognomina* in -*ius*, derived from the participle *amans*), *Aminia*,[44] *A]mpel[(i)us* (?)[45] (which, otherwise, could be the *nomen Ampel(l)i(u)s*; Kovács argues that 'the *cognomen Ampelius* is a typical Christian name'[46], although the variants of the anthroponimy occur several times in classical inscriptions as well[47]), *Aspalia*,[48] *As]terius* (?),[49] Βασιλιανός[50] ('it is its first Pannonian occurrence'[51]), *Bassus*,[52] *Bo]nonia* (?),[53]

as a fashionable case, as demonstrated by the facts that pagans also used several of them, see I. Kajanto, *The Latin Cognomina* (1982), 286-7.

[41] See A. Ferrua, 'Epigrafia Cristiana (under the voice of)', in *Enciclopedia Cattolica* V (Città del Vaticano, 1949-1950), column 436; I. Kajanto, 'On the problem of "Names of humility" in early Christian epigraphy', *Arctos* 3 (1962), 45-53.

[42] See the inscription of *Artemidora* in the footnote 27 along with: **1)** CIL III, 10232; H. Dessau, *Inscriptiones Latinae Selectae* (ILS), I-III (Berlin, 1892-1916), 9205; ILCV 2182 and **2)** CIL III, 14340². The name is quite frequent: A. Pasqualini, 'Iscrizioni inedite della IV regio augustea dai mss. di Antonio Ludovico Antinori', in L. Gasperini (ed.), *Scritti sul mondo antico in memoria di Fulvio Grosso* (Roma, 1981), 493-505, 503; H. Solin, *Die griechischen Personennamen in Rom. Ein Namenbuch*, I-III (Berlin and New York, 1982), 147-8; *Onomasticon provinciarum Europae Latinarum* IV (2002), 103 and the *Appendix*, 197.

[43] See note 40. The name *Am[a]ntius*, hypothesized in CIL, is purely conjectural and widely attested, see: I. Kajanto, *The Latin Cognomina* (1982), 255; ILCV III, 9; *Onomasticon provinciarum Europae Latinarum* I² (2005), 88.

[44] See note 42. The name is quite attested; in Pannonia appears only here. See *Onomasticon provinciarum Europae Latinarum* I² (2005), *Appendix*, 336.

[45] RIU 122; CIGP, cat. no. 187; P. Kovács, 'Christian Epigraphy in Pannonia' (2008), 498. See also I. Kajanto, 'Onomastic Studies in the early Christian Inscriptions of Rome and Carthage', in *Acta Instituti Romani Finlandiae* (Helsinki and Helsingfors, 1963), 84.

[46] P. Kovács, 'Christian Epigraphy in Pannonia' (2008), 498 and notes 20-1.

[47] See *e.g.*: AE 1982, 842; AE 1997, 1307; CIL III, 7050 (= CIL III, 14192⁵); CIL VI, 402; CIL VIII, 5337; CIL IX, 1912.

[48] CIL III, 4219; V. Pârvan, *Istoria Crestinismului Daco-Roman* (Bucharest, 1911), 40-1 and note 169; ILCV add., 352; RIU 128; T. Endre, *Lapidarium Savariense* (2011), 198. The name is attested only here and seems to be an *unicum*.

[49] ILJ 3082. The name is recorded very often. See also ILCV III, 16; H. Solin, *Die griechischen Personennamen in Rom. Ein Namenbuch*, Corpus Inscriptionum Latinarum. Auctarium. Series nova 2 (Berlin and New York 2003²), 1205-6; *Onomasticon provinciarum Europae Latinarum* I² (2005), 189 and *Appendix*, 340.

[50] See note 18. See also W. Pape, *Wörterbuch der griechischen Eigennamen* (Braunschweig, 1911), 200; H. Solin, *Die griechischen Personennamen* (1982), 1010; A. Mócsy, 'Nomenclator Provinciarum Europae Latinarum et Galliae Cisalpinae cum indice inverso', in *DissPann* III/1 (1983), 45; *Onomasticon provinciarum Europae Latinarum* I² (2005), 273.

[51] CIGP, 50.

[52] See note 32. The name is attested in diverse regions. See *Onomasticon provinciarum Europae Latinarum* I² (2005), 275-77 and *Appendix*, 345.

[53] The name is conjectural and occurs quite often. See also *Onomasticon provinciarum Europae Latinarum* I² (2005), 310 and *Appendix*, 347.

Calvena[54] (as a *cognomen*), *Cara*,[55] *Celsina*,[56] *Crescentia*,[57] *Dalmatius*,[58] *Desiderius*[59] (a name derived from the noun *desiderium*), *Domnica*,[60] *Dorot*[*heus* or *Dorot*[*thea*,[61] *Felicissima*,[62] *Flavianus*,[63] *Florentinus*,[64] *Fortunata*,[65] ʻ*Fronto*,[66] *Gaianus*,[67] *Gaius*,[68]

[54] See note 11. The female name *Calvena* is rarely attested. In both CIL IX, 3538 and AE 2005, 1698 *Calvena* is recorded as a *nomen*. See note 11 and P. Kovács, 'Christian Epigraphy in Pannonia' (2008), 496 and references.

[55] See note 11. The name is regularly attested.

[56] CIL III, 4220; E. Desjardins and F. Rómer, *Monuments épigraphiques du Musée National Hongrois, Magyar Nemzeti Múzeum* (Budapest, 1873), no. 207; Von Lajos Balla *et alii*, in András Mócsy and Tihamér Szentléleky (eds), *Die Römischen Steindenkmäler von Savaria* (Amsterdam, 1971), 160; RIU 78; T. Endre, *Lapidarium Savariense* (2011), 143. The name is well known.

[57] See note 48. The name is quite attested.

[58] See note 35. The name is regularly testified in diverse areas. See *Onomasticon provinciarum Europae Latinarum* II (1999), 92 and *Appendix*, 215.

[59] CIL III, 10233; ILCV 2181. Recurrent name. See also *Onomasticon provinciarum Europae Latinarum* II (1999), *Appendix*, 215.

[60] See note 56. The name is recorded in less than a dozen of inscriptions. See also *Onomasticon provinciarum Europae Latinarum* II (1999), 216.

[61] CIL III, 10231. In Pannonia the name occurs only here.

[62] CIL 3996a; ILCV 1449. Well-attested name. See also *Onomasticon provinciarum Europae Latinarum* II (1999), 137 and *Appendix*, 218.

[63] It appears twice **1)** see note 39 and **2)** CIL III, 4218; ILCV 2208; Von Lajos Balla *et alii*, in András Mócsy and Tihamér Szentléleky (eds.), *Die Römischen Steindenkmäler* (1971), 159; RIU 77; T. Buócz, *Lapidarium Savaria Museum, Museen des Komitats Vas* (Szombathely, 1994), 117, no. 109; T. Endre, *Lapidarium Savariense* (2011), 144. In **2)** the name might be also the well-known Celtic name *Elainus*, as it is actually written on the stone (one can experience the same degree of uncertainty about this name in the beautiful marble slab CIL XIII, 11032 = ILS 9215 = ILCV 554). It should be the only occurrence in Pannonia. The name *Flavianus*, however, is well attested; see its occurrence as *nomen/cognomen* in *Onomasticon provinciarum Europae Latinarum* II (1999), 144 and *Appendix*, 219. For the name *Elainus* see A. Holder, *Alt-Celtischer Sprachschatz*, vol. 1 (Leipzig, 1896-1907), 1411-141.

[64] CIL III, 4221; CIL III, 10934; ILCV 3298; RIU 82. The name is very frequent. See also I. Kajanto, *The Latin Cognomina* (1982), 28, 45-6, 189, 233; A. Mócsy, *Die Bevölkerung von Pannonien bis zu den Markomannenkriegen* (Budapest, 1959), 174; L. Barkòczi, *The Population of Pannonia from Marcus Aurelius to Diocletian* in *Acta Archeologica Academiae Scientiarum Hungaricae* 16 (Budapest, 1964), 312; A. Mócsy, 'Nomenclator Provinciarum Europae Latinarum' (1983), 128; H. Solin and O. Salomies (eds), *Repertorium nominum gentilium et cognominum latinorum. Editio nova addendis corrigendisque augmentata* (Hildesheim-Zurich-New York, 1994), 333; *Onomasticon provinciarum Europae Latinarum* II (1999), 148 and *Appendix*, 219.

[65] See footnote 27. Very recurring name; see also I. Kajanto, *The Latin Cognomina* (1982), 20, 72, 273; *Onomasticon provinciarum Europae Latinarum* II (1999), 150 and *Appendix*, 220.

[66] See note 56. The name is very frequently attested. See *Onomasticon provinciarum Europae Latinarum* II (1999), 153 and *Appendix*, 220.

[67] CIL III, 4197; RIU 79, A. Schober, *Die römischen Grabsteine von Noricum und Pannonien*, (Wien, 1923), 87; T. Endre, *Lapidarium Savariense* (2011), 96. The name is well attested.

[68] See note 67. The name is widely spread.

Gaudentius,[69] *Ge]rontia,*[70] *Hernilla,*[71] *Ianuaria,*[72] *Irenaeus,*[73] *Iodorus,*[74] *Irene,*[75] *Iustianus* or *Iustiane,*[76] *Iustinus/-a,*[77] *Kalendina,*[78] *Launio*[79] (I think that the

[69] Two inscriptions record the name *Gaudentius*: **1)** CIL III, 15181[2]; ILCV 3659 and **2)** see note 48. The name is well-attested. See also *Onomasticon provinciarum Europae Latinarum* II (1999), 161 and *Appendix*, 220.

[70] CIL III, 10235; VHAD, 10 (1908-9), 183, no. 385; ILCV 1125. H. Gračanin, *Svijet antičke žene u dva južnopanonska pokrajinska središta, Sisciji i Sirmiju* in *Scrinia Slavonica*, 4 (Srijem and Baranja, 2004), 56, no. 61 and note 149. The name is rare and in Pannonia is recorded only in this inscription.

[71] CIL III, 4190; E. Desjardins and F. Rómer, *Monuments épigraphiques du Musée National Hongrois, Magyar Nemzeti Múzeum* (Budapest, 1873), no. 135; ILCV *add.*, 401 and 2201; Von Lajos Balla *et alii*, in A. Mócsy and T. Szentléleky (eds), *Die Römischen Steindenkmäler von Savaria* (1971), 165; RIU 84; T. Endre, *Lapidarium Savariense* (2011), 149. The name is recorded only here and is an *unicum*. See also *Onomasticon provinciarum Europae Latinarum* II (1999), *Appendix*, 222.

[72] CIL III, 3986; AIJ 571; CIGP, cat. no. 70. Recurrent name. See also A. Mócsy, *Die Bevölkerung von Pannonien* (1959), 176; L. Barkòczi, *The Population of Pannonia* (1964), 314; I Kajanto, *The Latin Cognomina* (1982), 29-30, 60-1, 218; A. Mócsy, 'Nomenclator Provinciarum Europae Latinarum' (1983), 148; H. Solin and O. Salomies (eds), *Repertorium nominum gentilium* (1994), 344; *Onomasticon provinciarum Europae Latinarum* II (1999), 189-90 and *Appendix*, 222.

[73] N. Duval, 'Sirmium, 'Ville imperial' ou "Capitale"?' (1979), 83-4 for the inscription; A. Benvin, *Muka sv. Ireneja Srijemskoga, Ranokršćanski portret biskupa mučenika* in *Diacovensia*, vol. 2, no. 1 (Zagreb, 1994), 90; U. Brandl and M. Vasic (eds), *Roms Erbe auf dem Balkan. Spätantike Kaiservillen und Stadtanlagen in Serbien* (Mainz, 2007), 21, fig. 3.

[74] See note 56. The name occurs only here and should be an *unicum*. See *Onomasticon provinciarum Europae Latinarum* II (1999), *Appendix*, 223.

[75] RIU 85; AE 1972, 402; T. Endre, *Lapidarium Savariense* (2011), 150. See *Onomasticon provinciarum Europae Latinarum* II (1999), 196 and *Appendix*, 223.

[76] RIU 633; J. Ceška and R. Hošek (eds), *Inscriptiones Pannoniae Superioris in Slovacia* (1967), no. 41; H. Friederike and L. Barnabás (eds), *Führer zum römischen Lapidarium in Bastion* (2002), 47. *Iustiane* could be either the vocative case of the male name *Iustianus* (which occurs several times in Pannonia – **1)** CIL III, 6010[77]; AIJ 342; M.J. Vermaseren, *Corpus Inscriptionum et Monumentorum Religionis Mithriacae* (Den Haag, 1956-1960), 1605; CIL III, 4238; **2)** CIL III, 10942; RIU 230; M.J. Vermaseren, *Corpus Inscriptionum* (1956-1960), 1638; AE 1948, 79; **3)** CIL III, 4239; CIL III, 10943; RIU 231; **4)** RIU 1502; G. Alföldy, 'Epigraphica Pannonica IV. Inschriften aus Székesfehérvár (Alba Regia, Stuhlweißenburg)', in *Studia Epigraphica Pannonica* 2 (2009-2010), 13-30, 25; AE 1941, 10; AE 2007, 1169 – and is attested in diverse regions of the *orbis Christianus antiquus*) or the female name *Iustiane* (which never appears in Pannonia), as it appears in these two inscriptions **1)** CIL VI, 11796; CIL VI, 34047; CIL XIV, *67[1]; **2)** CIL XIV, 1571. The form *Iustiana*, *e.g.*, in CIL III, 6627; CIL III, 14147; ILS 2483; E. Bosch, *Quellen zur Geschichte der Stadt Ankara im Altertum* (Ankara, 1967), 49; AE 2001, 2048 is related to a *centuria*. See also *Onomasticon provinciarum Europae Latinarum* II (1999), 209 and *Appendix*, 223.

[77] *Iustinus* and *Iustina* are recorded together in **1)** CIL III, 4197; RIU 79, A. Schober, *Die römischen Grabsteine von Noricum und Pannonien* (Wien, 1923), 87; T. Endre, *Lapidarium Savariense* (2011), 96, whereas **2)** CIL III, 4186; RIU 81; ILCV *add.*, 474; ILCV 1282; T. Endre, *Lapidarium Savariense* (2011), 146 and **3)** TRH 26; T. Endre, *Lapidarium Savariense* (2011), 151 bear the name *Iustina*. See also *Onomasticon provinciarum Europae Latinarum* II (1999), 209 and *Appendix*, 223.

[78] See note 32. *Kalendina* appears also on the inscription ILJ 370 (from *Noricum*). The other rare occurrences of the name bear *Calendina* (also in *Noricum* and Pannonia: CIL III, 4537, 4997, attesting the oscillation c↔k in these areas, which coexisted). See *Onomasticon provinciarum Europae Latinarum* II (1999), 22 and *Appendix*, 213.

[79] CIL III, 4222; RIU 83; ILCV *add.*, 670; *Römisches Österreich. Jahresschrift der Österreichischen Gesellschaft für Archäologie* (Wien, 2006), 1 = T. Endre, *Lapidarium Savariense*

uncorroborated name *Launionus* needs to be challenged), *Leo*,[80] *Lu]picina*,[81] *Macarius*,[82] *Macedonius*,[83] *Marcellianus*,[84] *Martinianus*,[85] *Maurus*,[86] *Maximana*,[87] *Maximī'n'us*,[88] *Maximus*,[89] *Nemesius*,[90] *Nunnane*,[91] *Paulinianus*,[92] *Paulinus*,[93]

(2011), 148. Two other inscriptions bear this rare name: **1)** CIL V, 8752; E. Pais, *Corporis inscriptionum Latinarum supplementa Italica* (Roma, 1884), 406; ILCV 460; ILS, 2802; G. Lettich, *Le iscrizioni sepolcrali tardoantiche di Concordia* (Trieste, 1983), 37 and **2)** P. Jung and N. Schücker (eds), *1000 gestempelte Sigillaten aus Altbeständen des Landesmuseums Mainz* (Bonn, 2006), 280. See also M. Handley, *Dying on Foreign Shores: Travel and Mobility in the Late-Antique West*, JRA Supplementary Series 86 (Portsmouth, 2011), 136, no. 498. For the name occurrence see *Onomasticon provinciarum Europae Latinarum* III (2000), *Appendix*, 174.

[80]   See note 63, **2)**. See the occurrence of the well-attested name in *Onomasticon provinciarum Europae Latinarum* III (2000), 22 and *Appendix*, 174.

[81]   ILJ 3028. The female name appears one more time in ICUR V, 13919. See also *Onomasticon provinciarum Europae Latinarum* III (2000), *Appendix*, 175.

[82]   See note 70. The name is very frequent. See also *Onomasticon provinciarum Europae Latinarum* III (2000), 42 and *Appendix*, 175.

[83]   See note 73.

[84]   CIL III, 3996 and *add.*, 114; VHAD, 10 (1908-9), 159, no. 351; ILCV 01449; AIJ 581; Ž. Demo (ed.), *Od nepobjedivog sunca do sunca pravde* (1994), 82, no. 39; J. Dresken-Weiland, *Repertorium der christlich-antiken Sarkophage 2. Italien mit einem Nachtrag: Rom und Ostia, Dalmatien*, Museen der Welt (Mainz, 1998), 110, no. 311 and plate 100, 5; AE 2006, 1033. V. Vukelić, *Prilog istraživ antičke Siscije. Prvi pisani spomen Severillina sarkofaga u ranom novovjekovlju i pokušaj rekonstrukcije nijegovog izvomog nalazišta* (Zagreb, 2006), 201-16, especially 202, 211-3. This is the only occurrence in Pannonia, even if the name is rarely attested in diverse regions. See also *Onomasticon provinciarum Europae Latinarum* III (2000), 53 and *Appendix*, 176.

[85]   CIL III, 10237; VHAD, 10, (1908-9), 177, no. 376; H. Gračanin, *Svijet antičke žene u dva južnopanonska pokrajinska središta* (2004), 57, no. 65. See *Onomasticon provinciarum Europae Latinarum* III (2000), 61 and *Appendix*, 176.

[86]   CIL III, 4002; Ž. Demo (ed.), *Od nepobjedivog sunca do sunca pravde* (1994), 116, no. 155; AE 2004, 1121; M. Milin, 'Tri beleške iz kasnoantičke istorije', *ZAnt* 54 (2004), 149-51. The name is frequent. See *Onomasticon provinciarum Europae Latinarum* III (2000), 68 and *Appendix*, 177.

[87]   VHAD, 10 (1908-1909), 191, no. 397; ILJ 3028. The name occurs only here and in ICUR V, 14461. See also *Onomasticon provinciarum Europae Latinarum* III (2000), *Appendix*, 177.

[88]   See note 71. For the name see *Onomasticon provinciarum Europae Latinarum* III (2000), 69 and *Appendix*, 177.

[89]   VHAD, 10 (1908-9), 191, no. 397; ILJ 3028. See also *Onomasticon provinciarum Europae Latinarum* III (2000), 70 and *Appendix*, 177.

[90]   See note 63, **2)**. The name is rare, for the occurrence see *Onomasticon provinciarum Europae Latinarum* III (2000), 97 and *Appendix*, 178. Here the name might be the *agnomen* of *Flavianus*, where both the names are connected by the simple *et*. See I. Kajanto, *Supernomina. A Study in Latin Epigraphy* (Helsinki, 1966), 10.

[91]   RIU 633; J. Ceška and R. Hošek (eds.), *Inscriptiones Pannoniae Superioris in Slovacia* (1967), no. 41. The name is an *unicum*.

[92]   See note 32. The name is recorded in less than thirty inscriptions. See its occurrence in *Onomasticon provinciarum Europae Latinarum* III (2000), 129 and *Appendix*, 180.

[93]   CIL III, 3991; AIJ 574; Ž. Demo (ed.), *Od nepobjedivog sunca do sunca pravde* (1994), 40. The occurrence of the *cognomen* is copious in diverse areas. See also *Onomasticon provinciarum Europae Latinarum* III (2000), *Appendix*, 180. Marija Buzov seems to allude to this inscription, when she writes about a 'tombstone erected for Paulinus, Lucerin's son', see M. Buzov, 'The

Pomentius,[94] *Propincus*,[95] *Quinti]lla*,[96] *Quin]tina*,[97] *Quintus*[98] (used as a cognomen), *Revocata*,[99] *Secundinus*,[100] *Severilla*,[101] *Surica*,[102] *Urbica*,[103] *Ursi-*

Topography and the Archaeological material of the Early Christian period in Continental Croatia', *Classica et Christiana* 5 (2010), 299-334, 313. But this reading does not convince. *Lucerinus* is recorded as a *nomen* in a classical inscription (AE 1996, 449 = AE 2003, 548) – the female *nomen Lucerina* appears in CIL IX, 1521. In CIL IX, 3110 or ICUR VIII, 21883 *Lucerinus/-a* is the sole name recorded. In several inscriptions it is uncertain whether *Lucerinus* could be the *cognomen* or, on the other hand, indicate the place of origin, *Luceria* (see *e.g.* AE 1983, 224 or the polyonymy *Egnatius Caecilius Antistius Lucerinus*); anyway, in this kind of names, one option does not rule out the other. I do not think that in our inscription *Paulini Lucerinis* represented the filiation, but just *Paulinus'* cognomen or the provenance. In late Roman onomastics it is not rare to find people with two *cognomina*. See A. Ferrua, *Epigrafia Cristiana* (Città del Vaticano, 1949-1950), columns 429-40; I. Kajanto, *Onomastic Studies in the early Christian Inscriptions* (1963); A. Ferrua, 'I nomi degli antichi cristiani', *La Civiltà Cattolica* 117 (1966), 492-8.

[94] See note 77, **2)**. The name, recorded only here, is an *unicum*. See also *Onomasticon provinciarum Europae Latinarum* III (2000), *Appendix*, 181.

[95] See note 11. The name is rare and, besides our text, is recorded in a small number of inscriptions: CIL III, 13382; CIL VI, 2408; CIL X, 3492; AE 1965, 35; AE 1983, 800. See also *Onomasticon provinciarum Europae Latinarum* III (2000), 167.

[96] It appears on two Christian epigraphs: **1)** CIL III, 10236; VHAD, 10 (1908-9), 190-1, no. 396; ILCV 3611 and **2)** J. Ceška and R. Hošek (eds), *Inscriptiones Pannoniae Superioris* (1967), no. 42; RIU 634; H. Friederike and L. Barnabás (eds), *Führer zum römischen Lapidarium in Bastion* (2002), no. 50. The name *Quintilla* is very frequent and in Pannonia appears in several inscriptions; see *Onomasticon provinciarum Europae Latinarum* IV (2002), 19 and *Appendix*, 193.

[97] See note 96, **1)**. The name occurs one more time in Pannonia. See *Onomasticon provinciarum Europae Latinarum* IV (2002), 19 and *Appendix*, 193.

[98] See note 75. The occurrence of the name is too regular to need further explanation. See *Onomasticon provinciarum Europae Latinarum* IV (2002), 20-1 and *Appendix*, 193.

[99] J. Ceška and R. Hošek (eds), *Inscriptiones Pannoniae Superioris* (1967), no. 42; RIU 634; H. Friederike and L. Barnabás (eds), *Führer zum römischen Lapidarium in Bastion* (2002), no. 50. The name appears on four more inscriptions from Pannonia: **1)** RIU 1227; B. Lörincz, *Die römischen Hilfstruppen in Pannonien während der Prinzipatszeit. I: Die Inschriften* (Wien, 2001), 359; **2)** RIU 1228; **3)** RIU 232; CLEPann 65; AE 1964, 10; **4)** P. Kovács and Á. Szabó, *Tituli Aquincenses* (2009), no. 634; AE 1965, 50; AE 1967, 377. See also *Onomasticon provinciarum Europae Latinarum* IV (2002), 28 and *Appendix*, 193.

[100] CIL III, 4222; RIU 83; ILCV *add.*, 670; *Römisches Österreich. Jahresschrift der Österreichischen Gesellschaft für Archäologie* (Wien, 2006), 1; T. Endre, *Lapidarium Savariense* (2011), 148. The name is very frequent. See I. Kajanto, *The Latin Cognomina* (1982), 292; *Onomasticon provinciarum Europae Latinarum* IV (2002), 58-9 and *Appendix*, 195.

[101] For the inscription see note 84. For the name occurrence see *Onomasticon provinciarum Europae Latinarum* IV (2002), 75 and *Appendix*, 195.

[102] See note 77, **1)**. The name is very rare and is recorded in a few inscriptions; see *e.g.*: CIL V, 5618; H. Merten, *Katalog der frühchristlichen Inschriften des bischöflichen Dom- und Diözesanmuseums Trier* (Trier, 1990), 1 = *Recueil des Inscriptions Chrétiennes de la Gaule* (Paris, 1975-), 94; *Hispania Epigraphica* (Madrid, 1989-), 182.

[103] See note 85. For the name see *Onomasticon provinciarum Europae Latinarum* IV (2002), 185 and *Appendix*, 200.

cinus/-a,[104] *Valentinus*,[105] *Varus*,[106] *Venan[tius* (?),[107] *Venatorinus*,[108] *Victor* (?),[109] *Victorinianus*,[110] *Victorinus/-a*,[111] *Volussius*.[112]

It is significant that, besides the inscription of *M(arcus) Iuvinian[us Con] stantian[us]*,[113] no *tria nomina* occur – which are sporadically still used in the 4th century in conservative areas, such as the Roman provinces –, whereas, as I have said above, the presence of *duo nomina* is remarkable. The male *gentilicia* that recur are: *Aurelius*[114] (five times); *Flavius*[115] (most probably five times); *Iulius*[116] (once); *Paulinus*[117] (here used as a *nomen*); *Iuvinianus*[118] (once) and *Nammius*[119] (once). Another fragmentary inscription[120] bears only *-ius*, which can be regarded as one of the many *nomina* ending in *-ius*.

---

[104] For *Ursicina* see note 42, 1); for *Urs[ici]nus* see note 37. The male name is frequent, whereas the female one is rare (it appears one more time in Pannonia). See also *Onomasticon provinciarum Europae Latinarum* IV (2002), 186 and *Appendix*, 200.

[105] See note 40. For the occurrence of the name see *Onomasticon provinciarum Europae Latinarum* IV (2002), 141 and *Appendix*, 198-99.

[106] VHAD, 10 (1908-1909), 186, Nr. 391; ILJ 3026.

[107] CIL III, 15136²; VHAD, 10 (1908-1909), 186-7, no. 392. *Venantius* is quite attested in diverse regions. In Pannonia it occurs one more time in CIL III, 3294 (= CIL III, 10275). See also *Onomasticon provinciarum Europae Latinarum* IV (2002), 153.

[108] See note 38. The name *Venatorinus* is an *unicum*. *Onomasticon provinciarum Europae Latinarum* IV (2002), *Appendix*, 199.

[109] VHAD, 10 (1908-1909), 203, no. 441; ILJ 3065. See the occurrence of the name in *Onomasticon provinciarum Europae Latinarum* IV (2002), 167-8 and *Appendix*, 199.

[110] See note 33. For the occurrence of the name see *Onomasticon provinciarum Europae Latinarum* IV (2002), 168.

[111] For the name *Victorinus* see note 62; for *Victorina* see note 106. Both the names are frequent and well attested. See *Onomasticon provinciarum Europae Latinarum* IV (2002), 168-9 and *Appendix*, 199.

[112] See note 58. The name occurs in various regions; in Pannonia it appears only on this inscription. See the occurrence of the name in *Onomasticon provinciarum Europae Latinarum* IV (2002), 183 and *Appendix*, 200.

[113] CIL III, 6446 = 10238; ILCV 2838. The *nomen Iuvinian[us* occurs only in this inscription and is an *unicum*. The name *Con]stantian[us]* is rare and is recorded in the following handful of inscriptions: 1) CIL III, 1466; 2) ILCV 3419b; 3) CIL V, 1622 (the consulate); 4) CIL XIII, 8333; 5) AE 1987, 975b (the consulate). See also the occurrence of the name *Constantianus* in *Onomasticon provinciarum Europae Latinarum* II (1999), 73 and *Appendix*, 209.

[114] See the inscriptions mentioned in the notes 11, 56, 63, 2). One of the *Aurelii* is recorded in CIL III, 10238, but it is uncertain whether it could refer to a man or a woman. See also *Onomasticon provinciarum Europae Latinarum* I² (2005), 238-49 and *Appendix*, 342.

[115] See notes 35, 39, 77, 2), 85-6. See also *Onomasticon provinciarum Europae Latinarum* II (1999), 145-7 and *Appendix*, 219.

[116] See note 29.

[117] See note 93.

[118] See note 113.

[119] See note 98.

[120] See note 106.

Regarding the female *nomina*, even if *Aurelia*[121] prevails (it recurs seven times), we can find three times *Aul[(i)a* (?),[122] twice *Flavia*[123] and only once *Aelia*,[124] *Valeria*[125] and *Herennia*.[126]

Finally a rare case of polyonymy has to be mentioned, since it denotes a certain conservatism: *Aelius Mucianus Bassus Paulinianus*[127] (Fig. 4), where the *nomen Aelius* is used as a *praenomen*, and the *cognomen Mucianus* as a *nomen*.

5. Out of the 139 inscriptions that we are examining, only 28 referred to men and 26 to women (only several inscriptions are dedicated to more than a single deceased; the remainder are too fragmentary to allow us to verify to whom the tombs belonged). Out of these 54 inscriptions, only 27 texts record biometric identifiers, which testify that in Pannonia, too, life expectancy at birth, considering the high rates of infant mortality, was not over 30 years on average, both for men and women.[128] According to the documentation, we can perform a small-scale statistical analysis that reveal both the not surprising abundant death of children (11 children died before the age of 10) and the death of a very old man, *Nammius Quintus*, who died at the age of 86, and that of his wife, *Aurelia Irene*, who died when she was 61 or 71.[129]

The following table gives the details of the number of deaths recurring in every single age group:

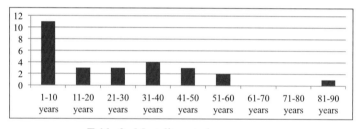

Table 3. Mortality rate by age group.

---

[121] See notes 42, 56, 71, 75, 77, **2)**, 103.

[122] See notes 96-7.

[123] See note 11.

[124] See note 78.

[125] See note 77, **3)**.

[126] See note 111.

[127] See note 32. For the occurrence of the names *Aelius* (*nomen* and *cognomen*) and *Mucianus* see *Onomasticon provinciarum Europae Latinarum* I² (2005), 33-8 and *Appendix*, 333; III (2000), 89 and *Appendix*, 178.

[128] R. Etienne, 'Démographie et epigraphie', in *Atti del III Congresso Internazionale di Epigrafia Greca e Latina* (*Roma 4-8 settembre 1957*) (Roma, 1959), 415-24.

[129] See note 98 and D. Mazzoleni, 'Custodes di cimiteri e di basiliche nelle iscrizioni cristiane', in *Kačić. Zbornik u Čast Emilija Marina za 60. Rođendan (Miscellanea Emilio Marin sexagenario dicata)*, 41-3 (2009-2011) (Split, 2009-2011), 316-7. The age of *Aurelia Irene* is erroneously written LXLXI on the gravestone. It can be either LXXI (due to the interpolation of L) or LXI (due to the dittography of the first two figures of the number).

Moreover, among the biometric data, the duration of marriage is also mentioned in two epigraphs,[130] but unfortunately, given the fact they are not combined with the indication of the lifespan of the deceased, this makes it impossible to detect the age at which the marriage was celebrated. We know that women used to marry quite early (between 14 and 21 years of age at Rome;[131] in Aquileia[132] women had an average age at marriage of 22 – between 14 and 35 anyway – and in Syracuse[133] probably between 15 and 18 years), while men's age of marriage has a broader range (between the age of 20 and 30 at Rome; later in Aquileia[134] and Syracuse[135]).

The *tituli* also record the rather generic expressions addressed to the deceased (husband, wife, children, parents, colleagues) to celebrate their virtues, drawn from the classical repertoire (worthy, very dear, very sweet). The spouses use stereotyped phrases to praise their mutual positive qualities, and terms such us: *coniux* or *coniunx*, *compar* (Fig. 5), *virginius*.

In contrast to the addition of many novelties both in the formulae and content, also the appearance of the invocation *Dis Manibus* has to be pointed out, which firmly continued to be used. In the inscription of *Aurelia Iustina* (Fig. 6) the dedication to the *Di Manes* – the underworld divinities invoked by pagans to identify and protect the tombs – appears in the very last line. This datum is not surprising, for it is broadly attested in diverse regions of the *orbis Christianus antiquus* (the *adprecatio* recurs, *e.g.*, in about 250 Christian inscriptions at Rome or even more persistently in Africa at the funerary basilica of Mactar and in the cemetery of Altava[136]), and allows the burial place to be placed under the protection of Roman law as a *res sacra*. The Christians, as well as the pagans, were afraid that their sepulchre could, after their death, be alienated or devastated, particularly when their burial places were in *sub divo* cemeteries and therefore difficult to protect.

6. Christian epigraphic production displays significant signs of the evolution of Latin and Greek in this Province. The texts are an extraordinary source to study the process of transformation in the consonant system and in the phonetic and morphosyntactic structures, as well as errors due to the distraction or ignorance of the stonecutter who transcribed the texts from the draft and the reflection of the spoken language. The documented phenomena in the Latin texts are:

---

[130] See notes 62 and 84.

[131] C. Carletti, 'Aspetti biometrici del matrimonio nelle iscrizioni cristiane di Roma', *Augustinianum* 17 (1977), 39-51.

[132] D. Mazzoleni, *Epigrafi del mondo cristiano antico* (Roma, 2002), 137.

[133] M. Sgarlata, *Ricerche di demografia storica. Le iscrizioni tardo – imperiali di Siracusa* (Città del Vaticano, 1991), 120-8.

[134] G. Cuscito, 'Valori umani e religiosi nell'epigrafia cristiana dell'Alto Adriatico', *Antichità Altoadriatiche* 2 (1972), 167-96, 195 and note 22. *Aurelius Fortunatus* probably got married over 30.

[135] In Syracuse *Sporus*, in all likelihood, got married at 41. See note 133.

[136] J. Marcillet-Jaubert, *Les inscriptions d'Altava* (Aix-en-Provence, 1968), 83-4, 217.

I) monophthongization of the diphthong *ae* into *e*, not only at the end of the word: *que, memorie, filie, ecclesie, bone, dulcissime, carissime, pientissime, Petronille, Kalendine, Celsine, Maximiane, Erenei*; II) hypercorrectness, *ae* in place of *e*: *<p>acae, maemoria*; III) metathesis between *i↔e*: *quiescet, fedeli, candeda, s[a]n(c)tisse[mi], verginius, cymiteri, Disiderium, Erenei*; IV) metathesis between *o↔u*: *cumpare, Martoria* (coexists together with the form *Martorya*); V) interchange *y↔u*: *martur, Surica* (coexists along with *Syrica*); VI) interchange *oe↔y*: *cymiteri*; VII) interchange *u↔i*: *duobis*; VIII) dropping of *m* at the end of the word: *beatu*; *marture*; *infane* for *infantem* (*error quadratarii* for the omitted *t*); IX) dropping of *h* at the beginning of word: *ic, abe, ortus*; X) dropping of the nasal before sibilant: *dolies*; XI) dissimilation, *m* being replaced by *n*: *conpar*; XII) the way to reproduce *x*: *vicxit*; XIII) elision of vowel in hiatus context: *Ladic(ense)* for *Laodicense, quesco*; XIV) epenthesis and anaptyxis: *interantem* for *intrantem* (idiotism for *intranti*), *Fortunatanem* (or *error quadratarii*); XV) syncope: *domnum, domnicarum*; sigmatic perfect in place of -*u*/-*v* perfect: *lanxit* for *languit*: 3rd declension, nominative plural of dental stems in -*is*: *innocentis* for *innocentes*; 3rd declension, nominative singular in -*or*: *custor* for *custos*; confusion over declensions (cases, agreement): *menserum* for *mensorum, qui* for *quae, beatum* for *beatus, Aelii* for *Aelius, Urbici* for *Urbica*; use of cum + accusative in place of ablative: *cum matronam suam*; in biometric formulae, mixture of accusative and ablative in the indication of years, months, days: *annis, menses, dies*.

The phenomena attested in the Greek inscriptions are: I) abridgement of αι into ε: Κέσαρος, κεῖμε; II) abridgement of ει into ι: βήτι *pro* βοήθει; III) interchange of labials: πύλαξον *pro* φύλαξον; IV) interchange of dentals: ἐθόθη *pro* ἐδόθη, βήτι *pro* βοήθει; V) elision of vowel in hiatus context: βήτι *pro* βοήθει; VI) dropping of ν at the end of the word (or *error quadratarii*): μνημί, τὴ *pro* τὴν; VII) iotacism/itacism: μνημί.

Eventually, with regard to numerals, the use of the *episemon* has to be mentioned in one inscription from *Sirmium*.[137]

7. Through reading the texts, one can become aware of the peculiar lexicon of the Christians in this Province.

Flavius Maurus is called *fidelis* in one inscription from *Certissia-Murs(i)a*[138] (Fig. 7). This term occurs five more times in the epigraphs from Pannonia (once at *Sirmium*, in the inscription of two children, *Petrus* and *Victorinianus*, who died at about 1 and about 5 years of age respectively[139] (Fig. 8); four times in *Savaria*: in the inscription that *Aelius Mucianus Bassus Paulinianus* and *Paulus* erected to their mother *Aelia Kalendina*;[140] in the inscription of the two *Aurelii*,

---

[137] See notes 96-7.
[138] See note 86.
[139] See note 33.
[140] See note 32.

conlactanei, *Flavianus* and *Leo*[141] (Fig. 9); on the tombstone that the *fideles Gaudentius* and *Crescentia* set up for their dearest daughter, who died *fidelis* at the age of 25,[142] to indicate that the deceased was baptized and therefore was a member of the community of the faithful. The fact that *fidelis* is referred both to adults and children, could confirm that in some circumstances – apart from any possible case of Baptism *in extremis* – paedobaptism could have become a common practice in Pannonia. At Rome, for instance, the practice of baptizing infants was not general; likewise a considerable number of people were baptized when still a child or adolescent.[143]

Those who could afford to set up a sepulchre bought a tomb for themselves and the members of their family during their lifetime, according to the custom that has always stimulated the dignity, the pride and the good name of the *familia* of which they were members. Humanity has always known how fugacious life is and how death hangs over everyone. Hence, fully aware of the ineluctability of death, people have attentively erected their sepulchre, while still alive. In fact formulae such as *vivus sibi suisque* or *sibi vivo, se vivo fecit* regularly recur both in classical epigraphs and in Christian inscriptions. A Latin inscription from *Sirmium* records that *Artemidora* built her tomb, when still alive[144] (Fig. 10). Other Christian inscriptions allude to the purchase of graves: *Aurelia Domnica* bought a tomb and dedicated an inscription both to her children and her husband, *Aurelius Iodorus*, who came from Greece (*ex regione Laodicense*)[145] (Fig. 11); *Aurelius Gaianus*, together with his children *Gaius*, *Iustinus* and *Surica*, bought the space for a tomb and erected a *titulum* to the wife and mother *Aurelia Iustina*;[146] *Flavius Flavianus* and his wife *Valeria Iustina* bought a sepulchre for their *innocens* child *Stercorinus*, who died when he was 13[147] (Fig. 12); the inscription of *Flavia Calvena* states that her mother along with her husband set up the tomb where she is buried;[148] the veteran *Iulius Herculanus* probably arranged a large tomb at his own expense (Fig. 13) and another veteran *Gaudentius*, along with his wife *Crescentia*, erected a tomb for their daughter *Aspalia* and for themselves.[149] Finally a fragmentary inscription from *Sirmium* could probably read (*vivus/-a*) *s*]*ibi p*[*osuit* (?).[150]

---

[141] See note 63, **2**).

[142] See note 57.

[143] J. Janssens, *Vita e morte del cristiano negli epitaffi di Roma anteriori al sec. VII* (Roma, 1981), 32-6 and 148-50.

[144] See note 27.

[145] See note 74.

[146] See note 77, **1**).

[147] See note 39.

[148] See note 11.

[149] See note 48.

[150] VHAD, 10 (1908-1909), 206, no. 452; ILJ 3076. *Vivus/-a* is just a conjecture, borne out by the recurrent formula that appears in many inscriptions. The formula 'sibi posuit' occurs without *vivus/-a* too.

With or without the mention of the *emptio* – which legally determined the inalienability of the tomb – the Christian epigraphs from Pannonia bear other precious and interesting information, mostly regarding the topography of the burial places. The mention, *e.g.*, of a cemetery (or one of its regions), rather than the indication of the sepulchre of a martyr – whose immediate proximity assures his/her intercession with God – or the allusion to a basilica sometimes constitutes the sole precious source we have for the historical reconstruction. The already mentioned *Artemidora*,[151] for example, was buried in *Sirmium*, by the tomb of *Syneros*, 'entering, to the right, between the tombs of *Fortunata* and *Desiderius*'. Other topographical details are in the *titulus* that *Aurelia Aminia*[152] has dedicated to her husband *Flavius Sanctus ex numero Iovianorum protector*, who died in Aquileia and was buried by the martyr *Syneros*. In this regard, I would like to draw attention to the suggestive, although not demonstrable, reflection of de Rossi:[153] the Acts of the martyr *Syneros* document that a lady, firmly admonished and mortificated by an elderly *Syneros* for her suspicious manners, brought him before the Governor. She was the wife of a *domesticus imperatoris*, who boasted to be *lateri regis adhaerens*. According to de Rossi this office is that of the *domesticus protector*, the same as *Flavius Sanctus*. *Aurelia Aminia* could have remembered that *Syneros* was martyred because of the *protector sacri lateris'* wife and, venerating the saint or commending the husband – who was a *protector* –, to him, in a way made amends for the malefaction of the woman who accused him and was occasion of his glorious death.

Macedonius, along with his wife, set down their inscription '*in basilica domini nostri Eirenei*'[154] (incidentally I think that the current reading of some lines of this epigraph needs to be called into question. I would rather suggest to read the lines 1-3 '*In basilica domini n* | *ostri Erenei (h)a(n)c mem* | *oriam posuit* – with '*Erenei*' pro '*Irenaei*' and '*ac*' pro '*hanc*', as it appears in one inscription from Salona[155] – and in the last two lines, the corrupted form of the name of *Macedonius'* wife. I do not assume that the sign between the two names on the slab may be a cursive '*Z*',[156] for it cannot be but a punctuation mark. I would propose to read the name in the last line *A{a}mmete {E}Vena(n)ti(a)*, with the vowel *e* inaccurately added at the beginning of the name by prosthesis or dittography[157] [Fig. 14]).

---

[151] See note 27.

[152] See note 42, **1**).

[153] G.B. de Rossi, 'Il cimitero di S. Sinerote Martire in Sirmio', *Bullettino di Archeologia Cristiana* (Roma, 1884-85), 147-8.

[154] See note 73.

[155] N. Gauthier, E. Marin and F. Prévot (eds), *Salona IV, Inscriptions de Salone chrétienne IVᵉ-VIIᵉ siècles, Salona IV, Natpisi starokršćanske Salone, IV.-VII. st.*, vols. *I-II*, Collection de *l'École française de Rome, 194/4, Niz 'Salona' Arheološkog Muzeja – Split, 12. Rome/Split: Ecole Française de Rome/Arheološki muzej Split*, vol. I, 82 (= CIL III, 9567; ILCV 838; ILJ 2375).

[156] A. Benvin, 'Muka sv. Ireneja Srijemskoga. Ranokršćanski portret biskupa mučenika', *Diacovensia* 2, no. 1 (Zagreb, 1994), 90.

[157] *Amme(s) Venantia*: the very rare *cognomen Amme(s)* is attested in two inscriptions from Rome and one from Venosa – CIL VI, 24196; 24358 and L. Chioffi, *Caro. Il mercato della carne*

Another deceased, who was deposed in a funerary basilica that remains unknown, is most probably mentioned in the last line of a fragmentary inscription from *Certissia-Murs(i)a*. It reads: *depositu]s ad basi[licam*.[158]

Unfortunately the topographical information provided in those epigraphs, not being corroborated by any archaeological evidence, is useless and mute in order to detect and reconstruct the arrangement of the *ad sanctos* burial places and their connection both with the tomb of the martyr and the cemetery.

8. The dedicators of the inscription sometimes refer to the inscription itself with the technical term *titulus*, both in verse and in prose epigraphs.[159] We have already seen it in the inscription of *Aurelia Aminia*.[160] In one of the most interesting Christian verse inscriptions from *Savaria*, it is said: '*Volussius* and *Sabatia liberti* wrote and placed the *titulus* to *Flavius Dalmatius*',[161] who was a *vir perfectissimus* (an honorary predicate and title of rank of the *Equites,* above the rank of *egregius* (*vir egregius*), but under the one of *eminentissimus*) (Fig. 15). The formula to indicate that 'Somebody has dedicated a title to somebody else' is *ponere titulum*[162] (which recurs only once in our documentation. The same verse inscription of *Flavius Dalmatius* bears the formula *scribere titulum* too[163]). This expression has a very high incidence of occurrence in the inscriptions of the 5th-6th centuries from Trier (about 96%)[164] and can be considered the peculiar feature par excellence of its epigraphic praxis (with or without the expression '*pro caritate*'). Apart from these inscriptions from *Gallia Belgica*, also several 2nd-3rd centuries epigraphs from *Germania* (*superior* and *inferior*) bear this formula, especially in military context.[165]

nell'occidente romano. Riflessi epigrafici ed iconografici (Roma, 1999), 78 –, always in nominative; a ---]*natia Ammis* is attested in Rome (CIL VI, 26429). This should be the only occurrence of the name in Pannonia. The *cognomen Venantia*, here corrupted with the vowel added at the beginning of the word, is isolated and appears in **1)** CIL XIII, 884; 2302 and **2)** CLE 718. For names composed of two juxtaposed *cognomina*, see note 93. On the other hand, the male name *Venatius* or *Venantius* appears quite frequently in various regions, even if the latter recurs more often than the former (see also the note 107).

[158] CIL III, 4005; Ž. Demo (ed.), *Od nepobjedivog sunca do sunca pravde* (1994), 104, no. 118.

[159] The term is more frequent in poetry: see, *e.g.*, P. Colafrancesco and M. Massaro (eds), *Concordanze dei Carmina Latina Epigraphica* (Bari, 1986), 827-30. Rarer in prose inscriptions: ILCV 2185, 2800, 4983; ICUR I, 1677; IX, 24385; *Recueil des inscriptions chrétiennes de la Gaule antérieures à la renaissance carolingienne* (RICG) (Paris, 1975-), XV, 148; D. Nuzzo, 'La denominazione della tomba nelle iscrizioni cristiane di Roma. Possibili elementi per la ricostruzione di una identità collettiva', *Vetera Christianorum* 42 (2005), 123-4.

[160] See note 42, **1)**.

[161] See note 35.

[162] See note 42, **1)**.

[163] See note 35.

[164] RICG, I, 43-4; C. Carletti, *Epigrafia dei cristiani in Occidente dal III al VII secolo. Ideologia e prassi* (Bari, 2008), 122-3.

[165] CIL XIII, 5382, 6906, 6947, 6967.

A fragmentary inscription from *Sirmium* bears the expression '*ponere titulum memorationis*',[166] which should probably be a hapax legomenon within the entire epigraphic record.

At other times the inscription is referred to as *memoria* and occurs several times in formulae like '*ponere memoriam*',[167] which is not a specifically Christian formula and, apart from Pannonia (*inferior* and *superior*), is quite attested in various regions, especially in *Dalmatia, Hispania citerior, Moesia inferior* and *Venetia et Histria*.

Otherwise the term *memoria* too can designate the burial itself, in such formulae like: *facere memoriam*.[168]

The above-mentioned Greek inscription of Βασιλιανός, dated to 352, also explains why the inscription has been set down and dedicated: ἐδόθη εἰς τὴν μνημί. So it was placed not only as a memorial, μνημεῖον, but also to remember one's own dear departed and for a deep sense of *pietas* towards them, as the inscription of *Flavia Calvena*[169] records. The same idea of commemoration is expressed in one Latin inscription from *Savaria* that reads in the first line: '*Bene memorandae coniugi*'. *Flavius Pomentius* dedicated this inscription against his own wishes and will, *contra votum*, a classical final formula that became quite popular in the epigraphic praxis of Christians too, particularly in Rome, Milan, Aquileia and *Gallia citerior*, mostly, but not only, in the case of children who predeceased the parents.[170]

The tomb is therefore the place of remembrance, where one can express auspicious wishes and prayers for the dead. In *Savaria* the introductory formula *bonae memoriae*, 'of good memory', is so common (it occurs five times out of 15 inscriptions), that can be easily regarded as a funerary peculiar formula of the epigraphic custom of the area[171] (the occurrence of this phrase is isolated in the other cities of Pannonia,[172] whereas is frequently attested in the inscriptions from Milan and Pavia). An inscription bears the variant *in D(o)m(ino) bon(a)e memori(a)e,* which might be an *unicum*.[173]

---

[166] VHAD, 10 (1908-1909), 186, no. 391; ILJ 3026.

[167] See notes 11, 32, 71, 73, 77, **2**), 85.

[168] See notes 27, 56, 79. The inscription in the notes 86, 96, **1**) and: **1**) VHAD, 10 (1908-1909), 391, no. 197; ILJ 3028; **2**) VHAD, 10 (1908-1909), 197, no. 419; ILJ 3046 and **3**) VHAD, 10 (1908-1909), 202, no. 438; ILJ 3062 bear the word *memoria*, but the slabs are too fragmentary to understand if they mention the formula *memoriam facere* rather than *memoria ponere* – as I can state, *e.g.*, for the inscription in the note 96, **1**) – or other such formulae that occur in Pannonian inscriptions.

[169] See note 11.

[170] See ILCV 4194-4210.

[171] See notes 39, 56, 77, **1**), 80 and the inscription CIL III, 10935; RIU 86; T. Endre, *Lapidarium Savariense* (2011), 153.

[172] CIL III, 3397 (from Nagyteteny); CIL III, 10611 (from Albertirsa); RIU 237 (from Janossomorja).

[173] See note 32.

A study on the nomenclature of the burial places is anything but sterile, if one tries to understand whether several terms were used to indicate a tomb in general or a specific kind of burial place. Such a study – in which excavation data and *in situ* inscriptions are useful and necessary, if not crucial – conducted on the Christian inscriptions from Rome, for instance, has furthermore revealed that the term *locus* is so frequent, that it can be easily considered peculiar to the epigraphic praxis of Rome, where the term, typologically speaking, does not designate a specific sepulchral structure, but and individual space defined by the nominal element. This locative definition does not indicate an autonomous and isolated space, not a distinct monument, but a part of a unitary complex, a part of the community cemetery.[174] Likewise, *e.g.*, the term τόπος is peculiar to Syracuse epigraphic custom[175] and *mensa* to the African praxis (*Mauretania Sitifensis* and *Numidia*).

In Pannonia only a few inscriptions mention the name of the tomb, so that such a survey will not yield firm results. Besides conventional terms such as *memoria* or the synecdochical use of *titulus* to indicate the burial space, other designations are: **a)** *locus*[176] (three times in our documentation); **b)** *arca*[177] (in the same inscription after a few lines it is generically redefined as *sedes*, set up by the husband after his wife's death, *post obitum*. *Arca*, which generally indicates the sarcophagus, is a technical term in the cemetery of Manastirine,[178] where it alternates with the rarer term *sarcophagus*[179]) (Fig. 16); **c)** *sepulcrum*[180] in one inscription from *Siscia*, which records that *Victorinus* buried his wife *Felicissima* in their tomb, probably a *bisomum* or a large tomb for two.

In another fragmentary inscription from *Siscia* the tomb is denominated *domus aeterna*,[181] eternal house (in the sense of eternal rest inside the tomb, as being an irrevocable condition *post mortem*[182]) (Fig. 17). The phrase *domus aeterna*, or the analogous formula *domus aeternalis*, appears in Roman classical

---

[174] D. Nuzzo, 'La denominazione della tomba nelle iscrizioni cristiane di Roma' (2005), 134.

[175] My MA thesis, unpublished, defended at the University of Catania in 2008, entitled *Osservazioni sulla prima comunità cristiana di Siracusa attraverso l'epigrafia funeraria*, 102-3; C. Carletti, *Epigrafia dei cristiani in Occidente dal III al VII secolo* (2008), 97, 120-1.

[176] See notes 34, 37 and **1)** CIL III, 14340[7].

[177] See note 84.

[178] See, *e.g.*, ILJ 2354, 2361, 2366, 2369, 2470, 2479, 2497, 2539, 2541-43, 2545-47.

[179] See, *e.g.*, ILJ 2400, 2402, 2405, 2409, 2425, 2469, 2510.

[180] See note 62. H. Gračanin, *Svijet antičke žene u dva južnopanonska pokrajinska središta* (2004), 33, no. 25 claims that *dominus Victorinus* means 'husband' and 'possessor' of *Felicissima*. To say the truth, it is well known that also in epigraphy such words as *dominus/-a* (or in Greek κύριος/-α) are common endearment words the spouses addressed each other, meaning '(my dear) sir' or '(my dear/good) lady'.

[181] See note 69, **1)**.

[182] G. Sanders, *Lapides memores. Paiens et chrétiens face à la mort: la témoniage de l'épigraphie funéraire latine* (Faenza, 1991), 300.

epigraphs – especially frequent in Africa[183] – and sporadically lives on, with an unaltered meaning, in the Christian epigraphic praxis.[184] In one inscription from *Aquincum* the burial is called *domus securitati*,[185] which, as it has already been pointed out, is the crasis of a longer and very frequently used pagan formula in Pannonia: *domo aeternae et perpetuae securitate*.[186]

9. Death and the concept of dying are very rarely exhibited in the Pannonian inscriptions. They are related to the notion of death considered in the active sense of 'departing' and 'ending life'. In a fragmentary inscription[187] from *Sirmium* the passage of the soul or spirit to the other world is indicated by the widespread expression *reces*]*sit in pac*[*e* (or other homologous verb). This formula, which is an *unicum* in Pannonia, does not have an eschatological connotation, but seems to be a retrospective element that indicates the state of peace of the deceased in relation to one's faith at the time of the death (that is *in pace cum ecclesia*) or the peace within the sepulchre. On the other hand, two inscriptions,[188] although one is just a fragment of three letters, bear the expression *defunctus est*, which, likewise such verbs as *fungi* and *complere*, expresses the idea of death as 'completing' the office and duties of life. *Flavius Sanctus* died in Aquileia and then was buried in close proximity to the sepulchre of Syneros in *Sirmium* (the tombstone of *Fl. Sanctus* is not the only testimony of people who died on foreign shores in our documentation. Several inscriptions[189] record the presence of foreigners, immigrants, travelers who died far away from homeland – in particular coming from Greece, Syria and the Balkans – and prove to be of extraordinary importance to delineate both the aspects and the dynamics of late Antique mobility).

10. To indicate that the deceased was resting or lying in the tomb, the Christians in Pannonia used the identifying-locative formula *Hic requiescit* or *quiescit*[190] (which probably recurs five times), without the irenic wish *in pace*, whereas a

---

[183] R. Lattimore, *Themes in Greek and Latin epitaphs* (Urbana, 1962), 166-69; G. Sanders, *Lapides memores* (1991), 303 and note 33.

[184] ILCV 3650-56 and Sanders,

[185] See note 11.

[186] A. Brelich, 'Aspetti della morte nelle iscrizioni sepolcrali dell'impero romano', in *Dissertationes Pannonicae*, Ser. I, Fasc. 7 (Budapest, 1937), 64-5; P. Kovács, 'Christian Epigraphy in Pannonia' (2008), 496.

[187] See note 11.4.

[188] See note 42, **1)** and VHAD, 10 (1908-1909), 179-80, no. 379; ILJ 3023.

[189] See notes 18 and 50, 56, 79 and CIGP, cat. nos. 132 and in all probability 209. For further mentions of travellers or foreigners in late Antique inscriptions from Pannonia see: M. Handley, *Dying on Foreign Shores* (2011), 136 (where the improbable *Frontonus* and *Launionus* at p. 136, nos. 496 and 497 respectively, must be read *Fronto* and *Launio*; see also notes 66 and 79).

[190] See notes 25, 29, 33 and **1)** VHAD, 10 (1908-1909), 194, no. 409; ILJ 3036; **2)** VHAD, 10 (1908-1909), 196, no. 417; ILJ 3044.

Latin inscription from *Sirmium* bears the *incipit* phrase '*in pace quiescit*'.[191] In Pannonia, according to the evidence, the initial phrase *hic requiescit/quiescit* is inserted within a context that has not totally broken with the habit of the dedicatory structure that normally characterize the 2nd-3rd centuries epigraphic praxis and is not already crystallized into that initial module, which will occur, broadly standardized, in the 4th-5th centuries Latin inscriptions.

The date of death/burial, according to the late Antique epigraphic custom that had also spread to Christian formularies[192] and has often been regarded as being specifically Christian,[193] is introduced, most of all, by *depositus/depositio* (which likely occurs six times) at the end or in the body of the text.[194] I am of the opinion that the phrase '*depositus/depositio* + name of the deceased' appears in the initial lines of a fragmentary inscription from *Certissia-Murs(i)a*[195] (the D most probably was in the missing piece of the slab) (Fig. 18), as it is recorded, for instance, in two inscriptions from Milan[196] or another one from *Clusium*.[197] The conjectural reading '*o]pt[imae memoriae*' proposed by the previous scholars needs to be challenged and rejected. Several epigraphs show the expression '*D(is) M(anibus)* + *et memoriae* + *nomen* (in genitive case) + adjective (one of the habitual epithets, such as *optimus*, etc.)' or the stereotyped one '*Aliquis* + *memoriae* + adjective (*bonae*, *optimae*, etc.)', the adjective and *memoriae* can recur inverted as well, *e.g.,* '*optimae memoriae*'. And yet, apart from an inscription from *Massilia*,[198] which seems to bear the formula '*optimae memoriae*' in the starting line – although I think that its actual initial line is missing –, no inscription, to my knowledge, carries such a phrase. It could be a hapax, but there is a certain space between the *P* and *T* to think that one could reasonably read '*optimae memoriae*'.

It is rare in Pannonia to find the other locative formula that may appear at the beginning of the first line, '*Hic iacet*', which probably recurs once[199] (a Greek inscription bears the phrase in the form ἐνθάδε κεῖμε, *pro* κεῖμαι, not in the initial line yet[200]). Also the variant '*In hoc loco iacet*' occurs only once.[201]

---

[191] See note 70.

[192] See C. Carletti, 'Nascita e sviluppo del formulario epigrafico cristiano: prassi e ideologia', in I. Di Stefano Manzella (ed.), *Le iscrizioni dei cristiani in Vaticano* (1997), 143-64; *id.*, 'Dies mortis-Depositio: un modulo 'profano' nell'epigrafia tardoantica', *Vetera Christianorum* 41 (2004), 21-48.

[193] See, *e.g.*, V. Cipollone, ICI, XI, pp. XIV, 77.

[194] See note 158; **1)** CIL III, 10234; ILCV 513; **2)** CIL III, 10240; AE 1986, 602 and **3)** CIL III, 10252;

[195] See note 93.

[196] G. Cuscito, ICI, XII, pp. LXIX, 9-10, no. 1 and 104-5, no. 93.

[197] V. Cipollone, ICI, XI, no. 28.

[198] CIL XII, 477; CLE 1784.

[199] VHAD, 10 (1908-1909), 195, no. 411; ILJ 3038.

[200] CIGP, cat. no. 132.

[201] See note 37.

The formula '*hic positus*',[202] appears twice (Fig. 19) and probably once in the variant *in hoc loco positus*[203] (a different and plausible reading of CIL III, 14340[7] could be also: *In hoc loco positus | est Innocens. In pace*).

11. The variety of occupations attested in the written texts, revealing how work was considered a social obligation and an essential component of life,[204] is a valuable element for the reconstruction of the composition of the heterogeneous early Christian communities. The inscriptions that record the mention of professions and occupations can be found from the end of the 3rd and the mid-4th centuries onwards, rarely in earlier periods.[205] In Pannonia only a small group of inscriptions indicates the activity and professions carried out by the deceased during their lifetime. One inscription mentions two *pictores*, painters, who while pilgrims died in *Savaria*[206] (Fig. 20); the already mentioned inscription of Βασιλιανός, witnesses he was a πραγματευτῆς, probably a Syrian wandering merchant;[207] a fragmentary inscription from *Sirmium* bears the mention of an unknown *agens in rebus*.[208] Finally an inscription from *Savaria* records a *custos cymiteri, Nammius Quintus*[209] (Fig. 21), thus far the only attestation of this profession in the entire epigraphic record.

Attestations also occur of famous individuals who held important roles in public administration, worked in the centres of power or were of aristocratic and of well-off families.[210] In a defective inscription from *Carnuntum*,[211] after a reference to the reparation of a grating (*cancellus*) to fulfill a vow (*[h]oc est votu[m]*), the commissioners and dedicators probably appear: a *tribunus*, a *praefectus* and an *act(u)arius*. As we have already seen, a *vir perfectissimus ex protectore* is also present.[212] Two more inscriptions mention the title *protector*:[213] the already seen

---

[202] See notes 38 and 64.

[203] See note .

[204] A. Quacquarelli, 'L'educazione al lavoro', in S. Felici (ed.), *Spiritualità del lavoro nella catechesi dei Padri del III-IV secolo. Convegno di studio e aggiornamento, Roma 15-17 marzo 1985* (Roma, 1986), 15; V. Grossi and A. Di Berardino, *La chiesa antica: ecclesiologia e istituzioni* (Roma, 1984), 211-2.

[205] C. Carletti, 'Nascita e sviluppo del formulario epigrafico cristiano: prassi e ideologia' (1997), 143-64; D. Mazzoleni, *Epigrafi del mondo cristiano antico* (2002), 39-48 and 73-84.

[206] See note 79.

[207] See note 50.

[208] See note 194, **1**). See also: Mark A. Handley, 'Two Hundred and Seventy-Four Addenda and Corrigenda to the Prosopography of the Later Roman Empire from the Latin-Speaking Balkans', *Journal of Late Antiquity* 3.1 (2010), 124.

[209] See note 98.

[210] See the other ones who lived in the 3rd-6th centuries in Mark A. Handley, 'Two Hundred and Seventy-Four Addenda and Corrigenda' (2010), 113-57.

[211] See note 43.

[212] See note 35.

[213] J. Diesner in *Paulys Realencyclopädie der classischen Altertumswissenschaft* (RE), XXIII,1, 1957, columns 1113 ff. (especially 1115); L. de Blois, *The Policy of the Emperor Galienus*, Studies of the Dutch Archaeological and Historical Society 7 (Leiden, 1976), 44-7.

inscription of *Flavius Sanctus ex numero Iovianorum protector*[214] and the one of *Flavius Pomentius*, who presents himself as *et vector nam et protector*.[215]

Even the military are mentioned, who belonged to diverse specialities: *Maximinus* was a *centurio*[216] (Fig. 22). *Aurelius Propincus* a *miles legionis II adiutricis p(iae) f(idelis)*[217] and *Iulius Herculanus* a *veteranus*.[218]

As with other elements that only recur gradually, at first sporadically, and then with greater frequency, in formulae, references to the members of ecclesiastical hierarchy spread from the fourth century onwards, not only in epitaphs, but also in votive and dedicatory inscriptions.[219] The scarce documentation we possess – which, apart the gravestone of *Dionisia vidua*[220] (Fig. 23), found in *Brigetio*, comes exclusively from *Sirmium* – however provides information both on the diverse functions of the clergy and ecclesiastical ranks in Pannonia, and includes members of both the so-called 'major orders' (a *diaconus*[221] and maybe a bishop from the 'Church of *Sirmium*'[222]) and the so-called 'minor orders' (*Ursicinus*, an *exorcista*[223] [Fig. 24]; the dedicator of the inscription is probably *Laurentia*, a *[sa]nctimonia[lis]*, who *fecit commemorationem*). In all likelihood another inscription could be numbered among these, the one I have already mentioned of *Dionisia vidua*, who might have been a 'sacred widow'. But it is not certain, since no epigraphic evidence has emerged to prove that sacred widows were consecrated and lived in a community, in a sort of monastic regime. They were only designated with the term 'widow', which may suggest that these faithful somehow lent their service to the community or chose to remain a widow and absolutely faithful to a single husband.[224]

The *famula Christi* recorded in one inscription[225] from *Siscia*, sure enough, is not a member of the Church hierarchy, given the fact that this term emphasizes only the spirit of service that animated the deceased when still alive, who submitted herself to the Lord, on the basis of scriptural passages such as

---

[214] See note 42, **1**). Arnold H. M. Jones, J. Morris and J. Martindale (eds), *The Prosopography of the Later Roman Empire*, Volume I, A.D. 260-395 (Cambridge, 1971), 802; Mark A. Handley, 'Two Hundred and Seventy-Four Addenda and Corrigenda' (2010), 114, 129.

[215] See note 77, **2**); Mark A. Handley, 'Two Hundred and Seventy-Four Addenda and Corrigenda' (2010), 141; Arnold H.M. Jones, J. Morris, J. Martindale (eds), *The Prosopography of the Later Roman Empire* I (1971), 712.

[216] See note 71.

[217] See note 11.

[218] See note 29.

[219] C. Carletti, 'Nascita e sviluppo del formulario epigrafico cristiano: prassi e ideologia' (1997), 155-6.

[220] See note 28.

[221] See note 70.

[222] CIL III, 14340³.

[223] See note 37.

[224] G. Stahlin, 'χήρα' in *Theological Dictionary of the New Testament* 9 (Grand Rapids, 1974), 453-4; J. Janssens, *Vita e morte del cristiano negli epitaffi di Roma* (1981), 210-4.

[225] See note 84.

Ps. 108:25; 133:1; *Luke* 1:38.48; *Titus* 1:1; *Acts* 2:18. According to Kovács the bilingual inscription of *Ampe(l)li(u)s*[226] (Fig. 25) found in *Savaria* would bear the expression δοῦλος θεοῦ, servant of God, which stresses the same idea of service and submission as the epithet *famula Christi, servus/-a Dei* or *ancilla Christi*.

Only the inscription of *Florentinus*,[227] a seven-year-old boy, who *requiem adcepit in deo patre nostro et (C)hristo eius* (who 'received rest in God our Father and in His Christ'), refers to the state of the deceased in the afterworld and contains traces of the creed, which the infant – in all probability already baptized or member of a Christian family – has been taught.

Sometimes the deceased invite who passes by or the surviving family members not to forget them, asking for prayers: *Tu qui (h)ic oras | Iustiane | in mente (h)abe Nunnane(m) ma | trem t[uam*[228] (Fig. 26). The living wish the deceased to live in God[229] (Fig. 27), the real life in Christ and peace, *pax/requies*, in the tomb.[230]

Another inscription,[231] in all probability the latest one of our texts, records the desperate and heartfelt prayer that God did not fulfill, since the Avars sieged successfully the city and destroyed it. It reads:

Κ(ύρι)ε, β(ο)ήτι τῆς πόλεος κὲ ῥύξον τὸν Ἄβαριν κὲ πύλαξον τὴν Ῥωμανίαν κὲ τὸν γράψαντα. Ἀμήν.

From the remarks I have presented, which do not fully cover all of the noteworthy elements in the Christian inscriptions from Pannonia, the exceptional value of these inscribed monuments should already be evident. Along with liturgical, hagiographical and literary sources, they allow us to have insights into the early Christian communities of this Province and understand several of the little-known aspects, such as, *e.g.*, religious feelings and affections towards people, concepts of death, language, level of education, and unpublished 'histories'. Small daily events that 'history' usually does not record.

---

[226] See note 45.

[227] See note 64.

[228] See note 91.

[229] See notes 55, 71-2, 80 (the epigraph in the note 72 bears the Greek word ζήσης (= *vivas*) written in Latin characters (*zaesis*).

[230] See notes 30, 70, 85 (the last-mentioned text is full of slips and misspellings, but it is really hard to accept in the third line the reading of the name *Inacae*, argued by J. Brunšmid and H. Gračanin. I would read the wish *in (p)acae*, due to the well-known phenomenon of hypercorrectness; the same phenomenon occurs in the seventh line of the same epigraph, where '*maemoria*' appears for '*memoria*'), 96. The wishes might have occurred in **1)** CIL III, 4004; Ž. Demo (ed.), *Od nepobjedivog sunca do sunca pravde* (1994), 103, no. 115 and **2)** ILJ 3031 (see note 36).

[231] See note 19.

PLATE I

Figure 1. Inscription of *Flavia
Calvena* (CIL III, 13382).

Figure 2. Inscribed tile (CIGP cat. no. 138).

PLATE II

Figure 3. Inscription of *Felicissima*
(CIL III, 3996a).

Figure 4. Inscription of *Aelia Kalendina*
(CIL III, 4217).

Figure 5. Inscription of *Flavius Martinianus*
(and daughter?) (CIL III, 10237).

Figure 6. Inscription of *Aurelia Iustina* (CIL III, 4197).

PLATE III

Figure 7. Inscription of *Flavius Maurus* (CIL III, 4002).

Figure 8. Inscription of *Petrus* and *Victorinianus* (Roman Imp. Towns, 349, no. 156).

Figure 9. Inscription of two *Aurelii* (CIL III, 4218).

Figure 10. Inscription of *Artemidora* (CIL III, 10233).

PLATE IV

Figure 11. Inscription erected by *Aurelia Domnica*
(CIL III, 4220).

Figure 12. Inscription of *Stercorinus* (TRH 26).

Figure 13. Inscription set down by *Iulius Herculanus* (CIL III, 3551).

PLATE V

Figure 14. Inscription dedicated by *Macedonius* along with his wife
(Duval 1979, 83-4, no. 156).

Figure 15. Inscription of *Flavius Dalmatius* (CIL III, 4185).

Plate VI

Figure 16. Inscription of *Severilla* (CIL III, 3996).

Figure 17. Inscription of *Gaudentius* (CIL III, 15181[2]).

Plate VII

Figure 19. Inscription of *Venatorinus* and
Martoria (ILJ 283).

Figure 18. Inscription of
Paulinus Lucerinus
(CIL III, 3991).

Figure 20. Inscription of *Launio* and *Secundinus*
(CIL III, 4222).

Figure 21. Inscription of *Nammius Quintus*
(RIU 85).

G.S. BEVELACQUA

PLATE VIII

Figure 22. Inscription of *Maximinus* (CIL III, 4190).

Figure 23. Inscription of *Dionisia* (RIU 632).

Figure 24. Inscription of *Ursicinus* (AE 1996, 1256).

PLATE IX

Figure 25. Inscription of *Ampelius*
(RIU 122).

Figure 27. Inscription
of *Ianuaria*
(CIL III, 3986).

Figure 26. Inscription of *Nunnane* (RIU 633).

The Orphic Singer in Clement of Alexandria and in the Roman Catacombs: Comparison between the Literary and the Iconographic Early Christian Representation of Orpheus

Fabienne JOURDAN, Paris, CNRS, UMR 8167 'Orient et Méditerranée'

ABSTRACT

To exhort the Pagans to convert to Christianity, Clement of Alexandria praises Christ as a new and better Orpheus. For this purpose, he resorts to the figure of Orpheus as the singer whose miraculous song charms even wild animals. In the Roman catacombs of the third and fourth centuries, the Christians represent also Orpheus as a singer surrounded by animals. After an overview of Clement's method to depict Christ as a new Orpheus in order to describe the Word as a new and powerful song and an examination of the possible meanings of the pictural representation of Orpheus in early Christian art, the question of the possible link between the literary and the iconographic representation is dealt with. Even though no actual influence can definitely be traced between the two, it appears that a common method of addressing a well-educated audience is used in both cases and that the motif of the Golden Age which seems to permeate the pictural representations find an echo in Clement's 'apocalyptic' manner of praising the Christian Mystery.

In his *Exhortation to the Greeks*,[1] Clement of Alexandria is the first one to draw the portrait of Christ as a new and better Orpheus.[2] This portrait's main characteristic is that it is essentially built on the same legendary image as the one used in the iconography, namely that of the singer and of his miraculous power to charm wild beasts, trees and even stones with his songs.

We are certainly more familiar with a comparison between Orpheus and Christ based on their respective descent to the underworld. But the interpretation of Orpheus' journey into Hades to bring back Eurydice as an allegorical picture

---

[1] This article is the written version of the conference I held at the Department of Theology and Religious studies at Kings' College on May, 26, 2011 at the invitation of Markus Vinzent and Allen Brent as part of their BARDA research project on 'Early Christian Iconography and Epigraphy'. I have kept the original form and most of its content. I am grateful to Piotr Ashwin-Siejkowski, Allen Brent, Carol Downer and Markus Vinzent for their valuable comments and to Philippe Charles for checking the English. I would also like to apologize for referring mostly to my own works, but the topic of the conference was very close to the one in theses books and I didn't want to clutter up the footnotes with too many references the reader can easily find there.

[2] See Fabienne Jourdan, *Orphée et les Chrétiens*, 1, Anagôgê 4 (Paris, 2010).

Studia Patristica LXXIII, 113-127.
© Peeters Publishers, 2014.

of Christ's journey into hell and his victory over death does not appear before the Middle Ages.[3] Early Christian authors who used the figure of Orpheus focussed mostly on its religious nature, namely Orpheus' status as founder of Greek religious institutions and more precisely the Mysteries. But more generally they also see in him the founder of paganism itself. It is striking for us modern scholars that they do not make of Orpheus the doctor of a small sectarian group, but the creator of the Greek religion itself. This picture is certainly based on three features: the pagan representation of the character, the consideration of the Mysteries as the most tangible pagan way to have contact with the gods, but it is also based on the Christian perception and presentation of Orpheus as a barbarian, as the Christians themselves were indeed represented, a barbarian the Jews claimed had become a convert to monotheism and that conversion eventually led him to sing the Biblical message. So, in their polemics with the Pagans and with this complex picture in mind, the early Christian writers made use of the figure of Orpheus in the following three ways:[4] First, they attacked the poet and his verses directly in order to denounce the atrocity and impiety of pagan traditions.[5] Secondly and in contrast to this, other writers pointed out certain of the merits of Orpheus and his works, but also with a view to discrediting Greek traditions. For instance, they praised Orpheus as the barbarian inventor of many Greek cultural institutions, in order to deny any originality to the Greek culture itself[6] – we must not forget that after the Jews, the Christians were also perceived as 'barbarians' and sometimes even described as such; so, in this context, Orpheus has something in common with them. Finally, a last group of Christian polemists presented Orpheus and his poems as real models that 'sing', if I may put it this way, in agreement with the Biblical message. For this last purpose, they relied on the Jewish-Hellenistic forgery just mentioned which ascribed to Orpheus a poem praising the only God.[7]

[3] The picture appears for the very first time in the *Moralised Orpheus*. See John Block Friedman, *Orpheus in the Middle Ages* ([Cambridge, 1970] New York, 2000), 86-146. Celsus, the enemy of the Christians, proposed such a comparison in the second century, but in order to denounce Christ as a charlatan similar to Orpheus. See Origen, *Against Celsus* II 55.

[4] I am summarizing the conclusions of *Orphée et les chrétiens*, 1 and 2, Anagôgê 4 and 5 (Paris, 2010 and 2011), here 2, 13-8 and 243-58. Detailed references and examples are given there.

[5] This is the attitude typical of Athenagoras (*Embassy for the Christians*), Tatian (*Address to the Greeks*), Theophilus of Antioch (*Apology to Autolycos*), the Pseudo-Clementine novel, Origen (*Against Celsus*) and Gregory of Nazianzus (*Discourses, Poems*). We also find it in Clement of Alexandria (*Exhortation to the Greeks*), Eusebius of Caesarea (*Preparation for the Gospel*) and Theodoret of Cyrus (*Cure of the Greek Maladies*). It should also be noted that the reference to Orpheus nourished the polemics against the so-called heretics who were accused of imitating pagan sources. On this point, see the summary in F. Jourdan, *Orphée et les Chrétiens*, 2 (2011), 215-6.

[6] This attitude is typical of Tatian (*Address to the Greeks* 1,1). We also find it in Theodoret of Cyrus (*Cure of the Greek Maladies*).

[7] This attitude is that of Pseudo-Justin (*De monarchia, Address to the Greeks*), Clement of Alexandria (*Stromateis*), Cyril of Alexandria (*Against Julian*) and of the *Tübingen Theosophy*. We also find it in Eusebius of Caesarea (*Preparation to the Gospel*). In the same way, Orpheus

These different attitudes are not exclusive and can be found in the same work. But Clement of Alexandria is the only early Christian writer who introduces the image of the singer (Eusebius will follow him in his *Eulogy of Constantine*[8]) and who makes the most of it in order to depict Christ as a new Orpheus. And this is how he transforms Orpheus himself into a prefiguration of the Lord.

In this context, what is at stake is the possible link between the literary and the iconographic representation of Orpheus as singer in the early Christian tradition. More precisely the questions which arise are the following: How does this picture of Orpheus, which was so central for Clement, appear in Christian iconography? What meaning does it have there or, more precisely, in what way is it linked to Christ? Finally is there any connection at all between Clement's singing Orpheus and the cither-playing Orpheus of the catacombs?

The first step to take to answer these questions is to shed some light on the way Clement creates his picture of a new Orpheus by using the image of the singer, and how, by doing so, he transforms Orpheus into a prefigurative counterpoint to Christ. Then an overview of the early Christian iconography of Orpheus will enable us to go through the possible meanings of the mosaics. Eventually a short comparison might be drawn between the painters' aims and Clement's.

I. Christ as a new Orpheus in Clement of Alexandria's *Exhortation to the Greeks*

Clement depicts Christ as a new Orpheus by making use of two features of the character, namely,[9] first, the picture of the cither player and, even more precisely, of the singer who fascinates even wild animals; and secondly, the picture of the founder of the Mysteries and of the poet who wrote texts for these cults. As poet Orpheus was also seen as the priest who reveals these cults and, through them and their sacred objects, provides the possibility to perceive something of the gods themselves.

By applying such characteristics to Christ, Clement portrays him as a new and better Orpheus, while bringing into being a new kind of pagan Orpheus, namely the Orpheus who becomes the prefiguration of Christ. How exactly does he go about this?

Clement's method is original. He does not resort to allegory.[10] If he had done so, it would have led him to assert that Orpheus *does* represent Christ with

---

could also be praised as a valuable model of Christian 'orthodoxy' against the heretics, see Didymus the Blind, *On the Trinity* II 27 (PG 39, 756,4-7).

[8] II 14, 4-5. See also *Theoph. Syr.* III 39.

[9] I am here summarizing the conclusions of *Orphée et les Chrétiens* (2010), 1.

[10] On this point, I disagree with Maria Tabaglio, 'La cristianizzazione del mito di Orfeo', in *Le metamorfosi di Orfea* (Verona, 1999), 78-80. See F. Jourdan, *Orphée et les Chrétiens*, 1 (2010), 262-3.

pagan features and that these features need only be correctly interpreted so that their highly Christian meaning can be seen. The use of allegory concerning Orpheus as singer does not appear before Eusebius.[11] Eusebius follows Clement in resorting to the portrait of Orpheus,[12] but he lives in a period in which Paganism represents a less serious threat to Christianity and therefore he can use the mythological figure more easily to evoke Christ directly. Likewise, Clement does not use typology, the theological method through which a character of the past is interpreted as foreshadowing a figure of more recent history. At the time, this method is only used to enhance the relationship between the Old and New Testaments. In this context, David is a type of Christ, but Orpheus is not.[13] Nor does Clement have any predecessors among the Gnostics for this depiction, even if the Gnostics sometimes exploit Orphic lore, namely the verses attributed to Orpheus.[14] He does not even have any predecessors among the Jews. Admittedly, the Jews ascribed a Testament or Sacred Discourse to Orpheus in which the poet is supposed to have praised the only God.[15] But they were making use of the figure of the religious founder and not of the cither player charming animals. Moreover, the Jews did not draw comparisons between David and Orpheus, at least, according to our sources, not before Clement. Of course, we have two mosaics in which David is represented as a lyre player reminding us of Orpheus, the mosaic of Doura-Europos and that of Gaza. But first, these pictures are not unequivocal and even if we are sure that David is depicted, we are not sure that Orpheus is too: his portrait could have been used by the artist as a pattern, but it was not necessarily the intention of those who commissioned the mosaics to show any links between the two musicians. Secondly, these pictures were made after Clement (the mosaic of Doura-Europos dates from 260 A.D. and that of Gaza from 508 A.D.) and they may well have been influenced by Christian iconography. Because of the Biblical link between David and Christ, the Christian link between Christ and Orpheus as musicians could easily have been extended to David and Orpheus and have thus spread.[16]

---

[11] See the texts mentioned in note 8.

[12] Eusebius' text is a rewriting of the beginning of the *Exhortation to the Greeks*.

[13] For a typological use of Orpheus in the Middle Ages, see Jean-Michel Roessli, *Postface à John Block Friedman, Orphée au Moyen Âge* (Fribourg, 1999), 308.

[14] The source of information on this point is essentially constituted by the Heresiologists and Gnostic detractors, see for instance Pseudo-Hippolytus, *Refutation of all Heresies* V 1, 4 and 20, 4-5 (on this text see F. Jourdan, *Orphée et les Chrétiens*, 1 (2010), 265-8 with updated bibliography). In this context, it is difficult to evaluate whether and to what extent the Gnostics really made use of Orphic lore.

[15] On this text, see F. Jourdan, *Poème judéo-hellénistique attribué à Orphée* (Paris, 2010), with updated bibliography.

[16] On the debate about these pictures, see F. Jourdan, *Orphée et les Chrétiens*, 1 (2010), 366-73, with updated bibliography. For another presentation and interpretation of the question, see J.-M. Roessli, *Postface* (1999), 297-305; *id.*, 'Imágenes de Orfeo en el arte judío y cristiano', in *Orfeo y la tradición órfica. Un reencuentro*, Religiones y mitos 280 (Madrid, 2008), 180-7.

The originality of Clement's process lies in fact in the goal of his *Exhortation to the Greeks*, which was to urge the Pagans to convert to Christianity. Clement himself describes his method as follows: to make use of pagan imagery in order to convince his listeners that the new religion is superior to their old traditions.[17] This method consists of three stages: a critical or oppositional stage; a transpositional one, and finally a full appropriation of pagan lore. These three stages are developed in the following way.

Clement begins by emphasizing three major oppositions between Orpheus and Christ. He presents Orpheus as a sophist and magician whose words are deceitful and thus lethal,[18] whereas Christ is shown as the real enchanter whose incantations are salutary.[19] Then he contrasts Orpheus as a man who is not a real man[20] (certainly alluding to the pederasty attributed to him) with Christ as the perfect man *par excellence*, that is as the only human being who really resembles God because he *is* God.[21] The third opposition consists in presenting Orpheus as the idolatrous founder of paganism and thereby as the servant of Satan,[22] while Christ is depicted as the priest of the only God and thereby as revealing the only valid religion.[23]

The second stage, I called the transpositional stage, is essentially based on comparisons using Orphic imagery to enhance the depiction of Christ. Two examples can be given, the first concerning Orpheus the singer, the second the religious founder. So, whereas the song of Orpheus is said to have charmed wild animals, the Word of Christ or Christ the Word is depicted as having charmed the wildest animals, that is human beings themselves.[24] Following the Biblical text, Clement can even add that the new Song can turn stones into human beings, that is non-believers into believers.[25] The second example pertains to the religious imagery. At the beginning of his book, Clement describes the Mystery of Eleusis and the cults of Dionysos which are linked to the name of Orpheus as shameful and lethal,[26] but in the middle of the book he uses this imagery and 'converts' it to describe in an apocalyptic manner the choir of the Just who sing of the only God.[27] In this light, Christ appears as a better and superior hierophant.[28]

---

[17] *Exhortation to the Greeks* XII 119,1.
[18] *Ibid.* I 3,1.
[19] *Ibid.* XI 115,2.
[20] *Ibid.* I 3,1 (ἄνδρες τινὲς οὐκ ἄνδρες).
[21] *Ibid.* I 7,1; 8,4; X 107,3; XI 113,2. See also *Stromateis* VI 14,114.4; VII 14,84.2.
[22] *Exhortation to the Greeks* I 3,1; 7,4; II 13,3 and 5.
[23] *Ibid.* I 3,2; XI 111,2-3; XII 120,2.
[24] *Ibid.* I 4,1.
[25] *Ibid.* I 4,2 and 4.
[26] *Ibid.* II 17,2; 21,1; 74,3. For the condemnation of the Mysteries, see *Exhortation to the Greeks* II.
[27] *Ibid.* XII 119.
[28] *Ibid.* XII 120,1.

The final stage can be described as the appropriation of the imagery tradition-ally linked to Orpheus, without alluding to it any longer. At this stage, Christ is described on the one hand as the agent of metamorphosis (an activity which is highly orphic)[29] and, on the other hand, as the Mystery itself.[30]

This last stage is inextricably linked with the conversion of Orpheus himself which occurs in the middle of the book when Clement mentions the Jewish-Hellenistic forgery. Clement quotes a series of verses which fit well with his exhortative message so that the words of this converted Orpheus already announce the final exhortation attributed to Christ.

Through this whole process, Orpheus becomes a prefiguration of Christ, namely through the intermediary of Clement's words, it is Christ himself who metamorphoses Orpheus into his own pagan predecessor.

This method uses the two features of the figure already mentioned, namely Orpheus' status as an enchanting singer and as a religious founder, but the most important is definitely the first and the whole of Clement's composition is actu-ally based on the metaphor of the song. The song provides him with an image ideally suited to the evocation of the Word and Clement invests the latter with all the powers ascribed to Orpheus by the pagan tradition. But these powers are now superior because of their Christian origin. Consequently, the Word or the *Logos* not only corresponds to the Reason so highly praised by the Greeks, but also to the Biblical Word in all its meanings, that is a Word endowed with creative, prophetic and salutary powers. Finally the Word or the new Song, according to the Biblical phrase, is Christ himself. It is exactly in this choice of the song as intermediary to evoke the Word that Clement's originality lies bringing together Orpheus and Christ.

Clement's creation of this link between Orpheus and Christ is a temporal one; it implies a reading which develops in time. In contrast, the iconography offers an image which is extended in space and carries with it another way of seeing things.

II. Orpheus in early Christian iconography

Christian iconography[31] emerges at the beginning of the third century by borrow-ing its motifs from popular Roman art. In this pagan art, during the Hellenistic

---

[29] *Ibid.* XI 114,4.

[30] *Ibid.* XI 111,2-3. See also *ibid.* XII 120,1.

[31] On the Pagan and Christian iconography of Orpheus, see for instance, for the most recent publications, Ilona Julia Jesnick, *The image of Orpheus in Roman mosaic*, BAR International Series 671 (Oxford, 1997); Laurence Vieillefon, *La Figure d'Orphée dans l'Antiquité tardive, De l'archéologie à l'histoire* (Paris, 2003); *id.*, 'Les mosaïques d'Orphée dans les maisons de l'Antiquité tardive. Fonctions décoratives et valeurs religieuses', *Bulletin de l'École française de Rome*, Antiquité, 116/2 (2004), 983-1000; J.-M. Roessli, 'Imágenes de Orfeo' (2008), 187-226;

period, the cither player surrounded by animals has become a real cliché which flourishes in the third and fourth centuries. In this context, the picture is always similar: Orpheus is represented frontally, holding the lyre in his left hand and playing with his right hand or just holding the plectrum. He is invariably placed in the middle of the picture, surrounded by animals. The variety of these animals is in keeping with the predilection of Roman art for representing animals. Orpheus wears Phrygian clothes. The fact that he is seated is remarkable because it contrasts with the representation of professional musicians. The idea is perhaps to show Orpheus as the hieratic figure of the wise man before his audience.

The ten most important Christian representations of Orpheus belong exactly to the period when the pagan image was flourishing. These representations are six frescoes in the Roman catacombs and four sarcophagi.[32] The significance of the fact that these pictures originate from burial sites is not to be overestimated, because in the period, most occurrences of Christian art appear in burial sites. The Christian image is similar to the pagan. The only difference lies in the fact that sometimes Orpheus' audience is composed only of peaceful animals, such as birds and ewes. If there is no other means to distinguish the Christian from the pagan portrait, the Christian context, however, is in most cases explicit because of the presence of Biblical scenes around the picture: close to the musician, we can see Daniel in the lions' den and the resurrection of Lazarus three times each and Moses hitting the rock four times. Each time, Orpheus occupies a privileged place in these compositions.

The examination of three of these frescoes[33] leads to the question of their meaning in the Christian context.

A. *The evidence*

1. Saint Callixtus

The mosaic of the cemetery of Saint Callixtus is the oldest picture, usually dated from the beginning of the third century. It is situated in the middle of a vault. Orpheus is shown frontally seated, playing the lyre and wearing a long-sleeved, high-belted tunic and a long cloak. He has the Phrygian cap on his head. This picture belongs to the group of pictures where Orpheus is represented only with peaceful animals. On the right stands a sheep turning its head toward him, and there may have been a second sheep on the left, in the portion of the painting which is now obliterated. The figure is set within an octagon which is part of a geometric pattern of concentric circles and half-circles – a

Miguel Herrero de Jáuregui, *Orphism and Christianity in Late Antiquity* (Berlin and New York, 2010), 118-23.

[32] For references, see the works mentioned in the previous note.
[33] For more details, see the works mentioned in the note 31.

Fig. 1. Orpheus, Saint Callixtus catacomb, Rome, early 3rd c.

characteristic type of catacomb painting. Here the only indication of the Christian context, apart from the presence of only peaceful animals, lies in the fact that the construction of the catacomb began with Pope Zephyrinus (203-218) and was completed under Pope Callixtus (218-228).

The Christian context of the two following pictures is much clearer because of the presence of Biblical scenes surrounding the representation of Orpheus.

2. Saint Peter and Marcellinus

In the catacomb of Peter and Marcellinus, Orpheus appears twice. From the first mosaic only a sketch remains, but the second one is well preserved. So the

Fig. 2. Orpheus, Peter and Marcellinus catacomb, Rome, early 4th c.

mosaic represented on figure 2 dates back from the beginning of the fourth century (310-330) and is painted in the tympanum of the left arcosolium. Orpheus is shown in the same dress and in the same frontally-seated position as in the mosaic of Saint Callixtus. With his left hand he touches the lyre which is resting on a rock. He seems, however, to have halted in his playing since his right hand in which he holds the plectrum is held out towards his left, while his large eyes gaze into the far distance. The figure is flanked by two trees which are bending towards him. In the tree on the right perches a bird of prey with outstretched wings. It may represent an eagle. The nature of the bird on the left is impossible to determine. There are no quadrupeds, but there may have been some in the lost part of the painting. Naturally, we do not know their nature, peaceful or ferocious.

3. Saint Domitilla

In the catacomb of Domitilla, there were two representations of Orpheus too. The first one only is known through the sketch of an archaeologist. The pre-served picture dating from the end of the fourth century (*ca.* 360 AD) and situated on the tympanum of an arcosolium, resembles the one just described. It represents Orpheus in the usual dress and pose. Two slender trees form a

Fig. 3. Orpheus, Domitilla catacomb, Rome, around 360 AD.

frame around the figure and have several birds on their branches, including a peacock. On the right stand a lion, a camel and a sheep; on the left there might be an ostrich and another camel.

B. *Interpretation of the pictures*

Two questions arise from the scrutiny of these pictures. The first one pertains to the identity of the figure represented: Is it Orpheus? Is it Christ? Or is it an Orpheus-Christ? The second concerns the meaning of the presence of this cither player in the catacombs. According to the assessment given above of Clement's picture of Christ as a new Orpheus, an additional question can even be raised, that of the link between the literary and the iconographic representations.

1. Orpheus or Christ?

As for the first question, it seems obvious that Orpheus and not Christ or even the good Shepherd is represented, especially since sometimes Christ and the good Shepherd are themselves represented in the same places. It can therefore be said that even if this picture of Orpheus is intended to make visitors think of Christ, it is not actually a portrait of the latter.[34] The possible connection to Christ must however be more deeply examined. It is certainly made possible by the fact that the figure of Orpheus is what I would call a neutral but live symbol (the notion of neutral symbol is borrowed from Theodor Klauser,[35] that of live symbol from Erwin Goodenough[36]). By neutral but live symbol I mean a figure which, on the one hand, is no longer tainted by the pagan idolatrous connotation, so in this sense, it is neutral and can therefore be used by the Christians, on the other hand, sufficiently 'live' to have kept its own ancient meaning easily taken on and renewed by the borrowers, exactly like the lyre, for instance, which became a Christian symbol.[37] As such, the figure of Orpheus can be associated with a complex of motifs such as harmony, peace and perhaps also salvation. This complex of meanings is proof enough that the portrait does not convey a unique meaning.[38]

The different and possible reasons for the presence of this picture in the catacombs must therefore be analysed. What kind of thoughts can the visitors seeing Orpheus in the Christian burial have had?

2. The meaning of Orpheus' presence in the catacombs

Why did the commissioners of the paintings choose to represent Orpheus? Six of the answers proposed by the scholars to this question can be examined.[39]

The first explanation consisted in recalling the Jewish-Hellenistic legend of the conversion of Orpheus and of the poem praising the only God which is attributed to him.[40] The problem with this idea is that the pictures do not present Orpheus as a religious figure, but just as a cither player. They do not show him as a priest or as teaching something to Museus, and that is why this explanation does not seem very convincing.

The second explanation aimed at enhancing the burial context. It was actually a twofold explanation. For researchers like John Block Friedman,[41] Orpheus

---

[34] For a similar conclusion, see L. Vieillefon, *La Figure d'Orphée* (2010), 148-54 and M. Herrero, *Orphism and Christianity* (2010), 120-1.

[35] 'Studien zur Entstehungsgeschichte der christlichen Kunst I', *JbAC* 1 (1958), 20-51; *id.*, 'Studien zur Entstehungsgeschichte der christlichen Kunst IV', *JbAC* 4 (1961), 128-45; *id.*, 'Erwägungen zur Entstehung des altchristlichen Kunst', *ZKG* 76 (1965), 1-11.

[36] *Jewish Symbols in the Greco-Roman Period*, 12, Bollingen Series 37 (New York, 1965), 73.

[37] Clement of Alexandria, *Instructor* III 11,59.2.

[38] M. Herrero, *Orphism and Christianity* (2010), 119.

[39] For another presentation of the debate, see J.-M. Roessli, 'Imágenes de Orfeo' (2008), 213-26.

[40] It was the interpretation of Antonio Bosio in the seventeenth century (*Roma Sotteranea. Opera postuma* [Roma, 1632], 627-31). See also A. Wrzésniowski, 'The Figure of Orpheus in Early Christian Iconography', *Archeologia* 21 (1970), 112-23; E. Goodenough, *Jewish Symbols*, 5 (1956), 103-11, and 9 (1964), 89-104. See also Henri Stern, 'Orphée dans l'art paléochrétien', *CArch* 23 (1974), 8-9.

[41] *Orpheus in the Middle Ages* ([1970] 2000), 39-40.

and Christ played the role of a psychopomp protecting the dead from evil influences – an explanation that actually does not really fit the pictures themselves as they do not show Orpheus as the shepherd of souls, nor does it seem to fit with the representations of peaceful animals only. The second theory linked with the burial context is more general and proposes to see in Orpheus the vehicle of the concept of immortality.[42] Here, too, we must be cautious because it is not the meaning obviously conveyed by the image of the cither player surrounded by animals. André Boulanger seemed to be right then when he wrote that 'the cither player of the catacombs is not the doctor of Orphism, the prophet of immortality and of monotheism'.[43]

A third hypothesis is based on supposing the influence of a previous Jewish representation bringing together Orpheus and David.[44] I have already expressed some doubts about the existence of such a comparison in Jewish circles before the Christian association between Orpheus and Christ. Moreover the figure of David as psalmist and lyre player did not predominate among Christians in the first centuries.[45] However, it cannot be ruled out that the visitors thought of David when they saw Orpheus in the catacombs.[46]

According to the fourth explanation, the picture of Orpheus stands as a representation of the Good Shepherd.[47] Of course, this interpretation seems to be very convincing when only peaceful animals and mainly ewes are painted. But firstly, it is not always the case and secondly, there already existed a Christian representation of the Good Shepherd which did not need to be replaced by a pagan figure and which was even sometimes present in the sites we are dealing with.[48] In addition, Orpheus' dress is not that of a shepherd, and he has a cither instead of the syrinx which is certainly more characteristic of a shepherd.[49] Of course it cannot be excluded that the picture of the Good Shepherd came to

---

[42] See Henry Leclercq, *Manuel d'archéologie chrétienne* (Paris, 1907), 127-8.

[43] André Boulanger, *Orphée. Rapports de l'Orphisme et du Christianisme* (Paris, 1925), 163.

[44] See Kurt Weitzmann, 'The Psalter Vatopedi 761', *Journal of the Walter's Art Gallery* 10 (1947), 38; *id.*, *Greek mythology in Byzantine Art* (Princeton, 1951), 6 and 93; H. Stern, 'The Orpheus in the Synagogue of Dura Europos', *The Journal of the Warburg and Courtland Institutes* 21 (1958), 1-6; *id.*, 'Un nouvel Orphée-David dans une mosaïque du VIᵉ siècle', *CRAI* (janvier-mars 1970), 63-79; *id.*, 'Orphée dans l'art paléochrétien' (1974), 1-16; J.-M. Roessli, *Postface* (1999), 306-7.

[45] See Robert Skeris, *XPΩMA ΘEOY, On the Origins and Theological Interpretation of the Musical Imagery used by the Ecclesiastic Writers of the First three Centuries, with special Reference to the Image of Orpheus* (Altötting, 1967), 229, n. 413.

[46] J.-M. Roessli, 'Imágenes de Orfeo' (2008), 226, supports the view that the Christian images of Orpheus in the catacombs represent Christ the Saviour as David's heir.

[47] See Giovanni Battista De Rossi, 'Nuovi scoperti nel cimitero di Priscilla per le escavationi fatte nell'anno 1887', *Bulletino di archeologia cristiana* (1887), 29-35; J.B. Friedman, *Orpheus in the Middle Ages* ([1970] 2000), 41-3.

[48] It was the case in the catacombs of Saint Petrus and Marcellinus I for instance.

[49] Even if it is not always the case, see J.-M. Roessli, 'Imágenes de Orfeo' (2008), 218-23.

the mind of the visitor, especially when there were only ewes around Orpheus.[50] But it was certainly not the prime intention of the commissioners of the mosaics to use the picture of Orpheus to represent the Good Shepherd.

Charles Murray supports the thesis that texts such as Clement's influenced the iconography.[51] This fifth hypothesis is really difficult to accept because there is no evidence that Clement's book was well known at all and more precisely in Rome. However if the iconography did not influence Clement (we have no proof that he knew of any Christian pictures of Orpheus), they may well have influenced Eusebius – because in the period of the bishop of Caesarea, the Christian pictures were effectively known.[52] But what is interesting in Murray's hypothesis is the link drawn between Clement's procedure and that of the painter or of the commissioners. According to Murray, the picture was the vehicle of the Greek conception of the wise and of culture, images without any real equivalent in Biblical scenes. In this specific case, the representation of the cither player could even have been thought of, as it is in Clement, as the means of conveying the idea of the power of the Word. It is difficult to assert that the writer and the painter were pursuing the same aim, but the idea of a similar method used to reach the public is worth considering.

The last hypothesis, and, in my view, the most convincing one, consists in recalling the meaning of the Orphic picture in the Roman context. Catacombs were built and financed by rather rich Christians in Rome. They were there to honour the dead and in these cults families had meals and spent some peaceful time there. Moreover they were used during the time of persecutions as refuges and were therefore perceived as oases of peace and dream. It just so happened that in the same Roman period, the miracles of the cither player were intimately linked with the representations of the Golden Age and its imagery of peace, the motif of animals leaving peacefully together was borrowed from it too and applied to the legend of Orpheus by Ovid and Seneca.[53] It is certainly through the combination of this archeological context with this mythological framework that the image of Orpheus integrated Christian iconography, perhaps as an echo of the messianic prophecy of another Golden Age which was to be brought by a descendant of David. Indeed, the background of the Christian picture of the singer enchanting animals could come from *Isaiah* (11:6-7):

The wolf also shall dwell with the lamb, and the leopard shall lie down with the kid; and the calf and the young lion and the fatling together; and a little child shall lead

---

[50] About the connection between the image of Orpheus and that of the Good Shepherd, see the recent analysis of J.-M. Roessli, 'Imágenes de Orfeo' (2008), 218-24.

[51] Charles Murray, 'The Christian Orpheus', *CArch* 26 (1977), 20-1; *id.*, *Rebirth and Afterlife*, International Series 100 (Oxford, 1981), 43-4, 120-1. It was also the thesis of A. Bosio, see note 40.

[52] See J.-M. Roessli, 'Convergence et divergence dans l'interprétation du mythe d'Orphée, de Clément d'Alexandrie à Eusèbe de Césarée', *RHR* 219 (2002), 503-13.

[53] Godo Lieberg, 'Arione, Orfeo ed Anfione. Obsservazioni sul potere della poesia', *Rivista di umanita classica e cristiana* 5 (1984), 139-56.

them. And the cow and the bear shall feed; their young ones shall lie down together: and the lion shall eat straw like the ox.

The confluence of these prophecies with the bucolic tradition, already obvious in Virgil (at the beginning of the *Fourth Eclogue* for instance), was well received by the Christians.[54] With the latter, however, the secular pagan myth of the Golden Age, referring to the perfect beginning and echoing Hesiod's *Works and Days*, acquired a messianic and eschatological dimension which the Christians considered as manifested in the *adunata* or miracles characteristic of the last days as they were previously conceived by the Jews. For the Christians, these *adunata* announced an era of peace begun with the new Creation, *i.e.* with the Incarnation of Christ. So in both pagan and Christian imageries, having tame and wild animals leaving peacefully together could have been perceived as one of these *adunata* or miracles promising the coming of the Golden Age, an Age that had actually already begun for the Christians. In this context, the picture of Orpheus as an enchanting cither player may have been seen as recalling Christ's activity as promoter of this promised peace. When the audience was composed only of peaceful animals, it may have represented the achieved state of peace produced by the song, that is by the Word which makes of all animals its flock of sheep, in other words believers.

This last interpretation is naturally not the only one possible. More than one meaning of the figure may have motivated the choice of Orpheus in each site and, conversely, from one site to the other, different reasons may have led the painter or the commissioner to choose this figure. In addition, the possibility of the free association of ideas plays a major part in the iconography, which is less the case in literature. But, despite all these reservations, the motif of the Golden Age as a vehicle to evoke Christianity certainly played a crucial role in the decision to represent Orpheus in the Christian catacombs: Orpheus could, indeed, have been thought of as the image representing the creator of peace who necessarily made visitors think of Christ. This is exactly where we can perceive the link between the painted Orpheus and Christ or at least the figure of Christ as the one intended to make people think of.

III. Conclusion: the literary and iconographic Christian Orpheus

As a conclusion the comparison between Clement's Orpheus and the Orpheus of the catacombs can be drawn.

Clement's text does not seem to have influenced the pictures. Conversely it is difficult to imagine that he himself was influenced by them. Of course, a Christian picture of Orpheus, from which there would not be any more traces left because

---

[54] M. Herrero, *Orphism and Christianity* (2010), 122.

of the loss of many pieces of art due to the passing of time or to the rising water table,[55] could have existed in Alexandria in Clement's time.[56] But Clement does not make any explicit reference to such a picture and the mosaics we know were made later in Rome. Moreover, the principal topic and theological context are not exactly the same in each case: on the one hand, the pictures seem to promote the image of the Golden Age, on the other hand, Clement wants to enhance the role of the Word through the image of the song. But it is first and foremost the process which is similar, that is, by addressing a well-educated audience, to take on the values conveyed by the pagan figure as a positive and live symbol in order to praise Christianity. The pagan picture of Orpheus does not contain this meaning in itself. Neither is it allegorical. As in Clement, it has to be previously integrated into a Christian context to acquire this new meaning. It is in this sense that Clement's and the painters' methods show similarities.

Furthermore, the meaning of both types of representation is not so very different. Clement does not completely ignore the myth of the Golden Age linked to the figure of Orpheus. In his *Exhortation to the Greeks*, this motif, with its Christian eschatological dimension, is precisely bound up with the topic of the song and even more precisely of the New Song borrowed from John's Apocalypse.[57] In this framework, Christ's miracles could be interpreted as these *adunata* which announce the coming of a new Golden Age created by the Word. Since in this book Christ is shown as a new and better Orpheus, the motif of Golden Age announced by the miracles of the pagan Orpheus has been completely appropriated by the Christian discourse. Conversely, without being directly influenced by Clement's text, the Christian iconography of Orpheus seems to deliver a message which by certain features resembles it: the cither player, and perhaps more precisely the singer (in the fresco of Saint Peter and Marcellinus, indeed, Orpheus does not play, but seems to be singing) who transforms his listeners into peaceful creatures, could have been conceived as conveying the idea of peace, that is certainly also of salvation and resurrection.

But whereas the text, with its linear and temporal development, can in itself transform the pagan image to convey a clear new meaning of it, the pictures, because of their spatial, motionless dimension, let the visitors accomplish this transformation process themselves, with all the ambiguities such a liberty implies. It is indeed the role of the visitor to conjure up for themselves the Christianisation of the symbol achieved by Clement, here thanks to the context in which they encouter this symbol.

---

[55] One may think of the Kom el Shoqafa paintings of the third century which are known only from copies in the 1860's. See Jean-Yves Empereur, *Alexandria, Jewel of Egypt* (New York, 2002), 54.

[56] See the hypothesis of J.-M. Roessli, 'Imágenes de Orfeo' (2008), 215.

[57] *Exhortation to the Greeks* XII 119. On this topic, see F. Jourdan, *Orphée et les Chrétiens*, 1 (2010), 426-32.

From Catacomb to Sanctuary: The Orant figure and the Cults of the Mother of God and S. Agnes in Early Christian Rome, with Special Reference to Gold Glass[1]

Eileen Rubery, Cambridge, UK

ABSTRACT

Much of the surviving early Christian imagery is found in the catacombs of Rome. Amongst this material gold glass discs, largely made in the 4th century, provide a unique collection of portraits of the early Christian saints. This paper explores the surviving examples of female figures in the orant pose within this collection, and demonstrates that images of S. Agnes are three or four times more common than those of Mary, the Mother of God. Material from the numerous scattered sources of details on gold glass is then arranged in tables based on their iconography. These gold glass images are then contrasted with panel and monumental paintings of the same two saints in the 5th-8th centuries in Rome, where images of Mary now predominate and images of Agnes are largely confined to her cult sites. In several of these examples Mary is depicted seated, with the Christ-child on her lap, but a number in which she is still in the orant pose are also found. It is within this orant iconography that, at the beginning of the 8th century, the uniquely Roman iconography of 'Maria Regina' (Mary crowned as an Empress) appears. This crowned image of Mary continues to be popular through into the second millennium, but the orant pose that originally accompanied it is soon dropped and replaced by the seated Mary (now wearing a crown) with the Christ-child in her lap. Having outlined and interpreted the key examples of these iconographies this article suggests the initial popularity of S. Agnes was probably due the support given to her cult by the Constantinian dynasty at the end of the 4th century. They, largely through the efforts of Constantina, the sister of Constantine the Great, initiated the building of a church at the catacombs of S. Agnese, they supported the papacy in the restoration and decoration of the church and they built an imperial mausoleum on the site. Constantina and her sister, Helena, were laid to rest in this Mausoleum in two magnificent porphyry sarcophagi. Once that imperial linked became attenuated, however, the cult of Mary expanded to become the major female focus of Christian devotion. The extent to which this expansion was stimulated in Rome by the arrival of the Byzantines in the second half of the 6th century is considered in detail. In the East, the orant iconography of Mary persisted and developed further to include an image of the Christ-child enclosed

[1] This article has been developed from the paper, 'From Catacomb to Sanctuary: the Orant figure and Rome's Virgin Saints', presented by the author at the conference, *Early Christian Art, an international conference with special regard to the Early Christian Cemetery* in Sopianae, Pécs, Hungary, at the Celia Septicharo Centre, Pécs, Hungary, 24-25, May, 2012.

in a mandorla on the chest of the orant Mary, but this iconography does not appear to have developed widely in the West, although examples from Constantinople did enter the West, most probably via Venice.

I. Introduction

It is not easy to identify the earliest stages in the development of the cult of 'Mary, Ever-Virgin, Mother of God' (to use her final, full title).[2] The Gospels describe her role in the incarnation and the birth of Christ, provide fleeting glimpses of her during Christ's childhood and during his ministry, and identify her as present at the foot of the cross and with the disciples at Pentecost.[3] Her voluntary agreement to the incarnation (which she is probably the only human being to witness) was an essential prelude to the implementation of God's plan for the salvation of mankind, but is reported only in the *Gospel of Luke*.[4] In *Matthew* it is Joseph who is reported to have direct engagement with the angel.[5] Only *John*, the latest of the gospel writers, reports Mary's instrumental role in initiating Christ's ministry by stimulating his first miracle, the changing

---

[2] For a recent discussion of the evidence for the early existence of her cult which warns against placing too much weight on the paucity of direct evidence for an early date see John Mc Guckin, 'The early cult of Mary and Inter-Religious Contexts in the Fifth Century Church', in Chris Maunder (ed.), *The Origins of the Cult of the Virgin Mary* (London, 2008), 1-22 esp. 1-2 and his note 2 on p. 20 which draws attention to the *Sub Tuum Praesidium* in the liturgy which comes from a 3rd century Egyptian Papyrus and is still used as the concluding prayer in Compline. McGuckin supports this third century date. This text calls Mary 'ever chaste' (which it is probably reasonable to see as equivalent to 'ever-virgin'), 'Only Blessed', 'Mother of God' and 'Protector of those who invoke you' ('Under thy compassion we take refuge, Theotokos [Birthgiver-of-God]; do not disregard our prayers in the midst of tribulation, but deliver us from danger, O ever Pure, ever Blessed One'). The terms 'Ever-virgin' and 'Mother of God' were therefore in common usage considerably earlier than the date at which they were formally conferred upon Mary at the Council of Ephesus in 431 (Mother of God) and at the Council of Constantinople of 553 (Ever-Virgin).

Further evidence that the term 'Ever-virgin' was in use long before 553 comes from Pope Sixtus III who addresses her as Virgin Mary in his dedicatory inscription in Santa Maria Maggiore:

'VIRGO MARIA TIBI XYSTUS NOVA TECTA DICAVI DIGNA SALUTIFERO MUNERA VENTRE TUO.

'TU GENITRIX IGNARA VIRI TE DENIQUE FETA VISCERIBUS SALVIS EDITA NOSTRA SALUS,

('I, Sixtus, have dedicated a new temple to you Virgin Mary, worthy of honour because of your salvific maternity.

'Mother without having known a man, you conceived our Salvation.)

The inscription and this translation are taken from Herbert Kessler and Johanna Zacharias, *Rome 1300* (Newhaven and London, 2000), 157.

[3] *Luke* 1:27-55; *Matth.* 1:16.18-25; *Luke* 2:5-48; *Matth.* 2:11; *Mark* 15:40-6; *John* 19.

[4] *Luke* 1:26-38.

[5] *Matth.* 1:16.18-25.

of water into wine, at the wedding at Cana.[6] Each gospel does include her in at least one event relating to Christ's birth, ministry and passion, but in none of these references does the story particularly enhance Mary's standing. The occasion on which Christ sends her and her companions away, saying that he regards his followers as his mother and brothers and sisters, not his blood relatives, occurs in *Mark* and *Luke*[7] and is presumably intended to emphasise the collegiate nature of the followers of Christ and his attitude towards them. It in no way implies that he saw any particular role for his mother in his mission on earth. The reference to Christ being ignored in Galilee and 'only' being the son of Joseph and Mary, which provokes Christ's comment that a prophet is 'not without honour except in his own country' occurs in *Matthew* and *John*,[8] and again provides information on the way Christ's ministry was perceived and received rather than on Mary's role. Again this story provides at best a neutral view of Christ's perception of his mother. Her presence at the foot of the cross at the crucifixion marks the end of his ministry, but is only reported by John, the last of the Evangelists.[9] All the other evangelists report the scene at the foot of the cross or the entombment without mentioning Christ's mother, instead mentioning sundry other mothers and Marys.[10] The *Gospel of John* does specifically describe Christ's instructions to S. John to take care of Mary and John's acceptance of this responsibility, as one of Christ's final acts.[11] But Mary is not specifically mentioned by him as one of the Marys at the tomb three days later,[12] and although almost invariably depicted in the *iconography* of the Ascension, the gospels do not describe her as present there either.[13] She is, however, present with the disciples in the post Ascension community that gathers in the upstairs room in Acts and is therefore presumably present when the Holy Spirit descends on them at Pentecost.[14]

In contrast, if one looks at the apocryphal sources excluded from the 'Canon', stories of Mary and the Holy Family abound and clearly enjoyed wide circulation (if judged by the number of surviving copies).[15] The best known of these sources is the *Proto-Evangelion of James*, dated by Elliot to sometime in the second century and particularly popular in the East.[16] In addition to this source, a significant number of other texts of varying dates provide lively tales of

---

[6] *John* 2:1-11.

[7] *Mark* 3:31-4; *Luke* 8:19.

[8] *Matth.* 15:54-6; *John* 6:41-3.

[9] *John* 19:25-8.

[10] *Matth.* 27:55-6; 27:61; *Mark* 15:40.46; *Luke* 23:49-56.

[11] *John* 19:25-8.

[12] *Matth.* 28:1-10; *Mark* 16:1-11; *Luke* 24:1-11.

[13] She was probably intended to represent *Ecclesia* in Ascension iconography.

[14] *Acts* 1:14; 2:1-4.

[15] J. Keith Elliott, 'Mary in the Apocryphal New Testament', in C. Maunder, *Origins* (2008) 57-70.

[16] J.K. Elliott, 'Mary in the Apocryphal New Testament' (2008), 59.

Mary's conception, infancy, experience of rearing the young Christ and death.[17] Indeed, notwithstanding Pope Gelasius' (492-496) decree specifically *excluding* the *Proto-Evangelion* from the Canon,[18] it is these stories that in due course provide much of the material incorporated into the emerging iconography of the life of Mary.

One might even wonder whether Pope Gelasius' edict was in fact stimulated by the increasing use of this source in the developing iconography of her cult, since the mosaics at S. Maria Maggiore, commissioned by the papacy about 60 years previously do incorporate numerous elements of these stories in their iconography.[19]

While her role is further developed in the writings of the Patristic Fathers, many of whom wrote specific works on her, it is her formal recognition at the Council of Ephesus in 431 as *Theotokos* or 'bearer of God' that is frequently seen as the key event providing the significant stimulus to the development of her cult. This is notwithstanding the fact that, as I and others have pointed out elsewhere, the issue at stake at this Council was not *her* status, but rather that of Christ. This means that, in truth, any increase in her perceived importance at Ephesus was a by-product of the much higher profile decision taken at that Council on the status of her son.[20]

Several sources provide evidence of the development of her cult even before Ephesus. The well-known *Akathistos* hymn, frequently attributed to Romanos Melodos in the 6th century, is now thought by many to have had its origins much earlier, probably around the time of, or shortly after, Ephesus.[21] Its diverse origins, and many later additions, however, make it difficult to identify within it the earliest forms of address used for the Virgin.

As well as the boost resulting from Ephesus, the cult of the virgin in the fifth century received considerable stimulus in the East from the Imperial family. A church in the Daphne Palace dedicated to the virgin and close to the throne

---

[17] J. Keith Elliott, *The Apocryphal New Testament* (Oxford, 1993), esp. 46-163; 689-724; Stephen Shoemaker, *Ancient Traditions of the Virgin Mary's Dormition and Assumption* (Oxford, 2002).

[18] Decree number 16 of the 'Gelasianum de libris recipiendis et non recipiendis;' see S. Benko, *The Virgin Goddess: Studies in the Pagan and Christian Roots of Mariology,* (Leiden, 2004), 200 and Chris Maunder, 'Editorial', in C. Maunder, *Origins* (2008), x.

[19] Mary's responsibility for spinning the veil of the temple with red silk, for example, is described in the *Proto-Evangelion* and depicted in the Annunciation scene.

[20] Eileen Rubery, 'The early iconography of Mary: the mosaics of the triumphal arch at S. Maria Maggiore, Rome in the context of the writings of Cyril of Alexandria and the Council of Ephesus of 431', *SP* 72 (2014), 279-325; J. McGuckin, 'Early Cult of Mary' (2008), 1-22 esp. 1-4; Richard Price, 'The *Theotokos* and the Council of Ephesus' (2008), 89-105, both in C. Maunder, *Origins* (2008).

[21] Vasiliki, Limberis, *Divine Heiress: The Virgin Mary and the Creation of Christian Constantinople* (London, 1994), 89-97.

room was probably built in the first half of the 5th century.[22] The Augusta Pulcheria (414-453) gained a reputation for being particularly devoted her cult and held a Virginity Festival at court in 428/429. Patriarch Proclus (434-446) of Constantinople, wrote an oration to the Virgin for this event, in which he addressed the Virgin as 'Theotokos, the unstained treasure of Virginity'. He went on to write several other sermons lauding the Virgin Mary.[23] At the end of the 5th century, during the reign of Leo I (457-474) a mosaic centred on the Virgin Mary flanked by the Imperial family was placed in a sanctuary in the Blachernae convent at Constantinople. The Blachernae already held the relic of the Virgin's robe, obtained by Empress Verina (died 484). In this mosaic Emperor Leo I is recorded with the 'official' imperial family (Empress Verina, Empress Ariadne and her new-borne son, the future Leo II) positioned either side of the image of the Virgin.[24] As Grabar explains, the way these figures are arranged (Verina is described as 'prostrate' before Mary and holding Leo II 'as if he was her own child'), and the absence of Ariadne's husband, Zeno, the father of the child, who was not as yet an Augustus, suggests the image commemorated a service in which Verina, in the presence of the *ruling members* of the Imperial family, asked the Mother of God to protect the new-borne Augustus, Leo II, and so ensure the continuation of the dynasty. Here we have a clear example of the Mother of God being treated as an intercessor before Christ, an example of the use of an image in cult activity at the end of the 5th century. Probably Mary was chosen in preference to Christ as the intercessor here because, as the Mother of God, a direct parallel could then be established between the birth of Leo II to Ariadne, and the birth of the Christ-child to Mary for it is clear from related stories from this period that, in general, images of Christ were more popular than those of Mary at this time.[25]

From these beginnings, it is clear that, by the early seventh century her cult is well established in the East. The contemporary poet, George of Pisidia records how in 622, Emperor Heraclius, while campaigning in his war against the Persians, made it widely known that he carried with him a precious icon of the Virgin, in this way intending to demonstrate to the military that he was campaigning with the aid of God.[26] Heraclius, as he led his army towards

---

[22] Bissera Pentcheva, *Icons and Power* (Pennsylvania, 2006), 12, quoting André Grabar, 'Remarks sur l'iconographie byzantine de la Vierge', *Cahiers Archéologique* 24 (1977), 169-78; see also Constantine Porphyrogenitas, *De ceremoniis*, trans. Albert Vogt (Paris, 1940), 1,1,5 and note at 1,2,38.

[23] V. Limberis, *Divine Heiress* (1994), 51-2, 86-9. The sermons are in PG 65, 681 and 788.

[24] André Grabar, *L'iconoclasme Byzantin* (Paris, 1984), 27 and note 4, 58-60; A. Wenger, *Revue des Études Byzantines* 10 (1952/3), 51-9.

[25] The rest of this section in Grabar gives a good idea of the relative popularity of images of Christ and images of Mary in the 5th and 6th centuries in such elite contexts.

[26] George of Pisidia, *Exped. Pers.* 1, verses 139-154; 2.24-26; 2.74-79; 2.86 (Pertussi pp. 91, 97, 100, 101), and in Walter E. Kaegi, *Heraclius: Emperor of Byzantium* (Cambridge, 2003), 113.

Constantinople to claim it from the unpopular Phocas, is also reported to have been crowned Emperor in Herakleia by Stephanos, the Metropolitan of Kyzikos, using a crown (*stemma*) taken from the church of the Virgin of Artakes.[27] This again suggests he was aware of the benefits of providing visual evidence of his special devotion to the Virgin at this testing time.

In Rome, it seems the development of the cult of Mary progressed somewhat more slowly, possibly because of the strong links there with the two major apostles, Peter and Paul. Following Ephesus, the dedication of the papal church of S. Maria Maggiore occurred and it seems highly likely, as McGuckin has concluded, that the outcome of Ephesus *did* result in some significant stimulation of her cult in the West.[28] However, imposing *iconic* images of Mary only survive in Rome from the 6th century, and when all the material is taken together, the major expansion of her cult in the west appears to largely coincide with the arrival of Justinian's army under the control of Narses, and the final return of major parts of the west to the rule by the Eastern Empire.[29] The extensive building programme undertaken at Ravenna, for example, with its procession of female saints led by the three kings towards the enthroned Mary and the Christ-child, is a particularly striking example of the expansion of the cult of saints in relation to women that occurred at this time.[30]

What was the second or third church in Rome[31] to be dedicated to Mary, the church at the foot of the Palatine Hill called S. Maria Antiqua, is usually thought to have been consecrated sometime in the second half of the sixth century.[32] However, the probable date of the earliest Christian fresco that survives in this complex, a fresco that may well have pre-dated the establishment of a church on the site, is from the *middle* of the sixth century which again coincides with the arrival of Narses (478-573) and the Byzantine military in Rome and the return of the city to Byzantine control.[33] This fresco depicts a striking image of Mary, enthroned as an Augusta in elaborate gemmed Byzantine garments, holding the Christ-child dressed in gold and probably originally flanked by two angels offering them victory wreaths (Figure 10).[34] Narses was another

---

[27] W. Kaegi, *Heraclius* (2003), 48.

[28] J. McGuckin, 'Early Cult of Mary' (2008), 1-22 esp. 1-4.

[29] E. Rubery, 'Early Iconography of Mary' (2014).

[30] Giuseppe Bovini, *Ravenna Mosaics* (London, 1978), 36-7.

[31] The other church dedicated to Mary (in 609) was S. Maria ad martyres, in the converted Pantheon. Permission for the dedication was given by the Eastern Emperor, Phocas, and an icon of Mary and the Christ-child (probably donated by the Emperor given its eastern appearance) still survives in the church. See Carlo Bertelli, 'La Madonna del Pantheon', *Bolletino d'Arte* 46 (1961), 24-32.

[32] Gordon Rushforth, 'S. Maria Antiqua', *Papers of the British School at Rome* I (1902), 1-123, esp. 23.

[33] G. Rushforth, *S. Maria Antiqua* (1902), 20-5.

[34] *Ibid.* 67. For coloured images of this fresco see Josef Wilpert, *Die Römischen Mosaiken und Malereien der Kirchlichen Bauten vom IV. bis XIII. Jahrhundert*, 4 vols. (Freiburg im Breisgau,

military general whose particular devotion to the Virgin Mary is recorded in the sources.[35] Once Narses had completed the conquest of Italy he is reported to have spent a considerable time residing on the Palatine in Rome, apparently preferring this to residing at the administrative centre of the West in Ravenna.[36] This would have placed him close to S. Maria Antiqua, which is situated at the foot of the Palatine Hill and connected to the imperial palaces on top of the hill by a well-built ramp.[37] The Liber Pontificalis entry for Pope Pelagius (552-561) reports that Narses assisted the pope in bringing order to Rome after the ravages of the wars, and that he also assisted in the rebuilding of the churches, including that of the SS Apostoli.[38] This raises the possibility that the re-conquest of the West by the Byzantines provided a further stimulus to her cult, first in Ravenna and Rome and then more widely in Italy.

Surviving Christian iconography from the first two hundred years after the crucifixion is sparse,[39] but even in the third and fourth centuries, when an abundance of Christian imagery occurs on sarcophagi, in surviving frescoes in the catacombs and on other media such as gold glass in the catacombs,[40] Mary is more noticeable by her absence than her presence.[41] Her only regular appearance in funerary imagery in the catacombs is in images of the Adoration of the Magi, where arguably her function is more to provide a suitable support for the Christ-child as the symbol of the incarnation than to be present in her own right. The only surviving attempt to depict Christ in the Adoration of the Magi *without* Mary as his support is the image in the second register on the left on the triumphal arch at S. Maria Maggiore, created shortly after the Council of Ephesus, where the diminutive Christ-child sits alone on a spectacularly large

1917), vol 4, Plates 151 and 133 for the fresco *in situ* on the apsidal arch, and Plate 134 for a reconstruction of the full original composition.

[35] Evagrius Scholasticus, *Ecclesiastical History*, trans. E. Walford (London, 1846), book iv. Chapter XXIV: 'Those about the person of Narses affirm that he used to propitiate the Deity with prayers and other acts of piety, paying due honour also to the Virgin and mother of God, so that she distinctly announced to him the proper season for action; and that Narses never engaged until he had received the signal from her'.

[36] Initially Narses appears to have developed good relations with Pope Pelagius I and his successor John III (561-574) and he is reported to help them rebuild the Roman churches including that of the SS Apostoli (*Vita* of Pelagius). Later he runs into difficulties and the people petition Justinian to remove him, making it necessary for Pope John to petition him to return to Rome after he has left it. (*Vitae* of Pelagius I (556-561) and John III (561-574): Louis Duchesne (trans.), *Liber Pontificalis* I (Paris, 1955), 303-4, 304-5. English translation at Raymond Davis, *The Book of the Pontiffs* (Liber Pontificalis) (Liverpool, 1980), 61 and 61-2.

[37] G. Rushforth, 'S. Maria Antiqua' (1902): a plan of the complex is at p. 18, where the ramp is identified as HHKK, A description of the topographical arrangements is at p. 21.

[38] *Vita* of Pelagius I (556-561): Louis Duchesne (trans.), *Liber Pontificalis* I (1955), 303-4.

[39] Paul Finney, *The Invisible God* (Oxford, 1994), 99-145.

[40] Raffaele Garrucci, *Storia degli Arte Italiano*, vols. 1-6 (Prato, 1876).

[41] Geri Parlby, 'The origins of Marian art in the Catacombs and the problems of identification', in C. Maunder (ed.), *Origins* (2008), 41-56.

Figure 1. Christ enthroned without the physical support of Mary in the Adoration of the Magi narrative scene in the second register of the triumphal arch 'Nativity of Christ' at S. Maria Maggiore, Rome, (circa 430 AD). On the left of his throne sits Christ's mother dressed in the 'virginal' golden robes she was depicted in the Annunciation in the top register of the mosaic, while on the right of his throne she sits as his mother, wearing a *maphorion* and holding a white handkerchief or *mappa* in her left hand (Photo: copyright E. Rubery).

throne (Figure 1).[42] Although a striking image, this was clearly not subsequently regarded as a particularly successful composition since, notwithstanding the high profile this church had in Rome (and probably elsewhere since Rome was a major focus for pilgrimage) the scene does not appear to have ever been copied. Indeed, one can postulate that the arrangement was a particular conse- quence of the Council of Ephesus and specifically linked to a desire to portray Mary in both of her named situations: as the Virgin Mary on the left side where she is dressed in identical fashion to her virginal figure in the Annunciation in the top register, and on the right as 'Mother of God', wearing a *maphorion*, and holding the senatorial *mappa* in her left hand, to indicate that the salva- tion of mankind has indeed now commenced (Figure 1), so drawing attention to her newly authorised name at Ephesus. Elsewhere, in the Roman Catacombs, frequent images of Mary holding the Christ-child and flanked by the magi

---

[42] For a detailed discussion of the possible background and meaning of this iconography see E. Rubery, 'S Maria Maggiore' (2014); for an image of the entire mosaic see Plate XLVII opposite p. 198, and for a colour images of this detail of the mosaic see Plate XLIX in Carlo Cecchelli, *I Mosaici della Basilica di S. Maria Maggiore* (Turin, 1956).

(between two and four magi occur) occur but otherwise Mary is rarely depicted in early catacomb art in Rome.[43]

So how, when and why did her cult develop? Chris Maunder, in his Editorial to 'The Origins of the cult of the Virgin Mary' concluded that 'there is scant evidence of a cult of Mary before the late 4th century'. He suggested that before then the pagan cults of Isis, Cybele, Demeter/Ceres and Artemis/Diana filled the emotional space she subsequently came to occupy.[44] John McGuckin, in the same book, in his discussion of the development of the early cult of Mary, also stresses her ability to absorb other female cultic images such as that of Isis.[45] In my contribution to the above book I considered ten images of Mary linked to the Roman papacy and produced up to 707 AD (the end of Pope John VII's time as Pope).[46] Only one source, the images of Mary in the narrative cycle on the triumphal arch at S. Maria Maggiore already mentioned, come from as early as the fifth century and the images of Mary in this narrative cycle can be viewed as incidental to the main storyline, which is the nativity of Christ.[47]

The earliest iconic images of Mary in my collection, both attributed to the 6th century, were linked to the church of S. Maria Antiqua in the Roman Forum, (the 'Palimpsest Madonna' on the right side of the main apse, already mentioned above and shown at Figure 10[48] and the fragment of the panel painting of the 'Madonna di San Luca', now in the sacristy of the basilica of S. Francesca Romana on the edge of the Roman Forum.[49] Additional 6th century iconic images of Mary in Rome, not specifically associated with the papacy, are the 'widow Turtura' fresco panel in the catacombs of Commodilla, which is usually dated to the first half of the 6th century on the basis of the entry in the Liber Pontificalis which attributes the restoration of these catacombs to Pope John I (523-556) and to the style of the fresco which resembles, for example, the mosaics of Pope John IV (640-642) in the Lateran Baptistery. The Turtura fresco appears to be the work of a local family.[50] In Ravenna, as already mentioned, roughly

---

[43] See G. Parlby, *Marian Art in the Catacombs* (2008), 41-56 for a discussion of this. There are two claimed examples of Mary in the catacombs of Priscilla where she is not part of an Adoration of the Magi scene (Mary holding Christ and an Annunciation: see Figures 1, 2 & 7 in Parlby's paper) but both are open to alternative interpretations and neither give her any particular prominence.

[44] C. Maunder (ed.), *Origins* (2008), ix-xvii; x-xi and Chris Maunder, 'Origins of the Cult of the Virgin Mary in the New Testament', in the same volume, 23-39.

[45] J. McGuckin, 'Early Cult of Mary', in C. Maunder (ed.), *Origins* (2008), 1-22, 7-9.

[46] Eileen Rubery, 'Pope John VII's Devotion to Mary: papal images of Mary from the 5th to the early 8th century', in C. Maunder (ed.), *Origins* (2008), 155-204, esp. Table 1, 156-7.

[47] For a more detailed description of the background and likely meaning of these images see E. Rubery, 'S Maria Maggiore' (2014).

[48] G. Rushforth, 'S. Maria Antiqua' (1902), 66-7.

[49] Pico Cellini, 'Una Madonna molto antica', *Proportioni* 3 (1950), 1-6 and Plates I-IX.

[50] See H. Stuart Jones, 'The catacomb of Commodilla', review of *Atti della R. Accademia dei Lincei, Serie V: Notitie degli Scavi di Antichità, 1905, JTS* 7 (1906), 615-20, esp. 618 which

contemporaneous with these images in Rome, and produced in response to the re-conquest of Ravenna by Justinian's armies, we find an enthroned Mary flanked by four angels and attended by the three magi and 22 female saints in the nave at St'Apollinare Nuovo.[51] The opposite wall of this nave complements these figures with an enthroned Christ flanked by angels and approached by a similar procession of male saints. These two sets of mosaics also draw our attention to an additional group of early Christian figures, now attaining greater importance, the martyr saints.[52] These mosaics also remind us that a major focus of the early Christians following the issuing of the Edict of Milan in 312, was a desire to remember and pay homage to those martyred for their faith during the persecutions. If the role of images of early saintly female figures is looked at from this perspective, then a social environment in which Mary, the Mother of God, might even appear less significant than the female martyrs who died for their faith as a source of iconography becomes intriguingly possible.

In my article on early papal images of Mary, I divided the ten images under discussion into four overlapping categories:

– Mother of God
– Virgin Saint
– Empress
– Orant.[53]

As I point out in this article, most of the surviving 'Mother of God' images depicting the Madonna and Child are further expressions of the incarnation of Christ and are variants of the 'Adoration of the Magi' iconography. Here I want to focus particularly on the last of my four categories: 'Mary as Orant'. This iconography, extremely prevalent in the catacombs of both Christians and pagans, is of particular interest in relation to the growth of the cult of Mary because it is the only type in which Mary is usually depicted alone, without the Christ-child. Furthermore, since this is also clearly an intercessionary pose, it is particularly likely to reflect a cultic purpose and to have links to the wider issue of the way that female saints are depicted.

I shall divide the rest of this article into four parts. In the first part I shall consider the early history of the orant pose and its likely meaning, both in

provides the Latin text of the inscription that accompanies it. For a coloured image of this fresco see J. Wilpert, *Die Römische Mosaiken und Malereien* (1917), Plate 136; for further information on the fresco see E. Russo, 'L'affresco di Turtura nel cimiterio di Commodilla, l'icona di S. Maria in Trastevere e la piu antiche feste della Madonna a Roma', *Bolletino dell'instituto storico Italiano per il medio evo e Archivio Muratoriano* 88 (1979), 35-85.

[51] For an image see Giuseppe Bovini, *Ravenna Mosaics* (London, 1978), 26-38.

[52] For a fuller discussion of the rise of the cult of saints in Late Antiquity see Peter Brown, *The Cult of the Saints* (Chicago, 1981).

[53] E. Rubery, *Papal images of Mary* (2008), 180-3.

general and more specifically in Christian terms. In the second part I shall consider the development of the orant image of Mary in the frescoes and sarcophagi in the catacombs. In the third part I shall focus in particular on the collection of images in gold glass from the Roman catacombs that depict Mary, Agnes and other female figures. These artefacts possess two great advantages from an analytic point of view. Firstly the frequent presence of an inscription, often including a name, reduces the difficulties in identifying the person(s) portrayed. Secondly, given the large number of surviving examples from a relatively short period of time (around 500 examples, probably mostly from the second half of the 4th century[54]) some judgements on the popularity of the different saints depicted can be made from the frequency with which various figures occur.[55] In the fourth section I shall consider images of the Virgin Saints and Mary in Rome in the early churches and on icons up to the early 8th century, so that these earlier images can be placed in the context of later developments.

II. The Early History of the Orant Figure

The catacombs are one of the richest surviving sources of orant imagery, some pagan, others clearly of early Christian origin. The pose necessarily assumes the adjacent presence of a higher authority, usually implied and situated above the figure, somewhere in the heavens, and the orant action invokes the assistance of this power in the journey into the after-life. The pose is an ancient one that can be traced back as far as classical times. The Empress Livia, for example, is shown adopting the orant pose as a priestess in the first century sculpture found in the Basilica of Otricoli (Figure 2), and, if the attribution of this iconography to the sculptor, Euphranor, active in the 4th century BC is correct, then it is an even more ancient pose.[56] Furthermore the pose is one naturally adopted by anyone imploring a favour in an emotional context and ultimately reflects spontaneous human behaviour.

---

[54] John Bradley, *Late Roman Gold-glass and its Contexts,* a dissertation submitted for a Bachelor of Arts degree at Royal Holloway, University of London, September, 2008, lists around 500 in Appendix 2.

[55] It is of course important to realise that the gold glass selected for use in the catacombs may not reflect the totality of gold glass produced in Rome at this time. Also that collection of examples will not have been random, a clear preference for exploring Christian catacombs and those with interesting images and other contents has clearly been present in the past, and many of the catacombs continue to include large areas that have yet to be examined.

[56] Database of Ancient Art. Inv. No. 637, Museo Pio-Christiana, Gallery of the Busts: Details on label.

Figure 2. Sculpture of Empress Livia dressed as a priestess in the Orant pose (from the Basilica of Otricoli, excavated 1778-1779). The statue is thought to date from the first century AD, probably after her death in 29 AD. The iconography is attributed to the sculptor Euphranor, who was active in the mid 4th century BC. (Inv. No. 637, Museo Pio-Christiana, Vatican Museum, Gallery of the Busts) (Photo: copyright E. Rubery).

According to Eusebius, Constantine was shown in this pose in portraits of the emperor placed over the entrance to the palace in certain cities, no doubt to emphasise how imperial rule involved a direct dialogue with God:

'His portrait also at full length was placed over the entrance gates of the palaces in some cities, the eyes upraised to heaven, and the hands spread out as if in prayer.'[57]

The final phrase suggests that the form of orant pose used here was of Constantine with his hands spread out to form a cross and this would have usefully echoed the contemporary emphasis on the cross as the key Christian symbol of the Constantinian dynasty. The widespread use of orant figures in secular as well as religious decorations at this time is clear from the presence of several orants in the *Sala dell'Orante* under the church of SS Giovanni e Paolo on the Celian Hill in Rome (Figure 3).[58] The context of this fresco is most consistent with a secular, non-Christian meaning, for the surrounding images are of masks, goats, vegetative designs, hippocampi and other religiously neutral subjects. While the rinceaux forming the border below the upper register could be used to refer to Eucharistic Christian rites, they are equally compatible with pagan Dionysiac rites or with being simply an indication of plenty and contentment. The lower sections of the walls are decorated with *faux opus sectile* marble panels and other geometric decorative features. The overall style and iconography is typical of the mid-4th century.

This room was part of a complex of houses in a 4th and 5th century *insula* under the present Basilica of SS Giovanni e Paolo, that belonged to Roman elite families.[59] Although this room was almost certainly secular, close by was a smaller chamber, approached by a narrow staircase and corridor, in which the orant figures clearly figure in an early *Christian* scene (probably second half of the fourth century). This chamber contains, as its focus, a fresco with a standing male orant figure framed by two drawn curtains and surrounded by a number of kneeling figures who are performing obeisance (Figure 4). The use of curtains here suggests an important person is being portrayed. Emperors, for example, are often depicted flanked by curtains which can be closed to hide them until they are opened with a flourish to display the ruler.[60] The figure

[57] Eusebius, *Life of Constantine,* Book IV, Chapter XVI. English translation from Philip Schaff and Henry Wace (eds), *Nicene and Post-Nicene Fathers of the Christian Church,* second series, Vol. 1, *Eusebius,* 544.

[58] Hugo Brandenburg, *Ancient Churches of Rome* (Turnhout, 2005), 155-62.

[59] *Ibid.* The arrangements in this building are complex and not completely worked out. Brandenburg provides a useful discussion of the uncertainties and some good quality illustrations.

[60] A. Grabar, 'Une fresque Visigothique et l'Iconographie du Silence', *Cahiers Archéologique* 1 (1947), 122-8 referring to the icon from the Blankernae Convent in Constantinople depicting the orant virgin enthroned with the Christ-Child on her lap. This icon was kept behind curtains that were only drawn once per week to reveal the image to faithful, and the arrangement of the curtains in the illustration of this icon in the Evangeliary of Etchmiadzin from the 6th century (Figure 2 in Grabar's paper) closely resembles that found in SS Giovanni e Paulo; in the fourth

Figure 3. The room of the orant in the Roman houses under the Basilica of SS Giovanni e Paolo, Rome. The orant here has arms outstretched so that the body forms a cross. However, overall the decorations of the room are most consistent with a secular function. The other images along the top of the walls and on the vault are of masks, goats, vegetative arrangements, sea monsters and other religiously ambiguous subjects The rinceaux of the border underneath are most probably intended merely to be decorative. The lower half of the walls is decorated with *faux opus sectile* marble panels and other geometric decorative features consistent with a late 3rd or 4th century date (Photo: copyright E. Rubery).

Figure 4. This small *Confessio* has been created on the platform above what appear to be martyrs' tombs (although the rules about bringing relics inside the city walls at this time make it likely the relics contained in them would be at best contact relics) and is decorated with Christian paintings from the second half of the fourth century, including an orant figure on the end wall with two figures doing proskynesis on either side. The side walls depict scenes of the martyrdom of saints (Photo: copyright E. Rubery).

therefore probably represented a cult saint and its lack of a halo would not be unusual at this period.[61] This orant's arms are bent at the elbow, the lower arms being extended at right angles to either side, with the palms exposed to the viewer. The sidewalls of this space are decorated with further figures dressed in contemporary clothes, some of whom are female. Above and on the left wall is a paradisiacal scene and on the right wall, in the top register, male and female figures are kneeling on the floor with their hands tied behind their backs awaiting martyrdom. The executioner is probably behind them although only his legs survive. Since at this date contemporary burial laws would not have permitted the bones of a saint to be held inside the walls of the city, presumably cult worship took place here in the absence of human relics (brandei could have been substituted for such remains), but there can be little doubt that this is a Christian cult site. The relationship of these frescoes to the graffito naming three saints: Cyprian, Justina and Theocristus and the later small shrine containing the bones of saints Giovanni e Paolo, possibly martyred in the time of Julian the Apostate (who later give their name to the basilica built above these houses) is unclear.[62] But these two orant figures at the same site usefully demonstrate the range of secular and religious contexts in which an orant figure could be used in the 4th century.

III. Images of Orants in frescoes and sarcophagi in the Catacombs

It is in the catacombs in Rome that we find the richest collection of orant figures, and their distribution makes it clear that this image was a key part of burial iconography for both pagans and Christians at this period. Examples occur in frescoes, on sarcophagi and on gold glass.[63] In the catacombs of Priscilla, for example, the cubiculum of the *Velatio* dating from before the 3rd century, includes a lunette with a central orant figure with covered head,

---

century; Gregory of Nazianzus also described how the bishop on his throne was hidden behind a curtain in the apse during the service (PG 36, 563) and this arrangement is illustrated in an image from the Philocalian Calendar drawn by Grabar in his Figure 3. Similarly in the mosaic panel of Augusta Theodora at S. Vitale in Ravenna (for a colour image see Robin Cormack, *Byzantine Art* [Oxford, 2000], 61) curtains are being drawn back to reveal the imperial figure of the Augusta as she enters the sanctuary.

[61] Hans Belting, *Likeness and Presence* (London, 1994), 80-5, who also discusses the various issues surrounding the way this building functioned and developed in some detail. The relatively rare use of halos in the fourth century is also clear from the numerous examples of saints minus halos in the gold glass discussed in Section IV below.

[62] See H. Belting, *Likeness and Presence* (1994), 82-5; H. Brandenburg, *Ancient Churches* (2005), 155-62 for relevant discussions and P. Franchi di Cavalleri, 'Dove furono seppolti i SS. Cypriano, Giustina e Teoctisto?' Note agiografiche 8, *Studi e Testi* 65 (Rome, 1935), 335-8.

[63] Vincenzo Nicolai, Fabrizio Bisconti and Danilo Mazzoleni, *The Christian Catacombs of Rome: History, Decoration, Inscriptions* (Regensburg, 2002).

Figure 5. An orant figure flanked by a marriage scene (left) and a mother and child (right) and above with birds and a peacock. From the catacombs of Priscilla, Rome. The lack of any overtly Christian iconography in the scene makes it compatible with a pagan burial site (Photo: copyright E. Rubery).

arms bent at the elbow, wearing a typically loose tunic (Figure 5). To the left are grouped three figures: a larger seated man, and a smaller couple who hold a scroll between them.[64] On the right a seated woman feeds a small baby. One possible interpretation is that the left group represents the marriage of the dead woman and the right group the birth of her child. The surrounding decorations of birds and a peacock, symbols frequently used to suggest regeneration and renewed life, are compatible with a pagan site where images of the key events in the life of the defunct woman: her marriage and the birth of her child, are evoked as the defunct, placed centrally in the orant pose, implores the gods to assist her in her journey through the afterlife. There is nothing in the decoration of this space that marks it as the site of a Christian burial although this cannot be ruled out. In contrast, the nearby *Capella Graeca* has, amongst a number of Christian iconographies, an 'Adoration of the magi' on the vault, suggesting the site belonged to a Christian family.[65] The orant figure on the left here has been interpreted as Susannah with the elders, Susannah employing the orant pose to

---

[64] Fabrizio Mancinelli, *Guide to the Catacombs of Rome* (Florence, 2012), 52-3.
[65] Sandro Carletti, *Catacombs of Priscilla* (Rome, 2012), 29-35.

Figure 6. Fresco of the child Nonnosa between her father and mother in the hypogeum of Teotecno in the catacombs of S. Gennaro, Naples, circa sixth century (Photo © Biblioteca Hertziana – Max-Planck-Institut für Kunstgeschichte, Rome).

implore God to witness her innocence from the charges of adultery made by the elders.

Many of the orant figures in the catacombs have a somewhat ascetic appearance, wearing clothes that appear somewhat dishevelled, perhaps intended to indicate emotional distress. But a fresco in a lunette from the Catacombs of S Gennaro in Naples, dated to the end of the 5th or beginning of the 6th century, depicts three elite, extremely well-dressed orant figures (Figure 6).[66] The central figure, *Nonnosa,* frontally posed, looks directly at the viewer. Her bent arms raise her hands to around shoulder height, again with the palms facing towards the observer. She is dressed in a richly decorated vermilion under-tunic decorated with a faint patina suggestive of pearls. The garment is fixed below the bust by a belt with a circular buckle, also decorated with pearls. Around her

---

[66] Umberto M. Fasola, *Le Catacombe di San Gennaro a Capodimonte* (Rome, 1975), 96, 102: Figure 68.

neck are more pearls in two rows on a black collar, and her black hair is bound
with a further row of pearls. Above her head an elaborate 'crown', probably in
fact a candelabra, is suspended, perhaps to make up for her small size when
compared with her two companions, identified by the inscription as her parents.
This composition focuses on the early death of their child although, according
to the inscription, Nonnosa's parents, Ilaritas and Teotecnus, are now also
dead.[67] Although also frontally posed, their hands and bent arms are turned
outwards, illustrating a common variant of the orant pose. The mother's head
is covered by a dark veil, her upper body and arms are covered by a dark cloak
and underneath she wears a dark under-tunic. The father is more brightly
dressed in a plum/pink garment through which the cuffs of the cream under-
tunic are visible, decorated with two bands of embroidered cloth. A further
embroidered panel is attached to his upper right shoulder. His shoulders are
covered with a cream cloak decorated with a pattern that might be of leaping
hinds in gold. It is pinned at his right shoulder, though probably not with an
elite fibula. He may also be wearing a decorative band around his head. At each
edge, beyond the adult figures two narrow green shoots, presumably indicating
fertility and growth, perhaps indicating the hoped for regeneration of the family in the after-life, can be seen. The 'crown' above the girl's head may remind
one of the victory wreath held by the hand of God above Christ's head in
Christian apses in Roman churches, but in fact the iconography does not make
the religious beliefs of the family explicit and the entire composition is consistent
with a pagan or Christian family. The image shows how the orant pose can be
adopted by the dead person, by a relative or intercessor, by either sex, and at
any age, for the inscription says Nonnosa died at a little over two years.[68]

Images of orants commonly occur on the sides of Christian sarcophagi.
The iconography of the three young men in the fiery furnace characteristically
depicts them in the orant pose, and Daniel adopts a similar pose in the lions'
den (Figure 7a and b).[69] Orants can be depicted alone, simply framed by strig-
illations, or surrounded by narrative scenes from the Old and New Testament
(Figure 7c) where the central orant figure is not named. These orant figures are
usually anonymous and most probably represent either the exhortations of
the defunct or of a representative of the defunct to their god. The final scene
of Daniel destroying the Temple of Bel is a rare example.[70] I have, however,
found no orant image of Mary on any of the sarcophagi I have examined in

[67] U. Fasola, *San Gennaro* (1975), 96 and Legend to Plate Va opposite p. 72.

[68] Tania Velmans, 'Un portrait familial de la catacomb de Naples et ses rapports avec la tradition byzantine', *Bollettino di Storia dell'arte dell'Università degli studi di Salerno* 3/4 (1974),
3-9.

[69] See the collection of sarcophagi in the Museo Pio-Christiana in the Vatican Museums for
examples.

[70] The image of Daniel destroying the serpent in the Temple of Bel was understood as a prefiguration of Christ's coming and victory over the demonic serpent. This sarcophagus was entire

Figure 7. **a:** Fragment of a sarcophagus depicting Noah in his ark and the three young men in the fiery furnace, each in the orant pose, on the front of a sarcophagus: **b:** Fragment of a sarcophagus depicting Daniel in the Lions' Den and the raising of Lazarus. **c:** A complete side of a sarcophagus depicting (from left to right): The miracle at Cana, the curing of the blind man, raising of the son of the widow, an orant figure, the multiplication of loaves, the haemorrhaging woman, and the prophet Daniel destroying the Temple of Bel and killing the dragon with poison. This sarcophagus was found under the pavement in Old S. Peter's Basilica.
All sarcophagi are in the Pio-Christian Museum, in the Vatican Museums (Photo: copyright E. Rubery).

Rome. Indeed, as was the case for frescoes in the catacombs discussed above, depictions of Mary are essentially confined to the Adoration of the magi iconography. The sarcophagi, therefore reinforce the evidence from the frescoes.

IV. Images of Orants in the Gold Glass from the Catacombs

The final significant source of images from this early period is the over 400 examples of images found on the bases of glass vessels whose bases were decorated with gold leaf sandwiched between two layers of glass. The original objects were usually glass cups or bowls, made largely if not entirely in the

when first exposed but was reduced to just the front in 1757 on being transferred to the Museum of Benedict XIV (details from the label to the sarcophagus in museum).

4th century. The vessels, or fragments of the original vessels, were then embedded in the mortar surrounding the tiles used to seal the *loculi* in the Roman catacombs.[71] These provide one of the largest collections of named early Christian images[72] and include a small but valuable group of orant images of Mary and other female saints including, in particular, St Agnes. This group of images has not been quantitatively assessed before in the context of the development of the cult of the Virgin Mary.[73] The habit of using these objects to decorate *loculi* appears to have been restricted to Rome, since almost all surviving examples can be traced back to that city, and the largest collection of them are held by the *Museo Sacra* of the Vatican museums, with significant additional collections in England in the British Museum and the Ashmolean Museum.[74] Other individual examples can be found in some Italian city museums and occasionally in collections in other European cities.[75] Some examples are still *in situ* in the catacombs.[76] Grig identifies 140 gold glasses of 'religious portraits' (although she does not say exactly what her criteria for this classification were) and says that these images make up 50.5% of her collection.[77] She identifies 63 images of Peter and 58 of Paul,[78] and states that there are 15 examples of depictions of Agnes but no examples of depictions of Mary in her sample.

Bradley identifies 16 examples of gold glass bearing images of Agnes, including all varieties of spelling.[79] Two of these he lists as of 'non-catacomb

---

[71] The major catalogues of these objects are Charles Morey, *Gold Glass of the Vatican Library* (Vatican City, 1959); Raffaele Garrucci, *Vetri ornati di figure in oro trovati nei cimiteri dei Cristiani primitivi di Roma* (Roma, 1858) updated in Raffaele Garrucci, *Storia della arte Christiana nei primi ottosecoli della Chiesa* III (Prato, 1876); Stephanie L. Smith, *Gold Glass Vessels of the Late Roman Empire: Production, Context and Function*, Dissertation for degree of Doctor of Philosophy (Graduate School, New Brunswick Rutgers, The State University of New Jersey, 2000); John Bradley, *Late Roman Gold-glass and its Contexts*, a dissertation submitted for a Bachelor of Arts degree at Royal Holloway, University of London, September, 2008. See also Lucy Grig, 'Portraits, Pontiffs and the Christianisation of Fourth Century Rome', *Papers of the British School at Rome* 72 (2004), 203-30 for some summaries of the types of images depicted.

[72] L. Grig, 'Portraits' (2004), 203-30, esp. 204 says there are over 500 examples of gold glass, Bradley, *Late Roman Gold Glass* (2008) lists 511 examples.

[73] Smith, Grig and Bradley all provide lists of the Gold Glass examples they have tracked down that supplement the early work of Morey and Garrucci. Unfortunately the differing ways the material is presented in each case (reflecting the aspect of the topic of interest to each author) makes cross comparisons time-consuming, and I have not attempted this.

[74] Those catalogued in early lists as at Pusey House are now in the Ashmolean Museum.

[75] C. Morey, *Gold Glass* (1959), see esp. the four unnumbered pages following p. 79.

[76] For example the orant figure from the Catacomb of Novaziano in Rome.

[77] L. Grig, 'Portraits' (2004), Table 1, 206.

[78] Unfortunately the iconography and/or sources of the additions made to the Morey catalogue are not stated, so it is not possible to work out from her figures how many examples of gold glass these figures represent, especially given that many pieces include two or more named figures. Morey, for example, lists 42 specimens with Peter and Paul on the same gold glass.

[79] J. Bradley, *Late Roman Gold Glass* (2008), Appendix 2: p. 42.

provenance'. One of his examples includes Mary with Agnes, both in profile and staring at each other across a Chi-Rho sign, reproduced here as Figure 9e, and also included in Morey as no. 265.[80]

Before considering the examples of the various saints of interest it is important to deal with the issue of the variability of the spelling of the names in the inscriptions on these discs. It is clear from an examination of the whole corpus of material that any given name could be spelt in a variety of ways on gold glass. Within this context the name of S. Agnes appears particularly variable. Around half of the examples have what appear to be variants of the name Anne or Anna. For example in Table 1 we find ANNES (R 10), ANNE (three times: R 9; R 12; R 34) and ANNI (once R 11). One might assume that these refer to the cult of S. Anne, the mother of Mary, except that the cult of S. Anne, is first recorded in Constantinople in the 6th century, when Procopius mentions a church there built by Justinian.[81] The earliest images of S. Anne in Rome are in Santa Maria Antiqua, where a probably mid-7th century fresco of her holding the child Mary is found on the right wall of the sanctuary.[82] No church dedicated to her is recorded in Rome until the church of S. Anne alla Marmorata is listed in the catalogue of the 'anonymous of Turin' in the 16th century.[83] It is therefore unlikely that these glasses celebrated the cult of S. Anne. Morey and Grig both assume that they are really mis-spelt variants of Agnes. I have continued this convention and score these variants as Agnes.

Table 1 lists 22 examples of the female Saint Agnes, allowing for the variants in spelling mentioned above, with the Morey number (where present) listed in the second column after my own 'R' number and the Garrucci (1876) number (where present) listed in the fourth column. The increased number of examples here when compared with the earlier compilations largely derives from building on the accepted variability of the way Agnes' name is spelt, plus a more rigorous search of fragments of gold glass for pieces that include AN or NE and/or where the accompanying image suggests that originally it was this saint that was depicted.[84]

Similarly MARA (R 19; R 22) occurs twice as a variation of MARIA and it seems reasonable to apply the same arguments to misspellings of Maria as are being applied to misspellings of Agnes, so these two variants have been

[80] See E. Rubery R 1 in Tables 1 and 2.

[81] Wladimir de Grüneisen, *Sainte Marie Antique* (Rome, 1911), 533-4; Procopius, *De aedificans* 1. 3. 11: Loeb, Classical Library, Buildings, 40/41: 'In that section of the city which is called Deuteron he erected a most holy and revered church to St Anna, whom some consider to have been the mother of the Virgin and the grandmother of Christ'.

[82] G. Rushforth, *Santa Maria Antiqua* Papers of the British School at Rome 1 (1902), 1-123, esp. 66-7.

[83] Mariano Armellini, *Le Chiese di Roma dal sec. IV al XIX* (Vatican City, 1891), 47-69.

[84] See reference 85 for discussion of the variability of spelling of names in these artefacts.

accepted as MARIA.[85] Morey omits R 19 from his 'Subject Catalogue' (pre-
sumably on the basis of the inaccurate spelling) but includes it in his 'Inscription
Index' under MARA. Bradley lists R 19 under 'Secular figures: Orant Female'.
In contrast Morey no. 59 is the example of a married lady called MARA. The
presence of her husband on her right makes it quite clear that she is not intended
to be the Mother of God. The inscription here reads AMADA E ABAS MARA
GERMANVS VIVAS.[86] This could either be an example of a miss-spelling of
MARIA or of a woman whose name was MARA.

i. *Images of Agnes with Mary* (Table 1 and Table 2)

The relatively high number of 'Agnes' figures (22) compared with those of
'Mary' (6) draws attention to the paucity of images of Mary in early Christian
art already noted in frescoes and sarcophagi in the catacombs.[87] Only two of
the 22 examples of Agnes in Table 1 (R 1 and R 22) depict both AGNES and
MARIA. R 1 is a profiled figure of AGNES opposed to a similar image of
MARIA. Each looks at the other across a Chi-Rho sign situated above a vertically placed rotulus (Figure 9e). Both women are veiled. This gold glass is
small, with a diameter of 5.3 cm and described by Morey (no. 265) as the base
of a cup.[88] It is not part of the Vatican collection but is held in the Museo
Civico in Bologna. Neither Garrucci (no. 191.8) nor Morey give a site of origin.
The chi-rho sign situated between the figures invokes the presence of Christ
above the two figures, so maintaining the usual hierarchical relationship
between Christ and his saints. However, later iconography would be inclined
to give a higher status to Mary than to Agnes. Neither of the heads of the two
figures is nimbed, nor are they in an orant pose. They probably hold martyr's
crowns in their covered hands.

R 22 (Figure 9f) is only recorded by Garrucci (no. 191.2) who does not
provide details of size, origin or present whereabouts. From the figure it would
appear to be a larger piece than R 1. It shows the two women frontally posed,
without halos, both with topknots and dressed in tunics under pallia. Both hold
their hands in the orant pose at shoulder height, and the two figures are enclosed
within two toothed circles, produced by pulling a series of semicircles away
from the inner circle to form the outer band.

---

[85] For some discussion of this issue see R. Garrucci, *Storia della arte* III (1876), 144, in the
discussion of Gold Glass in Plate 178.11.

[86] C. Morey, *Gold Glass* (1959), 15 and Plate IX.

[87] Note that in total there are only 21 items of gold glass bearing images of Agnes and/or
Mary since number 1 and 22 are the same object scored respectively for its image of Agnes and
Mary.

[88] C. Morey, *Gold Glass* (1959), 47.

Table 1. Images of the female saint, Agnes on Roman Gold Glass

R No.* Morey* No; D = Diameter (where available)	Inscription(s) and description of the Image	Present Site; Find site if known; (Figure where present) Garrucci** Number (where present)
1 265 D = 5.3 cm	AGNES and MARIA facing profile busts with chi-rho sign between	Museo Civico, Bologna (Figure 9e) Garrucci 191.8
2 82 D = 8.85 cm	AGNE Orant between two trees	Vatican Collection (Figure 8a) Garrucci 190.5
3 83 D = 8.0 × 7.3 cm	ACNE (Orant) + PETRVS & PAVLVS – busts only	Vatican Collection (Figure 8b) Garrucci 190.4
4 221 D = 7.7 cm	AGNNES with two doves still embedded in cement in the catacomb	Rome, Cemetery of Panfilo (Figure 8c) Not in Garrucci
5 226 D = 6.8 cm	AGNE with two trees Still in cement	Rome, Cemetery of Novaziano (still *in situ*) Not in Garrucci
6 283 D = 10.1 cm	CHRISTVS AGNES LAVRENTIVS (difficult to read)	Pesaro: Museo d'Arte Garrucci 191.6
7 425 (Fragment) D = 4.8 × 6.0 cm	AGN ES Only top edge of disc with name and edge of halo and top of head survives	Cologne: Romisch Germanisches Museum Not in Garrucci
8 75 D = 8.8 cm	PETRVS ANNES (Orant) PAVLVS ZESES in a square border	Vatican Collection (Figure 8d) Garrucci 190.1
9 84 D = 7.7 cm	AN NE Orant and nimbed with two plants	Vatican Collection (Figure 8e) Garrucci 191.3
10 246 D = 8.9 cm	AN NES orant, nimbed between two plants	Florence Museo Nazionale Garrucci 190.2
11 409 (Fragment) D = 6.5 × 4.0 cm	ANNI BONI: Just letters no figure pose	Paris: Petit Palais Not in Garrucci

12	412 (Fragment) D = 5.5 × 5.2 cm	AN NE Orant	Paris: Petit Palais Not in Garrucci
13	85 (Fragment) D. 7.8 cm	AN GNE Orant	Vatican Collection Garrucci 191.æ
14	121 (Fragment) D. 4.3 × 2.5 cm	NE Indeterminate	Vatican Collection Not in Garrucci
15	124 (Fragment) D. 2.2 × 2.4 cm	NE Orant	Vatican Collection Not in Garrucci
16	248 (Fragment) D. 9.5 cm	AN	Florence: Museo Nazionale Garrucci 191.7
17	77.111 Newark Museum	AN	Newark Museum (Taken from Bradley Appendix 2)
22		AN N EMA RA Two standing orant figures both in tunics & pallia, neither nimbed. Enclosed in two toothed circles of gold	Garrucci 191.2
27	85 D = 7.8 cm	ANGNE (Orant) plus 2 doves	Vatican Collection Garrucci 191.1
32	Largish disc	PETRVS and PAVLVSA with N E between Orant and Paulus all enclosed in square frame with small foliage swirls.	Garrucci 190.3 From the Cemetery of Ponziano
34		AN NE Similar composi- tion to 9, but a smaller disc and no halo.	Garrucci 191.4
35		VINCENTIVS AGNES POLTVS. Similar to No. 6 in composition	Garrucci 191.5

*　**R. No.** = number assigned in this paper;
　Morey No. = number assigned in C. Morey, *Gold Glass* (1959).
**　**Garrucci No.** = that used in the Plates and the text inked to the Plates in R. Garrucci, *Storia della arte* III (1876).

Table 2. Images of Mary the Mother of God, Ever-Virgin, on Roman Gold Glass

R No.* Morey* No; D = Diameter (where available)	Inscription(s) and description of the Image	Present Site; Find site if known; (Figure where present) Garrucci** Number (where present)
18 Not in Morey	MARIA Orant between two plants with two doves behind her shoulders on two columns	Vatican Collection according to Garrucci (Figure 9c) Garrucci* 178.10
19 33 D = 6.5 cm	MARA Orant, nimbed between two plants	Vatican Collection (Figure 9b) Garrucci 178.11
20	MARIA Orant with Peter and Paul	Wolf Collection, Stuttgart (Figure 9d) Garrucci 178.7
21	MARIA between Peter and Paul	From Northcote and Brownlow (1879) (Figure 9a) Garrucci 178.6 where it says it is from the catacombs of St'Agnese.
1 265 D = 5.3 cm	AGNES and MARIA facing busts with chi-rho sign between	Museo Civico, Bologna (Figure 9e) Garrucci 191.8
22	AN N EMA RA Two standing orant figures both in tunics and pallia, neither nimbed.	Garrucci 191.2 (Figure 9f)

*   **R. No.** = number assigned in this paper;
    Morey No. = number assigned in C. Morey, *Gold Glass*, (1959).
** **Garrucci No.** = that used in the Plates and the text inked to the Plates in R. Gar-
    rucci, *Storia della arte* III (1876).

In addition, Garrucci, (1876) includes four more discs bearing an image of
Mary (Table 2 lists all six examples with their Garrucci (1876) numbers in
column 4.[89]

---

[89] For the Garrucci numbers of these examples see Table 2.

ii. *Images of Mary with Peter and Paul*

Two images (R 21 and R 20) depict MARIA between PETRVS and PAVLVS (Figure 9a and d respectively). R 21 is Plate XXII.1 from Northcote and Brownlow who provide no details of provenance.[90] This disc appears identical to Garrucci Plate 178.6, who reports that the object came from the Catacombs of St' Agnese fuori le mura.[91] R 20 forms part of the Wolf collection held in Stuttgart and appears in rather pristine condition (as far as can be judged from the image in the catalogue).[92] Peter stands on the left of the disc in R 20 and on the right in R 21. Both examples appear to have identical decorative patterns enclosing the figures to that found in R 22, suggesting they could all be from the same workshop or craftsman. Mary adopts the orant pose in both examples but in Figure 9a she holds her hands unusually low, at hip height, with open palms facing the viewer, while in Figure 9d she holds them either side of her head. In both cases there is an established floor level, in Figure 9a two rotuli are placed vertically between the three heads, in Figure 9d the background between the two figures includes a few gold blobs and possibly a couple of schematic pieces of vegetation.

Mary's hair is loosely drawn back and she has a small top-knot in Figure 9a. She is neither veiled nor nimbed. The three figures are of equal height, the male figures being togate. Mary appears to be using her outstretched hands to involve the two saints, while the two saints both point with the index finger of their right hand, to their left shoulder. Paul, on the left, could be pointing to Mary, but Peter, on the right appears to be pointing to his name. Both Peter and Paul are clean-shaven and with identical features instead of possessing their more usual individual characteristics.

Figure 9d shows Mary as an orant with her arms bent and her hands held either side of her head, with the palms displayed. She is flanked by two smaller figures of PETRVS and PAVLVS, each holding a stubby scroll between their two hands. Mary in wearing a veil and a cloak over a tunic and her hair is parted in the middle, so there is no top-knot. The feet of the two male figures are remarkable. Each left foot in encased in a heeled shoe that appears to cover the entire foot and resembles those worn by Agnes in R 2 (Figure 8a), that of PAVLVS encroaches on the inner ring of the boundary of the disc. The left foot of each of the two males appears bare and the divisions of the toes are visible. Like Paul's left foot, Peter's right foot encroaches on the gold rim. This is the only example of a disc in which a section of the image extends into the rim of the design. As with the previous example, the two apostles are clean-shaven and

---

[90] J. Spencer Northcote and W.R. Brownlow, *Roma Sotterranea, Part Two: Christian Art* (London, 1879), 305-6 and Plate XXII.1 opposite p 312.

[91] R. Garrucci, *Storia della arte* III (1876), 143 and Plate 178.6.

[92] E. Marianne Stern, *Roman, Byzantine and Early Medieval Glass: 10 BCE – 700 CE* (Ostfildern, c. 2001), 139-40 and Catalogue no. 66, 170, and 179 with a plate.

Figure 8. Note: Figures are not all to the same scale.
Examples of gold glass containing figures labelled Agnes:
a = gold glass R 2;
b = gold glass R 3;
c = gold glass R 4.
Examples labelled Annes or Anne, but probably meant to represent Agnes:
d = gold glass R 8;
e = gold glass R 9.
Example of orant figure DVLCIS ANIMA or 'sweet soul':
f = gold glass R 25.

not differentiated, but both are smaller than Mary. Mary's left foot also wears a heeled shoe, her right foot is difficult to interpret, but the two feet here are similar to those of Agnes in R 2 (Figure 8a). The catalogue gives the provenance of this disc as the Borgia Collection in Rome. It does not include any details of its catacomb of origin.[93] Garrucci lists it as 178.7, mentioning the Borgia provenance but not where it was found. It is not in Morey. No measurements are available for R 21, but R 20 has a diameter of 8.6 cm. The border as with the two previous examples, consists of a circle with serrations facing outwards matched by a pattern of small gold 'cup-shaped' decorations forming an outer circle. Altogether the apparently pristine condition of this example must raise some suspicions about it genuineness, no real judgement on this is possible without direct inspection (which has not proved possible). Stern says that it was mentioned by Arevalo in the poems of Sedulius of Rome in 1794.[94]

Two examples of an orant Agnes flanked by Peter and Paul (Table 1 R 3 and R 8; Figure 8b and d) survive. Both are quite different in their organisation from the two examples of Mary with Peter and Paul (Figure 9a and d). In Figure 8d, three figures of equal size are enclosed in a linear *square* frame outside of which the names of the saints PETRVS ANNES PAVLVS are inscribed, while in Figure 8b PETRVS and PAVLVS are positioned below AGNE, with the letters of their names almost forming a halo around their heads and only the upper half of their bodies being included in the disc. Once again as with those depicting Mary with the apostles, the apostles are clean-shaven and not differentiated from each other, except through their inscriptions.

iii. *Mary alone as an Orant*

R 19 (Figure 9b) is part of the Vatican collection and depicts MARA as an orant, nimbed and standing alone flanked by two small trees. The disc is a little larger than that of Agnes and Mary facing each other (R 1), at 6.5 cm, but, given its rather small size, more likely to come from the base of a cup than a bowl. Here Mary wears a loose patterned under-tunic belted under the bust, not dissimilar to that worn by Nonnosa in the catacombs of S. Gennaro in Naples (Figure 6) and by Agnes or the un-named female saint in all six of the examples in Figure 8. A shawl is draped over MARA's arms and hangs down either side inside the two flanking trees. A similar arrangement of a shawl occurs with Agnes in R 2 (Figure 8a), although here the shawl also passes over Agnes' head); in R4 (Figure 8c) and in R 9 (Figure 8e). In R 4 the arms are held out in the orant pose at bust level. This is a common position for Agnes or for unnamed saints although the hands can also be either side of the head. In all cases the palms face the viewer.

---

[93] E.M. Stern, *Early Medieval Glass* (2001), 170.
[94] *Ibid.*

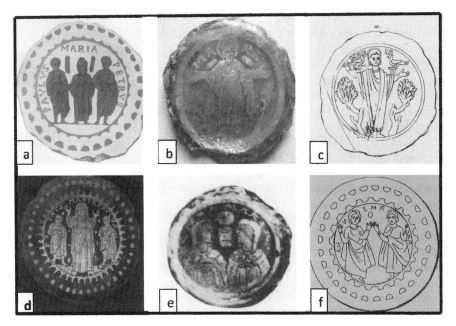

Figure 9. Note: Figures are not all to the same scale.
The six pieces of gold glass bearing a named image of Mary.
a = R 21: MARIA flanked by Paul and Peter;
b = R 19: MARA as an orant standing alone flanked by foliage;
c = R.18: MARIA as an orant standing alone flanked by foliage with two birds on her shoulders;
d = R 20: MARIA in the orant pose flanked by Peter and Paul;
e = R 1: Agnes and MARIA as busts facing a chi-rho sign;
f = R 22: Anne and MARA frontally posed in orant position.
(Photos: copyright E. Rubery).

In Figure 9b MARA is nimbed and this is the only example of a gold glass in which she is nimbed. Agnes is nimbed in Figures 8c and e, but not elsewhere in Figure 8. She is also nimbed in R 10 (Garrucci 190.2). Mary is flanked by two small trees in both images of her alone as an orant (Figures 9b and c) and in Figure 9c she also stands in front of columns on which two doves are perched. In the images of Agnes standing alone as an orant a similar range of compositions are found: with doves resting on pillars in Figure 8c and trees flanking her body in Figure 8a and e. Agnes has a shawl draped around her arms in Figure 8a, c and e, just as Mary has in Figure 9b. This example is in the Vatican collection and is only slightly bigger in diameter than Figure 9e, which depicts Mary and Agnes. Both are examples of gold glass composed of three layers of glass. As with Figure 9b, Morey suggests this disc originally formed the base of a cup. Morey does not identify this as bearing an image of Mary, and omits her from his subject list of images of Mary.[95]

R 18 (Figure 9c) is the final example of an orant gold glass bearing the name of Mary. It is only described by Garrucci who, nevertheless, ascribes it to the Vatican collection. I have never seen it on display. The drawing in Garrucci shows an orant MARIA with the hands held somewhat higher than R 19 at Figure 9b, but again with palms facing the viewer, flanked by two birds (presumably intended to represent doves). The one on the right appears to be standing on a column while the arrangement on the left is unclear. Two trees sprout from the ground, ending below her hands. Mary appears from the drawing to be standing on the inner rim of the circle of gold that bounds the scene. She is wearing what looks like a toga that narrows towards the lower hem, and is not wearing a veil. There is a double line around her head, which probably indicates a cap, but one of the lines could be intended to indicate a small halo. Garrucci does not provide diameters of the pieces, but from the drawing this would appear to be of similar size to Figures 9b and e.

Taken altogether these six examples do not suggest that depictions of Mary in the gold glass selected for the catacombs were popular. In Figure 9 the two most convincing examples, (b) and (e), are of relatively small size, and Figure 9c, from the size of the drawing, may also be of similar small size. The example in the Wolf collection (R 20) is of dubious provenance, R 18 is only available at present in a drawing in Garrucci, who attributes it to the Vatican although it does not figure in Morey's catalogue. Only one of the five images is nimbed. The presence of the two chief apostles, Peter and Paul either side of Mary in (a) and (d) makes it highly likely the intention in these two was to depict the Mother of God, not a lady whose name happens to be Mary. The example where MARIA is depicted alone and not nimbed (R 18) leaves open the possibility that the figure was intended to simply represent an elite lady named MARIA. Similarly the example labelled MARA could be meant to represent a member of a family bearing that name although the presence of a halo makes that less likely.[96]

Overall this small collection of ladies labelled with variants of MARIA (Table 2 and Figure 9) permits us to draw the firm conclusion that Mary, the Mother of God was rarely depicted on the gold glass that ended up in the catacombs in the fourth century. Furthermore, when females bearing this name (or variants of it) were depicted alone or with other saints, the iconography

---

[95] This is probably an error in the compilation of the table rather than a reflection on the status of the object, as these tables, compiled by Ferrara during the editing of the book prior to publication, while useful, are not entirely reliable.

[96] See p. 149.

most closely resembled that of the more popular (in terms of gold glass image production) Virgin Saint Agnes.

iv. *Images of S. Agnes in gold glass*

22 examples of surviving Gold Glass include an image of Agnes (Table 1) if we accept (as was discussed above) that the wide variety of miss-spelt versions of names beginning with 'A' were all intended to represent S. Agnes. Apart from Agnes, few other named female saints are found. There is one example of Peter and Paul flanking 'Peregrina' (R 33, Table 3). Agnes herself, if accompanied, is usually flanked by SS Peter and Paul, although there is one example of Agnes flanked by 'VINCENTIVS' and 'POLTVS'[97] (R 35) and one example of Agnes flanked by 'CHRISTVS' and 'LAVRENTIVS' (R 6). Seven of the examples bearing variants of Agnes have only survived as a fragment, usually making reconstruction of the iconography almost impossible. There are also over 14 examples of gold glass where an unnamed female orant is depicted (Table 3 and Figure 8f).

There are ten examples (Table 1: numbers 4-10, 13, 27 and 35) where the inscription clearly specifies Agnes, notwithstanding some degree of mis-spelling: The range of iconography includes the types already found for Mary, with the saint appearing alone as an orant, with the apostles Peter and Paul either smaller than she is or the same size or paired with Mary. In two cases (Figure 8c from the Catacombs of Panfilo and Figure 8e; Morey 84, the figure has a halo. The Catacomb of Panfilo Agnes is a particularly splendidly dressed example of the saint as an elite virgin, somewhat resembling Nonnosa (Figure 6). She is dressed in a tunic decorated with elaborate swirls and has pearls in her ears and around her top-knot. These embellishments also remind us of the image of Mary as the Virgin in the mosaics of the triumphal arch at S. Maria Maggiore (Figure 1 and Cecchelli Plate XLIX).[98] In addition to these examples, Agnes appears as the central figure flanked by other saints on two occasions, (nos. 6 and 35) in the first example being flanked by Vincentius and Poltus (the latter probably intended to be read as Hippolytus) and in the second case, flanked by Christus and Laurentius.

Additional examples of Agnes are almost certainly present amongst the fragments of gold glass. R 14 and R 15 in Table 1 have the last two letters of their inscription surviving as …NE which is compatible with Anne or Agne. One of these (R 15, Morey 124), is an orant, the other is too incomplete for the pose to be determined. R 16 and R 17 retain only AN…, again compatible with AGNES but also consistent with ANIMA or ANONE.

---

[97] Possibly intended to be Hippolytus.
[98] Carlo Cecchelli, *I mosaici della basilica di S. Maria Maggiore* (Torino, 1956).

Table 3. Images of female figures in the orant pose on Roman
Gold Glass where the figure is un-named or ambiguously named in the
inscription (Selection)

R No.* Morey* No; D = Diameter (where available)	Inscription(s) and description of the Image	Present Site; Find site if known; (Figure where present) Garrucci** Number (where present)
11 409 (Fragment) D = 6.5 × 4.0 cm	ANNI BONi	Paris: Petit Palais Not in Garrucci*
14 121 (fragment) D = 4.3 × 2.5 cm	..NE Pose cannot be determined	Vatican Collection
15 124 (fragment) D = 2.3 × 2.2	..NE Orant – right hand visible	Vatican Collection
16 248 (fragment) D = 9.5 cm	AN Left head and left arm in orant pose on a female figure	Florence: Museo Nazionale
17 77.111 Newark Museum	AN	Newark Museum (Taken from Bradley Appendix 2)
23 379 (fragment) D = 11.4 cm	DIGNTIASAMIC(orum) Male and female orants with chi-rho sign	Pusey House/Ashmolean Garrucci 194.3
24 411 (Fragment) D = 5.0 × 4.0 cm	ZHCAIC ANIMA BONA	Paris: Petit Palais
25 48 D = 8.6 cm	DVLCIS ANIMA PIE ZESES VIVAS Female Orant with two plants	Vatican Collection Garrucci 178.8 Figure 8f
26 57 (fragment) D = 6.4 × 3.6 cm	(pie zes) ESBENE(dictorum) Good Shepherd with part of an orant figure visible underneath	Vatican Collection Garrucci 171.5
28 165 small disc D = 2.0 cm	Laterally posed veiled headed figure of woman with outstretched hands at shoulder height	Vatican Collection Garrucci 178.1

29	334 small disc D = 2.5	Laterally posed woman with outstretched hands at shoulder height and belt/ veil blowing in the wind	From British Museum Garrucci, 178.2
30	small disc	Frontally posed woman with orant hands at shoulder height and veil	Garrucci 178.9
31	small disc	Frontally posed veiled woman with orant hands at shoulder height and two trees either side of her	Garrucci 178.12 Found in the Garden of S. Eusebius.
33	largish disc	PETRVSPAVLVS P ER EGRI NA. Peter and Paul both point to Peregrina, centrally in the orant pose. A small flower is situated on the left of Peter and a second flower between Peregrinus and Paulus. All are enclosed in a square frame.	Garrucci 190.6

*   **R. No.** = number assigned in this paper;
    Morey No. = number assigned in C. Morey, *Gold Glass*, (1959).
** **Garrucci No.** = that used in the Plates and the text inked to the Plates in R. Garrucci, *Storia della arte* III (1876).

One example of a gold glass disc (R 33, Table 3) bears a completely different named female orant: 'PEREGRINA' between SS Peter and Paul. This is a name that Garrucci was unable find any trace of elsewhere in early Christian art.[99]

Finally a group of similarly posed female images bear more generalised inscription. The word ANIMA (soul) (Table 3, R 24 and R 25) is common but numerous other variants also occur. Another largish fragment in poor condition, bears the inscription DIGNITISAMIC(orum) and a male and a female orant with a chi-rho sign between them (Table 3: No 23). Many of these fragments are in poor condition so that details of the figure(s) depicted are unclear. As well as named saints being used to invoke support for the deceased person, these suggest that more general invocations to God to care for the soul of the dead person were sometimes made, somewhat similar to the more anonymous

---

[99] R. Garrucci, *Storia della arte* III (1876), 170.

images of orants that were common in a pagan context, as in the cubiculum of the *Velatio* in the catacombs of Priscilla (Figure 5).

From this analysis it can be concluded that, in the fourth century (the period when gold glass was being made)[100] the virgin Mary, Mother of God, the virgin saint, Agnes, and various anonymous female orant figures were treated in a very similar fashion iconographically. They could all be depicted flanked by the two main apostles, Peter and Paul, flanked by doves as evidence of constancy,[101] or alone. From the evidence of the Vatican collection and the additional material assessed by Morey, Garrucci and other writers in the field, it would appear that by far the most popular female cult saint to be invoked at this period in connection with the burial of the dead was Agnes not Mary. The most elaborately decorated image of a female saint in the collection is the example of Agnes found in the Catacombs of Panfilo (R 4). Here she is depicted as an elite virgin, nimbed, richly dressed in a tunic with an elaborately embroidered overgarment, with her hair and ears decorated with pearls and flanked by two doves on columns. No comparably elaborately dressed image of Mary survives in gold glass. While the total number of surviving examples of female figures are not great, the dominance of S. Agnes over S. Mary in these glasses from the catacombs is unmistakable, suggesting that the Marian cult in the fourth century was as yet not fully developed, while that of S. Agnes flourished.

V. Images of the Virgin Saints including Mary in Rome in the early churches and on icons up to the early 8th century

To assess how the cults of these two saints subsequently developed, we shall now consider the way these two saints were subsequently portrayed in surviving iconic images *outside of* the catacombs up to the early 8th century in Rome. In this way a wider perspective can be gained on the iconography that followed these gold glass discs and the relative prominence of the cults of Mary and Agnes after the 4th century be assessed.

Images of S. Agnes

The situation with respect to images of S. Agnes outside of the catacombs is both intriguing and informative. Only one significant major image of her

---

[100] E.M. Stern, *Early Medieval Glass* (2001), 170.

[101] The widow Turtura, in the inscription attached to the fresco in which she stands in front of the enthroned Virgin and child in the Catacombs of Commodilla, remained unwed for 36 years after the death of her husband and was consequently likened to a turtle dove who had no other love after the death of its mate: B. Bagatti, *Il Cimiterio di Commodilla o dei martiri Felici e Adautto* (Vatican, 1936), 42.

Figure 10. Drawing of the enthroned Mary, dressed as a Byzantine Empress, holding the Christ-child and flanked by two angels. This is on the right side of the apsidal arch at S. Maria Antiqua in Rome. The vertical line A_____A marks the existing left edge of the fresco, which is congruent with the edge of the present apse. It is presumed that before the enlargement of the niche in the apsidal wall to form the present full apse, there was a second angel on the left of Mary. This is lightly sketched in on the left of the lin A_____A. (Drawing copyright E. Rubery).

survives in Rome from this period, at the catacomb church of St'Agnese fuori le mura on the Via Nomentana. Here in the 7th century apse mosaic, against a uniform gold background, the patron for the mosaic, Pope Honorius (625-638) with Pope Symmachus (498-514) stand either side of a centrally placed image of Agnes, nimbed and dressed in a blue tunic covered by an elaborately decorated Y-shaped over-garment and collar (Figure 11).[102] Agnes does not adopt the orant pose here, but holds a white shawl on her left arm, and a scroll tied with a ribbon, bearing a cross, between her two hands. A red fire billows around her

---

[102] Walter Oakeshott, *The Mosaics of Rome* (London 1967), Plate XVI opposite p. 148 and Figure 87. The present basilica was built by Pope Honorius, the one referred to in the *vita* of Pope Liberius is now thought to be the large 'catacomb' church whose footings can still be seen adjacent to the present church and to which the surviving Mausoleum of S. Costanza was originally attached: R. Davis, *Pontiffs* (1989), xxxiii.

Figure 11. *Left:* The apse at St'Agnese fuori le mura depicting Agnes flanked by the two popes with the hand of God above her head. *Right:* Detail of Agnes showing her elaborately be-jewelled over garment and collar, and decorated head=dress resembling that of Mary in S. Maria Antiqua in Figure Ten (Photo: copyright E. Rubery).

feet, recalling one of the elements of her martyrdom. Pope Honorius, who, according to the inscription was the patron for the production of the mosaic, holds a model of the church in his hands, while Pope Symmachus holds a codex. At the apex of the conch, above a starry sky, the hand of God can be seen conferring a martyr's crown on Agnes.

Elements of this image of Agnes bear strong similarities to certain aspects of the fresco of Mary enthroned with the Christ child and Angels found on the right side of the apsidal arch at S. Maria Antiqua (Figure 10, mentioned in the Introduction above) although by the time this mosaic was made, that image had long been covered with later frescoes.[103] But this is not the first Roman church to have been built adjacent to the catacombs of St'Agnese. The remains of an earlier 4th century church, to which the Mausoleum of S. Costanza was originally attached, can still be seen in the grounds of the present church.[104] No information on the decoration of the apsidal conch of this earlier church survives, but given that it was common practise in Rome to repeat earlier iconography when a new

[103] G. Rushforth, PBSR I (1902), 1-123, esp. 66-8.
[104] R. Davis, *Pontiffs* (1989), xxxiii.

building replaced an older one, it is quite possible that the figure of Agnes on the present apse reproduced an image of her from the earlier catacomb church and that the image in that earlier church *was* based upon the image of the enthroned Mary on the apsidal arch at Santa Maria Antiqua before the fresco was obliterated.

Until the 9th century in Rome, the apses of titular churches were commonly decorated with a central figure of Christ flanked by S. Peter and S. Paul, and/or beyond them by the titular saint(s) of the church and/or the patron(s).[105] There is no evidence of a saint, whether male or female, being placed in the centre of the apse, *instead* of Christ in Rome until the 9th century. The presence of the hand of God above Agnes, exactly mimicking the usual arrangements for central images of Christ in apses in Rome at this period, is even more unusual for Roman apses in the early medieval period.[106] The earliest surviving apsidal conch of a major Roman church that shows Mary in the centre is that in S. Maria Domnica, commissioned by Pope Paschal I (817-824) probably sometime around 820. Even here there is no hand of God at the apex of the apse. Instead, Christ, enthroned with his apostles, forms a band across the upper portion of the apsidal arch, representing the authority that Mary in the apse is addressing on behalf of mankind from her position in the conch of the apse below Him.[107]

The martyrdom of S. Agnes occurred in Diocletian's reign (245-311) and an inscription from her place of burial in the Catacombs, commissioned by Pope Damasius (366-384), is displayed at the foot of the stairs that lead to the present church.[108] From behind the apse it is still possible to directly access the catacombs linked to the church, and it is this connection that I suggest explains the unusual iconography of this apse. For if the main service being held in this church was the rite for the burial of the dead before the body was laid to rest in the catacomb dedicated to S. Agnes, then it would be natural for the dead person and their family to want the service to be carried out in the invoked presence of *that* saint. Placing an image of S. Agnes in the centre of the apse would then have made liturgical sense, in the same way as placing an image of Christ in the centre of the apse of a titular church made liturgical sense in churches where the Eucharist was the service celebrated most frequently at the main altar.

---

[105] These all take as their model the original apse at S. Peter's where Christ is flanked by Peter and Paul: W. Oakeshott, *Mosaics* (1967), Figure 29. See for example the apsidal conch at SS Cosma e Damiano, H. Kessler and J. Zacharias, *Rome 1300* (2000), 98.

[106] This iconography does, however, occur in the 6th century in the Basilica at Poreč (Ann Terry and Henry Maguire, *Dynamic splendor: the wall mosaics in the Cathedral of Eufrasius at Poreč and in three surviving churches in Cypress* [Pennsylvania, 2007]) and in three surviving small churches commonly dedicated to the seventh century in Cyprus: Andreas Stylianou and Judith A. Stylianou, *The Painted Churches of Cyprus* (Cyprus, 1987), 43-52.

[107] W. Oakeshott, *Mosaics* (1957), 203-4 and Plate XX opposite p. 204.

[108] W. Oakeshott, *Mosaics* (1957), 148.

Figure 12. *Left*: Engraving of the central section of the mosaic in Pope John VII's
funerary chapel in Old S. Peter's. The centre was an image of Mary as an orant, receiving the model of his church from Pope John. (Engraving from Vat. Lat, 11988 70v-71r).
Right: The surviving mosaic fragment of the orant Mary crowned as an Empress, now
in the church of S. Marco in Florence (Photo: copyright E. Rubery).

In the funerary chapel in Old S. Peter's commissioned by Pope John VII
(705-707) around 706, an orant image of Mary is situated immediately behind
the altar (Figure 12). Three inscriptions included in the mosaic say:

- That Pope John had built the chapel (+IOHANNES INDIGNVS EPISCOPVS
FECIT+;
- Describes John as the servant of the Mother of God (BEATAE DEI GENE-
TRICIS SERVVS);
- And dedicates the chapel to the Mother of God (DOMVS SCAE DEI GENI-
TRICIS MARIAE).

In addition an epitaph placed in the chapel made it clear that Pope John intended this chapel to be the final resting place for his body.[109]

The mosaic of the orant Mary, crowned as an Empress, but wearing clothes not dissimilar in design to those worn by the orant figures of the saints in the gold glass, but now decorated with Byzantine gems and pearls, survives and is now kept in the Basilica of San Marco in Florence, having been transferred there when Old S. Peter's was pulled down in the 17th century.[110] This is irrefutable evidence that by the beginning of the eighth century the cult of Mary had been endorsed by the Papacy and was flourishing in Rome. It also suggests that the papacy now saw Mary not just as a female saint but also as the equal of the Imperial Byzantine Empresses of the East.

At least two additional images of Mary depicted as an orant are known to have been produced in the period up to 707 in Rome:

– In the chapel of S. Venantius in the Lateran Baptistery, where she is situated under a giant bust of Christ in the mosaic in the apsidal conch leading towards Christ a procession of the saints whose relics had been translated to the chapel from Dalmatia. These relics had been moved on the orders of Pope John IV (640-642) who had the chapel be built and decorated specifically to receive them.[111]
– In the icon of Mary often called the *Madonna Avvocata,* now in the church of San Sisto Vecchio, possibly dated to the 8th century, where Mary poses in profile and adopts the orant pose used by the parents of Nonnosa in the fresco in the catacombs of S. Gennaro in Naples (Figure 5).[112]

So, as the cult of Mary developed in Rome, and images were placed in churches and chapels rather than in catacombs, images of her as an orant continued to be popular, and indeed, in Old S. Peter's, led to her depiction as an Empress, interceding with Christ for the soul of the defunct Pope John VII.

VI. The Relationship between the cult of S. Agnes and the cult of Mary

This examination of images of S. Agnes and Mary, the Mother of God in the Roman catacombs clearly demonstrates that Agnes dominated and Mary was very

---

[109] H. Kessler and J. Zacharias, *Rome 1300* (2000), 212-4; E. Rubery, 'Papal images of Mary', in C. Maunder (ed.), *Origins* (2008), 155-204, esp. 158-9, Figure 2 and front cover; W. Oakeshott, *Mosaics of Rome* (1957), Figure 108.

[110] Vat. Lat. 11988 folios 70v and 71r; E. Rubery, 'Papal images of Mary', in C. Maunder (ed.), *Origins* (2008), the cover image, 155-204, esp. 158, 159: Figure 2 and 174-8 including Figure 17 and Table 2d.

[111] E. Rubery, 'Papal images of Mary', in C. Maunder (ed.), *Origins* (2008), 155-204, esp. 172-3 and Figure 2; W. Oakeshott, *Mosaics* (1957), Figure 99 and 101.

[112] E. Rubery, 'Papal images of Mary', in C. Maunder (ed.), *Origins* (2008), 155-204, esp. 173-4, Figure 16 and Table 2d.

much a minor figure in 4th century gold glass from the Roman catacombs. Images of Mary were also rare in frescoes and sarcophagi in the catacombs in this early period, except when Mary was represented as part of the Adoration of Christ by the Magi. However, by the 6th-9th centuries, when panel paintings and monumental paintings become the main vehicle for decorating the churches that now replace the catacombs as the site for the burial of the dead, Mary, the Mother of God dominated and images of Agnes were largely confined to her titular cult site. The early prominence of images of Agnes could be seen as evidence of widespread popularity of this cult Rome in the 4th century, a prominence that subsequently declined as the cult of Mary developed in Rome in the sixth and seventh centuries. Given that the cult of Mary developed somewhat earlier in the Byzantine East than it did in the West, several writers have suggested that the increase in the prominence of the cult of Mary in the second half of the sixth century in Rome and the West was at least in part a consequence of the re-conquest of the West by General Narses on behalf of Emperor Justinian from around 550.[113]

However, when this pictorial information is integrated with the literary material from the same period in Rome, the situation with respect to the cult of Agnes appears more localised. The Liber Pontificalis (LP), or book of the biographies of the popes, tells us that, around the time of manufacture of these gold glass discs, Pope Liberius (352-366), having been recalled from an exile of over three years by the 'Arian' Emperor Constantius II (337-61), stayed at the church of S. Agnese fuori le mura with the Emperor's sister, Constantina Augusta.[114] The scribe tells us that Liberius hoped Constantia would intercede with Augustus Constantius and so enable him to return to his post of Pope without having to accept the 'Arian' doctrine then espoused by Constantius II. (The papacy at that time adhered to the doctrine of the anti-Arian and anti-Eusebian bishops).[115] From this and other sources we know that Liberius eventually temporarily gave in to Constantius and appeared to embrace the 'Arian' faith, but that the death of Constantius in 361 allowed him to return Rome and to return the Western church to the anti-Arian doctrine.[116] Liberius' biographical entry also mentions that it was the imperial family that originally stimulated the construction of the first church at the catacombs of Agnese and that Pope Liberius also decorated the tomb of St'Agnese with marble tablets.[117]

---

[113] John Osborne, 'The cult of Maria Regina in Early Medieval Rome', *Acta ad Archaeologiam et Artium Historiam Pertinentia* 21 (2008), 95-106; B. Pentcheva, *Icons and Power* (2006).

[114] Louis Duchesne (trans.), *Liber Pontificalis* I (Paris, 1955), 207-10.

[115] *Vita* of Pope Liberius: Louis Duchesne (trans.), *Liber Pontificalis* I (1955), 207-10; Raymond Davis (trans.), *The Book of Pontiffs* (Liber Pontificalis) (1989), 29-30; J.N.D. Kelly, *Dictionary of Popes* (Oxford, 1986), 30-1.

[116] *Ibid.*

[117] Latin = *Platonis marmoreis*. Little of this earliest church survives. The LP records in Pope Symmachus' *Vita* (498-514) that he repaired the whole basilica, mentioning in particular that the

This raises the possibility that the high number of gold glass discs from this period bearing the name of Agnes were specifically stimulated by the high profile given to the basilica and catacombs of St'Agnese by the presence there for a period of a year or so, of an Empress and a Pope? Was the use of these symbols in a funerary context in some way linked to the dispute between the papacy and the emperor? Could the preparation of these discs be linked in any way to the various changes in doctrinal policy that clearly took place during this rather tumultuous period? Could the image of S. Agnes even have acted as a covert symbol of support for the embattled Pope and the anti-Arian doctrine? Unfortunately the dating of these glasses within the second half of the 4th century is not well developed so it is not possible to identify when any particular glass was made. However, a more detailed study of the sources from this period does throws additional light on events. Emperor Constantius II's sister, Constantia, daughter of Constantine the Great, was indeed an Augusta and is indeed credited, earlier in the Liber Pontificalis, with stimulating her father, Constantine the Great, to build and endow the basilica of S. Agnes.[118] But after Constantina married her second husband, Constantius Gallus, in 351, the couple were sent to Syria and Antioch to defend part of the Eastern Roman Empire from the Persians. In 354 they were recalled to Rome by Constantius, but on the way back Constantina died in Bithynia.[119] Constantina was indeed then buried 'on the Via Nomentana at Rome', and this statement by Ammianus Marcellinus is usually taken to mean that she was buried at St'Agnese.[120]

These additional facts make her involvement in the dispute between Liberius and Constantius impossible since this dispute only started after her death. They do, however, demonstrate the strong link that existed in the fourth century between the imperial family and the St'Agnese site. Indeed Constantina's body is thought to have been placed in the large porphyry sarcophagus now in the Vatican Library. These facts therefore confirm that some stimulation of the cult of S. Agnes by the imperial family in the second half of the 4th century probably

---

apse was liable to collapse. This does not refer to the present building, built by Pope Honorius around 625, but probably to the earlier building whose remains can now be seen on the right as one approaches the entrance to the Mausoleum of Costanza (R. Davis [trans.], *Pontiffs* [1989], xxxiii). The Mausoleum was probably originally attached to this earlier church. Pope Honorius I (625-638) built 'from the ground up' the present basilica and decorated the apse with its present mosaic (LP 72.3 of *Vita of Honorius*; R. Davis [trans.], *Pontiffs* [1989], 65-7). The fact that this church was placed under the control of the clerics of S. Vitale by Pope Innocent I (401/402-417) suggests that this early church was not a regular parish church but rather a catacomb church that needed to source its clergy from outside (R. Davis, *Pontiffs* [1989], 32-4).

[118] *Vita* of Pope Sylvester (314-335), R. Davis (trans.), *Pontiffs* (1989), 34:23, p. 22.

[119] A.H.M. Jones, J.R. Martindale, and J. Morris, 'Constantina 2', *The Prosopography of the Later Roman Empire* (Cambridge, 1971), 1.222.

[120] Ammianus Marcellinus, Walter Hamilton (ed.), *The Later Roman Empire (A.D. 354-378)* (Middlesex, 1986), 41.

occurred.[121] The imperial family and Pope Liberius could indeed have worked together to establish and maintain S. Agnese as an important burial site. The building of the imperial Mausoleum adjacent to the ancient basilica on the orders of Constantius following a request from Constantina demonstrates their particular association with the site, an association that would have increased its profile in Rome. These imperial links could undoubtedly have encouraged increasing popularity for the cult of S. Agnes in Rome, even if the story of the Augusta's residence at the site during Liberius' dispute with Constantius is a fiction.

When trying to reconstruct events surrounding gold glass it is important to remember that almost certainly its primary function had nothing to do with the catacombs. From the large collection of images of family groups that also survive, it is clear that dishes bearing these artefacts were frequently (probably usually) made for general household use. Only following damage to the bowl, or perhaps following the death of those depicted on the disc, would the glass object be used as a marker in the catacombs. Therefore if the imperial family felt a particular link with the cult of S. Agnes, they might also have created series of cups and/or bowls bearing her image in gold on the bases. Such objects are unlikely to have been particularly expensive. There is a clear subset of gold glass portraits that are made to a high standard, but the majority of examples, while attractive, are likely to have been made by relatively unskilled craftsmen, if the quality of the design and the spelling of the inscriptions is anything to go by. Such objects would have been attractive gifts and been suitable for incorporating into household objects, such as tableware to be used at dinners and other ceremonial events. This would inevitably also result in a supply of broken glass vessels which might then be used to decorate burial sites. Objects bearing imagery linked to the cult of St'Agnese, especially if specifically commissioned by the imperial family for personal use or as personal gifts to others in the imperial court, would be valued by lesser mortals even if damaged and discarded. Embedding these discs in the cement of the loculi in the catacombs as markers for their friends and relatives in the catacombs could have provided an additional 'imperial' aura. Furthermore, given Constantine's belief in his special relationship between himself and Christ and his position as Christ's 'Gerund' on earth, it is quite possible that courtiers and the public would perceive a saint commanding such imperial support as particularly likely to be effective in interceding with Christ in the afterlife precisely *because* of her close links with the imperial family.

We know that the most elegant gold glass image of Agnes came from the Catacomb of Panfilo, not the catacomb of St'Agnese, and that R 21, an image of Mary between Peter and Paul, came from the Catacombs of S. Agnese (Table 2). But unfortunately the origins of most surviving examples of gold glass were not recorded. R 5, depicting an orant Agnes between two trees is still *in situ* in

---

[121] L. Duchesne (trans.), *Liber Pontificalis* I (1957), 208, note 10.

the catacombs of Novaziano (Table 1). But neither Morey nor Garrucci in his *Storia della arte* III provide any information on the site of origin of the rest of the pieces in these tables. Of the 12 examples in Table 3 (an incomplete list of unnamed orant figures) a site of origin is only provided for number R 31, a frontally posed woman flanked by two trees in a small disc, identified as from the Gardens of Eusebius,[122] and for No. 32, identified by Garrucci as from the Cemetery of Ponziano and depicting an image of Peter and Paul either side of an orant with isolated letters A N and E between Paul and the orant.

VII. Conclusions

As the above analysis has clearly shown, the orant iconography of Mary can be traced back to the ubiquitous orant figure in sepulchral art, who, from the earliest periods interceded with the heavenly powers linked to whichever faith the dead person had followed. The art of the catacombs in the 3rd and fourth centuries reveals, however, that Mary did not come to occupy this role to any significant extent until relatively late in the development of her iconography. The images on gold glass (Table 3) suggest that, in the fourth century, in most cases, orant figures continued to be anonymous or personifications of the soul or spirit. The only exception to this rule was S. Agnes, who appears to have enjoyed a period of particular popularity (Table 1) that coincided with references to links between her cult, the Imperial family and the papacy in contemporary written sources. It seems likely that the imperial family owned the land on which her catacomb was situated, and this (perhaps plus the attractiveness of her hagiographic legend which involved the martyrdom of an innocent twelve year old young girl and her sister), possibly encouraged imperial support for her cult. Her cult entered the Roman calendar in 336 and Pope Damasius (366-384) dedicated one of his epitaphs (now placed at the bottom of the stairs leading to the basilica of S. Agnes) to her.[123] S. Agnes' popularity in gold glass does not appear to have been parallelled by comparable images of her on sarcophagi.[124] The catacombs of St'Agnese were not generally frescoed and images of her elsewhere in the catacombs are also rare.[125] Coincidentally the feast day of S. Panfilo, the saint who gave his name to the catacomb where the most elaborate gold glass image of S. Agnes remains *in situ* embedded in its

---

[122] R. Garrucci, *Storia della arte* III (1876), 144.

[123] Fabrizio Bisconti, *Primi Cristiani* (Vatican City, 2013), 109-13, esp 109.

[124] An image of her in orant pose on the side of a sarcophagus dated to the 4th century and from the catacombs of St'Agnese is reproduced in F. Bisconti, *Primi Cristiani* (2013), 111.

[125] One does occur in the Catacombs of Commodilla in the cubiculum of Leone, (an administrator in the food and revenues department in Rome) where she is depicted in orant pose with a single lamb on her left: F. Bisconti, *Primi Cristiani* (2013), 108.

172   E. RUBERY

original cement (R 4), is 21 January,[126] the same as the feast day for S. Agnes. Did these two catacombs perhaps become linked in some way because festival processions took place to them both on the same day?

Taking all these considerations into account, the following conclusions appear justified. Firstly, notwithstanding the popularity of the early apocryphal stories about Mary, it seems clear that, by the 4th century, Mary had not achieved a significant role in the rites surrounding the burial and subsequent remembrance and support of the souls of the dead. In contrast, at this early date Agnes appears to have attained a position of sufficient significance for more gold glass discs bearing her image to have survived than did for Mary or for any other female saint. The site of the catacombs of St'Agnese clearly had a special significance for the imperial family, given the presence there of their imperial mausoleum, and they may have originally owned this site.[127] For this reason the cult probably also enjoyed an enhanced status with others at the imperial court and even with those outside the immediate court circle. It is possible the widespread use of her image on bowls and glasses resulted in a wider availability of fragments that could be used to mark loculi in the catacombs and so explains the preponderance of her image at this period. Notwithstanding this, however, we should remember that images of the two apostles Peter and Paul are over three times more numerous in the catacombs than any female saint,[128] and that examples of other female saints at this time appear negligible (confined to Mary and Peregrina in this survey).[129]

Turning to the iconography of orant images in particular, it is clear that the 'pagan' orant image continued to be popular, important and frequently used in Christian burials. The fact they they this iconography had been used for pagan religious rites does not appear to have affected its widespread popularity. The presence of the two major apostles on gold glass was also frequent, but it is interesting that they could be depicted supporting Agnes *and* Mary, and that no images of these two saints supporting either of the two apostles have survived. This is another pointer supporting the probable exceptional high status of Agnes in the 4th century in Rome.

Inscriptions in the early Christian catacombs do not suggest that the orant figure was particularly associated with invocations to speed the soul of the dead

[126] Agostino Amore, *I Martyri di Roma* (Vatican City, 2013), 19-21.
[127] F. Mancinelli, *Catacombs of Rome* (2012), 92.
[128] L. Grig, 'Portraits' (2004), Table 1, p. 206 identifies around 60 images each of S. Peter and S. Paul, presumably in many of these, both images were present on the same object.
[129] Apart from Agnes and Mary there is only one other female figure depicted in these 'Christian' discs, PEREGRINA, flanked by Peter and Paul (R 33: Table 3) a name that has no particular associations in Rome. In addition there is one disc with Agnes in the centre (R 35) flanked by two lesser known male saints: VINCENTIVS and (? hypPOL[I] TVS (See Table 1).

person towards paradise.[130] From their inscriptions most Christians in this early period appeared certain their dead relative would make their transfer to paradise satisfactorily, and this was reflected in their inscriptions. A mosaic inscription from the Catacombs of Panfilo, for example simply invokes the help of the 'saintly, good and blessed martyrs' in a non-specific way.[131]

The dresses and decorations worn by most images of the two female saints were not particularly elaborate. The richest clothes were worn by the figure of Agnes from the Catacombs of Panfilo, where she wears pearl earrings and a pearl and gem decorated collar that reminds one of the dress of the mother of God in the triumphal arch mosaics of circa 430 in Santa Maria Maggiore (Figure 1). Gold glass images do not include any signs of imperial crowns or imperial sceptres or globes.

Finally, taking a wider perspective, we see from this data that, in the fourth century there was a much greater fluidity in the imagery in the gold glass found in the catacombs than was present outside the catacombs by the 6th century and later. R 6 (Table 1) a disc with Christus on the left of Agnes with Laurentius on her right, would not be iconographically acceptable in the 7th and 8th centuries. Clearly at this early period, a more fluid attitude to status was possible. Agnes could be the focus of the composition and the male apostles be relegated to her supporters, even Christ could be placed in the lateral 'supporting' position beside S. Agnes (as we see in R 6 in Table 1). Reducing the size of supporting images, whoever they represented, was also quite acceptable, as we see in R 3 in Table 1. These gold glass discs do indeed provide a unique insight into the range of iconography that was acceptable in this relatively early period when the 'rules' of Christian imagery were still developing. This paper has only looked at images of female saints, a small fraction of the *ca.* 500 examples of gold glass that has survived. But this detailed study has exposed some unique features of the art of this period, and a more detailed study of some of the other larger groups of gold glass would undoubtedly also produce further insights into the way the earliest Christian imagery developed in Rome.

Images of Mary become widespread in the second half of the sixth century (Figures 10 and 12 and the Turtura Fresco). In the 6th-early 8th century images of Mary develop in a number of different ways. First of all, in the 7th century, the orant Mary is depicted interceding with a rather stern figure of Christ (possibly intended to indicate his return to judge mankind in the second coming) in the apse of the chapel of S. Venantius in the Lateran Baptistery. Here possibly Mary represents little more than an extension of the intercessionary function of the pagan orant, but by leading the other male saints, she is clearly now positioned to indicate a status above theirs.

---

[130] See the survey of early catacomb inscriptions in F. Bisconti, *Catacombs of Rome* (2002), 147-85, esp. 172-4.

[131] F. Bisconti, *Catacombs of Rome* (2002), 173, Figure 123 ICUR X, 26350.

It is not until the beginning of the eighth century that we see the development of what comes to be known as the 'Maria Regina', or image of Mary crowned as an Empress. The earliest example of this depicts her in orant pose, but now dressed in pearl and gem covered clothes.[132] This imagery is at odds with the simple, ascetic image more usually found for the pagan orant. The earliest such image in Rome was commissioned by Pope John VII in 706 for his funerary chapel at Old S. Peter's.[133] Her crown here is clearly closely modelled on that of the Empress Theodora in the sixth century mosaic panel at San Vitale in Ravenna.[134] Here she is still without the Christ child, and in Rome this separation of the orant image of Mary from the Christ-child is maintained. However, in Constantinople, further developments follow so that the image of Mary at the Blachernissa convent, believed to have originally been deposited there by Empress Verina, is depicted in later images with the Christ child suspended over Mary's chest in a mandorla, finally reuniting Christ with his intercessor and mother, Mary.[135]

Further examples of crowned images of Mary continue to occur through the time of Pope Hadrian I (in S. Maria Antiqua), through the 11th century (in the apse at S. Francesca Romana) and on into the 14th century with the apse at S. Maria Maggiore.[136] In some of these examples Mary loses the orant pose and is crowned and enthroned with the Christ-child on her lap. In other words she has returned to the 'Adoration of the Magi' type, but has retained her crown.

---

[132] J. Osborne, 'Maria Regina in Rome' (2008), 95-106.

[133] Figure 12: Detail from the engraving in Vat. Lat, 11988 70v-71r.

[134] R. Cormack, *Byzantine Art* (2000), 61.

[135] For a marble icon depicting this iconography see Ernst Weitzmann, *The Icon: Holy Image* (London, 1978), 24, Figure A, originally from Constantinople but now in the church of S. Maria Mater Domini in Venice, which Wietzmann dates to the 11th century.

[136] J. Osborne, 'Maria Regina in Rome' (2008), 95-106.

Some Theological Considerations on the Visual Representation of the 'Suffering on the Cross' in the First Half of the Fifth Century

Luise Marion FRENKEL, Cambridge, UK

ABSTRACT

This article offers some new perspectives to the puzzling scarcity of crucifixes in early Christian iconography, discussing the theological implications of the depiction of Christ's torso and the role of the fifth-century Christological debates in providing a framework which made uncontroversial appreciation possible. It presents a cleaner distinction between various uses of the cross, arguing for the theological and semiotic difference of a symbolic representation of the cross, the narrative depiction of the crucifixion and the crucifix (or the crucified) as a Christian symbol. Resorting to literary evidence related to liturgical practices, drawn mainly from homilies, but also some treatises, it is argued that this last type only became understood and accepted when the Christological debates had clarified the relation of human and divine in Christ, providing the language and the basis for a symbolic depiction of Christ's death on the cross.

The aim of this article is to contribute to scholarship on Christian figurative representation of the crucifixion in iconographic and literary media, and to suggest that the late appearance of crucifixes is only the more noticeable aspect of the difficulty to render Christ's death. The incipient visual depiction of the crucifixion was nurtured by the recurrent liturgical description of the Passion events, and developed concomitantly in several regions multi-faceted responses to an exegetical narration centred on detailing the suffering and passibility. The theological debates made it possible for a later preacher like Leontius of Constantinople (c. 485 – c. 543) to say in a Pascal Homily that 'Christ, our Lord, asleep in death for three days, did not close the eyes of divinity', as a lion on guard, the visual analogue to the image of the divinity that keeps watch and does not remain bound to the body, overpowered by death.[1] This does not apply fully to early crucifixes or to narrative depictions of the crucifixion.[2]

---

[1] ὁ δεσπότης Χριστὸς καθευδήσας ἐν τῷ θανάτῳ τριήμερον τοὺς τῆς θεότητος ὀφθαλμοὺς οὐκ ἐκάμμυσεν· Leontius of Constantinople, *In S. Pascha hom.* II, 6, 17. Michel Aubineau (ed.), *Hesychius de Jerusalem, Basile de Seleucie, Jean de Beryte, Pseudo-Chrysostome, Leonce de Constantinople. Homélies pascales: cinq homélies inédites*, Sources chrétiennes 187 (Paris, 1972), 28, 440.

[2] The earliest, fifth-century, examples of Christian crosses with a torso are discussed in Felicity Harley, 'The Crucifixion', in Jeffrey Spier (ed.), *Picturing the Bible: The Earliest Christian Art*

A preliminary version was presented under the title 'Fifth-century Greek homiletics and the iconography of the crucifixion: initial considerations' at a workshop[3] of the project 'Early "Christian" Epigraphy and Iconography: A new approach to Doelger's classical project'. Its inquisitive context motivated reflecting over the fragmentary visual sources, the accompanying weighty questions and the recent approaches and explanations for the first examples of crucifixions in Early Christian iconography, while researching the Christological debate. It builds on the central visual evidence, a selection of patristic sources on iconography, and on Christological documents mainly related to the First Council of Ephesus (431) and its immediate aftermath. The article remains an early attempt to come to terms with the complexity of the symbol of the cross, pondering on several potential reasons why it was scarcely present, and, when it was present, how it may have been seen and understood.

1. Period and Area

The focus of this study falls on the first half of the fifth century. To this period are dated the first examples of visual representation of the crucifixion, apart from a few controversial objects.[4] The wish to discuss iconography pre-dating the Council of Chalcedon lessens the relevance of some well-known early crucifixions, such as illuminated manuscripts like the Rabulla Evangeliar.[5] It leaves a select body of evidence, challenging in its visual diversity, regional spread, and debatable dating. The Christological conflict leading to the Council of Chalcedon happened in these decades, not only through the key doctrinal and political events, best exemplified in the major synods and councils, but also, in many areas, by means of the awareness and, occasionally, the involvement of the Christian population in the debate.[6] The bishops spread their views not only

(New Haven, Conn., 2008), 227-31; Allyson Everingham Sheckler and Mary Joan Winn Leith, 'The crucifixion conundrum and the Santa Sabina doors', *HThR* 103 (2010), 67-88; Antonella Ballardini, 'La "crocefissione" nella porta della basilica di S. Sabina in Roma', in Boris Ulianich and Ulderico Parente (eds), *La croce: iconografia e interpretazione: secoli I-inizio XVI: atti del convegno internazionale di studi, Napoli, 6-11 dicembre 1999* (Napoli, 2007), 271-92; Dina Tumminello, *La crocifissione del portale di S. Sabina e le origini dell'iconologia della crocifissione* (Roma, 2003).

   [3] 14 February 2012, at the British School at Rome.

   [4] A few extant amulets, seals, rings and graffiti bear images that are crucifixions or which have been related to early Christian representations of the crucifixion. These objects, their chronology and their relation to the earliest crucifixions are reassessed in A.E. Sheckler and M.J.W. Leith, 'The crucifixion conundrum' (2010). They are potent reminders of the cultural variety of Late Antiquity, the fluidity of religious affiliations and the ambiguity of visual material.

   [5] An account of the late rise of crucifixion iconography derived mainly from later examples, like the Rabbula Evangeliar, the Fieschi Morgan Staurotheke, and the Palla of Sant' Apollinare Nuovo can be found in Klaus Wessel, 'Die Entstehung des Crucifixus', *ByzZ* 53 (1960), 95-111.

   [6] For an overview of the theological and historical events, see Christianne Fraisse-Coué, 'Le débat théologique au temps de Théodose II: Nestorius', in Charles Pietri, *et al.* (eds), *Naissance*

through sermons and hymns, but also by fostering liturgical developments which involved the faithful. Moreover, Marian devotion developed significantly at this time, contributing to a renewed interest in narrative details of the life of Christ.[7] Thus, also the population of dioceses only marginally affected by the conflict between 'Cyrillians' and 'Orientals' could be familiar with topics debated in the Christological controversy.

It is well known that, through the exchange of letters, the conflict which had sparked between Alexandria and Constantinople was brought to the attention of the see of Rome. The first half of the fifth century was a politically troubled period in the Western Roman Empire, not the least considering the various Germanic incursions. In the aftermath of the Trinitarian and anti-Arian debates of the fourth century, Christology did not become the main bone of contention at Western synods unlike those in the East, and this is reflected in the sermons, letters and other means of communication with which the church spread theological topics among the population. Nevertheless, theological insights associated to the Christological crises were present in the West, and at least the see of Rome was involved in the conflicts between Eastern bishops. Also the universal scope of imperial laws endorsing the Cyrillian Council divulged the matter.

The article mainly discusses the relation of iconography with the Christological debate in the environs of Alexandria, and is complemented by often studied visual examples from Rome. Constantinople would, in theory, be the ideal source of visual material closely related to the heritage of Roman art associated with imperial monuments, as well as to the support of the imperially endorsed theology. However, most visual material did not survive Iconoclasm, the Arab presence and natural catastrophes, and it is difficult to use Constantinople to counterbalance Alexandria. The few surviving literary descriptions can be variously interpreted and even if the historical accuracy of chronology, or attribution to direct imperial patronage could be circumvented for this study, the ambiguity of vocabulary (for example, whether cross or crucifix) and the thin line between description of concrete things and (theological) interpretation,[8] encourage resorting to Rome instead.

---

d'une chrétienté (250-430), Histoire du christianisme des origines à nos jours 2 (Paris, 1995), 499-550. The pastoral dimension of the debate can be seen in John Anthony McGuckin, *St. Cyril of Alexandria: the Christological controversy: its history, theology, and texts* (Crestwood, N.Y., 2004); Michael Redies, 'Kyrill und Nestorius: Eine Neuinterpretation des Theotokos-Streits', *Klio* 80 (1998), 195-208.

[7] Vasiliki Limberis, *Divine Heiress: the Virgin Mary and the creation of Christian Constantinople* (London, 1994); Jan Harm Barkhuizen, *Proclus, Bishop of Constantinople – Homilies on the life of Christ* (Brisbane, 2001).

[8] For example, the descriptions in pilgrims' accounts, not least Egeria's Pilgrimage, or in Choricius of Gaza, and the references to devotional and liturgical uses, for example, in the seventh-century Rule of Mar Dādisho.

2. Iconography of Christ and representation of suffering

It is well known that Christ is not represented explicitly during the first centuries, making it difficult to identify early Christian iconography univocally, in its rather late development. From the third century onwards, a significant body of objects can be described as carrying Christian art with increasing certainty, especially from the second half of the fourth century on. A century later, the time this study focus on, Christian art was widespread insofar as large scale examples, visible on a daily basis, were available in most regions of the Roman empire. The imperial basilicas in Rome and Constantinople were adorned with mosaics, paintings, reliefs, sculptures, and churches and other Christian buildings in general were decorated with visual elements that carried some more or less Christian content.[9] It is likely that Christian iconography could also be seen in other venues, increasing the range of 'public' images.

'Public' is not the anachronistic concept defined by the opposition to 'private', but a term with which to characterise, for example, the images shared by the audience of a preacher. The ideal 'public' image would be visible concomitantly to the discourse, but the concept is also applied to anything a bishop could mention in a sermon with the expectation that his congregation had seen or could go and see, for example, to check details he was mentioning. Thus, iconography accessible to only a few, for example, because of its location or its size, will not be considered here.

'Public' images then form a set of objects which could carry a message that might be endorsed or stand in contradiction with the oral or written theological discourse. In the case of crucifixions, although there is no evidence of large scale crucifixes from this period, the hypothesised small scale exemplars were probably 'public', possibly even used in churches. Therefore, it cannot be expected that they would be fostered if they conflicted or contradicted the preaching of a bishop, or the theology endorsed synodically.

Christian theological digressions on images arose early. A substantial body of texts attests various objections,[10] but it does not help to explain the late appearance of crucifixions. The legacy of the fourth-century Trinitarian debates was similarly rich for both the Christological and the Iconographic debates, not the least because it had expanded the exegesis of the opposition between a God of the Old Testament which remains hidden from sight of men, and Christ

---

[9] Fabrizio Bisconti, 'Progetti decorativi dei primi edifici di culto romani: dalle assenze figurative ai grandi scenari iconografici', in Federico Guidobaldi and Alesandra Guiglia Guidobaldi (eds), *Ecclesiae Urbis, Atti del Congresso internazionale di studi sulle chiese di Roma (IV-X secolo)* (Roma, 2002), III 1633-58.

[10] Preserved especially in sources from the iconoclastic disputes, since excerpts from earlier literature were used to uphold claims based on the authority associated to their authors. See Paul J. Alexander, 'The iconoclastic council of St Sophia (815) and its definition (horos)', *DOP* 7 (1953), 35-66.

in the New Testament, through whom God becomes visible. However, the arguments raised in the first centuries address little the representation of suffering in Christian iconography.

Many of the arguments advanced by scholarship to explain the scarce rendition of suffering in Christian imagery in general resort to wider anthropological and social concerns. Thus, it has been suggested that Christian visual art was understood as primarily consolatory, and that therefore representation of suffering, especially of the death on the cross, was not conducive.[11]

Another recurring opinion builds on the chronological overlap of the rise of an imperial church, and what seem to be the first representations of Christ,[12] and the possibility of interpretatively equating Christ and emperor, especially in the large scale figurative examples of apsis mosaics in Rome and Constantinople.[13] According to this, Christ was always represented imperially, and in the victorious emperor iconography 'suffering' was not appropriate.[14] Among the arguments, it is claimed that when Christians felt at ease to use the Roman imperial imagery to depict their Ruler, and it was no longer symbolising the oppressor, they were faced with an imagery that did not include 'suffering kings'. Secondly, arguing that the cult of the emperor was, roughly speaking, replaced with a 'we honour you as our ruler on earth, as we honour Christ as our Saviour in eternity', which would visually translate to 'when we depict Christ in our churches and worship him, we remember you, and pray for you', it would be unfitting to encompass suffering in this semiology.[15] Finally, Stoic arguments on the relation of social structure and nature accounted for a view of the Roman emperor as bearer of the *lógos*, and of the *lógos* as the principle of divine order in nature as well as in society. Stoic ideas on the relation of matter and spirit would also permeate the discourse and iconography of both pagans and Christians, and their relation to the object of the linguistic or visual discourse.[16]

---

[11] See Robin Margaret Jensen, *Understanding Early Christian Art* (London, 2000), 133-4.

[12] By the early fourth century, images of Christ proliferated, even if the practice may not have enjoyed widespread support everywhere. Several arguments against the use of images for Christian themes, or in Christian religious buildings were advanced, but no significant debates arose, suggesting a silent majority did not object.

[13] For a classic account of imperial iconography in Byzantine art, see André Grabar, *L'empereur dans l'art byzantin: recherches sur l'art officiel de l'empire d'Orient*, Publications de la Faculté des lettres de l'Université de Strasbourg 75 (Paris, 1936). The analysis of the earlier examples suffers from positing a pre-existing sacred and monarchical Near Eastern art, and moreover from considering them part of the Byzantine tradition, minimising that it did not yet exist when they were made in a classical setting.

[14] Johannes G. Deckers, 'Constantine the Great and early christian art', in J. Spier (ed.), *Picturing the Bible* (2008), 106.

[15] On the absence of representation of suffering, see Herbert L. Kessler, 'Bright gardens of paradise', in J. Spier (ed.), *Picturing the Bible* (2008), 111-2, 114.

[16] Allen Brent, *Cyprian and Roman Carthage* (Cambridge, 2010), 81-114.

These very interesting and helpful approaches, mostly derived from the same main examples, fall short of a convincing general explanation for the limited visual representation of gruesome details of Christ's suffering. For one, the relevance of the strongly panegyric correlation of Christ and emperor should not be overestimated outside the capitals.[17] Then, the consolatory nature of Christian art seems at odds with the extensive literary material on suffering, which served to highlight the merits of saints as much as to emphasise the extent of God's demeanour.

Before discussing further problems of these general approaches, a selective description of the visual material will introduce a tentative classification of the semiotic meaning of crosses, with or without torso. In this perspective, the matter was not a conundrum for the artists, that is the artisans, but a set of questions which discouraged theological and political patronage of large scale representations and contributed to the survival of limited exemplars.

3. The Cross

The symbolic use of the cross is more elaborate than as a mere tag for Christians, but in the period under consideration at least this meaning was probably carried by even a very simplified and schematic cross. A viewer of a cross without a torso would interpret it as alluding to Christ, in a huge range of meanings. This sort of cross was alongside the Chi-Rho one of the earliest Christian 'symbols',[18] more related to the Pauline cross than to its function in the Passion cycle, in

[17] The influence of standards of imperial iconography has been used to explain the selection of 'Entry to Jerusalem' and 'Resurrection', but omission of the Passion events in the narrative cycle of the wooden lintel from El Mu'allaqa, one of the few examples of early sculptural cycle incorporated in architecture, insofar as 'the theme of triumph before and after the Passion was adequate for an imperial gateway'. See Alexander Badawy, *Coptic Art and Archaeology: The Art of the Christian Egyptians from the Late Antique to the Middle Ages* (Cambridge, Mass., 1978), 133; also, A. Grabar, *L'empereur* (1936), 210, 234-5. However, this conclusion is drawn from the comparison of a handful of examples from all over the Roman Empire, spread over three centuries. Likewise, it is difficult to give preference for the influence of the pagan cult of a Sun God via imperial iconography to explain the representation of both Sun and Moon in crucifixion scenes such as the Rabbula Evangeliar, considering the plethora of apocryphal narratives and legends which are attested in homilies, for example. See Martin Wallraff, *Christus verus sol: Sonnenverehrung und Christentum in der Spätantike*, Jahrbuch für Antike und Christentum. Ergänzungsband 32 (Münster, 2001), 165-6.

[18] See on this topic the contribution by Markus Vinzent in this volume. The complex relation of the cross with classical and imperial imagery is discussed in Rudolph H. Storch, 'The trophy and the cross: Pagan and Christian symbolism in the fourth and fifth centuries', *Byzantion* 40 (1970), 105-18, and with Egyptian hieroglyphs in László Török, *Transfigurations of Hellenism: Aspects of Late Antique Art in Egypt, A.D. 250-700*, Probleme der Ägyptologie 23 (Leiden, 2005), 17-30. Other Christian symbols, such as the lamb or Greek letters, were depicted on or next to cruciform symbols, see Jacob Stockbauer, *Kunstgeschichte des Kreuzes: die bildliche Darstellung des Erlösungstodes Christi im Monogramm, Kreuz und Crucifix* (Schaffhausen, 1870), 133.

agreement with recent remarks on the reduced importance of the narrative passages of the Gospels during the first centuries after Christ, which even question their existence.[19] Nevertheless, Paul's 'cross' is, evidently, that object on which Christ died. The early Christian writers gradually introduced a distinction between the cross and the crucified one, while occasionally taking the Cross metonymically for the Crucified, leading later to reflections on the object itself.[20] A visual cross associated to the Pauline texts is imbued with positive connotations, encompassing glory, glorification, revelation, salvation, redemption, lifting. The same applies to the qualities of Christ represented through the object. The connotations incorporate allusions, such as to royalty and precious materials, because of Old Testament typologies. An imperial patronage of Christianity was then an additional layer of meaning,[21] but unlikely a determining factor. It facilitated the social and financial support for large scale Christian visual representations, which do not seem to have more or less in common with the non-Christian use of the same media than had been the case with *stellae* and frescoes, for example.

Crosses with evident Christian connotation would have been visible in every day places, and ought to have figured prominently in the urban landscape, but a careful assessment of the origin and date of the extant crosses denies, rather than endorses claims that crosses were a prominent feature of the 'visual fanfare' which adorned the churches 'proliferating' in the late years of Constantine's reign and thereafter.[22] In the urban landscape accessible to all, crosses were not necessarily conspicuous, even if they were a frequent, if not constant adornment of buildings used for Christian worship, at least in the inside. Thus, Christians would be confronted with a significant variety, ranging from the ornate mosaics in Rome,[23] or the sculptures in churches in Egypt,[24] to more simple graffiti in martyria *et al.*

Without a representation of Christ on it, the cross was seen by Christians foremost as a sign of the glory, with which they identified themselves, and represented the redemption which gave them their identity. However, it seems that Christian art did not transition directly from cross to crucifix, that is, the symbolic representation of a torso on a cross. Rather, crucifixions are first seen in visual narrative cycles, representing moments of the Passion.[25]

---

[19] See Markus Vinzent, *Christ's Resurrection in Early Christianity and the Making of the New Testament* (Farnham, 2011).

[20] See Jean-Marc Prieur, *La croix chez les Pères (du IIe au début du IVe siècle)*, Cahiers de Biblia Patristica 8 (Strasbourg, 2006), 143, 196.

[21] A. Grabar, *L'empereur* (1936), 240-3.

[22] Kimberly Bowes, 'Christian worship', in Anastasia Lazaridou (ed.), *Transition to Christianity: art of late antiquity, 3rd-7th century AD* (New York, 2011), 53-7, 55.

[23] J.G. Deckers, 'Constantine' (2008), 95-100.

[24] A. Badawy, *Coptic art* (1978), 133-49.

[25] See also Rudolf Berliner, 'A Palestinian Reliquary Cross of about 590', *BProvidence* 9 (1952), 1-4.

4. Narrative crucifixion

4.1. *Narrative cycles*

The first visual representations of narrative cycles in the fourth and fifth centuries were contemporary to the development of most feasts and commemorations, which established a more or less uniform calendar of major celebrations into which regional feasts merged and settled. Many sermons for these feast days have been preserved, and they are key sources to trace this development, since some describe the novelty, even the chronology of the introduction of the celebration. Besides, festal sermons contain extensive paraphrases of Biblical narratives, for example, to discuss the particular significance and relation of one event in the entire life of Christ. This segmentation of the narrative did not alter the view shared by all major exegetical traditions that the existence of Christ with all its events and characteristics was what redeemed mankind.[26]

The rise of feast days celebrating particular events and the frequent mention, for example, in sermons, of a certain selection of key events encouraged the representation of scenes, while the attention to the importance of the whole, that is of the position of each event in the saving dispensation, fostered the elaboration of visual cycles, preferably all encompassing ones. Christ's existence was part of God's plan for his dealing with humanity, not isolatable from the Old Testament, although utterly different. In sermons, the narrative cycles often referred back to it for causative elements (as in the Fall requires redemption), comparisons, contrasts, and especially prefigurements. Likewise, the earliest extant visual cycles generally include scenes from the Old Testament, some of which already had a long tradition in Christian iconography.[27] An extended framework circumvented choosing between Annunciation, Nativity, or another scene as the first for New Testament cycles. At the other end of the narrative, the Resurrection was generally featured, not seldom as the last scene. Ascension and Pentecost were often not included, possibly reflecting the late development of these feasts. If the actions in the Resurrection accounts were easy to represent visually, theological issues with the representation of the resurrected Christ remained. A solution was to depict the cross and anagram instead of a human Christ, coming out of the grave with sleeping soldiers around as seen in the Sarcophagus of Via Salaria, for example. Soon, the visual choice to represent the resurrected with the same features of the scenes prior to the Passion predominated, even in cycles which skipped the crucifixion, going, for example, from the entry into Jerusalem to a scene figuring the Resurrected. The symbolic use of a cross or a Chi-Rho monogram in narrative scenes is attested in several

---

[26] Frances Margaret Young, *Biblical Exegesis and the Formation of Christian Culture* (Cambridge, 1997), 24-35, 180-90.

[27] Fabrizio Bisconti (ed.), *Temi di iconografia paleocristiana*, Sussidi allo studio delle antichità cristiane 13 (Città del Vaticano, 2000).

examples, and at least in the Roman milieu, the imperial connotations of the symbol could allow the reading of a Resurrection scene where the Chi-rho seems to trample the soldiers as a representation of a victorious Roman (emperor) trampling his enemies.

Also in Christian patristic literature, narrative cycles and detailed paraphrases were frequent arguments in the doctrinal debates. At the end of the first quarter of the fifth century, Greek authors resorted to passages which describe Christ's suffering so that by asserting his passibility, they could speak of a real humanity being part of his nature, while arguing he was not a mere man. However, Christ's death on the cross received less attention than Christ's birth in poverty, his refusal to have a cohort of guards protecting him, and especially his obedience. These scenes were paraphrased more often and discussed in greater detail than the time Christ spent on the cross within the Passion events. A certain lack of interest on the crucifixion is well exemplified in the Alexandrian tradition of exegesis of *Phil.* 2:5-11 where the first verses are often quoted literally and expounded at length, while the latter, on the Passion, are briefly retold and hardly expounded.[28] Elsewhere, these authors speak of the cross as a symbol of 'lifting', 'raising', thus of 'glory'.[29] The factuality of Christ's death is mentioned when referring, for example, to the descent to Hades, the opening of its doors, and the defeat of the Devil.[30]

4.2. *Crucifixions*

Frequent mention of the crucifixion and of the role of the Passion in the narrative cycles, as well as awareness of the length of the Passion accounts in the Scriptures probably created time and again a demand to see them in the visual cycles representing many scenes.[31] Solutions found for visual problems in other scenes that recurred in the cycles constrained artisans and theologians alike. In narrative cycles, the adult Christ was depicted with the same traits in all scenes, and, thus, a crucifixion would essentially represent the same Christ. The variety of the early examples, stemming from diverse areas, is suggestive of home grown solutions, which reflect their origin, including the chosen media, influenced by economical considerations.[32]

---

[28] Sebastian Schurig, *Die Theologie des Kreuzes beim frühen Cyrill von Alexandria: dargestellt an seiner Schrift „De adoratione et cultu in spiritu et veritate"*, Studien und Texte zu Antike und Christentum 29 (Tübingen, 2005), 114-38.

[29] Enrico Cattaneo, 'L'encomio della croce nell'omiletica greca (IV-VIII)', in B. Ulianich and U. Parente (eds), *La croce* (2007), 216-8.

[30] Thus, for example, Proclus, *Hom.* 11, PG 65, 781-8.

[31] Furthermore the few literary references to visual hagiograhical cycles suggest they included a representation of the martyrium of the saint. See Géza De Francovich and Valentino Pace, *Persia, Siria e Bisanzio nel Medioevo artistico europeo* (Napoli, 1984), 9-13.

[32] The impact of local traditions and material limitations has been used to posit a hypothetical precursor, see D. Tumminello, *La crocifissione* (2003), 71-3.

The cycles usually contained scenes which already associated to Christ concepts foreign to the imperial propaganda. For example, the Adoration was used in the Christological debate to illustrate the extent of God's descent. Preachers spoke of God's wish to become poor and subject to humiliation and denigration, whilst performing miracles that are beyond any prior example, and finally taking up human death, and thus redeeming mankind.[33] That is, the scenes finding their way into the decoration of the churches, liturgical objects or items with some devotional function, were also interpreted in connection with humiliation and lowering. Christians were steadily reminded, even outside the Christological debate, that the exalted God had saved them by becoming like the least man. Thus, imperial patronage ought not to be seen as a handicap for rendering scenes of Christ's suffering, like the crucifixion, since during the liturgies, at least in sermons, hymns and readings, the faithful were reminded that what was represented, for example, in the large scale mosaics in an apsis, was the same Christ who suffered, and had thus redeemed mankind.

There is no evidence of large scale narrative cycles of the Life of Christ,[34] although examples may have existed in fragile media like tapestries. Nevertheless, it seems some of the early small scale cycles were placed in liturgical settings, like niches, altars or lintels. Therefore, the inclusion of a scene of the crucifixion would make it visible to the congregation at the time they heard a sermon about the suffering and glory of Christ, his death on the cross and opening of the Doors of Hell, his remaining what he was, immortal, unseen and becoming what he had not been, seen and passible.

Both the carved doors of Santa Sabina and the so-called Maskell plaques are examples from Rome, dated to 420-430, that of Santa Sabina perhaps even from precisely 432, a year after the Council of Ephesus, two years after Cyril of Alexandria sent translations of Nestorian material to Rome, a time when Cassian might have been working on *De incarnatione*. Albeit being unambiguous portrayals of the crucifixion, both are not crucifixes strictly speaking, rather narrative depiction. Furthermore, both illustrate a moment in the story when Christ was still alive. Indeed, the Maskell counters the idea that a suffering Christ was not represented, since humiliation can be seen in Christ's eyes when compared to Mary's. Modern descriptions of early examples of crucifixions[35] reveal their hermeneutic and semiotic complexity, insisting on the absence of suffering

---

[33] Sarah Coakley, 'Does Kenosis Rest on a Mistake? Three Kenotic models in Patristic exegesis', in C. Stephen Evans (ed.), *Exploring kenotic Christology: the self-emptying of God* (Oxford, 2006), 246-64.

[34] There is no evidence to corroborate hypothetical frescoed predecessors for the illuminations of manuscripts like the Rabulla Evangeliar, see, however, D. Tumminello, *La crocifissione* (2003), 58.

[35] Conflicting attempts to pinpoint the specific scene are found in D. Tumminello, *La crocifissione* (2003), F. Harley, 'The Crucifixion' (2008), A.E. Sheckler and M.J.W. Leith, 'The crucifixion conundrum' (2010), K. Wessel, 'Die Entstehung' (1960). These attempts are dismissed by Marcus Mrass, 'Kreuzigung', in Klaus Wessel and Marcell Restle (eds), *RBK* 5 (Stuttgart, 1995), 354.

while taking pains to point out the specific moment of the Passion being represented. Even if unintentional, the interpretative ambiguity may have been handy for liturgical use, allowing various references. The first representations generally share a narrative aspect, and point to the artist's wish to picture Christ both nailed to the cross, and in the position known as *orans*. The examples are described as narratives, evidencing their link to visual and homiletic cycles of Christ's life.

4.3. *The* Orans

Characterising early examples of Christ crucified as *orans* may be influenced by later crucifixes which are basically an *orans* in front of a cross. Also, describing the image of the torso in the crucifixion scene as an *orans* helps to categorise it in the iconographic vocabulary of early Christianity. It seems, however, that the attempt to represent a scene where Christ speaks or intercedes led the artisan to use a visual clue for speech, intercession or prayer, which could be conciliated with the constraints imposed by the cross. Thus on the carved wood doors of Santa Sabina and especially on the so-called Maskell ivory plaques, the arms are horizontal.[36]

Rather than seeing an early attempt to represent a crucifix, these crucifixions ought perhaps to be placed in the semiotic language of Late Antiquity, where in theatre as in visual arts speaking on behalf was related to the body language encapsulated in the *orans* imagery. Accepting the narrative character and the need of a visual clue for the event makes it unnecessary to connect crucifixion with martyrdom, as often attempted in early Christian iconographical studies which explore visual similarity even if examples are far removed in space and time. Christ is then said to be represented as a paradigm for martyrs, since he faced death courageously, to achieve salvation for mankind.[37]

This connection has been attractive since it would also help to explain the absence of suffering of Christ on the cross, endorsing the *orans*-like position as being related not to the narrative gesture, but to its use in Christian iconography, in several contexts and regions.[38] Common in all the Hellenistic world,

---

[36] Christ crucified is not an *orans* image if the *orans* typology is described more strictly: K. Wessel, 'Die Entstehung' (1960), 99.

[37] Such was the case of the description of an early Coptic crucifix at a major exhibition (London, 2011), which conciliated an outreach character with providing quite accurate information, especially in the catalogue, which unfortunately does not mention that object: Martina Bagnoli (ed.), *Treasures of Heaven: Saints, Relics, and Devotion in Medieval Europe* (New Haven, Conn., 2010).

[38] The *orans* image had a long background with several parallel sources. In the fifth century, it was still employed for non-Christian images too, and as such visually well represented in most areas. See L. Török, *Transfigurations* (2005), 273. Also the inscriptions on *stellae* can often not be described as 'Christian' with certainty, for example Alberto Tulli, 'Le stele copte del Museo Egizio Vaticano', *RAC* 6 (1929), 127-44, 131.

orantes were also frequent in Egyptian art, often with reference to the Egyptian Gods. Low reliefs on *stellae* with a depiction of the deceased in the common position of prayer (hence the name) predominated there.[39] In Rome, the iconography was similar, but the range of meanings larger, including a tendency to balance it with Pietas, in sarcophagi as well as in imperial monuments. The custom of representing the deceased 'alive' as *orans* corresponds literally to the predominance in epigrams and other media, of texts about the deceased which speak of the afterlife or refer to his life.

Whichever scene with Christ on the cross was represented like *orans*, it probably was meant to stand for a moment of enunciation with an intercessory or promising character, reminiscing that Christ saved mankind. On behalf of human beings, Christ died on the cross. However, the portrait of a living Christ predominated. Claiming Christian artists resorted to the *orans* iconography and to the context of the martyr's cult,[40] that is, that they largely used the visual language they were familiar with to express new ideas and themes, especially when they were not themselves acquainted with the concepts involved, implies that these paradigms were to some extent a handicap to represent suffering. This premise suggests that if the intention was to portray suffering, these would not have been the adopted formats, and thus it is inferred that there was no intention to portray suffering.

4.4. *Death and suffering*

The absence of gruesome details ought to be related to the choice of representing Christ at moments when he was still alive. It is not yet the *Christus triumphans,* which in the always relevant distinction of torsos can be opposed to the *Christus patiens.* This dichotomy between crosses with living and dead torsos suggests a preponderance of one or the other type in various regions at different moments, and schematises their relation to concomitant theological problems and devotional trends.[41] However, the early Christian *Christus triumphans*

---

[39] A. Badawy, *Coptic art* (1978), 127-31. However, Török, *Transfigurations* (2005), 56-8 highlights the influence of Western models.

[40] Anachronistic terms used in studies of Christian iconography to describe a martyrs' imitation of Christ, and that martyrs 'gave their life for others' simplify the cultural background and the theological foundation of the martyr's cult and overemphasise its importance as well as that of pilgrimages. Only thus can it be suggested, concerning the iconography of Christ, that artists would easily invert the logic of the parallel between a martyr's and Christ's death to find a visual solution. It ought to be seen as a coincidence that the crucifixion was depicted only once martyrdom was not a real or imminent danger. If the representation can be taken as a token that the faithful were coming to terms with Christ's death and its value, that is due to the subsequent theological debates.

[41] In the East, both types largely coexisted not only during the Christological controversies of the fifth century, but also in the aftermath of the iconoclastic crises. Some examples are discussed

represented an event, part of a narrative cycle, and not yet the 'veiling divinity of Christ'.[42]

The details that differentiate between a living and a dead torso would be indistinguishable depending on the setting (position, light), and could be overseen on purpose. Any torso on a cross can from a certain distance seem a dead body. While aiding a preacher speaking on the 'obedience to the death on the cross' (*Phil.* 2:8), Christ dead on the cross would easily conflict with slogans like 'Do not attribute suffering to God!'[43] On the other hand, the large eyes and serenity, soon typical in Coptic crucifixes, that seem an ideal representation of impassibility, stand in contradiction to equally frequent exhortations not to deny the suffering. Thus crucifixion scenes in a church or a shrine, or in the environs of the bishop's audience, seen in daily life, could be objects the faithful may have struggled to conciliate with the theological discourse. They were reminded that 'He remained what he was, and became what he was not'.[44] They were also dissuaded from trying to think about the divinity and the humanity in Christ, of Christ, because this was deemed to divide Christ, at least in an 'Alexandrian' exegesis. Visual representation of the crucifixion seem inevitably to fail to convey both messages.

A representative excerpt prior to the Council of Ephesus I which details the inherent contradiction of a narrative iconography of the crucifixion is found in Theodotus of Ancyra's Homily I. The sufferings, the nailing of the sins to the cross, the death on the cross 'having been appropriated by God took their power for great successes from (his) divinity, becoming as God's own, but they did not impair the essence of divinity, which always remained in its own impassibility. [...] How did the cross crucify sin, or (how) did death break up the tyranny of death, unless these things had become of God and had taken from that the power, while he appropriated our things, (yet) did not suffer in nature?'[45]

---

in Alexander Kazhdan and Henry Maguire, 'Byzantine hagiographical texts as sources on art', *DOP* 45 (1991), 1-22, 10-1.

[42] M. Aubineau (ed.), *Hesychius* (1972), 29.

[43] For example, in Cyril of Alexandria, *In S. Joan.* VIII 27-8, ed. Philip Edward Pusey (Oxford, 1872), 317.

[44] '[...] we say both that he remained what he was, and became what indeed he was not. For remaining by essence what he was, he accepted sufferings, having united himself to the suffering nature.' [...] λέγομεν καὶ μένειν αὐτὸν ὃ ἦν, καὶ γεγονέναι ὅπερ οὐκ ἦν. τῆι γὰρ οὐσίαι μένων ὃ ἦν, ἐδέξατο πάθη, ἑαυτὸν ἐνώσας φύσει τῆι παθητῆι. Theodotus of Ancyra, *Hom.* II 5, ed. Eduard Schwartz ACO I 1/2 (Berlin, 1927), 83. See also Cyr., *ep. ad Nestorium* III (*ep.* 17) 3, ed. E. Schwartz ACO I 1/1 (Berlin, 1914), 35; and Luigi I. Scipioni, *Nestorio e il concilio de Efeso. Storia, dogma, critica*, Studia Patristica Mediolanensia 1 (Milano, 1974), 79.

[45] ταῦτα τὰ πάθη οἰκειωθέντα θεῷ τὴν μὲν ἰσχὺν τῶν τοσούτων κατορθωμάτων ἐκ θεότητος ἔλαβεν, ὡς θεοῦ ἴδια γεγενημένα, οὐσίαν δὲ θεότητος οὐ παρέβλαψεν ἐν τῆι ἑαυτῆς ἀεὶ μένουσαν ἀπαθείαι. [...] πῶς δὲ σταυρὸς ἁμαρτίαν ἐσταύρωσεν ἢ θάνατος θανάτου τὴν τυραννίδα διέλυσεν, εἰ μὴ ταῦτα γέγονε θεοῦ καὶ παρ' ἐκείνου τὴν δύναμιν ἔλαβεν οἰκειωσαμένου τὰ ἡμέτερα, οὐ παθόντος φύσει; Theod. Anc., *Hom* I 4, ed. E. Schwartz ACO I 1/2 (1927), 83.

An image of a living Christ displaying no suffering on the cross shrinks from representing Christ's 'death', like the paraphrases on the Passion by theologians involved in the Christological debate which become more figurative when nearing the death on the cross. They do not give material and circumstantial details about the body on the cross as they would add elsewhere when describing the life of Christ. Instructed by Paul's interpretation of 'Christ crucified' as 'Christ the power of God and the wisdom of God', Cyril, for example, wrote already before the Council of Ephesus that 'the Lord did not suffer unwittingly, but purposely and knowing that not only he was dying, but also by what means: and he denominated the cross death.'[46] Furthermore, that: 'the death on the cross is a summit, associated with honour and glory.'[47]

5. The Crucifix

The representation of Christ on the cross, taken directly from the narrative crucifixion did not become widely used as a stand alone image, despite its message of Christ interceding for a man or for mankind, or of speaking to the Father, among other meanings, which would seem fitting for several devotional contexts, whether monastic reflection or domestic prayer. A more abstract and typified image spread, suggesting that the problems posed by the conflicting message of narrative crucifixions in view of the Christological content spoke against them.

The better known example and traditional views of fifth-century ecclesiology have made some attempts trying to link the first images of crucifixion to the Christological debates very focused on the importance of Rome, both as a visual innovator and a theological and church-political player.[48] The scholarly debate around the crucifixion on the doors of Santa Sabina helped to highlight that the first crucifixions are contemporary with the Christological debate. Much has been made of an inscription which linked the foundation to the involvement of Cælestine in a council with all the best bishops of the world. Early modern descriptions preserved extensive details, and explored its possible meanings manifoldly.[49]

---

[46] οὐκ ἀγνοῶν ἔπαθεν ὁ Κύριος, ἀλλ᾽ ἑκὼν καὶ εἰδὼς οὐ μόνον ὅτι ἀπέθνησκεν, ἀλλὰ καὶ ποίῳ τρόπῳ· τὸν σταυρὸν δὲ ὠνόμασε θάνατον. Cyr., *in S. Joan*. VIII 33; ed. P. E. Pusey (1872), 324.

[47] [...] ὕψος εἶναι τὸ ἐπὶ εὐκλείᾳ καὶ δόξῃ νοούμενον, τὸν ἐπὶ τῷ σταυρῷ θάνατον. Cyr., *in S. Joan*. VIII 32; ed. *ibid.*, 324.

[48] A theological impediment, albeit lacking an in-depth analysis of contemporary sources, was cited by J. Stockbauer, *Kunstgeschichte des Kreuzes* (1870), 155-7. The influence of Rome in the Christological debate is highlighted by A.E. Sheckler and M.J.W. Leith, 'The crucifixion conundrum' (2010), 86-8; D. Tumminello, *La crocifissione* (2003), 26-32; and Boris Ulianich (ed.), *La Croce: dalle origini agli inizi del secolo XVI* (Napoli, 2000), 15-7.

[49] Preserved in Giovanni Giusto Ciampini, *Vetera monumenta: in quibus praecipue Musiva Opera, sacrarum, profanarumque, Aedium structura, ac nonnulli antiqui ritus dissertationibus iconibusque illustrantur* (Roma, 1690), 186-95, with an illustration on Tab. XLVIII.

The crucifixion is hard to see from the floor in its current position, while inscriptions such as that found in Santa Sabina are easy to read from beneath. The text witnessed a self-representation of Rome that developed only after the Council of 431, but is echoed and applied to all early Christianity by many scholars.

In fifth-century Egypt, apart from a Hellenic tradition, usually identified with Alexandria, where Greek and Roman models were followed, a more endogenous vein dialogued with traditional Egyptian visual models. A proto-Coptic visual language was developing, marked by 'rigid frontality strongly stylised with smooth flattened broad areas, large eyes bordered by heavy lids, deeply inset, often inlaid, pupils, hair treated in ribbed style symmetrical about the axis of the face.'[50] The Christian emphasis on frontality and huge eyes, usually raised to heavens or starring at the viewer, whether in sculptural imperial portrays or in textiles[51] was also rendered literarily, for example, during the Council of Ephesus in 431: 'the soul looks through the eyes, and reveals itself, in the face, how it is.'[52]

If the Egyptian milieu is promising for the abundance of visual and discursive sources, it also demands caution with its inherent diversity as well as the pace of changes, which transfers to the use of the term Coptic.[53] Early in the fifth century, Alexandria was still a strong centre of Hellenistic culture, and there was no clear division between a Greek speaking and visually Hellenic Alexandria and a Coptic inland. Most literary sources about Christianity in Egypt are in Greek, while being supplemented by numerous Coptic papyri. Coptic language and art was not restricted to the inland, rather it was also used in Alexandria. A simplistic urban and inland dichotomy cannot be ascertained, however different characteristics predominated in each setting. The cities championed Greek thought and language, and remained in contact with the recent developments, especially in Constantinople and the East. Hellenic characteristics predominated in urban iconography, and art produced for the major Egyptian centres tried to follow the fashions of the capitals, including Rome, as exemplified by fifth-century Jewish and Christian frescoes.[54]

The extent of use of Coptic language in Christian liturgy is unclear, but was probably significantly larger where Greek was less well known and used than in cities like Alexandria. Since monasticism likewise flourished in non-urban

---

[50] A. Badawy, *Coptic art* (1978), 125.

[51] Mary Charles-Murray, 'The emergence of Christian art', in J. Spier (ed.), *Picturing the Bible* (2008), 60.

[52] እንተ፡ አዕይንት፡ ታስተጋይጽ፡ ነፍስ፡ ወታርኢ፡ በገጽ፡ ዘከመ፡ ሀለወት። Theod. Anc., *Hom.* VI, ed. Bernd Manuel Weischer, *Homilien und Briefe zum Konzil von Ephesos*, Qērellos 4.1 (Wiesbaden, 1979), 122.

[53] L. Török, *Transfigurations* (2005), xxv-xxvii.

[54] Steven Fine, 'Jewish art and biblical exegesis in the Greco-Roman world', in J. Spier (ed.), *Picturing the Bible* (2008), 33-42.

areas, it used Coptic language and art widely. In the fifth century, however, there is no independent Coptic aesthetic or liturgy, and no independent church where Coptic is the primary language and where a markedly monophysite theology is espoused. Rather, the bishops from Egypt were better or worse speakers of Greek, and fostered the imitation of the iconography of the imperial capitals as much as they could afford. At the same time, they were familiar with Coptic art and language not the least to fulfil their pastoral duties towards those who spoke no Greek. Cyril of Alexandria, for example, may have referred to images which bore the characteristics usually associated with Coptic art.

It can be said that a cross with a torso is not a narrative representation but a crucifix when it stands for the salvation which God granted to men by taking up all that is human, including death, which Christ suffered on the cross. Without an associated narrative, crucifixes could represent the 'death on the cross', and the image did not conflict with Christology but stood for it and what was crucial for Christians.

With the transition from a crucifixion scene to a crucifix, there was a visual representation that avoided the problems of a narrative framework, corresponding to the fifth-century exegesis. A cross with a torso was then no longer a symbol of honour and glory for Christians;[55] as a crucifix, it stood for an array of theological ideas, evidencing their tension and dialogue.

The loss of most narrative meaning also allowed that the *orans*-like iconography of the crucifixion which spread in Egypt representing the death on the cross could coexist with the ongoing use of *orans* in traditional ways. Through the similarity to *orans* used in the iconography of saints for their intercessory role, crucifixes could echo visually their role to represent Christ redeeming mankind by dying on the cross, having taken up all that is human.

6. Iconography

The persisiting conflict between images and content probably contributed to the reticence against the visual representation of Christ, and kept the iconographic debate alive. When it flared up, the iconoclasts could find also in texts of the fifth century, when the use of images in the sacred buildings steadily increased and explored new avenues, many complaints and arguments against their presence in churches, expanding on earlier reflections on image, likeness and the imitative nature of art, for example, by Origen and the Cappadocian fathers. Christ depicted dead on the cross, or even as just asleep, could seem to represent foremost his humanity and in the crucifixion it would not be possible to

---

[55] K. Wessel, 'Die Entstehung' (1960), 101, 107.

see his divinity. Thus, it could lead the viewer to divide Christ. Albeit in thought only, this was not tolerable for many bishops.[56]

On the other hand, the impassible representation, especially using the *orans* typology, aesthetically preferred,[57] also had problems, as reflected in Leontius' preaching, quoted above. He renders Christ's death as a three days long sleep, during which Christ did not close the eyes of his divinity. Mentioning only his divinity was tantamount to distinguishing the divinity and the humanity of Christ.[58]

The lack of suffering is theological; it is neither iconographical nor political; it is not lack of ways to depict death on the cross, or unwillingness to represent Christ suffering because of the emperor. Rather, with the Christological debate on the agenda, preachers were, for example, making the suffering real and vivid in words, while reminding the audience of the limitations of human nature to apprehend God even after what was unseen became seen. Thus the easier alternative, of reading a torso as representing Christ not suffering, could contradict the preacher who was reminding the audience of the realness of the pains and struggles.

Eventually the Christological controversy explained the soundness of depicting Christ's death, representing the 'taking up suffering'. Until Chalcedonian and anti-Chalcedonian formulations spread, tension remained in the meaning of a crucified Christ, since it ought to reflect what happens to Christ on the cross. Either representation could be interpreted as showing only one of the natures: if dead, then it is the humanity, which took up our death. If living, watchful, it is the divinity, which shatters the doors of hell. Bishops were unwilling to leave the intellectual activity that could open such sound theological interpretations unregulated. This may explain the scarcity of representations of the crucifixion,

---

[56] 'All who grant the union of divinity and humanity, would agree with us that concerning what has been united, it is no longer called one but two, if you again divide by concept and examine each according to itself. Do not split the union!, for it is impossible both to watch the union and to examine each according to itself at the same time. What has been united became one indissolubly and no longer becomes two.' Καὶ ταῦτα ἡμῖν συνομολογήσειαν ἂν ἅπαντες οἱ ἕνωσιν ὁμολογοῦντες θεότητός τε καὶ ἀνθρωπότητος· τὸ γὰρ ἑνωθὲν οὐκέτι δύο, ἀλλ' ἓν ὀνομάζεται, τῇ δὲ ἐννοίᾳ πάλιν [εἰ] διαιρεῖς καὶ ἕκαστον κατ' ἰδίαν σκοπεῖς. οὐκοῦν λύεις τὴν ἕνωσιν· ἀδύνατον γὰρ ἅμα καὶ φυλάττειν τὴν ἕνωσιν καὶ ἑκάτερον κατ' ἰδίαν σκοπεῖν, ἀλλὰ τὸ ἑνωθὲν ἀλύτως ἓν γέγονε καὶ οὐκέτι γίνεται δύο. Theod. Anc., *Hom.* I 7, ed. E. Schwartz ACO I 1/2 (1927), 83-4.

[57] The *Christus dolens* typology had few proponents in the East. It was criticised for blending (συγκαταμείγνυμι) suffering to Christ's nature (characterised as ἁπλός and ἀνείδεος) by Ignatios, the Deacon, for example. See *Ignatii diaconi Vita Tarasii*, 416 ed. Ivar A. Heikel, ASSF 17 (Helsingfors, 1891).

[58] Also Choricius of Gaza introduces the description of the Passion scenes in a narrative cycle in the sixth-century St Sergius church in Gaza reflecting that 'art knows how to represent God in human disguise', *Laudatio Marciani* I, 72, ed. Richard Foerster and Eberhard Richtsteig (Leipzig, 1929); trans. Cyril Mango, *The Art of the Byzantine Empire 312-1453: Sources and Documents* (Toronto, 1986), 67.

until after Chalcedon the majority of the viewers would be familiar enough with the matters at stake to read the image conventionally, so that not only the cross was the Glory, but the torso was the Word.

In crucifixes, the Word could be represented, not any more an event in the Life of Christ, who is the incarnate Word of God. Rather, on them the Word was depicted at the crucial stage of the sin redeeming victory over the Devil. It was a visual solution for Cyril's argument approved as orthodox in Ephesus I: 'According to the same manner we consider the dying; for the *lógos* of God is by nature immortal, incorruptible, life and life-giving; and since contrariwise his own body, by the grace of God, as Paul says, tasted death for all, it is said that he himself suffered death for us, not as if going towards an experience of death approaching his own nature (for it is madness to say or think this), but because, as I just said, his flesh tasted death.'[59]

Chalcedon allegedly clarified how to speak and represent the suffering of Christ in relation to his divinity, and sanctioned overtly representing Christ in human events. This endorsed a proliferation of large scale images of Christ crucified, from the mid-fifth century onwards, as in the Western mosaics, such as St Apollinare in Classe.[60] Christ's torso no longer conflicted with either 'Christ taking up our death', or 'the non suffering God'. Not even the developing 'monophysitism' hindered the proliferation of depictions of the crucified.[61] Also in monasteries, crucifixes would adorn the churches, shrines and cells, and in so far as the frescoes of Abu Hennis[62] may be representative of a larger phenomenon, the utility of visual images may have won the day, and the reticence to visual representation of the crucifixion subsided.

Placing the problems of representation of the crucifixion in the context of the contemporary Christian theological debates and visual and artistic environment contributes to the re-reading of Dölger's 'classical project' by showing the ongoing dialogue with the artistic environment in Late Antiquity. The imperial patronage gave the necessary means, including setting and funding, to represent the cross as symbol of Christ's majesty and power with great opulence. Neither the panegyric comparison of emperor and Christ, nor artistic limitations had been hindering large scale crucifixes. Rather, theological problems had to

---

[59] κατὰ τὸν ἴσον δὲ τρόπον καὶ ἐπὶ τοῦ τεθνάναι νοοῦμεν. ἀθάνατος μὲν γὰρ κατὰ φύσιν καὶ ἄφθαρτος καὶ ζωὴ καὶ ζωοποιός ἐστιν ὁ τοῦ θεοῦ λόγος· ἐπειδὴ δὲ πάλιν τὸ ἴδιον αὐτοῦ σῶμα χάριτι θεοῦ, καθά φησιν ὁ Παῦλος, ὑπὲρ παντὸς ἐγεύσατο θανάτου, λέγεται παθεῖν αὐτὸς τὸν ὑπὲρ ἡμῶν θάνατον, οὐχ ὡς εἰς πεῖραν ἐλθὼν τοῦ θανάτου τό γε ἧκον εἰς τὴν αὐτοῦ φύσιν (ἀποπληξία γὰρ τοῦτο λέγειν ἢ φρονεῖν), ἀλλ' ὅτι, καθάπερ ἔφην ἀρτίως, ἡ σὰρξ αὐτοῦ ἐγεύσατο θανάτου. Cyr., *Ep. ad Nestorium* II (*Ep.* 4) 5, ed. E. Schwartz ACO I 1/1 (1914), 27.

[60] H.L. Kessler, 'Bright gardens' (2008), 128.

[61] P.J. Alexander, 'The iconoclastic council' (1953).

[62] H.L. Kessler, 'Bright gardens' (2008), 126. Little monumental Coptic art has been preserved, but can be supplemented, for example, with embroideries that echo their visual language, see Dorothy G. Shepherd, 'Late coptic embroideries', *BClevMus* 37(3) (1950), 46-8.

be surpassed. Pioneering depictions of Christ crucified dialogued with late antique communicative structures and classical art, circumventing incompatibilities to complete narrative visual cycles of Christ's life. If the early crucifixions in narrative cycles avoided the theological conflict by pointing to a moment of the Passion when Christ was still alive, the theological debate gave the semantic material for the iconography to be further refined and turn to crucifixes, where a living torso represents Christ redeeming death on the cross. Independent developments were ground breaking and provided a visual repertoire which was not enough to avoid semiotic contradictions inherent to the narrative being portrayed. When the visual representation of Christ crucified lost most of its narrative message, crucifixes could arise and stand for the Christological solutions.

Zoltán Kádár and the Early Christian Iconography of Roman Pannonia.
Some Problems of Interpretation

Levente NAGY, Pécs, Hungary

ABSTRACT

Zoltán Kádár was an outstanding expert of Early Christian art iconography of Roman Pannonia in 20th-century Hungary, his fundamental book about this topic was published in 1939. It is, however, high time to re-evaluate some of his interpretations. This contribution deals with four unsolved iconographical problems of Early Christian art in Roman Pannonia. In the case of each questions I try to show at first the answer or proposed interpretation of Zoltán Kádár. This is followed by other answers given in later literature to these days (including my own interpretations) in order to show the way to a new iconographical survey.

Zoltán Kádár was an outstanding expert of Early Christian art and iconography in 20th-century Hungary. Hungarian research was very influenced by his book on the iconography of the Early Christian monuments of Pannonia, published in 1939.[1] He took part in many international conferences on Early Christian archaeology mostly in the 1960s, where he presented his most important iconographical observations printed earlier, or slight modifications of them.[2] In the beginning of the 21st century it is high time to re-evaluate Early Christian representations found on casket-mounts, small artefacts, or wall paintings. Some observations of Zoltán Kádár can be held as outdated by now, but he had also some essential ideas which still provide a good basis for new interpretations. My contribution deals with four unsolved iconographical problems of Early Christian art in Roman Pannonia in the hope to find better founded solutions. Dealing with these four iconographical questions, I try to show at first the answer or proposed interpretation of Zoltán Kádár. This is followed by other answers that can be found in subsequent literature to these days, and I include my own interpretations, which are considered by myself only as

---

[1] Zoltán Kádár, *Pannónia ókeresztény emlékeinek ikonográfiája (L' iconografia dei monumenti paleocristiani della Pannonia)* (Budapest, 1939).

[2] A fundamental summary of this period is Zoltán Kádár, 'Lineamenti dell' arte della Pannonia dell' epoca di antichitá tarda e paleocristiana', *Corso di cultura sull' arte Ravennate e Byzantina* XVI (1969), 179-201.

Studia Patristica LXXIII, 195-218.
© Peeters Publishers, 2014.

possible solutions within the framwork of Late Antique iconographical conventions of Early Christian art and the biblical contexts of the representations as well.

My first question is: who is represented by the four busts on the barrel-vault in the St. Peter and Paul burial chamber of the Late Roman – Early Christian northern cemetery of Sopianae, or who is starring at us from a paradisiac landscape, as we have learnt from the paper of Professor Zsolt Visy (fig. 1)?[3] In the 1930s it seemed to be not so hard for Zoltán Kádár to find an answer. The popular danish archaeologist, Ejnar Dyggve happened to excavate the Early Christian Marusinac cemetery of Salona at that time, and the architectural analogies of the *loculus* in the Sopianae hypogaeum with the Marusinac *mausoleum* containing the relics of the martyr Anastasius seemed to be obvious.[4] Behind the *fenestella* of the northern wall, martyr relics could be placed, and the heads in the medaillons belonged to unknown martyrs, so the *hypogaeum* should have been an Early Christian *heroon*, where the figures of the two apostles with the sign of Christ symbolise his resurrection (*anastasis*) and that of the hero buried here.[5] Zoltán Kádár called therefore the scene of Peter and Paul

---

[3] Zsolt Visy, 'The Paradise in the Early Christian cemetery of Sopianae', being published in this volume; see also Ferenc Fülep, *Sopianae. The History of Pécs during the Roman era and the Problem of the Continuity of the Late Roman Population*, Archaeologia Hungarica 50 (Budapest, 1984), 39; Zsolt Visy, 'Recent Data on the Structure of the Early Christian Burial Buildings in Pécs', *Acta Classica Universitatis Debreceniensis* 43 (2007), 137-55, 146; Krisztina Hudák and Levente Nagy, *A Fine and Private Place. Discovering the Early Christian Cemetery of Sopianae*, Heritage booklets 6 (Pécs, 2009²), 53; Krisztina Hudák, 'The Iconographical Program of the Wallpaintings in the Saint Peter and Paul Burial Chamber of Sopianae (Pécs)', *Mitteilungen zur Christlichen Archäologie* 15 (2009), 47-76, 60.

[4] Ejnar Dyggve, 'Das Mausoleum in Pécs', *Pannonia* 1 (1935), 62-77, especially 67, 69-70, 75. Another researchers later seemed to accept the possiblity of this interpretation, too: Helmut Buschhausen, *Die spätrömische Metallscrinia und die frühchristlichen Reliquienaltäre*, Wiener Byzantinische Studien IX (Wien, 1971), 16; F. Fülep, *Sopianae* (1984), 41; Wolfgang Schmidt, 'Spätantike Gräberfelder in den Nordprovinzen der römischen Reiches und das Aufkommen christlichen Bestattungsbrauchtums. Tricciana (Ságvár) in der Provinz Valeria', *Saalburg Jahrbuch* 50 (2000), 213-441, 292; Olivér Gábor, 'Sopianae ókeresztény egyházai [The Early Christian Churches of Sopianae], *Janus Pannonius Múzeum Évkönyve* 50-52 (2005-2007) [2008], 118; Renate Pillinger, 'Early Christian Grave Paintings in Niš, between East and West', *Niš & Byzantium. The Collections of Scientific Works* X (Niš, 2011), 35; Levente Nagy, *Pannóniai városok, mártírok, ereklyék. Négy szenvedéstörténet helyszínei nyomában (Cities, Martyrs, Relics in Pannonia. Discovering the Topography of Four Pannonian Passion Stories)*, Thesaurus Historiae Ecclesiasticae in Universitate Quinqueecclesiensi 1 (Pécs, 2012), 177-82, English: 225-6. Despite the rejection of the existence of a basilica discoperta in Marusinac, the chronology of the cult complex of Anastasius martyr established by Ejnar Dyggve can be still accepted today: Emilio Marin, 'Solinska crkva i njezini mučenici. Istraživanja i otkrića (The Church of Salona and Its Martyrs. Research and Discoveries)', in Darija Damjanović (priredila), *1700 godina svetih srijemskih mučenika. Zbornik radova s međunarodnog simpozija o 1700. obljetnici Sirmijsko-panoniskih mučenika (304.-2004.)*, Zbornik posvećen pokojnom doc. dr. sc. Andriji Šuljaku (Đakovo, 2011), 140.

[5] Z. Kádár, *Pannonia ókeresztény emlékeinek ikonográfiája* (1939), 4, 10-5, 58-9.

an *anastasis*-representation.[6] The symbols of eternal life and resurrection are clearly visible in this Christian funeral context, but the strong relationships of the ancient hero cult with the cult of the saints have been outdated at the latest since 1981, when Peter Brown published his book about the cult of the saints, simply due to the development of the methodology of Late Antique history of religions.[7] Recently Krisztina Hudák did not exclude the possibility from the point of view of an iconographical analysis of the heads (fig. 2), that the four men should represent a group of four Pannonian martyrs, the so-called *IV sancti coronati*, whose cult was present in Rome in the SS. Pietro e Marcellino catacomb.[8] Hudák stressed also the similarities of the style of some details and ornaments between the Via Labicana catacomb and the Sopianae hypogaeum.[9] Possibly due to the iconographical conventions of the individualized heads of busts depicted in the medaillons in Roman funerary art, Endre Tóth argued for an interpretation of four dead men, who were buried there.[10] Other scholars argued for a symbolic or cosmological meaning of the four persons, regarding them as allusions to the four Gospels, four seasons, four edges of the world, four winds, or to the four rivers of Paradise.[11] Last year, when I read a paper about the after life interpretations of the paintings in Sopianae at the international conference "Norico-pannonian autonomous towns" in Szombathely, I tried to summarize the three main theories and the possible arguments against them as follows:[12]

1. Are these heads idealised anonyme portraits, *i.e.* personifications of symbolic ideas (happiness, seasons, Gospels, *etc.*)? My problem with these interpretations is, that they do not fit the iconographical conventions of Roman and Early Christian funerary art. The heads in Sopianae are not equally young, not

[6] Z. Kádár, *Pannonia ókeresztény emlékeinek ikonográfiája* (1939), 6-8, 58. István Bugár provides a new theological analysis of the Peter-Paul scene from Sopianae: István Bugár, 'Theology on Images? Some Observations on the Murals in the Peter and Paul Burial Chamber of Pécs', this volume, 281-95.

[7] Peter Brown, *The Cult of the Saints* (Chicago, 1980), 5-8; Friedrich Wilhelm Deichmann, *Einführung in die christliche Archäologie* (Darmstadt, 1983), 54-5.

[8] Levente Nagy, *Pannóniai városok, mártírok, ereklyék* (2012), 153-77, english: 225-6; Krisztina Hudák and Levente Nagy, *A Fine and Private Place* (2009²), 82-5.

[9] Krisztina Hudák, 'The iconographical program' (2009), 64-70.

[10] Endre Tóth, 'Sopianae a késő császárkorban' [Sopianae in the Late Roman period], *Jelenkor* XLIV (November 2011), 1134.

[11] Friedrich Gerke, 'Die Wandmalereien der Petrus-Paulus Katakombe in Pécs (Sopianae)', *Forschungen zur Kunstgeschichte und christlichen Archäologie. Neue Beiträge zur Kunstgeschichte des 1. Jahrtausends* I/2: *Frühmittelalterliche Kunst* (Baden-Baden, 1954), 190-1; Csaba Pozsárkó and Zsolt Tóth, *Pécs in den römischen Zeiten. Wegweiser zu den Schauplätzen des Welterbes in Pécs* (Pécs, 2011), 35.

[12] Levente Nagy, 'Jenseitsvorstellungen und ihre Interpretationsprobleme im spätrömischen frühchristlichen Gräberfeld von Sopianae/Pécs', Lecture at the fifth international conference 'Autonomous Towns in Noricum and Pannonia' on the 25th october 2011. The publication is forthcoming in the proceedings of the conference.

idealized, and the analogies of similar individualized heads of busts in medaillions can be interpreted mostly as representations of the deceased.[13] I show *exempli gratia* five of them on murals from both pagan and Christian contexts, *i.e.* from the Via Latina catacomb,[14] the Domitilla catacomb,[15] the burial chamber of Aelia Arisuth from Oea,[16] from another burial chamber from Or-ha-ner,[17] all 4th century, and from the Via Portuense *hypogaeum*, 2nd century A.D.[18] (figs. 3-7).

2. Could these heads point to busts of members of a family buried in the chamber? As Ferenc Fülep, and Krisztina Hudák pointed out in their papers, the small hypogaeum could have been built originally for one deceased.[19]

3. Are these busts indeed representations of deceased men, *i.e.* martyrs in Paradise? Could the *loculus* behind the northern wall have been a place for their relics, according to the analogy of the *hypogaeum* of the Anastasius-Mausoleum of Salona? The famous painting on the barrel vault of the *cubiculum* 3 in the SS. Pietro e Marcellino catacomb with similar composition, like the northern wall and barrel vault of the St. Peter and Paul Burial Chamber, with Peter, Paul, Christ, and Christ once more as the lamb venerated by the four most famous martyrs of the catacomb (Peter, Marcellinus, Tiburtius, Gorgonius) was taken as analogy already by Krisztina Hudák.[20] Now I would like to add another analogy on a gold-sandwich glas from Rome, with the head of Christ in the middle of the composition, and with four busts in the four corners,

---

[13] K. Hudák, 'The iconographical program' (2009), note 67; R. Pillinger, 'Early Christian Grave Paintings in Niš' (2011), 33; L. Nagy, *Pannóniai városok, mártírok, ereklyék* (2012), 177, english: 226; fig. 30.

[14] Antonio Ferrua, *Katakomben: Unbekannte Bilder des frühen Christentums unter der Via Latina* (Stuttgart, 1991), 149.

[15] Pasquale Testini, *Le catacombe e gli antichi cimiteri cristiani in Roma*, Roma cristiana II (Bologna, 1966), fig. 171; This analogy was also taken by K. Hudák, 'The iconographical program' (2009), note 94.

[16] Ranuccio Bianchi Bandinelli, *Rome. La fin de l'art antique*, L'universe des formes (Paris, 1970), fig. 243.

[17] Talila Michaeli, 'Funerary Lights in Painted Tombs in Israel: from Paganism to Christianity', in Carmen Guiral Pelegrin (ed.), *Circulacion de temas y sistemas decorativos en la pintura mural antigua. Actas del IX Congreso Internacional de la Association Internationale pour la Peinture Antique (AIPMA)*, Zaragoza-Catalayud 21-25 septiembre 2004 (Zaragoza, 2007), 203-8, 533. This analogy was taken by Dorottya Gáspár, *Christianity in Roman Pannonia. An Evaluation of Early Christian Finds and Sites from Hungary*, British Archaeological Reports International Series 1010 (Oxford, 2002), 73, figs. 210-1.

[18] R. Bianchi Bandinelli, *Rome. Le centre du pouvoir. L'art Romain des origines a la fin du deuxième siècle*, L'universe des formes (Paris, 1969), fig. 99.

[19] F. Fülep, *Sopianae* (1984), 41; K. Hudák, 'The iconographical program' (2009), 64.

[20] Vincenzo Fiocchi Nicolai, Fabrizio Bisconti and Danilo Mazzoleni, *Roms Christliche Katakomben. Geschichte-Bilderwelt-Inschriften* (Regensburg, 2000²), fig. 144; K. Hudák, 'The iconographical program' (2009), fig. 18.

interpreted as heads of martyrs (fig. 8).[21] The only problem with this idea is the absence of written sources about any cult of martyrs in Late Roman Sopianae. Archaeological research was until now not able to find a cemetery basilica built for the cult of martyrs,[22] although the best analogies of the Late Roman period are the Early Christian cemetery of Sopianae in Salona and the one in Naissus which have their own martyrs and funerary basilicas by the end of fourth, beginning of fifth century.[23] The question is still open to discussion.

My second iconographical question is: what kind of plant can be seen above Jonah, thrown up by the monster on the eastern wall of the Petrus and Paulus burial chamber in Sopianae (fig. 9)? Imre Henszlmann discussed already as early as in the year 1873 the possibility of identifying the plant to be a gourd tree or ivy leaves or a *qiqeion* read in the hebrew original text of Jonah in the Old Testament.[24] If the plant is indeed an ivy, a possible *terminus post quem* of the painting can been defined, namely a dating after the years 389 to 392, when Jerome had finished translating the book of Jonah. The paintings of the burial chamber would then be dated to the very end of the 4th century which would also fit the style and analogies of the portait-like heads on the barrel-vault.[25] This theory was examined by György Heidl in the year 2005, when he identified the depicted plant with the *qiqeion*, mentioned in the hebrew version of the book of Jonah, a plant growing in Palestina. Since Jerome published his commentary of the book of Jonah in the year 397, where he tried to explain his translation of *qiqueion* to *hedera* instead of the well-known *cucurbita*, György Heidl suggested this year as the new *terminus post quem* of the whole icono-graphical program of the burial chamber after 397.[26]

Zoltán Kádár chose another solution. He regarded the ivy leaf as a dionysic motiv in a clearly Christian context, a sign of a so-called dionysiac syncretism, where the Jonah figure lying under the ivy should have been based on a prototype,

[21] Geffrey Spier (ed.), *Picturing the Bible. The Beginnings of Christian Art* (New Haven, London and Fort Worth, 2007), 219, Kat. Nr. 45.

[22] K. Hudák and L. Nagy, *A Fine and Private Place* (2009), 76-9, 85-6.

[23] Emilio Marin (coord.), *Salona IV. Inscriptions de Salona Chrétienne, IVᵉ-VIIᵉ siècles I,* Collection d'École Française de Rome 194/4 (Rome and Split, 2010), 16-8; Emilio Marin, 'Solinska crkva i njezini mučenici' (2011), 139-40; Miša Rakocija, 'Paleobyzantine Churches of Niš. Preliminary Survey', *Niš & Byzantium. The Collections of Scientific Works* V (Niš, 2007), 127-33; R. Pillinger, 'Early Christian Grave Paintings in Niš' (2011), 30-5.

[24] Imre Henszlmann, 'Die altchristliche Grabkammer in Fünfkirchen'. *Mitteilungen der Kaiserlichen und Königlichen Central-Commission zur Erforschung und Erhaltung der Baudenkmale* 18 (1873), 65-6, note 29.

[25] Krisztina Hudák, 'The Chronology of the Paintings in the Saint Peter and Paul Burial Chamber in Sopianae', in Szilvia Bíró (ed.), *Ex officina… Studia in honorem Dénes Gabler* (Győr, 2009), 228-30.

[26] György Heidl, 'A pécsi 1 számú sírkamra Jónás-freskója és Szt. Jeromos Jónás-kommentárja' [The fresco of Burial Chamber Nr. 1 in Sopianae, and the commentary of St. Jerome about the Book of Jonah], *Katekhón* 2 (2005/1), 221-35.

the lying Bacchus depictions in earlier Greek-Roman art.[27] His main argument, however, according to which the second panel of the eastern wall near Jonah should be a dionysiac scene, can hardly be substantiated, as we can not find any bacchic-representation on the panel, there is only a part of the hip of a possibly naked figure.[28] Hence, instead of a dionysiac imagery on the eastern wall, I can identify Jonah's plant rather as gourd than ivy which needs further discussion.

Actually I do not know, whether the commissioner of the painting got to know the then recently published Christian literature, and especially whether he had access to and knowledge of the commentary of Jerome on the book of Jonah. Did he want to see, based on Jerome, here intentionally a *qiqeion* and not an ivy-leaf? It is also questionable, whether the painter was able to paint a plant from Palestina that he had never seen before, instead of the gourd tree which was well-known from pattern books, or the ivy, recently known from the new Bible text.[29]

My third question refers to an unusual representation on the so called syncretistic casket mount from the village Császár in northern Transdanubia. It has been found in a 4th century grave of a woman in 1901, together with a golden earring (type Facsády III B).[30] The woman has been put secondarily in a grave built from earlier tombstones and a stone altar, where another deceased was lying already, together with two glas flasks dated to the second half of

---

[27] Z. Kádár, *Pannonia ókeresztény emlékeinek ikonográfiája* (1939), 30.

[28] So thinks D. Gáspár, *Christianity in Roman Pannonia* (2002), 72, although she does not exclude the possibility of bacchic motifs beside biblical scenes as 'pannonian practice', because on the casket mount of Császár discussed below there are bacchic and biblical scenes together in the same iconographical program. Iconographical arguments against the bacchic interpretation: K. Hudák, 'The iconographical program' (2009), note 24. The identity of the naked figure (Daniel or Good Sheperd?) in the middle panel of the eastern wall of the burial camber was vigorously discussed by György Heidl, 'Remarks on the Iconography in the "Peter-Paul" (No. 1) Burial Chamber of Sopianae', and by Péter Csigi, 'Deliberate Ambiguities in Early Christian Wall Paintings in Sopianae', both contributions are published in this volume (pp. 219-35 and pp. 237-48). Although I do not think, that the biblical scenes were commissioned and elected by the owner of the *hypogaeum* as pure decorations by chance (nobody argued for this hypercritical interpretation during the discussions of the conference), according to my own opinion, placing of both representations of Daniel and Good Shepherd between the Fall and Jonah could have a theological background that may have been in the mind of the commissioner.

[29] Similar questions have been raised by Krisztina Hudák, 'The iconographical program' (2009), note 122. The answers for my questions I got from the paper of György Heidl, 'Remarks on the Iconography in the "Peter-Paul" (No. 1) Burial Chamber of Sopianae', this volume, 219-35. For the existence of pattern books in antiquity argued recently Michael Donderer, 'Und es gab sie doch! Ein neuer Papyrus und das Zeugnis der Mosaiken belegen die Verwendung antiker „Musterbücher"', *Antike Welt* 36 (2005/2), 61-8.

[30] Ede Mahler, 'Császári (Komárom m.) sírleletek' [Burial finds from Császár (County Komárom)], *Archaeológiai Értesítő* 22 (1902), 24-8, Fig. 4a; Annamária Facsády, *Aquincumi ékszerek (Jewellery in Aquincum)*, Az Aquincumi Múzeum gyűjteménye 1 (Budapest, 1999), 80, Table 5.

the fourth century.[31] The iconographical program of the casket, dated by Krisztina Hudák to the second third of the fourth century based on stylistic observations,[32] was examined in detail in my habilitation lecture at the University of Pécs, which has been published in the periodical *Mitteilungen zur Christlichen Archäologie* in Vienna (fig. 10). Three biblical salvation scenes, the Good Shepherd, Daniel, the sacrifice of Isaac, and two further mythological representations can be seen on the casket, I tried to interpretate the thiasos-scenery and the figures of the seven planetary gods as allegories of joy, hapiness, *gaudium in nomine dei*, and of a perfect creation during seven days provided by God.[33]

Let me also draw attention to the scene with a sitting figure, listened to by a crowd, whose interpretation was problematized in earlier research (fig. 11). The first publisher of the casket, József Hampel argued in 1902 for a representation of Joseph and his brothers from the book of Genesis.[34] Zoltán Kádár saw in 1939 a picture of the sermon of the mountain, where the Emperor-Christ was depicted as the judge at the Last Judgement, but he does not sit on a tribunal in order to be closer to the ordinary people, as a kind of a popular or democratic ruler.[35] The *maiestas domini* interpretation became popular in later Hungarian research, too, with allusion to the Last Judgement.[36] In order to understand this image, I tried to collect all analogies of the earlier mentioned representations in fourth century Christian iconography. The task was not so difficult, because the only surely Joseph-and sermon of the mountain representations are known from the Via Latina catacomb, cubiculum B (fig. 12)[37] and from the so called polychrome plate of Rome in the Palazzo Massimo dated to the preconstantinian period (fig. 13).[38] They do not seem to be good iconographical analogies to

---

[31] Ede Mahler, 'Császári sírleletek' (1902), Fig. 2-3.

[32] Krisztina Hudák, *Bibliai témák és szentábrázolások a sirmiumi Metropolia ókeresztény művészetében [Biblical figures and representations of Saints in the Early Christian Art of the Metropolia of Sirmium]*, M.A. Dissertation manuscript (Budapest, 2003), 33-4, 39.

[33] Levente Nagy, 'Bemerkungen zum ikonographischen Programm des frühchristlichen Kästchenbeschlags von Császár (Ungarn)', *Mitteilungen zur Christlichen Archäologie* 18 (2012), 61-90.

[34] József Hampel, Császári (Komárom m.) sírleletek [Grabfunde aus Császár (Komitat Komárom)], *Archaeológiai Értesítő* 22 (1902), 39.

[35] Z. Kádár, *Pannonia ókeresztény emlékeinek ikonográfiája* (1939), 34-5.

[36] Dorottya Gáspár, *Römische Kästchen aus Pannonien I-II*, Antaeus. Mitteilungen der Archäologischen Instituts der Ungarischen Akademie der Wissenschaften 15 (Budapest, 1986), I 146; D. Gáspár, *Christianity in Roman Pannonia* (2002), 34; K. Hudák, *Bibliai témák és szentábrázolások* (2003), 38.

[37] A. Ferrua, *Katakomben* (1991), 82, Abb. 67. The interpretation of the scene with the frontal sitting figure from the reliquiary casket from Milano found under the altar of the church S. Nazaro as Joseph and his brothers is not impossible, but uncertain: G. Spier, *Picturing the Bible* (2007), 262, Kat. Nr. 77.

[38] Guntram Koch, *Frühchristliche Sarkophage*, Handbuch der Archäologie (München, 2000), 162, fig. 16; Fabrizio Bisconti, 'Sermone della Montagna', in Fabrizio Bisconti (ed.), *Temi di*

the Császár casket, nor does the only sure Last Judgement representation on the sarcophagus in New York from the 4th century, with lambs and rams on each side of Christ (fig. 14).[39]

The best analogies of the iconographical type of the sitting person listened to by the crowd can be found in Pannonia and Dalmatia, on the casket of Bakonya (fig. 15),[40] on the dagger sheet of Pölöske (fig. 16),[41] on a gem stone from Carnuntum,[42] and a glas medaillon from Narona in the archaeological Museum of Split (fig. 17).[43] On the casket of Bakonya, presented during this conference by Zsolt Visy[44] and to be published in the periodical *Specimina Nova*, one reads under the sitting figure the inscription *dominus*, which refers together with the christogram on the casket of Császár to Christ, or to a Christian emperor. It is sure, that the iconographical antecedents of this imagery are the audience representations of Roman imperial art, called *"Kaiserliche Audienzszenen"* by Hans Gabelmann.[45] Regarding christogram, philosophers' dress, and the rotulus in his hand I tend to interpretate the picture not as a Christian emperor, but as an unusual type of the teaching Christ representations that have become popular on sarcophagi during the second third of the fourth century. Instead of the usual frontal composition these examples from Illyricum are depicted in

---

iconografia paleocristiana, Sussidi allo studio delle antichità cristiana 13 (Città del Vaticano, 2000), 279; Martin Büchsel, *Die Entstehung des Christusporträts. Bildarchäologie statt Bildhypnose* (Mainz, 2003), 17, Abb. 1; L. Nagy, 'Bemerkungen zum ikonographischen Programm' (2012), note 67.

[39] Joseph Engemann, 'Hirt', *Reallexikon für Antike und Christentum* 15 (1989), 604-7; G. Koch, *Frühchristliche Sarkophage* (2000), 182; fig. 20; L. Nagy, 'Bemerkungen zum ikonographischen Programm' (2012), note 69.

[40] Ferenc Fazekas, Olivér Gábor, Levente Nagy and Zsolt Visy, *A késő római kor és az ókereszténység Sopianae és Valeria területén – Geç Roma dönemindeki Sopianae ve Valeria-Erken Hristiyanlık – Sopianae and Valeria in the Late Roman Age-Early Christianity*. Specimina Nova dissertationum ex Instituto Historico Universitatis Quinqueecclesiensis, Supplementum 10 (Pécs, 2010), 38.

[41] Z. Kádár, *Pannonia ókeresztény emlékeinek ikonográfiája* (1939), 34, fig. 20; D. Gáspár, *Christianity in Roman Pannonia* (2002), 94; fig. 267.

[42] Franz Humer and Gabrielle Kremer (eds), *Götterbilder – Menschenbilder. Religion und Kulte in Carnuntum*, Ausstellung im Rahmen der Niederösterreichischen Landesausstellung 2011 "Erobern-Entdecken-Erleben im Römerland Carnuntum" im Archäologischen Museum Carnuntinum, Bad Deutsch-Altenburg 16. April 2011 bis 15. November 2012 (Wien, 2011), 432, Kat. Nr. 1035.

[43] Nenad Cambi, 'La figure du Christ sur les monuments paleochrétiens de Dalmatie', *Disputationes Salonitanae* 1970, 54, Fig. 4, but the identification of the scene as sermon of the mountain is – like in the case of the Császár casket – incertain, simply because of the absence of the hill or mountain, where the speaking figure (teaching Christ?) is sitting on.

[44] Zsolt Visy, 'The Paradise in the Early Christian Cemetery of Sopianae', this volume, 59-73.

[45] Hans Gabelmann, *Antike Audienz- und Tribunalszenen* (Darmstadt, 1984), 105-10, 156, 190-7, 211-21, Taf. 21, 23, 31, 33, 38-39, 54, 58, 62, 64; L. Nagy, 'Bemerkungen zum ikonographischen Programm' (2012), notes 73-9.

profile.[46] My interpretation is only a possibility that fits the conventions of Early Christian iconography, the question of the identity of the sitting figure is, however, open for discussion.

My last, but maybe most exciting question relates to an unusual Lazarus-representation of a casket mount in the Late Roman cemetery of Ságvár (southern Transdanubia) from the grave 54,[47] which can also be dated to the second third of the 4th century (fig. 18).[48] The scene is unusual not only because of the extremly small, bearded mummy of Lazarus: Christ has his staff, the *"virga thaumaturgica"* not in his right, but in his left hand, in his right hand he holds a long unusual thing. In an earlier contribution Zoltán Kádár saw the iconographical antecedents of the Early Christian Lazarus-representations in an Egyptianizing Roman art, especially in the depictions of Osiris: on a fresco from the *ecclesiasterion* of the Iseum in Pompeji there is a believer standing before the Osiris-statue depicted in an *aedicula*.[49] His idea has been partly accepted by later research, but rather stressing an influence of Hellenized Roman art of Alexandria on Early Christian iconography.[50] In 2010, at the conference of the Hungarian Patristic Society I held a lecture about the Lazarus depictions and more specifically about this particular piece from Ságvár,[51] while György Heidl presented another lecture about the interpretation of the wonder-making staff of Christ, not mentioned in the Gospels.

Examining the representations of the wonder making Christ, we rejected both the interpretation of Jesus as a sorcerer suggested by American scholars, especially that recently proposed by Thomas Mathews.[52] Instead, I tried to interpret the staff as a visual appearance of the resuscitating words of Christ, and maybe

---

[46] L. Nagy, 'Bemerkungen zum ikonographischen Programm' (2012), 71-7.

[47] Alice Sz. Burger, 'The Late Roman Cemetery at Ságvár', *Acta Archaeologica Academiae Scientiarum Hungariae* VIII (1966), 99, 105, fig. 2, 97, Pl. LXXXII, 1; W. Schmidt, 'Spätantike Gräberfelder' (2000), 357-8, 363-4.

[48] K. Hudák, *Bibliai témák és szentábrázolások* (2003), 15, 33-4, 44.

[49] Zoltán Kádár, 'Zur Frage der römerzeitlichen ägyptischen Elemente in der altchristlichen Ikonographie', in *Akten des VII. Congresso Internazionale di Archeologia Cristiana, 5-11 September 1965, Trier* (Città del Vaticano and Berlin, 1969), 575-8; Abb. 1.

[50] Jan Stanisław Partyka, *La résurrection de Lazare dans les monuments funéraires des nécropoles chrétiennes à Rome*, Travaux de Centre d' Archéologie Mediterranéenne de l'Académie Polonaise des Sciences 33 (Warszawa, 1993), 35-6, 92-3; Fred C. Albertson, 'An Isiac Model for the Raising of Lazarus in Early Christian Art', *Jahrbuch für Antike Christentum* 38 (1995), 123-32 (pls. 1-2), 127.

[51] Levente Nagy, 'Interpretationsprobleme des frühchristlichen Kästchenbeschlags mit Lazarus-Darstellung von Ságvár, Grab 54', *Specimina Nova dissertationum ex Instituto Historico Universitatis Quinqueecclesiensis* 2014, forthcoming

[52] Thomas F. Mathews, *The Clash of Gods. A Reinterpretation of Early Christian Art* (Princeton, 1999²), 54-69, notes 27-9; rejected recently by Vasiliki Tsamakda, 'Eine ungewöhnliche Darstellung der Heilung des Paralytikers in der Domitilla Katakombe: Zur Verwendung des Wunderstabes in der frühchristlichen Kunst', *Mitteilungen zur Christlichen Archäologie* 15 (2009), 25-45, 40, with further literature.

as a representation of the *logos*, the words of Jesus as well.[53] More interesting was the recently published solution of György Heidl, who could demonstrate with the help of some texts of Saint Ambrose, that the staff, as a picture of the transfigurating words of Christ can be connected to baptismal liturgy, where the priest is using it, too.[54]

The most important question in this context is: what is that strange thing in the right hand of Jesus? In the year 1968, Zoltán Kádár saw a snake in the right hand of Jesus, and he thought that Jesus defeated death and the satan represented in the form of a snake, and withholds evil from his resurrected friend Lazarus.[55] Zoltán Kádár had also another interpretation in mind: the picture could represent a syncretistic Asklepios-Christ figure as an allusion to the pagan god Asklepios,[56] who was able to heal people and also to resurrect the dead, according to an antique mythological tradition from the 4th century BC.[57]

Helmut Buschhausen and Dorottya Gáspár, both great experts of Late Roman casket mounts, rejected the identification of the strange thing as a snake, and instead argued for the identification of the thing as a pleat or ruck of the *pallium* of Jesus, who is dressed anyway in a tunica.[58] Jesus holds the edges of his well identified garments usually with his left hand. However, the thick pleat of a *pallium* hanging down to the earth in the palm of Jesus (and not on his arm or on his shoulder) has no good analogies in the Early Christian Lazarus imagery, especially not on the nearest analogies of the Lazarus-representation of Ságvár (Trier, Köln, Wiesbaden, Intercisa, Keszthely, München, figs. 19-21).[59] The mount itself is unfortunately too small, but if one tries to enlarge the

---

[53] The starting point of my interpretation was Claudia Nauerth, 'Heilungswunder in der frühchristlichen Kunst', in Herbert Beck and Peter C. Bol (eds), *Spätantike und Frühes Christentum, Ausstellung im Liebieghaus Museum alter Plastik Frankfurt am Main. 16. Dezember 1983 bis 11. März 1984* (Frankfurt am Main, 1983), 339-46, 339.

[54] György Heidl, *Érintés. Szó és kép a korai keresztény misztikában [Touch. Word and Picture in the Early Christian Mystic]* (Budapest, 2011), 183-210.

[55] Zoltán Kádár, 'A ságvári későrómai szinkretisztikus ládikaveret (La rappresentazione sincretistiche dello scrigno tardoromano di Ságvár)', *Archaeológiai Értesítő* XCV (1968), 92; Abb. 1.

[56] Z. Kádár, 'A ságvári későrómai szinkretisztikus ládikaveret' (1968), 92.

[57] See for example the poem of Isillos von Epidauros from the 4th c. B.C.: *Inscriptiones Graecae* IV, 1, 128; L. Nagy, 'Interpretationsprobleme des frühchristlichen Kästchenbeschlags' (forthcoming), with further written sources and literature.

[58] H. Buschhausen, *Die spätrömische Metallscrinia* (1971), 105; D. Gáspár, *Christianity in Roman Pannonia* (2002), 97.

[59] Sebastian Ristow, *Frühes Christentum im Rheinland. Die Zeugnisse der archäologischen und historischen Quellen an Rhein und Mosel* (Köln, 2007), Taf. 38c (Köln); 67d (Wiesbaden); Taf. 56 (Trier); D. Gáspár, *Römische Kästchen aus Pannonien II* (1986), Taf. LVI-LVII; D. Gáspár, *Christianity in Roman Pannonia* (2002), Abb. 135 (Keszthely-Fenékpuszta); D. Gáspár, *Römische Kästchen aus Pannonien II* (1986), Taf. LII; D. Gáspár, *Christianity in Roman Pannonia* (2002), Abb. 76c (Intercisa); Ludwig Wamser (ed.), *Die Welt von Byzanz – Europas östliches Erbe. Glanz, Krisen und Fortleben einer tausendjährigen Kultur* (München, 2001), 264, Kat. Nr. 400 (München).

published photos, the pleat of the pallium seems to have a triangular head with a small hole in the middle, perhaps really the eye of a snake. In 2010 I played with the idea, that if the strange thing is indeed a snake, the whole scene could have an eschatological meaning. Snakes are not only evil animals in Old Testament context:[60] the motiv of the healing metal snake raised by Moses[61] with its parallel text about the elevation of Christ in the gospel of John,[62] like the staff of Aaron and the egyptian magicians changing into snakes[63] could be well known biblical symbols for the pannonian Christian communities, too. In the prophecy of Amos one reads about snakes as punishing instruments of God on the day of the Last Judgement,[64] this Old Testament *locus* could be connected with the second arrival of Christ and the resurrection of the Dead at the Last Judgement as well. If this interpretation is right, the star and the christogram besides the head of Christ on the casket mount refers to the cosmic power of Christ resuscitating the dead, too. This is only one possible solution concerning the decoding of this unusual image, the meaning of the scene on the cascet mount of Ságvár is open for discusion, too.

In the end I would like to mention the new research project 'Frühes Christentum in Ungarn' of the University of Pécs, Department of Archaeology, under the leadership of Prof. Zsolt Visy, and the University of Wien, with Prof. Renate Pillinger. The aim of the project is a detailed monographical analysis of all the Early Christian structures and findings from the territory of present day Hungary. One of the tasks of this project is to evaluate the Early Christian iconographical programs on artefacts and paintings, that is to follow the path, that Zoltán Kádár had begun in the 1930s, and to write within the frames of this project a new Early christian iconography of the Pannonian artefacts. Valuable comments of colleagues dealing with Christian iconography will hopefully provide a great help to understand the unusual and problematic Early Christian images from Roman Pannonia.

---

[60] Wolfgang Kemp, 'Schlange', *Lexikon zur Christlichen Ikonographie* 4 (1972), 75-81, with further examples.
[61] *Num.* 21:6-9.
[62] *John* 3:14-5.
[63] *Ex.* 7:10-25.
[64] *Amos* 5:19; 9:3.

Fig. 1. The northern wall and the barrel vault of the St. Peter and Paul
burial chamber in Sopianae /Photo: András em Török.
Courtesy of the Pécs/Sopianae Heritage Nonprofit Ltd.

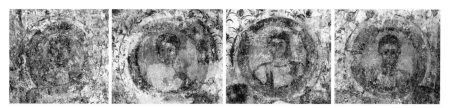

Fig. 2. The four heads in medaillons on the barrel vault. Photo: András em Török,
Courtesy of the Pécs/Sopianae Heritage Nonprofit Ltd.

Fig. 3. Head of a deceased in a medaillon from
the Via Latina Catacomb, Rome. Taken from
A. Ferrua, *Katakomben* (1991), 149.

Fig. 4. Head of the deceased in a medaillon from the Domitilla Catacomb, Rome. Taken from P. Testini, *Le catacombe* (1966), fig. 171.

Fig. 5. Head of the deceased Aelia Arisuth in a medaillon in her burial chamber from Oea. Taken from R. Bianchi-Bandinelli, *Rome. La fin de l'art antique II* (1970), fig. 243.

Fig. 6. Head of a deceased in a medaillon from a burial chamber, Kibbutz Or-ha-Ner. Taken from T. Michaeli, 'Funerary Lights in Painted Tombs' (2007), lámina 52, 19.

Fig. 7. Head of the deceased from the Via Portuense hypogaeum, Rome. Taken from R. Bianchi-Bandinelli, *Rome. La centre du pouvoir* (1969), fig. 99.

Fig. 8. Gold sandwich glas from Rome with the depiction of
Christ and four martyrs. Taken from G. Spier, Picturing the Bible (2007),
fig. 219, Kat. Nr. 45.

Fig. 9. Detail from the Jonah scene from the eastern wall of the St. Peter and
Paul burial chamber in Sopianae. Photo: András em Török, Courtesy of the
Pécs/Sopianae Heritage Nonprofit Ltd.

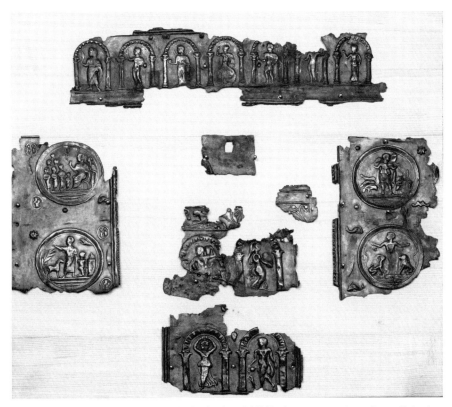

Fig. 10. Casket mount with mythological and biblical representations from Császár, grave Nr. 1. Photo: András Dabasi, Courtesy of the Hungarian National Museum©, Budapest.

Fig. 11. Detail from the Császár casket mount with the representation of a sitting
figure speaking to a crowd of people.
Photo: Renate Pillinger, Courtesy of the Hungarian National
Museum ©, Budapest.

Fig. 12. Painting of the Via Latina catacomb cubiculum B, with the representation of Joseph and his brother. Taken from A. Ferrua, *Katakomben* (1991), Abb. 67.

Fig. 13. Polychrome relief from Rome with the representation of the Sermon of
the Mount. Courtesy of Renate Pillinger.

Fig. 14. Sarcophagus from Rome (now in New York), with the representation of the Last Judgement. Taken from G. Koch, *Frühchristliche Sarkophage* (2000), Abb. 20.

Fig. 15. Casket mount with biblical representations from Bakonya. Courtesy of Zsolt Visy.

Fig. 16. Dagger sheet from Pölöske with the representation of a sitting figure speaking to people. Courtesy of the Liszt Ferenc Museum, Sopron.

Fig. 17. Glas medaillon with the depiction of a sitting figure (teaching Christ?).
Taken from N. Cambi, 'Le figure du Christ' (1970, n. 43.), fig. 4.

Fig. 18. Casket mount from Ságvár, Grave Nr. 54, with the depiction of the raising
of Lazarus. Photo: Renate Pillinger. Courtesy of the Hungarian National Museum©,
Budapest.

Fig. 19. Casket mount from Keszthely-Fenékpuszta with the depiction of the raising of Lazarus. Taken from D. Gáspár, *Römische Kästchen* aus *Pannonien II* (1986), Taf. LVII E.

Fig. 20. Detail from the so called Orpheus-casket mount from Intercisa.
Photo: Renate Pillinger, Courtesy of the Hungarian National Museum©, Budapest.

Fig. 21. Casket mount from München with the depiction of the raising of Lazarus.
Taken from E. Wamser (ed.), *Die Welt von Byzanz* (2001), Kat. Nr. 400.

Remarks on the Iconography in the 'Peter-Paul' (No. 1) Burial Chamber of Sopianae

György HEIDL, University of Pécs, Hungary

ABSTRACT

In this article I attempt to offer an interpretation of the logic and structure of the Biblical scenes appearing on the walls of Peter-Paul Burial Chamber in Pécs.[1] My understanding will at some important points differ from the most elaborated iconographical interpretation of these *al secco* paintings published by Krisztina Hudák.[2]

In fact there are substantial disagreements between us even in identifying some of the scenes. For in my view, the Jonah panel on the eastern wall includes not three but only two scenes of the Jonah cycle; the third panel in the southwestern corner represent the three Babylonian youths, and the central panel on the eastern wall, destroyed today, can most probably interpreted as a place of a New Testament scene.[3]

Sign of Jonah

The Jonah cycle, which is often represented in three scenes, is condensed into one frame. By grasping his leg, two sailors are throwing Jonah into the sea, probably into the mouth of the great fish as, despite the lack of details, can be inferred from the position of the monster's body. The image is damaged at the whale's head, but the curved, fork-ended tail of the fish, emerging from the water, is clearly seen (Fig. 1). The two front and two rear legs or fins can also be recognised. These are characteristics for the traditional dragon-like depiction of the monster.

Presumably, its head was dragon-like too, similarly to its representation on so many early Christian paintings and sarcophagi. In the top right corner of the image Jonah appears as a naked figure leaning slightly to the right. His sole touches the bows and, at the same time, the forked tail of the fish. He is surrounded by a plant's tendril.

---

[1] I would like to thank for my friend and colleague, John Voelker for the revision of the English text.

[2] Krisztina Hudák, 'The Iconographical Program of the Wallpaintings in the Saint Peter and Paul burial chamber of Sopianae (Pécs)', *Mitteilungen zur Christlichen Archaologie* 15 (2009): 47-76.

[3] See also, Krisztina Hudák and Levente Nagy, *A Fine and Private Place: Discovering the Early Christian Cemetery of Sopianae / Pécs*, Heritage Booklets 6 (Pécs, 2009), 46-7.

Studia Patristica LXXIII, 219-235.

Fig. 1. The Jonah panel (southeastern panel), Photo by László Tám.

Fig. 2. Jonah under the plant, Photo by László Tám.

The loin of the figure is hidden by a corner of the shroud covering his left hip. The right leg is slightly bent in knee, whereas the left crosses over the right shin. Jonah keeps his left hand stretched, but far from his hip, while supporting the head with his bent right hand (Fig. 2). The representation is considered a traditional *anapaumenos*, 'resting position', going back to pagan artistic patterns.[4] However, it is a hitherto unrecognised peculiarity of the *secco* in Pécs that while the artist painted the ship with the two sailors and the monster side view, Jonah resting under the plant tendril was represented top view, probably due to the lack of space. Therefore, the plant is painted semicircle around Jonah in order not to cover his body.

Special attention should be paid to the representation of the plant. It does not seem to be a gourd-tree (*cucurbita*), which was common in early Christian art, but rather an ivy (*hedera*). Thus, the image may testify a change related to Saint Jerome's translation of *Jonah*. In fact, the monk of Bethlehem made a seemingly slight change while breaking at this point with the Septuagint tradition. He named this plant in *Jonah hedera* instead of *cucurbita*. His process evoked the resentment of such contemporaries as Augustine and Rufinus, and caused even a minor storm within the bilingual Christian communities.[5] If we assume the effect of Jerome's translation on the artists or the patrons in Sopianae, then the painting cannot be dated earlier than 393 AD.[6]

There is, however, a work of Jerome's that seems more important with regard to the representation of the plant in our burial chamber, namely his *Commentary on Jonah*.[7] Answering his critics, Jerome endeavoured to justify his innovation and characterised in detail the ricinus castor oil plant, called *qiqueion* (קִיקָיוֹן) in Hebrew. As he admits, neither the *cucurbita* (pumpkin or gourd tree), nor *hedera* (ivy) really corresponds to the original. For *qiqueion* is a common

---

[4] Imre Henszlmann already noticed the *anapumenos* position, but he did not identify the figure as Jonah. See his 'Die altchristliche Grabkammer in Fünfkirchen', in *Mittheilungen der K. K. Zentralkomission* 18 (1873), 66, and *Pécsnek régiségei* [Antiquities of Pécs], part 3. *Monumenta Hungariae Archaeologica* vol. 2, part 1 (Budapest, 1873), 135. Zoltán Kádár, 'Pannonia ókeresztény emlékeinek ikonográfiája ('Iconography of the Early Christian Monuments of Pannonia')', *Regnum* (Budapest, 1938/1939), 3-58, especially 30. n. 130, refers to Henszlmann's view, but he regards Jonah as a standing figure.

[5] Rufinus, *Apologia contra Hieronymum* 2.39; Augustine, *Ep.* 71.3 and 82.5; Jerome, *Ep.* 112.22 and 115.1, *In Ionam* 4.6 with reference to the so-called 'Canterius' reproaching Jerome's translation.

[6] I. Henszlmann, 'Die altchristliche Grabkammer' (1873), 65, and *Pécsnek régiségei* (1873), 134-5 was the first to recall the early Christian debate concerning Jerome's *hedera* version in the context of the Sopianae panel, but he did not attempt to decide which plant was painted on it. Most recently K. Hudák, 'The Iconographical Program' (2009), 55 and K. Hudák and L. Nagy, *A Fine and Private Place* (2009), 48 considered the appearance of the ivy leaves as a possible influence of Jerome's translation.

[7] For a detailed discussion see, György Heidl, 'A pécsi 1 számú sírkamra Jónás-freskója és Szt. Jeromos Jónás-kommentárja' ['The Fresco of Jonah in Burial Chamber no. 1 in Sopianae and the commentary of St. Jerome on the Book of Jonah'], *Katekhón* 2 (2005/1), 221-35.

plant in Palestine that prefers sandy areas, grows from seed, sprouts very quickly, and rises high without any support. Its vine-like leaves shed thick shadow, and its roots are short so it withers soon. In contrast to this, pumpkin and ivy represent climber plants that can run high on support.[8]

The seemingly insignificant botanical differences gain importance in understanding the text. In *Jonah* we read that after Nineveh having repented, the prophet 'went out of the city, and made a booth for himself there. He sat under it in the shade, till he should see what would become of the city' (4:5).

It was only after that that God intervened. He appointed a plant and made it come up over Jonah. The natural shading was more appropriate than the booth made by Jonah, since the prophet was suffering under the former, 'he was exceedingly glad because of the latter' (*Jonah* 4:6). The *qiqueion* by itself and without support increased over the head of Jonah. What we can see in the early Christian representations of the scene does not, indeed, follow from the narrative. Numerous images suggest that Jonah first made the pergola which did not guard him against anything and then he was sitting under a simple frame while waiting for a plant to run up over him (Fig. 3). Even though Jerome's innovation was just as inappropriate to render the Hebrew *qiqueion* as the traditional *kolokynthe / cucurbita* version, it has merit that in taking into account the properties of the plant, he reconstructed the literal meaning of the Scriptural text more accurately than anybody else.

---

[8] *In Ionam* 4,6 (*SC* 323, 298-300): '*Pro cucurbita sive hedera, in hebraeo legimus «ciceion», quae etiam lingua Syra et Punica «ciceia» dicitur. Est autem genus virgulti vel arbusculae lata habentis folia in modum pampini et umbram densissimam sustinens. Quae Palestinae creberrime nascitur et maxime in arenosis locis. Mirumque in modum, si sementem in terram ieceris, cito confota surgit in arborem et intra paucos dies quam herbam videras arbusculam suspicis. Unde et nos, eo tempore quo interpretabamur prophetas, voluimus idipsum Hebreae linguae nomen exprimere quia latinus sermo hanc speciem arboris non habebat. Sed timuimus grammaticos, ne invenirent licentiam commentandi et, vel betias Indiae vel montes Boeotiae, aut istiusmodi quaedam portenta confingerent, secutique sumus veteres translatores qui et ipsi hederam interpretati sunt, quae graece appellatur κισσός; aliud enim quid dicerent non habebant. Discutiamus ergo historiam et, ante mysicos intellectus solam litteram ventilemus. Cucurbita et hedera huius naturae sunt ut per terram reptent et, absque furcis vel adminiculis quibus innituntur, altiora non appetant. Quomodo igitur, ignorante propheta, cucurbita in una nocte consurgens ubraculum praebuit quae naturam non habet sine perticulis et calamis vel hastilibus in sublime consurgere? «Ciceion» autem, cum in ortu subito miraculum praebuerit et potentiam ostenderit Dei in protectione virentis umbraculi, naturam suam secuta est.' In Ionam 4,6, 302.: 'Porro «ciceion», nostra arbuscula modica, cito consurgens et cito arescens, ordine et vita comparabitur Israheli radices parvas mittenti in terram et conanti quidem in excelsa sustolli, sed altitudinem cedrorum Dei et abietum non aequanti.' Jerome, Ep. 112.22 (to Augustine): 'Super qua re in commentario Ionae prophetae plenius respondimus hoc tantum nunc dixisse contenti, quod in eo loco, ubi septuaginta interpretes «cucurbitam» et Aquila cum reliquis «hederam» transtulerunt, id est κιττόν, in hebraeo uolumine «ciceion» scriptum habet, quam uulgo syri «ciceiam» uocant; est autem genus uirgulti lata habens folia in modum pampini, cumque plantatum fuerit, cito consurgit in arbusculam absque ullis calamorum et hastilium adminiculis, quibus et cucurbitae et hederae indigent, suo trunco se sustinens.'*

Fig 3. Jonah and the pergola, Aquileia, Theodorus basilica.

Jerome's remarks in his *Commentary* can shed new light upon the representation of the plant in the *Jonah* scene in Pécs. Here, the Prophet rests under a short-rooted plant, an offshoot with leaves, which bends over him in a natural arch (Fig. 2). Standing on its own root, the plant does not need any external support. There are, therefore, good reasons to suppose that the image was influenced by Jerome's commentary. If so, then the paintings can be dated after 397 AD.[9] This dating is in accordance with the conclusions of the recent critical studies of the style of the paintings.[10] At the same time, this particular representation of the plant indicates that the patrons and artists of the burial chamber were familiar with the literal meaning of the Biblical story. It is worth remembering this conclusion when we turn to the panel in front of the *Jonah* scene.

[9] Pierre Nautin, 'Etudes de chronologie hiéronymienne (393-397)', *Revue des études augustiniennes* 20 (1974), 251-84, esp. 252-3 and 269-73; Yves-Marie Duval (ed., introd., trans., comm.), *Jérôme, Commentaire sur Jonas*, SC 323 (Paris, 1985), 11-2; 21-2; 432. n. 18.

[10] K. Hudák dates the paintings *ca.* 392-400 ('The Iconographical Program' [2009], 63-4). Jerome's commentary on Jonah, with the description of the plant, was dedicated to Chromatius, the bishop of the town that played important role in christianising Pannonia in the late 4th century. Naturally, there was no need to give an exact representation of the *qiqueion*, a plant frequent in Palestine, but unknown in the area of Sopianae. It was enough to depict a plant, otherwise similar to the traditional imagery, with short roots and without any support. These are the two important characteristics outlined by Jerome for interpreting the literal meaning of the Biblical text. See K. Hudák ('The Iconograpical Program' [2009], 73, n. 122) who, at this point, seemed to misunderstand my arguments.

The three young men in the fiery furnace

Despite its poor condition, three men can be recognised on the picture in the southwestern corner (Fig. 4). They are wearing pants, cloaks, tunics, shoes, and probably Phrygian caps. They look like they are hastening somewhere. Their garments and hair style are different from the Roman fashion; that is to say, they represent eastern men in a way that is typical in the late Roman art. Two possible interpretations occur and both have supporters from long ago.

Fig. 4. Three youths or/and (?) magi (southwestern panel), Photo by László Tám.

According to the earliest view, the three figures represent the three magi. In 1804, József Koller stated that on the image the three magi were offering their gifts to the new-born Saviour (Fig. 5).[11] In fact, the second image of the western wall shows Mary and the Child, and the three men seem to turn towards them. Koller refers to a similar picture in San Pietro e Marcellino, published in Paolo Aringhi's *Roma subterranea novissima*, and supposed that the three men held oval platters in their hand with their gifts (Fig. 6).[12] If so, the image clearly

---

[11] Josephus Koller, *Prolegomena in historiam episcopatus Quinqueecclesiarum* (Posonii, 1804), 31.

[12] J. Koller, *Prolegomena* (1840), 31: 'Pictura Tab. II. Cubiculi XIV. Cemet. SS. Marcellini, et Petri ap. Aringhium, L. IV. C. XIV. pag. 347.'

Fig. 5. Three magi from Koller's
Prolegomena. Photo courtesy of Klimó
Library, Pécs.

Fig. 6. *Adoratio magorum* from Aringhi's *Roma subterranea novissima* (p. 46).
Photo courtesy of Klimó Library, Pécs.

Fig. 7. Flames on the Three youths/magi panel, Photo by László Tám.

depicts the magi known from the *Gospel of Matthew*. The question is, however, whether Koller, influenced by Aringhi's engravings, saw indeed or believed to see platters on the image. About sixty years later (in 1863), the plates at least no longer seemed so, as Imre Henszlmann writes who had played a pioneering role in another possible interpretation of the scene.[13]

On his own part Henszlmann identified the image as showing the three youths in the fiery furnace (*Daniel* 3).[14] In my view, he was right because the modern lighting and restoration made visible some red stripes at the feet of the figures which are clearly recognisable as tongues of flame. The presence of the flames clearly decides the issue (Fig. 7). It is not unparalleled that tongues of fire are represented without a furnace (*e.g.* Priscilla catacombe cubiculum of the *velatio*).

However, the 'three magi' interpretation emerges in the most recent literature and seems to be corroborated by the argument that the men proceed towards Mary and the Child. Therefore, the image is considered a typical portrayal of

---

[13] I. Henszlmann (*Pécsnek régiségei* [1873], 80.) mentions his visit in the burial chamber in 1863 where he was not able recognise the platters referred to by Koller.

[14] I. Henszlmann, *Pécsnek régiségei* (1873), 124; 128-30; 164-5 and *id., Magyarország ó-keresztény, román és átmenet stylü mű-emlékeinek rövid ismertetése* [A short Description of the Monuments of Early Christian, Romanesque and Transtiory Style in Hungary] (Budapest, 1876), 38.

Fig. 8. Three youths/magi and the lady with the child (southwestern panel),
Photo by András Török.

adoratio magorum. The main problem with this understanding is, however, that
the two images are definitely separated by frames (Fig. 8).[15]

Depictions of the three youths closely follow the Biblical text: 'These men were
bound in their mantles, their tunics, their hats, and their other garments, and they
were cast into the burning fiery furnace' (*Daniel* 3:21). From this point of view our
painting fits the tradition. The image is unusual only because the youths are not
portrayed in front as *orantes* but with a little side view as walking in the midst of
the fire. Although this representation seems to break with the iconographic patterns,
it is entirely faithful to the text. The Biblical account emphasises the opposition of
boundedness and freedom. The three youths were thrown bound into the fire but they
appeared loose and free to walk in the fiery furnace. In contrast to them, the king,
the lord of life and death, appears to be free, but he is a real slave of false gods.

A similar phenomenon was observed concerning the representation of Jonah. As
noted above, the image can testify to the fact that artists and/or clients faithfully
adhered to the iconographic patterns as long as the literal meaning of Scripture did
not disprove the traditional representations. The visual formulation of the story of
the three Babylonian youths can lead us to the same conclusion.[16] Moreover, on the

---

[15] K. Hudák, 'The Iconographical Program' (2009), 56-8; K. Hudák and L. Nagy, *A Fine and
Private Place* (2009), 48-50.

[16] I have already suggested considering a conscious ambiguity on the part of the painters/
clients while representing the three youths as those evidently recalling the three magi of the

Fig. 9. Noah (northwestern panel), Photo by András Török.

Pécs image, the youths are not simply walking, but their position and gestures reveal that there is a fourth person with them, 'the son of God' (*Daniel* 3:25) whom the Christians identified with Jesus. As we shall see, the artist painted this fourth person, Jesus, on the next panel, and therefore, he made the three youths turn towards Him. On the northwestern panel Noah also turns to this image (Fig. 9). The angel

Epiphany scene. Although in a separate panel they are turning towards Mary with the Child, which is to be regarded highly similar to the traditional scenes of *adoratio magorum*. See K. Hudák, 'The Iconographical Program' (2009), 58. n. 40. Ambiguity seems to be a characteristic of the Peter and Paul burial chamber in Sopianae. This can be grasped in relation to the plant of Jonah, as well as to the Lady figure on the middle panel of the western wall. For this latter panel, see the next footnote.

coming down from heaven saved the youths from dying, just like the Son of God descending from heaven and incarnated through the Holy Spirit and the Virgin Mary made the faithful free from the power of death. The three youths worship the only God who can bring salvation. During the persecutions the story of the Babylonian youths became a symbol of martyrdom, and later it could serve to visualise internal liberation and escaping from the fire of sins.

A missing image

Two scenes on the eastern wall of the burial chamber can be identified with certainty: the story of Jonah on the southeastern panel and in the northeastern corner, the traditional representation of the Fall, that is, Adam and Eve with the tree of the knowledge of good and evil. These two paintings are very heavily damaged, and the third in between them is completely destroyed. Since the earliest records already establish the fact of its devastation, any attempt to identify the original scene remains uncertain. There are, however, two reasons for attempting to formulate a hypothesis concerning the possible subject of the missing image. On one hand, options are limited. Starting from the size and a small part of the image, as well as considering the possible iconographical patterns, and mainly taking into account the arrangement and logic of the rest of the burial chamber's images, one may presume the subject of the middle panel. It is this latter aspect that, on the other hand, substantiates the investigation of the possible theme of the image.

The frame of the two middle panels on the eastern and the western walls is narrower than that of the extremes, which must have influenced the compositions. The panel's size precludes the possibility to paint, without upsetting asymmetry, such group scenes as the Fall, the three youths in the fiery furnace, or the Jonah cycle. Rather, one should suppose that the composition of the middle image of the eastern wall was similar in its structure to that of the opposite image on the western wall. On the western *secco*, damaged too, only the head and shoulders of a central female figure occur (Fig. 10). She is sitting and most probably takes a child in her lap since a small portion of the child's head is also shown. Such details are enough to safely conclude that Mary with the Child was painted on the central axis of the image.[17]

Let us consider its counterpart image on the eastern wall. A tiny remnant of this destroyed image affirms that a key figure was located in the axis of the image field (Fig. 11). As the colouring and the dark contour show the fragment

---

[17] The context seems to confirm this identification. However, a representation of a lady buried in the chamber cannot be excluded. This latter view is that of Prof. Renate Pillinger who kindly shared it with me via email correspondence.

Fig. 10. The lady with the child (middle panel of the western wall),
Photo by László Tám.

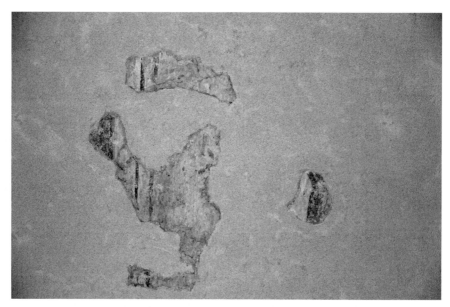

Fig. 11. A remnant of the middle panel of the eastern wall,
Photo by László Tám.

represents a part of a human body, but it is difficult to determine exactly which limb is involved.

In 1907, Ottó Szőnyi stated that the fragment seemed to be a portion of a leg, and supposed that it had belonged to a naked figure or someone wearing a short tunic.[18] The figure should have been standing in the focus of the image. Szőnyi argued for an image of Daniel in the lions' den. The assumption seems particularly appealing because in the early Christian mausoleum, discovered later in the same area, one can indeed see a scene of Daniel (Fig. 12). Moreover, an image of Daniel in the Peter and Paul burial chamber would nicely match with the other Old Testament images which symbolise the possibility of liberation.

The surmise is accepted by the most recent literature as well. However, Szőnyi himself changed his view and believed that the Good Shepherd was depicted within the framing.[19] This solution was accepted by Lajos Nagy who identified the remnant of the picture as the hip of the shepherd.[20] Whether or not it is a hip, its position really allows the assumption that a Good Shepherd might have been the central figure of the image. The modest amounts of data can support both surmises. At this point the investigation is hindered unless we take into account the comprehensive program of the paintings and the thematic and theological layout of the images.

The paintings of Peter and Paul burial chamber indicate regular symmetrical arrangement both on the walls and on the vault (Fig. 13). Entering through the narrow entrance cut into the southern wall, our sight is immediately directed by the gestures of the two Apostle figures towards the christogram painted over the *fenestella* on the northern wall. The christogram symbolises the risen Christ, because early Christian art did not represent Christ's passion and his resurrection directly. Symmetry rules the eastern and western walls as well. Three biblical scenes appear on both sides according to highly conscious compositional principles. Not only is it important what Biblical scenes are placed next to each other, but also which ones are facing each other. The three images on the western wall are considered the three youths in the fiery furnace, Mary and the Child, Noah and the ark. On the eastern wall, the Jonah scene appears in front of the three youths and the Fall scene in front of Noah. Consequently, as far as the western panels are concerned, there is a New Testament scene in between two Old Testament stories. One can rightly assume that on the eastern panels a New Testament scene was also painted in between the panels of the

[18] Ottó Szőnyi, *A pécsi ókeresztény sírkamra* [*The Early Christian Burial Chamber in Pécs*] (Budapest, 1907), 53-5.
[19] O. Szőnyi, 'A pécsi ókeresztény temető sírkamrái és kápolnája' ['The Burial Chambers and Chapel of the Early Christian Cemetery in Pécs'], *Magyar Művészet* 5 (1929), 537-44.
[20] Lajos Nagy, 'Pannonia Sacra', in *Emlékkönyv Szent István király halálának kilencszázadik évfordulóján* (Budapest, 1938), vol. I. 31-148, esp. 38.

Fig. 12. Daniel in the lion's den. Mausoleum, Pécs, Photo by András Török.

Fig. 13. Barrel vault of Burial chamber I, Photo by András Török.

Fall and Jonah. The assumption is confirmed by the different colouring of the frames. This phenomenon has not hitherto received special attention on the part of the interpreters. For in contrast to the yellow frames of the Old Testaments scenes, the two middle panels possess thick green framing, including Mary with the Child and the destroyed image in front of that. Thus, the frame of an Old Testament scene is always yellow, whereas that of the New Testament scene is pained green.

What could be the subject of the missing image within green framing? Compelled by the size of the surface, the panel needs a central figure on its axis. For reasons of content this figure should be someone from the New Testament. The Good Shepherd seems to be the most appropriate figure for this purpose.

Let us suppose that a Good Shepherd was painted on the middle panel of the eastern wall, and consider the iconographical program of the burial chamber! Imagine that we are standing in the geometrical centre of the oblong chamber back to the entrance! Possibly, this is the point where the sarcophagus was to be set. While standing at this point, we stretch out our hands sidelong and so, our body forms a cross-shape. Our sight falls exactly upon the christogram on the northern wall. There is a christogram above our head on the vault as well. Our left hand points to the Infant Jesus while our right hand to the Good Shepherd. The cross-shape is both horizontally and vertically outlined. In both cases the christogram appears on the height of the vertical shaft. Just as the cross appears in the two christograms, which include the X (*chi*), a symbol of cross, so the shape of the cross is the organising principle of the arrangement of the paintings. As the two shafts of the cross intersect four rectangular fields out of the space, so four Old Testament scenes can be seen in rectangular frame intersected by the two shafts of the cross.

The scene of the Fall (Fig. 14) indicates how and why death has dominated us and why we have lost the happy life. As opposed to this, the traditional scenes of the flight occur in the other three corners. They express the hope that we can escape from the power of death and regain the original blessedness, as Noah was saved from the flood, Jonah from the belly of the fish, and the youths from the fiery furnace.

Christians regarded these stories as prefigurations of Christ's life and the works of salvation. Noah prefigures Christ the Saviour. Jesus himself refers to the parallel between the days of Noah and the coming of the Son of Man (see *Matth.* 24:27 and *Luke* 17:26-7). As Noah saved the human race from extinction in his ark, so Christ saved human souls from spiritual death in his Church.

Jonah symbolises the Christ who descended into Hell. 'For as Jonah was three days and three nights in the belly of the whale, so will the Son of man be three days and three nights in the heart of the earth' (*Matth.* 12:39-41, see *Matth.* 16:4; *Luke* 11:29-32).

As far as the Babylonian young men are concerned, early Christian authors emphasise that their number symbolises the Trinity to whose knowledge Christ

Fig. 14. Fall (northeastern panel), Photo by László Tám.

has led us. On the other hand, the liberation of the youths was possible only through 'the Son of God', 'the Lord's angel' (see *Daniel* 3:49 and 92), who descended into the furnace. This element of the story was generally considered as a reference to the incarnation of God's Word.

Consequently, in accordance with the New Testament symbolism which is based upon the Old Testament (see *Jer.* 23:3-4; *Isa.* 40.11, *Ez.* 34:11-6; *Ps.* 23), it is probable that the Good Shepherd who lays down his life for the sheep (*John* 10:11, see *Luke* 15:4-6) was depicted in front of Mary and the Child as its counterpart image. Birth and death, Incarnation of the Word and Passion of the Shepherd are closely connected. It is logical why the Jonah scene was placed immediately by the Good Shepherd. Jonah symbolised the Saviour descending into the heart of the earth.

Considering the four Old Testament scenes, one of them reminds us of the cause of the Fall, and three refer to the elevation of the fallen men through the three principal works of redemption. Christ's incarnation is referred to by the three youths, His death by Jonah and His resurrection by Noah. What the Old Testament scenes indicate in typology the symbolism of the New Testament makes evident on the central images of the three walls: Mary with the Child near the three youths, the Good Shepherd near Jonah, and the christogram near Noah.

Deliberate Ambiguities in Early Christian Wall Paintings in Sopianae

Péter Csigi, London

ABSTRACT

The objective of this article is threefold. The first section includes new approaches to two questions concerning the wall paintings on the side walls of the Ss Peter and Paul Burial Chamber in Sopianae in Pannonia. The first research question is about a panel on the western side wall. In the scholarly analyses of the last two centuries, it was identified either with the Magi, or the Three Youths from the Book of Daniel. Using the theories of Th. Matthews and R. Jensen, this article aims to propose a new hypothesis about deliberate ambiguities of the depiction. The second research question is about the missing panel on the eastern side wall. Collecting parallel iconographical structures from the catacombs of Rome, my aim is to reflect on the probability of two options (Daniel or the Good Shepherd). The last section tries to contextualise the so called neutral elements of the Burial Chamber 'Korsós' or with the Jar.

1. The 'Ss Peter and Paul' Burial Chamber

The wall paintings of the Ss Peter and Paul Burial Chamber in Sopianae represent the pinnacle of Early Christian art in Pannonia.[1] Scholars dealing with this burial chamber have debated two main questions regarding the paintings on the side walls. The first one is about the picture of the three men in oriental clothes on the western side wall.[2] The other one is connected to the missing

---

[1] Giovanni B. de Rossi, 'Fünfkirchen in Ungheria. Camera sepolcrale sotterranea dipinta', in *Bullettino di Archeologia Cristiana*, Vatican, V (1874), 150-4, 150-2; Ferenc Fülep, *Roman Cemeteries on the territory of Pécs, Sopianae* (Budapest, 1977); Ferenc Fülep, *Sopianae: The History of Pécs during the Roman Era, and the Problem of the Continuity of the Late Roman Population* (Budapest, 1984); Krisztina Hudák, 'The Iconographical Program of the Wallpaintings in the St Peter and Paul Burial Chamber of Sopianae (Pécs)', in *Mitteilungen der christlichen Archäologie* (Vienna, 2009), 47-76; Krisztina Hudák, 'The Chronology of the Paintings in the Saint Peter and Paul Burial Chamber of Sopianae', in Szilvia Bíró (ed.), *Ex officina… Studia in honorem Dénes Gabler* (Győr, 2009), 225-38.

[2] Friedrich Gerke, 'Die Wandmalereien der Petrus-Paulus Katakombe in Pécs (Sopianae)', in *Forschungen zur Kunstgeschichte und christlichen Archäologie. Neue Beiträge zur Kunstgeschichte des 1. Jahrtausends* I/2: *Frühmittelalterliche Kunst* (Baden-Baden, 1954), 147-99, 151, 156; Krisztina Hudák, Levente Nagy, *A Fine and Private Place: Discovering the Early Christian Cemetery of Sopianae / Pécs*, Heritage Booklets 6 (Pécs, 2009), 49-51; György Heidl, 'A

Studia Patristica LXXIII, 237-248.
© Peeters Publishers, 2014.

panel in the middle of the opposite wall.[3] The next subsection examines with the first topic.

1.1. *Ambiguous imagery: The Three Youths or the Magi?*

On the western side wall, there are the three men portrayed in the first field. They turn towards the next panel. The main figure on the central picture panel of the wall is a woman holding an infant on her lap. The last panel portrays Noah in his ark. The picture of the three men is not in a good shape, but it is distinctly visible that they wear trousers, capes and probably the so called Phrygian caps, however, the outlines of the caps cannot be seen clearly. Their clothes suggest squarely that they are not Romans but Oriental people. They look as if they would be hurrying somewhere. According to some scholars[4] (especially the first researcher from the 19th century)[5], they are the Magi, who are bringing bowls to the infant Jesus, depicted together with his mother in the next panel. In their opinion, the first two pictures on the western wall belong together.

From the second half of the 19th century, when the pictures became much less observable, it was suggested[6] that they are the Three Youths from the Book of Daniel.[7] Later, the better lighting and the restoration of the wall paintings

---

három ifjú a tüzes kemencében' [The three youths in the fiery furnace], in *Pannon Panoráma* 2 (2005/5), 18-9.

[3] F. Gerke, 'Die Wandmalereien der Petrus-Paulus Katakombe in Pécs (Sopianae)' (1954), 153.156; K. Hudák, L. Nagy, *A Fine and Private Place* (2005), 44-5; György Heidl, 'Egy eltűnt kép nyomában' [Pursuit of a Lost Picture], unpublished.

[4] Ottó Szőnyi, *A pécsi őskeresztény sírkamra* [The Paleochristian burial chamber in Pécs] (1907), 62; F. Gerke, 'Die Wandmalereien der Petrus-Paulus Katakombe in Pécs (Sopianae)' (1954), 151; András Mócsy, 'A kereszténység kezdetei és a pogányság elhalása' [Beginnings of Christianity and decline of paganism], in A. Mócsy, Jenő Fitz (eds), *Pannonia régészeti kézikönyve* [Archaeological handbook of Pannonia] (Budapest, 1990), 262-4, 264; Zsuzsa Katona Győr, 'Az első keresztények a Dél-Dunántúlon az ókeresztény temetők tükrében – Sopianae' [First Christians in Southern Transdanubia in the light of Paleochristian cemeteries – Sopianae], in Zoltán Huszár (ed.), *Kereszténység és államiság Baranyában, Pécsvárad, 2000-2001* [Christianity and statehood in County Baranya, Pécsvárad, 2000-2001] (Pécs, 2000), 23-39, 27.

[5] József Koller (Josephus Koller), 'Prolegomena', in *Historiam Episcopatus Quinqueecclesiarum* (Posonium [Bratislava], 1804).

[6] Imre Henszlmann, 'A pécsi sírkamra „cubiculum"' [The burial chamber cubiculum in Pécs], in *Magyarország Ó-keresztyén, román és átmeneti stylű mű-emlékeinek rövid ismertetése* (Budapest, 1876), 37-9; Zoltán Kádár, 'Lineamenti dell'arte della Pannonia nell'epoca dell'antichità tarda e paleocristiana', in *XVI corso di cultura sull'arte ravennate e bizantina* (Ravenna, 1969), 179-201, 186; Ferenc Fülep, Alice Burger, 'Baranya megye a római korban' [County Baranya in the Roman era], in G. Bándi (ed.), *Baranya megye története az őskortól a honfoglalásig* [The history of County Baranya from the prehistory until the Hungarian Conquest] (Pécs, 1979), 223-328, 244; Endre Tóth, 'Sopianae a késő császárkorban' [Sopianae in late Roman Empire], *Jelenkor* 44 (2001), 1129-36.

[7] Shadrach, Meshach, and Abednego are men recorded in the book of *Daniel*. In 3:19-30, their narrative describes how they were sent into a fiery furnace because of their stand to exclusively

showed that there are reddish stripes under the feet of the three figures which look like tongues of flames. This fact could put an end to further discussion but it does not solve the problem of the orientation of the composition. The other problem is that the left one of the three figures 'has bent arms, as though they held out large, oval platters in their hands laden with their gifts.'[8] This fact should not be left without explanation.

Krisztina Hudák states that 'there is no indication of a double layer of painting. The painting had not been repainted'.[9] She is right when she excludes the possibility of the palimpsest of two paintings in her monograph relating to the early Christian cemetery of Sopianae. She argues that 'the paintings decorating the Sopianae Burial chamber betray [maybe reveal? P. Cs.] a sophisticated theological and iconographical background'.[10]

The problem is that the traditional depiction of the Three Youths in the Fiery Furnace shows them frontally, standing with hands lifted in prayer (*expansis manibus*).[11] But in the case of Sopianae, they turn to the middle panel. György Heidl[12] thinks that they are walking up and down in the fire as it is written in the Scripture.[13] In my opinion, the orientation of the three figures could be explained as follows. The iconographic importance of this orientation is confirmed by the picture on the opposite edge. Noah who is shown in his usual box-like ark turns to the centre as well. We can assume that the three pictures were composed together. This theory is supported by Robin Jensen who writes: 'Many of the 'fiery furnace' scenes are juxtaposed with a figure of Noah. […] The frequent connection of these two biblical images suggests that they should be understood as belonging together.'[14] Following this, Jensen discusses two possible interpretations of the two pictures. Both of them can be the symbol of salvation of the righteous or baptism and resurrection.[15]

Besides all of these explanations, it may well be possible that the first viewers of these wall paintings in the early 19th century were not totally wrong when

---

serve their God alone. By God's angel, they were delivered out of harm's way from this order of execution by the King of Babylon.

[8] K. Hudák, 'The Iconographical Program of the Wallpaintings' (2009), 55-6.

[9] K. Hudák, 'The Iconographical Program of the Wallpaintings' (2009), 58.

[10] K. Hudák, L. Nagy, *A Fine and Private Place* (2009), 50.

[11] Barbara Mazzei, 'Fanciulli ebrei', in Fabrizio Bisconti, *Temi di icongrafia paleocristiana* (Vatican, 2000), 177-8; Graydon F. Snyder, *Ante Pacem: Archaeological Evidence of Church Life Before Constantine* (Macon, GA, 1985), 54; Thomas F. Mathews, *The Clash of Gods. A Reinterpretation of Early Christian Art* (Princeton, NJ, 1993), 78; Robin M. Jensen, *Understanding Early Christian Art* (London - New York, 2000), 79, 82.

[12] György Heidl, 'A három ifjú a tüzes kemencében' [The three youths in the fiery furnace], in *Pannon Panoráma* 2 (2005/5), 18-9.

[13] 'He [King Nebuchadnezzar] replied, "But I see four men unbound, walking in the middle of the fire, and they are not hurt; and the fourth has the appearance of a god"' (*Daniel* 3:25).

[14] R. Jensen, *Understanding Early Christian Art* (2000), 80.

[15] R. Jensen, *Understanding Early Christian Art* (2000), 82-5.

they identified these three men with the Magi from the gospel of Matthew.[16] Such a theory should therefore be looked for that will explain all key iconographic details of the fragmented picture, which are essential in the identification of this painting. These elements are: the importance of the number three (the three figures), the orientation toward the next panel, the oriental clothes, the flame-like patches under their feet and the bent arms, probably holding a bowl. It is suggested that the identity of these three figures is intentionally kept ambiguous, a hypothesis which attempts to fulfil these conditions.

Thomas Matthews in his book *The Clash of Gods* noticed a transposition of the Three Youths in the Furnace into the iconography of the three Magi:

'The most startling detail of the scene is the identification of the three young men with the Magi. For the brave magicians, who turn with gestures of disgust from the image of the emperor, find before them the star of the Magi. Following the star, in the sequel image panel, they find the Christ Child on his Mother's lap and they worship him.'[17]

Matthews points to the example of a fourth-century sarcophagus relief from St. Gilles, France. In this picture, the Three Youths from the Book of Daniel and the Magi are conflated: three men in eastern clothing turn away from an idol and towards a star. It was supposed that the artists confused the figures of the three young men with the Magi because of the similarity of their dress.[18] But in Matthews opinion, 'this "mistake" was deliberate – the artists wanted to identify the two famous sets of three magicians.'[19]

Robin Jensen also supports this theory when she writes:

'This popular interpretation is reflected in art, which often links the three magi with the three Hebrew youths in the fiery furnace and with Daniel in the lions' den—all easterners (Daniel and the Hebrew youths lived in the Persian court) who used their gifts of prophecy, dream interpretation and perhaps even magic to resist the evil of pagan idolatry.'[20]

She also notes that 'images of the magi are often paired with the three youths or Daniel, as in the fourth-century catacomb of Marcus and Marcellianus, in Rome, where paintings of the magi and the three youths are grouped together.'[21]

Francesca Massara also confirms the strong connection between the two scenes when she states that the episode of the Three Youths in the Fiery Furnace is a *pendant* of the one of the Magi. She says relying on the *Dictionnaire d'archéologie*

---

[16] The Magi, also referred to as the (Three) Wise Men, (Three) Kings, or Kings from the East, were a group of distinguished foreigners who visited Jesus after his birth, bearing gifts of gold, frankincense and myrrh. Their story can be read in *Matthew* 2:1-12.

[17] Th. Mathews, *The Clash of Gods* (1993), 79.

[18] Henri Leclerq, 'Hébreux, Les trios jeunes', in Fernand Cabrol, Henri Leclercq, *Dictionnaire d'archéologie chrétienne et de liturgie* VI (Paris, 1925), 2107-26.

[19] Th. Mathews, *The Clash of Gods* (1993), 80.

[20] Robin M. Jensen, 'Witnessing the Divine', *Bible Review* 17.6 (2001), 24-32.

[21] R. Jensen, 'Witnessing the Divine' (2001), 29.

chrétienne et de liturgie[22] that the placement of the two episodes is usually motivated not only by a call for symmetry, but also a historical-symbolical reading of the two stories both with three people who renounce idolatry and embrace faith.[23]

So I propose that the artist in Sopianae deliberately produced such a composition with three men in oriental clothing, which could be interpreted as the Magi turning to the next panel with the Mother and the Child, and at the same time, as the Three Youths in the Fiery Furnace connecting to Noah on the opposite side of the wall. Otherwise, this technique, i.e. the combination of more scenes into a single composition, would not have been unfamiliar as a concept to the artist of this burial chamber. The depiction of Jonah on the wall on the opposite side is an excellent example, where he condenses what is usually depicted in more individual pictures into one panel.[24]

I believe that this is a masterful utilization of the potentiality of the two themes in one composition.

1.2. *The Missing Picture*

The picture areas of the eastern sidewalls are quite damaged. Of the picture panel portraying the scene of the Fall, only Eve's torso and some details of the tree survived. Adam's figure has completely vanished. The exact identification of the middle panel is not possible due to damage to the secco. Finally, the south-eastern corner panel tells the tale of Jonah condensed into one single picture area as I mentioned before.

The picture in the middle panel has perished. But there is a report about a fragment from the beginning of the 20th century. According to Ottó Szőnyi, 'there was a 10-cm-long fragment of a strong foot there, which was drawn with black contours and inclined at the knee. The upper part of the foot is 3.7, the lower 5.6 cm long'.[25] Proceeding from this fragment, he looked for a composition common among the catacomb paintings in Rome. In the centre, there is a nude or only a tunic-wearing figure and he finally found it in the depiction of Daniel.

---

[22] *Dictionnaire d'archéologie chrétienne et de liturgie* X, 2 (Paris, 1931), 979-1070.

[23] Francesca P. Massara, 'Magi', in Fabrizio Bisconti, *Temi di icongrafia paleocristiana* (Vatican, 2000), 207-8.

[24] The condensing composition of the Jonah panel is analysed by Friedrich Gerke ('Die Wandmalereien der Petrus-Paulus Katakombe in Pécs (Sopianae)' (1954), 157, 175) and by György Heidl ('A pécsi I. számú sírkamra Jónás-képe és Szent Jeromos Jónás kommentárja' [The Jonah picture in the burial chamber nr. I at Pécs and St Jerome's commentary on Jonah], in György Heidl, *A keresztény és a szirének* [The Christian and the sirens] (Budapest, 2005), 201-40, 201-8.

[25] O. Szőnyi, *A pécsi ókeresztény sírkamra* [The early Christian burial chamber in Pécs] (1907), 53.

Later Szőnyi suggested that it is possible that this fragment belonged to the hip of the Good Shepherd. This suggestion was shared by Lajos Nagy in the 1930s.[26] According to Friedrich Gerke, possible depictions present in a panel between the Fall and the cycle of Jonah might have been: the Good Shepherd, *orante*, the resurrection of Lazarus, or another salvation scene from the Old Testament.[27]

In the first decade of the 2000s, György Heidl further developed this theory. In his new hypothesis, a new approach to the question is put forward. In his lecture, at the conference of this volume, he suggested that the figure of the Good Shepherd should have been there because in this case there would have been a depiction of Christ in every central field of the burial chamber. If a viewer stood in the middle of the room, there would be a Christogram opposite him in the middle of the wall between Peter and Paul, another Christogram above his head on the ceiling, the child with his mother on his left hand side and another picture of Christ on the other side. Knowing that the Good Shepherd is one of the most traditional compositions of the Roman catacombs, what else could it be than the popular Good Shepherd? – claims Heidl.

Before trying to choose between Daniel and the Good Shepherd, I will take a broader approach to the question. My starting point comes from a statement by Jeffrey Spier. According to him, the Christian art of the 3rd and 4th centuries was marked by 'a use of a limited selection of concisely composed images, which were often juxtaposed in various ways'.[28] He suggests that the limited selection of pictures must have had a special meaning, but the images are almost never accompanied by explanatory inscriptions. However, based on the extant evidence, we can assert that 'certain biblical scenes appear with great frequency, others only occasionally, and some not at all.'[29]

'The consistency of the iconographic programs from tomb to tomb indicates that individual taste or personal whim played little role in the decoration of these places.'[30] So if we would like to make a well-substantiated hypothesis about the missing panel, we should turn to compositions of this kind. Since Graydon Synder states in his famous book *Ante Pacem* that 'early Christian archaeology refers primarily to Rome',[31] Aldo Nestori's collection[32] of the wall

---

[26] Lajos Nagy, 'Pannonia Sacra', in Jusztinián Serédi (ed.), *Szent István Emlékkönyv* (Budapest, 1983), 29-148.

[27] F. Gerke, 'Die Wandmalereien der Petrus-Paulus Katakombe in Pécs (Sopianae)' (1954), 156.

[28] Jeffrey Spier, 'The earliest Christian art: from personal salvation to imperial power', in Jeffrey Spier (ed.), *Picturing the Bible: The Earliest Christian Art* (London, 2007), 1-24, 8.

[29] Robin M. Jensen, 'Early Christian Images and Exegesis', in Jeffrey Spier (ed.), *Picturing the Bible: The Earliest Christian Art* (London, 2007), 65-86, 71.

[30] R. Jensen, *Understanding Early Christian Art* (2000), 27.

[31] G. Snyder, *Ante Pacem* (1985), 3.

[32] Aldo Nestori, *Repertorio topografico delle pitture delle catacombe romane* (Rome, 1975).

paintings in the different catacombs of Rome can provide a stable and reliable initiation for further considerations.

But before a more detailed analysis, a unique iconographical feature of the Sopianae cemetery needs to be mentioned. The 4th century brought forward a lot of innovation in Christian art. From the first decades of this century, the list of popular biblical scenes grew significantly both in funerary context and in church decoration as well. A lot of other episodes from the Old Testament were added to the former repertoire. Previously unknown passages from Genesis were depicted on the paintings in the Via Latina Catacomb (e.g. Abraham's visitors at Mamre and scenes from the life of Joseph) and from other books (Pharaoh's daughter finding Moses and the manifestation of the burning bush).[33]

But these changes do not affect the paintings in the cemetery of Sopianae. It is conspicuous how conservative the catalogue of the pictures is here. But Synder does draw our attention to the fact that 'early Christian art in other locations where the time lapse between them and Rome gives us a post-Constantinian date, but a pre-Constantinian style. […] The frescoes there repeat what has been found in Rome as third-century materials.'[34] The only exception in Sopianae could be the depiction of the Magi discussed in the former section. But if my hypothesis is appropriate, it is not the introduction of an absolutely fresh topic, but rather the expanded interpretation of an older form.

So taking into consideration this provincial phenomenon, I collected similar examples of the wall paintings of the Sopianae burial chamber in Rome.[35] I was not satisfied with the old argument that since the eastern wall is decorated only with Old Testament scenes, on the other side 'a similarly Old Testament scene (for example Daniel) is a more likely guess'.[36]

The details of this compilation can be found in the following chart. As it can be seen, there is no place in Rome where all of the pictures from Sopianae would appear in the same *cubiculum*. At the same time, there are such places where four of them occur together. (The numbers of these *cubicula* are written in italics.) Having examined these places, I can claim that there are four *cubicula*, where the Good Shepherd appears, but there are only two examples among them without the presence of Daniel. There are four instances when the picture of Daniel is there without the Good Shepherd.

---

[33] R. Jensen, 'Early Christian Images and Exegesis' (2007), 72.

[34] G. Snyder, *Ante Pacem* (1985), 33.

[35] A. Nestori, *Repertorio topografico delle pitture delle catacombe romane* (1975), 191, 192, 195, 198, 200, 203-4, 210.

[36] K. Hudák, 'The Iconographical Program of the Wallpaintings' (2009), 53.

Adam & Eve	Noah	Three Youths	Jonah	Woman with Child	Daniel	Good Shepherd
Aureli 1						Aureli 2
		Balbina 2			Balbina 2	
Callisto 37		Callisto 27	Callisto 2, 6, 21, 22, 23, 24, 25, 27		Callisto 2, 6, 28	Callisto 2, 3, 4, 6, 14, 21, 22, 23, 26, 45, 46
			Circo di Massenzio 1			
			Ciriaca 2			
				Commodilla 3	Commodilla 5	
Domitilla 33, 39 (?), 43, 51, 57, 69, 77	*Domitilla 3 e 10, 31, 43, 45, 62, 69*	Domitilla 31, 33, 62, 69	Domitilla 27, 30, 31, 36, 60 62, 74	Domitilla 54	Domitilla 3 e 10, 28, 31, 39 (?), 45, 62, 67, 69	Domitilla 23, 27, 34, 39, 42, 51, 63, 67, 70, 72, 73, 74, 75
		Ermete 4, 10	Ermete 3	Ermete 1	Ermete 3, 4, 9	Ermete 2, 3
Giordani 4, 7	Giordani 6, 7	Giordani 5	Giordani 6, 7, 11		Giordani 4, 6, 7, 12	Giordani 3
Giordani e Epimaco 1					Giordano e Epimaco 1	
Maius 8, 9, 17, 19	*Maius 8, 9, 12, 13, 16*	*Maius 5, 12, 16, 19*	*Maius 4, 5, 12, 13, 15, 16, 17, 19*	Maius 22	*Maius 4, 8, 16, 18, 19*	*Maius 4, 5, 6 (?), 7, 8, 9, 12, 15, 16, 17, 19*
	Marco e Marcell. 6	Marco e Marcell. 5	Marco e Marcell. 5			Marco e Marcell. 5
	Minus 1				Minus 1	
	Nuziatella 4					

	Panfilio 1			Panfilio 5		
Pietro e Marcellino 44, 51, 52, 57, 58	Pietro e Marcellino 15, 21, 22, 27, 28, 47, 48, 57, 64, 65, 67, 69, 71, 77, 78	Pietro e Marcellino 71	Pietro e Marcellino 15, 16, 18, 22, 27, 28, 29, 34, 35, 39, 45, 47, 49, 51, 53, 58, 64, 67, 69, 77		Pietro e Marcellino 11, 21, 24, 27, 29, 41, 42 (?), 51, 54, 57, 65, 71, 74, 77, 78, 79	Pietro e Marcellino 14, 15, 16, 19, 20, 21, 22, 28, 29, 34, 35, 39, 42, 45, 51, 53, 57, 62 (?), 64, 67, 71, 74, 76, 77, 78
	Ponziano 3	Ponziano 4				Ponziano 9
	Pretestato 19		Pretestato 8, 17		Pretestato 14, 17	Pretestato 3, 8, 15, 17, 19
Priscilla 32	Priscilla 1, 5, 39	Priscilla 7, 25, 39	Prisc. 5, 7, 9, 15, 32	Priscilla 10	Priscilla 39	Prisc. 5, 7, 9, 10, 13, 14, 15, 19, 22, 37
	Quatro oranti presso Vibia 2		Quatro oranti presso Vibia 2			
	Sebastiano 3		Sebastiano 3			Sebastiano 7 (?)
					Sta Croce 4	
			Tecla 2		Tecla 2	
				Valentino 1		
	Via Anapo 12, 14	Via Anapo 8	Via Anapo 8, 9, 10, 11		Via Anapo 8, 9, 10, 11, 14	Via Yser 5
						Via Anapo 7
Via Latina 1, 2, 3, 11	*Via Latina 1, 2, 13*	*Via Latina 1, 13*			*Via Latina 1, 13*	
Via Paisiello 1	*Via Paisiello 1*	*Via Paisiello 1*	*Via Paisiello 1*			*Via Paisiello 1*

There are different theories in the current literature that attempt to explain why those certain Old Testament episodes occur among the catacomb paintings with a significant frequency. A good summary of the different explanations is available in the book *Understanding Early Christian Art* by Robin Jensen.[37] I would like only to highlight five theories here:

- the theory of the lost illuminated manuscript of the Bible,
- the theory of deliverance from persecution,
- the theory of the *commendatio animae*,
- the theory of scriptural typologies and
- the theory of sacramental life.

Although these theories differ in many aspects, I presume that on the basis of any of them the former presence of Daniel could be argued with fewer problems.

Another argument would be that the closest parallel of Adam and Eve was found in the so called Early Christian Mausoleum in Sopianae, in the same cemetery. Therefore, we should take the fact into account that it is Daniel in the next picture to the one with Adam and Eve on in that burial chamber, and there is no depiction of the Good Shepherd there, at least in the condition as we know the chamber today (since its ceiling has been damaged totally).

On the basis of these two arguments, I join those researchers who assign higher likelihood to Daniel's depiction in the missing panel.

Robin Jensen presents a complex interpretation of early Christian pictures in her book, titled *Understanding Early Christian Art*. She presents the academic reception of many images which occur above all in funerary art. She thinks that images had multivalent meanings which did not exclude each other. She writes: 'interpretive systems cannot be applied immutably. Moreover, the nature of symbols is never to be restricted to one meaning only, and their possible interpretations are never mutually exclusive.'[38]

She researches the significance of several biblical stories on different levels and tries to make cross-references among them. There are some concepts which appear as nodal points in this interpretation matrix. The key terms of interpretation used by Jensen are creation and recreation, resurrection, rebirth, baptism, salvation, hope. She supposes that as 'baptism is an extraordinarily complex rite with expansive theological signification' as 'artistic references to this sacrament ought to be as layered or multifaceted as baptism itself'.[39] So on the grounds of her thoughts, I conclude that not only each biblical picture as an element has a multivalent interpretation, but the whole iconographic structure of this certain burial chamber in Sopianae bears a multilevel significance.

---

[37] R. Jensen, *Understanding Early Christian Art* (2000), 69-75.
[38] R. Jensen, *Understanding Early Christian Art* (2000), 87-8.
[39] R. Jensen, *Understanding Early Christian Art* (2000), 88.

2. 'Korsós' or the Wine Jar Burial Chamber

The next part is about the 'Korsós' or the Burial Chamber with the Jar, which contains decorative elements rather than single wall paintings.[40] The only figures found in the niche scooped into the northern wall of the burial vault are a jar and glass. The bluish green colour of the vessels shows that these are depictions of glass vessels. Both vessel types can be defined. The conic cup was very popular through the whole of the 4th century. The shape of the wine jar is more specific. It has one bail and its neck is cone shaped. The shape of the vessel is neither ball, nor coil, rather its belly looks like an egg standing on its broader side. Glass vessels whose shape is similar to the form of this painted one but not the same are more typically found in the southern rather than the northern part of Pannonia.

It is worth taking a look at the artefacts in the grave from Pannonia in the 4th century to see whether this composition of the wine jug and cup occurs only on a wall painting, or in reality as well. I would like to lean on the analysis of the Hungarian archaeologist, Endre Tóth in this respect.[41] There are a lot of Roman graves from the province of Pannonia which contained artefacts like a plate, a cup and in many cases also a jug. The presence of these vessels can be explained on the grounds of Roman funerary traditions. The custom of a funeral meal, which was shared by the mourners and the deceased, was commonly spread in the empire. The kitchen utensils were essentially used for eating and drinking at these funeral meals. It is very likely that they contained food and drink as it is indicated by the remains of animal bones near them in some cases and by the depictions carved in gravestones.

The presence of a cup and a jar in a grave is much more infrequent than the one of a plate and a cup. The different usage must indicate a different, i.e. symbolic meaning. The importance of this symbol is emphasized by the fact that its position is central in the burial chamber. Especially as the other paintings on the walls are only marble incrustation and vine tendrils. The connection of the wine jar and the cup to the *refrigerium* is obvious. But they also express the afterlife faith of the people who built or had the graves built. Because a jar and a cup are containers of liquids, it seems evidential that the intention was to protect the deceased, especially from thirst in the afterlife. It was a common belief in the Mediterranean region that the thirst of the one who roams and wanders in the other world must be alleviated by the ones who are alive. But

---

[40] Ferenc Fülep, Antal Fetter. 'Neuere Forschungen in der ausgemalten, frühchristlichen Grabkammer Nr. II. von Pécs', in *Janus Pannonius Múzeum Évkönyve* (Pécs, 1971), 91-103.; K. Hudák, L. Nagy, *A Fine and Private Place* (2009), 30-6.

[41] Endre Tóth, 'A pogány és keresztény Sopianae' [The pagan and Christian Sopianae], in *Specimina nova dissertationum ex Instituto Historico Universitatis Quinqueecclesiensis de Iano Pannonio Nominatae* (Pécs, 2006), 49-102, 71-82.

this theory was accepted not only by pagans but by Christians as well. Some examples are the parable of the poor Lazarus and the rich man from the *Gospel of Luke* (16:20) or Perpetua's vision of her brother, the child Dinocrates.[42]

So making allowance for the whole neutral iconographic program of this burial chamber and the possible interpretations of its core motif, the wine jar and cup, I presume that the religious identity of this grave cannot be done unambiguously. I suppose that what Fabrizio Bisconti ascertained about the vessel findings in the catacombs is true about these vessel symbols, too: 'their significance resided in their ambivalent and multivalent role that oscillated between decoration and funerary equipment.'[43] Probably, it is not an accident that there are no special Christian symbols in this tomb, which otherwise stands amongst graves that are full of biblical pictures or at least signed by painted Christograms. Nevertheless, I suppose that the decoration of this burial chamber is special in Sopianae because it could convey meaning to both a pagan and a Christian viewer at the same time. Also I would not exclude the possibility that the commissioners of this tomb were such people who could not or more probably did not want to choose a distinct and separate iconographic expression for their afterlife beliefs.

Summary

At the end of my article, I would like to stress that this presentation can only be regarded a snapshot of my research, as my study is still well in progress. My main purpose was to show that the iconographic methods which are well elaborated in the case of the Christian burial paintings in Rome can be successfully adapted to the provincial pieces of art of Pannonia. The current approaches of Christian iconography can help us with the global interpretation of the painted burial chambers of Sopianae. The primary and direct influence of the Roman catacomb paintings can be observed here, together with the effects of other regions of the empire.

---

[42] *Passio Sanctarum Martyrum Perpetuae et Felicitatis* 2.3, PL 3, 34.

[43] Vincenzo Fiocchi-Nicolai, Fabrizio Bisconti, Danilo Mazzoleni, *The Christian Catacombs of Rome: History, Decoration, Inscriptions*, 2nd ed. (Regensburg, 2002), 81.

Technical Observations on the Paintings in the St. Peter and Paul (No. 1) Burial Chamber in Sopianae

Krisztina HUDÁK, Hungary

ABSTRACT

This article deals with some details of technical observations on the paintings in the Saint Peter and Paul Burial Chamber of Sopianae dated to the end of the 4th century AD, which the author had a chance to examine in person. After trying to separate the painting agents, matters and brushwork of the two or three craftsmen who had worked at that place the author tried to suggest some solutions on some iconographical problems of the badly visible details of the paintings with the help of 4th century analogies.

I am indebted to early Christian research for writing this contribution. In the spring of 2003, some days before the official opening of the Cella Septichora Visitor Centre I had an exceptional chance to examine the paintings in person. It was an unforgettable experience for me. Now I try to demonstrate some details about my observations made at that time.[1]

In the course of my work I received a lot of photos made by the restorators, archeologists and photographers, and I had also the possibility to talk with the restorators dealing with roman wall painting techniques, Attila Pintér and Zsófia Kurovszky.[2] In my article I would like to share my observations and I try to separate the craftmen who worked in this special place.

1. The restorations

The burial chamber and the narthex were discovered in 1782.[3] The paintings found in the *hypogaeum* were restored several times. Due to the drawings

---

[1] First of all I must thank Olivér Gábor, the archeologist at the Baranya Megyei Múzeumok Igazgatósága [Directory of the Museums of County Baranya] in Pécs for this possibility.

[2] I thank them for their valuable comments on Roman fresco and *secco*-painting techniques. Attila Pintér was the restorer of the burial chamber in 2002-2003 (and of the so called mausoleum in the cemetery of Sopianae, St. Steven's Square in 1976-1977), Zsófia Kurovszky is a restorer who is specialized in wall-paintings of Roman Pannonia.

[3] The false date of the discovery (1780) known from the first publication of József Koller, *Prolegomena in historiam episcopatus quinqueecclesiarum* (Posonii, 1804), 25 has been revised and corrected at first by István Lengvári, 'Sopianae kutatásának története (The History of investigation of Sopianae)', *Jelenkor* 44 (2001), 1157.

Studia Patristica LXXIII, 249-279.

250 K. HUDÁK

and paintings made in the 19th century, the actual state of the paintings can be followed with the help of older illustrations as well. I think here in the first place of the drawings published by József Koller in 1804 (Fig. 1), and of the illustrations in the publication of Imre Henszlmann from 1873.[4] The first restoration campaign using modern technologies was made in 1939, in the contributions published after the second World War one can see the results of this restoration.[5] The last restoration utilizing the most advanced technologies was completed by 2003, by Attila Pintér.[6] This latest restauration work provided me with the possibility to examine the precise details of the technical execution.

2. The datation

In another essay of mine I have made a chronological comparison of the motives in the Peter-Paul burial chamber,[7] with the following results.[8]

```
Peter, Paul
and Christogram      ---------------------------------------------
Jonah's plant                                       ---------------------(?)
Mary's head                    ---------------------------
Barrel vault:
head in the NE corner                       -----------
head in the NW corner             -------------
head in the SE corner                        -----------------------
Suggestion of dating                        -------------
_____
AD               350  360  370  380      390    400    410
```

[4] J. Koller, *Prolegomena* (1804), 24-5; Imre Henszlmann, 'Die altchristliche Grabkammer in Fünfkirchen', *Mitteilungen der Kaiserlichen und Königlichen Central-commission zur Erforschung und Erhaltung der Baudenkmale* 18 (1873), 57-83.
[5] Ferenc Fülep, *Sopianae. The History of Pécs during the Roman Era and the Problem of the Continuity of the Late Roman Population,* Archaeologia Hungarica 50 (Budapest, 1984), 36; Pls. X-XIX.
[6] Attila Pintér and András Heitler, 'Újra megnyílt a Péter-Pál sírkamra Pécsett [The St. Peter and Paul Burial Chamber in Pécs is open again]', *Örökségvédelem* VII/5-6 (2003), 1-4.
[7] Krisztina Hudák, 'The Chronology of the Paintings in the Saint Peter and Paul Burial Chamber in Sopianae', in Szilvia Bíró (ed.), *Ex officina… Studia in honorem Dénes Gabler* (Győr, 2009), 225-38. The ivy winding around Jonah may reflect the impact of Jerome's translation yet again from the end of the fourth century. According to György Heidl, the presence of ivy-leaves would make the *terminus post quem* of the paintings after AD 392 (or 396-397), see the contribution of György Heidl in this volume. The painted frames of the side walls are wide-spread after 350 AD, see Krisztina Hudák and Levente Nagy, *A Fine and Private Place. Discovering the Early Christian Cemetery of Sopianae,* Heritage booklets 6 (Pécs, ²2009), note 160. Stylized acanthus leaves become particularly popular in the last quarter of the fourth century, the representation of the twin Apostles spread from Rome into the territories under the spiritual influence of the Church of Rome in the second half of the fourth century: Krisztina Hudák, 'The Iconographical Program of the Wallpaintings in the Saint Peter and Paul Burial Chamber of Sopianae (Pécs)', *Mitteilungen zur Christlichen Archäologie* 15 (2009), 47-76, 50.
[8] K. Hudák, 'The Chronology' (2009), 233.

The characteristic features of the so called 'Zeitstil'[9] and the topographical and geological situation of the burial chamber can provide a good basis for chronology.[10] The paintings of the Peter-Paul burial chamber cannot be dated much later, than the first years of the fifth century because the provincial urban society suddenly collapsed and impoverished as the result of intense barbarian raids. Wealthier families fled to Italy or the safer areas, and those who stayed could not afford to commission high quality burial paintings.[11]

3. Brief comments about the course of the painting

In the Roman era the basic technique of Roman wall-painting was fresco in Pannonia, as everywhere in the Empire.[12] The *secco* was much more rare than the fresco technique. The order of the *secco*-painting on the surface consists of two steps:

1st step: the painters prepared several layers (two or three) of foundations (*tectoria*). Their tools probably were brushes (*penicilli*). A white-greyish –white upper layer is laid on the lower layer(s), on a reddish-brown mixture of lime-water and chalk.

2nd step: a red (or rarely a black) painted or incised *sinopia* is made in the case of the *secco* work. In Pécs and in the case of the majority of roman wall-paintings, this underdrawing was made on the surface to outline the scenes and the main figures.[13] The red or black colours and the axial lines of the figures were then filled in with guide-lines and with different colours down to the last detail.[14] Further guide-lines were also employed to sketch out figures and figure-groups.[15] Mainly horizontal lines were drawn and the surface was divided into some horizontal stages.[16] These snapped lines can be incised and painted preparatory drawings.[17]

---

[9] Norbert Zimmermann, *Werkstattgruppen römischer Katakombenmalerei*, Jahrbuch für Antike und Christentum, Ergänzungsband 35 (Münster, 2002), 45.

[10] K. Hudák, 'The Iconographical Program' (2009), note 93.

[11] K. Hudák, 'The Iconographical Program' (2009), note 66.

[12] R. Ling, *Roman Painting* (Cambridge, 1991), 200.

[13] Preparatory drawings made by brush or incision can be identified with false-colour infrared photography. For the description of this technique and of its use for scientific investigations see Ioanna Kakoulli, *Greek Painting Techniques and Materials from the Fourth to the First Century B.C.* (London, 2009), 77-9.

[14] K. Hudák, 'The Iconographical Program' (2009), 62, note 57; I. Kakoulli, *Greek Painting Techniques* (2009), 8, 12. The technical observations of Kakoulli are valid to Roman painting as well, which was discussed in her book, too.

[15] R. Ling, *Roman Painting* (1991), 203.

[16] R. Ling, *Roman Painting* (1991), 203: 'Vertical divisions are less common, because Roman plaster was thick enough and well enough compacted to retain its moisture for long periods'.

[17] I. Kakoulli, *Greek Painting Techniques* (2009), 8. But there are no samples where there were any traces of preparatory drawing: I. Kakoulli, *Greek Painting Techniques* (2009), 12; on the basis of the book of Selim Augusti, *I colori pompeiani* (Roma, 1967), *non vidi*.

4. The question of repainting

There are no traces of a repainting in the Burial Chamber. Thus, because the painting had not been repainted again, it can be excluded that a representation of the Three Youths was later repainted as a Three Magi scene (I will deal with this problem later).

5. The colouring agents, matters, dyestuffs

The narthex, like all the paintings in the main chamber was at least partially covered in *al secco* wall paintings. According to the roman customs, the surfaces of the walls were first prepared with several layers of white colour foundation.[18] The lower part at the wall of the inner room is covered with a beige coloured layer. Painted fragments at the pediment of the narthex and in the small entrance room there was a *candelabrum* found during the 1939 restoration campaign (Fig. 30).[19]

In the case of Sopianae, the used techniques actually seem to follow somewhat simpler methods than those described for mural paintings by Vitruvius and Pliny the Elder.[20]

In Sopianae we do not have any published results of pigment investigations. One has no sure information about the contents of the different colours, so the following descriptions of the pigments are based only on analogies from investigated ancient paintings.

There were naturally occured earth pigments. Red (from ochre, red chalk), yellow (from yellow ochre[21]), black (from charcoal, powdered carbon), ochre (from iron-ochre), green (locally made from ochre and black), blue (mixed from yellow and green[22]), grey, beige, brown and their tints and tones (locally mixed from the main colours) were used for the painting. As a rule, one used glass bottles, capsules, palettes, paint-box, a mortarium with rubbing stone for

---

[18] I. Kakoulli, *Greek Painting Techniques* (2009), 8.

[19] F. Fülep, *Sopianae* (1984), 36.

[20] I. Kakoulli, *Greek Painting Techniques* (2009), 82.

[21] The use of red ochre was very common in the Greek and Roman World for the *sinopia*, in the case of yellow ochre the situation was very similar: Plinius, *Naturalis Historia* XXXIII 50; XXXV 31; Theophrastus, *De lapidibus* 51-3, cited by R. Ling, *Roman Painting* (1991), 207-9, see also Ralph Mayer, *The Artist's Handbook of Materials and Techniques* (New York, ⁵1991), 375. To the question of yellow ochre: I. Kakoulli, *Greek Painting Techniques* (2009), 53: 'It was also used as a secondary pigment in admixtures with other colours to produce different tonal variations ranging from light and dark yellow to dark brown green and red'.

[22] There was a real blue pigment around Mary's head (personal communication of Attila Pintér). The dyestuffs had been analyzed by the chemist Zoltán Szabó before the last restoration campaign, the documentation of the chemical analysis is preserved in the archive of the Gyula Forster National Centre for Cultural Heritage Management, inv. nr. 20725 and 33648.

grinding colours, knives, bronze scoops.[23] The colours have a strong accent to the identification the blurred scenes and figures.

6. The number of the painters and the division of labour during the painting

How many painters created the pictures? This question can only be raised by investigating the paintings of a *cubiculum*, if the quality, quantity, the actual technical condition of the murals allow us. If all these conditions are fullfilled, one can try to distinguish the face painter and his assistants from each other, who painted the decorative elements and the framing.[24]

Fortunately in our burial chamber all the conditions are given, because we have an amount of relatively well preserved painting fragments. Examining these *seccoes*, after the modern restorations had been removed one can distinguish on the cleaned surface at least two different painter's hands. The classical Morelli-method can be used for the identification of the individual artist based on the examination of the proportion of the figure, the fingers, the lips, the eyes, *etc.*[25] I try to distinguish the painters' hands on the basis of the brushwork and the modelling of hands:

1) The first hand would be called *Painter Nr. 1*. He worked on the tondo-heads, on the layout of some garments (Mary, three men, tondos), the elements of the barrel vault: peacocks, pigeons, bunches of flowers, some acanthus and other floral ornaments of the barrel vault (Fig. 2), and probably the head of the *ketos* in the Jonah-scene. He used sometimes very thin brushstrokes and used many colours. He liked to tinker away at the details.[26]

2) The second master's hand whom I call *Painter Nr. 2* painted the figures of Peter and Paul and their hands (Fig. 3), Eve, Jonah and the Noah-scenes and Mary's head (Fig. 4). He painted forms and frames with roughly sketched lines and tones, the *candelabrum* in the narthex (Fig. 30) and the

---

[23] R. Ling, *Roman Painting* (1991), 211.

[24] N. Zimmermann, *Werkstattgruppen* (2002), 46.

[25] R. Ling, *Roman Painting* (1991), 217.

[26] See for example the scene of the three men: 'Their garment is carefully decorated down to the smallest detail. Their green tunics have belts and ochre coloured borders. They wear narrow leggings and bright green shoes outlined in red to differentiate them from the leggings. The men wear scarlet cloaks, fastened together on their right shoulders with round brooches. A dotted yellow top is visible under the cloak of the man on the right'. Or see the garment of the female figure 'which is carefully decorated down to the smallest detail like the three men. On close inspection, red-green patches of colour become visible near the woman's neck, while the arms are covered with a white garment. The colourful dots that enrich the composition may allude to an applied ornament on the woman's cloak, a popular feature of Late Roman fashion', so K. Hudák, 'The Iconographical Program' (2009), 55-8.

contours of the scenes. Generally he used rather thicker brushstrokes, even for the elaboration of the faces also. His brushwork is sometimes very vivid.

In the case of the barrel vault of Sopianae, it is possible to separate a face-painter, who could be named as *pictor imaginarius*. He was a quality master and worked on the faces and details, while the other master, while his assistant (?) painted the background and the other parts of the figures and the scene. This one could be called *pictor parietarius*. I think, both of them were not only the painters of the details, but the plasterers, too.

I do not know, whether I am right to call *Painter Nr. 1* the *pictor imaginarius*, and his assistent as *pictor parietarius*.[27] Both seemed to paint faces in this burial chamber, but the head of Peter (Fig. 5) and the medaillon heads (Figs. 6-7) on the barrel vault were apparently painted by different hands. The working area was subdivided by the painters in the catacombs as well. Both painters made figures and perhaps decorative elements, too. They usually worked with the same painting technique in the same *hypogaeum*, but their style can be differentiated.[28] Apparently two or more brushes were used, broader brushstrokes can be seen at the girlands of acanthus leaves, and narrower lines at the details of the medaillon heads. The reduced size of the burial chamber allows me to suppose only two or three painters.[29] I have to assume at least two painters instead of one for practical reasons (for example because of the height of the room), too.[30]

Master and disciple, or the masters (like in our case) must have worked fast so that they may have finished this *hypogaeum* in a week.[31] As a rule a *pictor parietarius*, a *pictor imaginarius* may have one (or more) assistant(s), a plasterer worked in case of the more qualitative paintings.[32] There was a chief painter and his assistant. We can speak about an assistant and not about another painter itself, if no characteristic features of another painter's hand can be identified.[33] In the Sopianae burial chamber, however, both painters had their own characteristic brushwork-technique, therefore I do not think, that the assumed *Painter Nr. 2* was only an assistent.

[27] For main painters (face painters) and assistants in Antiquity see R. Mayer, *The Artist's Handbook* (1991), 365, 373; R. Ling, *Roman Painting* (1991), 204, 213, 215-7; Harald Mielsch, *Römische Wandmalerei* (Darmstadt, 2001), 17 who identified the *pictores imaginarii* in the *Edictum de pretiis* of Diocletian (7, 8, 9.) with portrait painters, earning 150 *denarii* against the *pictores parietarii*, earning only 75, like bronze sculptors.

[28] N. Zimmermann, *Werkstattgruppen* (2002), 173, 256.

[29] Roger Ling reckons with 3-4 painters in a workshop based on the division of labour: R. Ling, *Roman Painting* (1991), 215-6.

[30] N. Zimmermann, *Werkstattgruppen* (2002), 47.

[31] For various investigations concerning the spread of individual workshops and painters see H. Mielsch, *Römische Wandmalerei* (2001), 17.

[32] R. Ling, *Roman Painting* (1991), 215.

[33] N. Zimmermann, *Werkstattgruppen* (2002), 256.

7. The problem of the wandering painters

In previous studies, I have dealt with the possibility how to separate well known motifs from pattern books, and special iconographical solutions, due to the owner's desire, or to the painters' creative own ideas.[34] The appearance of identical Christian themes in distant places is often attributed to the activity of wandering artists[35] or workshops, working from pattern books.[36]

These similarities (both stylistic and thematically) were based on direct or indirect contacts.[37] No sure information is known, however, in Antiquity about the wandering painters who traveled through Italy and the Balkan lands or about their pattern books. Only their artistic products bear witness to their work.[38] A comparison between the brushwork or colours of the painters active in Sopianae and those of fourth century Roman catacomb paintings is also possible (Figs. 8-9),[39] the technical knowledge of the Sopianae artists equals that of other craftsmen active in the most important centers of Christian art.

In my other essays and in this contribution I collected some parallels of the figures, motives and scenes of the burial chamber.[40] Besides the well known biblical scenes from Italy and the provinces, identical decoration patterns of the barrel vault can be found both in Italy (Rome and Aquileia) and in the Balkans (Nis, Thessaloniki, Sofia, Serdica).[41] Politically as well as culturally, the provinces of Pannonia belonged to the western part of the Roman Empire. Sopianae

---

[34] K. Hudák, 'The Iconographical Program' (2009), 61-4; K. Hudák and L. Nagy, *A Fine and Private Place* (2009), 57.

[35] R. Ling, *Roman Painting* (1991), 213.

[36] Michael Donderer, 'Und es gab sie doch! Ein neuer Papyrus und das Zeugnis der Mosaiken belegen die Verwendung antiker "Musterbücher"', *Antike Welt* 36/2 (2005), 61-8.

[37] I. Kakoulli, *Greek Painting Techniques* (2009), 12.

[38] K. Hudák, 'The Iconographical Program' (2009), 63.

[39] 1. The hands of the Apostles look like the hands of St. Peter in the SS. Pietro e Marcellino-catacomb, cubiculum 3, and the hands in the fragment of the figure of Christ in the Giordani-catacomb: Johannes Georg Deckers, Hans Reinhard Seeliger and Gabriele Mietke, *Die Katakombe "Santi Marcellino e Pietro". Repertorium der Malereien*. Roma Sotterranea Cristiana 6 (Münster, 1987), colourpl. 2, no. 3; Pasquale Testini, *Le catacombe e gli antichi cimiteri cristiani in Roma*, Roma Cristiana II (Bologna, 1966), Fig. 167.

2. The brushwork of the heads of the Apostles resembles Moses head and the figures participating at a banquet, both found in the SS. Pietro e Marcellino-catacomb, see P. Testini, *Le catacombe* (1966), Figs. 156, 164; J.G. Deckers, H.R. Seeliger and G. Mietke, *Die Katakombe "Santi Marcellino e Pietro"* (1987), no. 75; Vincenzo Fiocchi Nicolai, Fabrizio Bisconti and Danilo Mazzoleni, *Las catacumbas cristianas de Roma. Origen, desarrollo, aparato decorativo y documentación epigrafica* (Regensburg, 1999), lámina 126.

3. The acanthus tendrils in *loculus* Nr. 69. of the SS. Pietro e Marcellino catacomb are similar to the Sopianae example, see J.G. Deckers, H.R. Seeliger and G. Mietke, *Die Katakombe "Santi Marcellino e Pietro"* (1987), no. 69.

[40] K. Hudák, 'The Iconographical Program' (2009), 47-61; K. Hudák, 'The Chronology' (2009), 226-33; K. Hudák and L. Nagy, *A Fine and Private Place* (2009), 39-61.

[41] See notes 51-5.

had iconographic connections with the Balkans, too.[42] (Roman painting techniques were strongly influenced by greek painting as well, Romans followed
the Greek painting tradition.[43])

8. Pattern books, desires of the owner and ideas of the painters

As I stressed earlier in my contribution, work was carried according to a preliminary plan in agreement with the patron and based on an iconographic drawing, the underdrawing, the *sinopia*. This draft always accorded to the desires of
the owner/commissioner.[44] From this point of view, one has to ask: were there
really pattern books used in the burial chamber?[45]

The patron's efforts to make not only figural depictions, but decoration
patterns of high quality, can be often observed in artistic programs.[46] The two
main components of these painted programs are the fulfilled needs of the
patrons and the possibilities and potentials of the painter itself.[47] Examining the
Sopianae figures and scenes I could distinguish three categories.

a) *pattern book-figures or -scenes*

These figures and scenes have good chronological and iconographical parallels
in early christian art:

1. Eve on the eastern wall[48]
2. Peter, Paul: representation of the two apostle figures according to their
   standardized iconography on the northern wall[49]

[42] K. Hudák, 'The Iconographical Program' (2009), 70-1.
[43] I. Kakoulli, *Greek Painting Techniques* (2009), 8, 12: 'The Roman paint layers also evidence strong Greek influence. The range of pigments and the techniques of application (mainly
based on layering of the colours) were very similar'.
[44] The draft was based on a contract of *locatio operis faciendi*: R. Ling, *Roman Painting*
(1991), 217.
[45] Based on the drawings depicting various animals on a late hellenistic egyptian papyrus,
Michael Donderer was sure, that the papyrus is the first known extant pattern book from the
ancient world: M. Donderer, 'Und es gab sie doch!' (2005), 62, Abb. 3.
[46] N. Zimmermann, *Werkstattgruppen* (2002), 260.
[47] N. Zimmermann, *Werkstattgruppen* (2002), 260.
[48] Only the head of Eve, the waistline of the Eve-figure and leafy branches of the tree were
preserved. Eve's hair on this painting gives the same windswept impression as the softly undulat-
ing locks of Pharaon's daughter and her ladies-in-waiting painted with similar quick brushstrokes
on the frescoes of *cubiculum* B of the Via Latina-catacomb representing the discovery of Moses
and dated to the second third of the fourth century. See Antonio Ferrua, *Katakomben: Unbekannte
Bilder des frühen Christentums unter der Via Latina* (Stuttgart, 1991), 81, Abb. 66; K. Hudák,
'The Iconographical Program' (2009), note 21.
[49] K. Hudák, 'The Iconographical Program' (2009), 47-51, with further literature; more
recently discussion about the analogy from the Jagodin Mala cemetery of Naissus, see Renate

3. the composition of the three men on the western wall[50]
4. Noah on the western wall[51]
5. the peacocks on the barrel vault (Fig. 10)[52]
6. bunches of flowers on the barrel vault (Fig. 11)[53]
7. some acanthus-variations on the southern wall and on the barrel vault (Fig. 12).[54]

Conclusions drawn from the representations of my category a): The painters were familiar with the well known biblical (salvation) scenes in Christian context, with the usual representation type of St. Peter and Paul connected to Rome, and with the rich and sophisticated animal and floral ornaments on the barrel vault.

b) *motifs according to the special desire of the owner*

These cannot be entirely reduced to the schemes from the assumed pattern books:

1. tondo-heads on the barrel vault, which are not entirely schematic (each figure has a different face and head-shape)[55]
2. rich elaborated barrel vault, effort to fill the space[56]

Pillinger, 'Early Christian Grave Paintings in Niš, between East and West', *Niš and Byzantium. The Collections of Scientific Works* X (Niš, 2011), 30-5.

[50] See *exempli gratia* adoration scenes in catacombs, sarcophagi in K. Hudák, 'The Iconographical Program' (2009), notes 24, 29; P. Testini, *Le catacombe* (1966), Fig. 139 (*Capella Graeca* from the Priscilla catacomb); Guntram Koch, *Frühchristliche Sarkophage*, Handbuch der Archäologie (München, 2000), Abb. 22, 41, 42, 46, 48, 75, 80. Similar composition with three barbarians bringing gifts to the Emperor on the northwestern side of the column base of Theodosius in Constantinople (Figs. nr. 18-22): Bente Kiilerich, *The Obelisk Base in Constantinople: Court Art and Imperial Ideology*, Acta ad Archaeologiam et Artium Historiam Pertinentia, Series altera Nr. X (Roma, 1988), Fig. 63.

[51] K. Hudák and L. Nagy, *A Fine and Private Place* (2009), 52, notes 145-6, for another Noah-representations on early christian paintings, mosaics, sarcophagi. Perhaps the best analogy of the Sopianae Noah can be seen in the *cubiculum* 69 of the SS. Pietro e Marcellino catacomb, see J.G. Deckers, H.R. Seeliger and G. Mietke, *Die Katakombe "Santi Marcellino e Pietro"* (1987), colourpl. 50, no. 67b.

[52] K. Hudák, 'The Iconographical Program' (2009), notes 49-52, with further literature.

[53] K. Hudák and L. Nagy, *A Fine and Private Place* (2009), 53, note 148.

[54] The arch surrounding the southern entrance wall is decorated with luxuriously curling tendrils and stylized leaves growing out from an acanthus motif, see K. Hudák, 'The Iconographical Program' (2009), 53, 59, 60; notes 33, 48, 49, with further analogies.

[55] K. Hudák, 'The Iconographical Program' (2009), 60, 61, notes 53, 54.

[56] The framing runs around bunches of stilized acanthus leaves with vine-tendrils filling in the space. The barrel vault measures 3.20 meters by 2.47 meters. (The diameter of the medaillons is 0.43 meter.): K. Hudák, 'The Iconographical Program' (2009), 59, 60, notes 48, 51, 52, with further analogies. For recently discussed analogies of the Christogram with wreath in the middle of the barrel vault from the Jagodin Mala cemetery from Naissus, see R. Pillinger, 'Early Christian Grave Paintings in Niš' (2011), Figs. 2-5, 8, 15, 19.

3. *hedera, qiqeion* or gourds at the Jonah-scene (Fig. 14)[57]
4. elaborated, detailed Jonah-scene according to the biblical text (but according to the composition of the figures, this representation belongs rather to my category c).

Conclusions drawn from the representations of my category b): The efforts to fill the space entirely on the barrel-vault, to make scenes completely fitting the bible texts, and to represent the medaillon heads with unique, individualized features.

c) *individual ideas/brain-waves of the painters*

There are other painted motifs, mostly details, which are neither well known schemes from pattern-books, nor special representations for the sake of the owner. They could reflect individual ideas of the painters appearing in the walls:

1. the christogram stands on the frame, as if on a socket, comprising colourful bands running around the loculus (Fig. 13),[58]
2. the Jonah-cycle is in one scene (3 in 1 solution),[59] where the sea is symbolized by long green lines in the lower part of the picture (Fig. 14). The first publisher of the paintings, József Koller saw already in 1804 two monsters below the ship of Jonah.[60] Imre Henszlmann, however, was not able to see them any more, therefore he explained the composition according to a gold sandwich glas from the Louvre with one monster (Figs. 15-6).[61] The two monsters below the ship are clearly visible after the latest restoration work. The composition of the Jonah cycle in two or three episodes in one scene on a relief from Asia Minor (Tarsus, Fig. 17), on the sarcophagus of Singidunum (Fig. 19) and on the glass plate of Podgoritza (Fig. 18), where the prophet is thrown up directly under his plant.[62] Good analogy of the

---

[57] For this problem see the contributions of György Heidl and Levente Nagy in this volume.

[58] Christograms standing on high columns with the two apostles on the two sides on a gold sandwich glas and on a passion sarcophagus, see Kurt Weitzmann (ed.), *Age of Spirituality. Late Antique and Early Christian Art. 3rd-7th century*. Catalogue of the exhibition at the Metropolitan Museum of Art, November 19, 1977, through February 12, 1978 (New York, 1979), Kat. Nr. 508; Friedrich Gerke, 'A passiószarkofágok kormeghatározása' [The Chronology of the Passion Sarcophagi], *Archaeologiai Értesítő* 52 (1939), Abb. 27.

[59] The three episodes in the story are compressed into a single picture on the Sopianae painting, probably due to the lack of space.

[60] J. Koller, *Prolegomena* (1804), Pl. XI.

[61] I. Henszlmann, 'Die altchristliche Grabkammer in Fünfkirchen' (1873), 66; Fig. 5; colour-plate: Geffrey Spier (ed.), *Picturing the Bible. The Earliest Christian Art* (New Haven, London and Fort Worth, 2007), 186, Cat. Nr. 14.

[62] Tarsus: G. Spier, *Picturing the Bible* (2007), 186-7, Cat. Nr. 15; Podgoritza: G. Spier, *Picturing the Bible* (2007), Fig. 4; Singidunum: G. Koch, *Frühchristliche Sarkophage* (2000), Abb. 194.

composition of the episodes of the Jonah-cycle in a single scene is an early christian gemstone probably from Syria (Fig. 20). On this gemstone the prophet is sitting under the plant next to the ship where he is swallowed by the *ketos* shown below the ship, like on the Sopianae painting.[63] For the huge beak-like head of the *ketos* in Sopianae (Fig. 23), there is also a good analogy from the Via Anapo Catacomb, niche nr. 9 (Figs. 21-2).[64]

3. The ornamental decoration of the barrel vault is a somewhat simplified variation of the acanthus leaves on the southern wall.
4. Maybe an aspiration could be observed concerning the connection of the panels of the three men (three Magi?) and the female figure (their eyes are at the same height, they turn to each other).

Conclusions drawn from the representations of my category c): The surely extant high-degree of individual creativity of the painters provides some kind of play with forms and figures, the pictures are prepared with meticulous care.

Summary of the conclusions, characteristic features of the paintings of the St. Peter and Paul burial chamber

The filling out of the unpainted spaces on the walls of some *cubicula* of the SS. Pietro e Marcellino catacomb with ornalental bands and ribbons between the loculi are generally characteristic as 'Lokalstil' to this cemetery, the decoration has a clear connection with the architectural form of the *cubiculum*.[65] We have these features in the St. Peter and Paul burial chamber, too. For example the framed acanthus leaves on the southern wall, around the entrance door, or on the edge of the barrel-vault along the frames of the garden landscape with Christogram and medaillon heads (Fig. 12). Concerning the 'Formschatz' of the paintings, following assumptions can be made:

– This 'Formschatz' is the common result of the desires of the owner, and the repertoire of the painters.[66]
– The desires of the commissioner can be usually connected to some kinds of patterns, models, types of representations, with creative additions, individual ideas of the painters from their own repertoire.[67] In Sopianae they worked with a traditional 'Formschatz' with the addition of a rich decoration asked by the owner, performed with demanding care. The execution reflects the

---

[63] G. Spier, *Picturing the Bible* (2007), 188, Cat. Nr. 18.
[64] V. Fiocchi Nicolai, F. Bisconti and D. Mazzoleni, *Las catacumbas cristianas de Roma.* (1999), 70, lámina II.
[65] N. Zimmermann, *Werkstattgruppen* (2002), 258.
[66] N. Zimmermann, *Werkstattgruppen* (2002), 263.
[67] N. Zimmermann, *Werkstattgruppen* (2002), 263.

financial possibilities of the comissioner,[68] who apparently did not spare money for the fine elaboration of the paintings.
– The colours have many shades.
– The more qualified the painter is, the more can he be independent from the traditional forms and patterns.[69] At least one of the painters employed here, was a qualified artist, he could have been rather expensive. If *pictores imaginarii* earned really twice as much money at the end of the fourth century, as one can read in the *Edictum de pretiis* of Diocletian one century earlier,[70] the employment of such (a) painter(s) means that the patron was a wealthy person.
– The desire of the patron for representation: the demand for painting is in itself a representation, like the imitation of expensive material with incrustations, marble imitations, the *candelabrum* in the narthex (Fig. 30), and so on. The carefully elaborated human figures reflecting desires of the owner for salvation and resurrection express demands for representation, too.[71]
– The use of a pattern book is also probable: the proportions of the scenes and figures are equal up to their analogies.[72]
– The pictorial themes are tasteful, their elaboration is provided with meticulous care.

9. The question of workshop

After the identification of the painters' hands and the examination of the paintings one has to deal with the questions of workshop and the so called workshop-style. In Sopianae unfortunately we have no more similar figural paintings dated to the same period, so we can not compare more pictorial programs as a workshop activity.[73]

The ascription to workshops can be made on the basis of favoured or characteristic, standard designs and motifs, compositions and colour schemes.[74] What kind of characteristic standard 'Formschatz' does appear in the *hypogaeum* and what does the term 'characteristic' mean in our case? How can we identify the exact needs of the patron in the artistic program?[75] A kind of regular collaboration of more masters, which we usually call 'workshop', as assumed by

---

[68] N. Zimmermann, *Werkstattgruppen* (2002), 263-4.
[69] N. Zimmermann, *Werkstattgruppen* (2002), 264.
[70] See my note 27.
[71] N. Zimmermann, *Werkstattgruppen* (2002), 261.
[72] Roger Ling rightly observed, that the 'lines' may in that case be reference-lines to enable the copyist to fix the position within the panel of specific details: R. Ling, *Roman Painting* (1991), 219. For pattern books see my note 36.
[73] For this problem see N. Zimmermann, *Werkstattgruppen* (2002), 47, 162.
[74] R. Ling, *Roman Painting* (1991), 216; N. Zimmermann, *Werkstattgruppen* (2002), 45.
[75] N. Zimmermann, *Werkstattgruppen* (2002), 45.

classical archaeologists in the houses of Pompeii and elsewhere in Roman painting, cannot be clearly demonstrated in catacomb art.[76] Using a less strict definition of 'workshop', this so-called 'Sopianae-workshop' has one or more (regularly collaborating?) face-painter master with high quality. According to the technical layout of the medaillon-heads on the barrel-vault one can also conveniently date the wall paintings. The technical execution at the paintings of the whole burial chamber is high, too. The inner room of the *hypogaeum* was entirely covered with exquisite *al secco* pastels, and the painters used many colours to detail the figures and scenes.

In the case of Sopianae we cannot speak of a regional workshop or local cemetery workshops, like in some of the Roman catacomb *cubicula*.[77] The painters seem to have left the cemetery after performing the single commission ordered by the owner of the funerary building, like the 'oberirdische' painters of the Via Latina catacomb, identified by Nirbert Zimmermann.[78] The same iconographical and technical features apparent in the Sopianae *hypogaeum* cannot be demonstrated elsewhere in the region, the so called Early Christian Mausoleum on the St. Stephen's Square with the representations of the Fall and Daniel have been dated earlier, to the middle of fourth century.[79]

10. Some iconographical observations on the wall-paintings. Problems and possible solutions

In case of the *al secco* technique there is a possibility for the painters to make a delicate precision work. Unfortunately the *secco*-painting very easily drops and powders away one by one. Thus the work, the protection of substance and the identification of the figures and scenes is very difficult for the restorer and the archeologist. In Pécs there is a further problem: the erosive force of the oozing rainwater arriving from the hillside.[80] And at the first place: the salt and some other minerals with water as dissolver and agent.[81] Due to the salt absorption and the dampness of the walls, paintings will crumble into powder after a while.[82] A highly important task for restorers was the prevention of the salt efflorescence on the paintings.

---

[76] N. Zimmermann, *Werkstattgruppen* (2002), 256; H. Mielsch, *Römische Wandmalerei* (2001), 17.

[77] N. Zimmermann, *Werkstattgruppen* (2002), 45.

[78] N. Zimmermann, *Werkstattgruppen* (2002), 257.

[79] K. Hudák and L. Nagy, *A Fine and Private Place* (2009), 26.

[80] Olivér Gábor, 'Ókeresztény jellegek a pécsi késő antik temetőben (Old Christian features in the Late Roman Cemetery of Pécs)', in Szilvia Bíró (ed.): *FiRKák I. Fiatal Római Koros Kutatók I. konferenciakötete.* Xantus János Múzeum, Győr, 2006. március 8-10 (Győr, 2007), 369, english: 377.

[81] A. Pintér and A. Heitler, 'Újra megnyílt' (2003), 3.

[82] A. Pintér and A. Heitler, 'Újra megnyílt' (2003), 3.

262   K. Hudák

The misterious grey plate

There is a very special detail which appears on the scene of the three men on
the western wall. In the hand of the figure at the left side seems a bigger, grey
plate with oval form. The thumb of the figure holds it (Figs. 24-5).[83] The type
of the plate has a characteristic late Roman form known from the recently
found silver treasure of Cibalae as well.[84] If the figure carries this plate towards
the female figure and his legs go towards her, in this case it would not be the
scene of the Three Youths in the fiery furnace, but that of the Three Magi.
Thus, the two panels are iconographically connected and the painter may have
left three panels on this wall, too, in order not to break the rhythm of the paintings.[85] In my other contribution I was not entirely sure, that the yellow stripes
at the feet of the magus of the left side would be tongues of fire.[86] Bigger oval
plates can be seen in the hands of the magi from the epiphany scenes of the
Domitilla and SS. Pietro e Marcellino catacombs,[87] but a stone relief from
München of uncertain provenience depicting a magus with a smaller plate is
perhaps the best analogy to the Sopianae painting (Fig. 26).[88] The form of the
plates is very similar on both representations. Considering the similar compositions of the three Babylonian youths and the three magi, like in *arcosolium* Nr. 5

[83] Plates were seen in the hand of the magi already by József Koller, who wrote the first
publication on the paintings: J. Koller, *Prolegomena* (1804), Tabula XI.
[84] Hrvoje Vulić, *Silver of the Antique City of Vinkovci. Archaeological Treasure Trove.*
Museum of Arts and Crafts, Zagreb May 18th – June 10th 2012 (Zagreb, 2012), colourplate.
[85] According to the rules of Roman fresco painting, subsequent panels separated by a frame
cannot create a narrative, cannot belong to the same story, since the presence of the frame closes
off the story, creating two independent scenes. Early Christian art often disregards this rule, so
that feet, hands, or plant ornaments are often painted on the bordering frame, thus, breaking up
the closed composition within the frame. Two separate panels, however, do not comprise a con-
tinuous story even in Early Christian art. There are examples when the panels are widened,
especially in representations of the Three Magi, or Epiphany. The details belonging to the scenes'
figure between the panels, and the internal relationship of the figures make them appear to belong
to the same story. In this way the scenes become comprehensible without dividing the painted space
into a double and a single panel: see K. Hudák and L. Nagy, *A Fine and Private Place* (2009),
note 137.
[86] K. Hudák, 'The Iconographical Program' (2009), 58.
[87] Umberto M. Fasola, *Die Domitilla Katakombe und die Basilika der Märtyrer Nereus und
Achilleus*, Römische und italienische Katakomben 1 (Città del Vaticano, ³1989), Fig. 16; Alexander Demandt and Joseph Engemann (ed.), *Imperator Caesar Flavius Constantinus. Konstantin
der Grosse. Ausstellungskatalog* (Trier and Mainz, 2007), 380. On the epitaph of Severa from the
Museo Lateranense there are flat plates in the hands of the magi: P. Testini, *Le catacombe* (1966),
Fig. 63.
[88] Ludwig Wamser (ed.), *Die Welt von Byzanz – Europas östliches Erbe. Glanz, Krisen und
Fortleben einer tausendjährigen Kultur* (München, 2001), 117, Kat. Nr. 150A. Claudia Behling
argued recently for the interpretation of the paintings as *adoratio magorum*, too: Claudia Behling,
'Kinder des Ostens. Spätantike und frühchristliche Kinderdarstellungen im heutigen Ost- und
Südosteuropa', *Acta Archaeologica Academiae Scientiarum Hungariae* 62 (2011), 163-73, 169.

in the SS. Marco e Marcelliano catacomb (Figs. 27-8),[89] perhaps only the grey plate can help to identify the three figures.

The phrygian cap of a man on the Three Magi-scene

Two longer brushstrokes above the face of the figure on the right may represent the rim of a hat. In this case it is not a phrygian cap.[90] This part does not make a change in the interpretation of the scene (Fig. 24).

The blotches behind the female figure's head

Two bluish-greenish blotches can be seen behind the woman's figure sitting on the western wall. Strength of their colour, plants come to mind, perhaps a palm tree, or flower baskets. Their colours do not allow further interpretations. These colours, the bluish-greenish blotches cannot belong to a human figure, for example because of the lack of the red and black colours (Figs. 4, 29). According to the composition of the scene with Virgin Mary and the small Jesus it would have been better if we had been able to interpretate the two blotches as male/ or prophets heads.[91] The palm tree or flower baskets namely do not make any sense from iconografical point of view.

The green tones on the paintings of the barrel vault

More shades of green can be observed which were simply mixed from black and yellow. It looks to me that the green frames around the tondos marked out for the imitation of a transcendent light around the laurel crown.[92] Further examination of the painting is needed to identify the original function of the double frame (Figs. 6-7).

Outlook

This is a kind of summary of all the observations about the paintings by autopsy, without using another special technology. I hope that this contribution will serve as an introduction to encourage further research.

---

[89] Joseph Fink and Beatrix Asamer, *Die römischen Katakomben*, Sonderhefte der Antiken Welt 28 (Mainz am Rhein, 1997), Abb. 56-7; K. Hudák, 'The Chronology' (2009), Fig. 5.

[90] In my earlier publications I stressed, that according to the early christian iconographical conventions the three oriental people should wear phrygian caps, but I had to admit, that these caps are not clearly visible: see for example K. Hudák, 'The Iconographical Program' (2009), 56.

[91] Because of iconographical considerations I thought earlier, that these blotches could be male heads of prophets: K. Hudák, 'The Iconographical Program' (2009), 58; K. Hudák and L. Nagy, *A Fine and Private Place* (2009), 51.

[92] K. Hudák, 'The Iconographical Program' (2009), note 48.

A next phase of scientific research is needed to investigate the origins and the transport of the pigments used by the painters' workshop with Zoltán Szabó's chemical analysis.[93] The false-colour infrared photography of the preparatory drawings is useful for the identification of the badly visible scenes and for further analysis of their iconographical connections. During this investigation new information can be provided about the processing of the painting. It is extremely helpful for the identification of the debated iconographical details, the painters' attribution, style, technique, work organisation in their workshop, or for the more precise dating of the paintings. The paintings are hermetically closed in the burial chamber in order to avoid the destroying effects of the dampness of the walls and salt efflorescence. Now the investigation of the murals is a complicated procedure for the archeologists and the restorers.

[93] See my note 22.

Fig. 1. The paintings of the St. Peter and Paul burial chamber published by Joseph
Koller, taken from J. Koller, *Prolegomena* (1804, n. 3), Tabula XI.

Fig. 2. The varrel vault of the St. Peter and Paul burial chamber,
photo: Attila Pintér.

Fig. 3. St. Peter on the northern wall,
photo: Attila Pintér.

Fig. 4. Virgin Mary on the western wall, photo: Attila Pintér.

Fig. 5. St. Peter on the northern wall, photo: András em Török.

Fig. 6. Medaillon on the barrel vault, photo: Attila Pintér.

Fig. 7. Medaillon on the barrel vault, photo: Attila Pintér.

Fig. 8. Apostle's hand on the northern wall, photo: Attila Pintér.

Fig. 9. Apostles' hands on the barrel vault of cubiculum 3, SS. Pietro e Marcellino catacomb, Rome, taken from V. Fiocchi Nicolai, F. Bisconti and D. Mazzoleni, *Las catacumbas cristianas de Roma* (1999, n. 38), lámina 126.

Fig. 10. Peacock on the barrel vault, photo: Attila Pintér.

Fig. 11. Bunches of flowers on the barrel vault, photo: Attila Pintér.

Fig. 12. Acanthus decoration on the barrel
vault, photo: Attila Pintér.

Fig. 13. Christogram on the northern wall, photo: Attila Pintér.

Fig. 14. Jonah scene on the eastern
wall, photo: Attila Pintér.

Fig. 15. Jonah scene on a gold-sandwich glass probably from Rome, taken
from G. Spier (ed.), *Picturing the Bible*
(2007, n. 59), 186, Cat. Nr. 14.

Fig. 16. Jonah scene on a gold-sandwich glass of fig. 19, drawing, taken
from I. Henszlmann, 'Die altchristliche
Grabkammer in Fünfkirchen'
(1873, n. 4), 66; Fig. 5.

Fig. 17. Stone relief probably from Tarsus, taken from G. Spier (ed.),
Picturing the Bible (2007, n. 59), 186-7, Cat. Nr. 15.

Fig. 18. Glass bowl from Podgoritza with biblical scenes,
taken from G. Spier (ed.), *Picturing the Bible*
(2007, n. 59), Fig. 4.

Fig. 19. Stone sarcophagus from Singidunum with biblical scenes, taken from
G. Koch, *Frühchristliche Sarkophage* (2000, n. 48), Abb. 194.

Fig. 20. Gold ring with gem stone with the Jonah scene probably from
Syria, taken from G. Spier, *Picturing the Bible* (2007, n. 59), 188,
Cat. Nr. 18.

Fig. 21. Jonah scene on the niche nr. 9 of the Via Anapo
catacomb, Rome, taken from V. Fiocchi Nicolai, F. Bisconti
and D. Mazzoleni, *Las catacumbas cristianas de Roma*
(1999, n. 38), lámina II.

Fig. 22. Jonah scene on the
niche nr. 9 of the Via Anapo
catacomb, Rome, detail of
Fig. 21.

Fig. 23. Jonah scene on the eastern wall
of the St. Peter and Paul burial chamber,
detail, photo: Attila Pintér.

Fig. 24. Three magi on the western
wall, photo: Attila Pintér.

Fig. 25. Three magi on the western wall,
detail, photo: Attila Pintér.

Fig. 26. Stone relief with a magus carrying a plate from unknown provenance, taken from L. Wamser (ed.), *Die Welt von Byzanz* (2001, n. 86), 117, Kat. Nr. 150A.

Fig. 27. Three Babylonian youths refusing the sacrifice from the SS.
Marco e Marcelliano catacomb, arcosolium no. 5, taken from J. Fink and
B. Asamer, *Die römischen Katakomben* (1997, n. 87), Abb. 56.

Fig. 28. Three magi and Virgin Mary from the SS. Marco e Marcelliano
catacomb, arcosolium no. 5, taken from J. Fink and B. Asamer, *Die
römischen Katakomben* (1997, n. 87), Abb. 57.

Fig. 29. Virgin Mary on the western wall during
restoration process, photo: Attila Pintér.

Fig. 30. Candelabrum in the narthex of the
hypogaeum after the restoration in 1939, taken
from F. Fülep, *Sopianae* (1984, n. 5), Pl. X.

Theology on Images?
Some Observations on the Murals in the Peter and Paul
Burial Chamber of Pécs

István M. Bugár, Debrecen, Hungary

ABSTRACT

First, I have to explain the title. I shall briefly argue that there is hardly any trace of any conceptual achievement in this period that could be termed as theology *of* images. At the same time, however, I cannot agree with those who at least intimate that there was no real interaction between learned theology and the production of Christian imagery in the early period. Theological ideas – as I shall argue – are consciously and emphatically reflected on objects of visual art. Can we take the aforementioned wall-painting in Pécs as evidence of this phenomenon, and if so, in what sense? What are the theological considerations that obtain a visual representation in this work of Christian art?

As for a Christian theology of images, the first candidates come from the first decades of the fifth century: Paulinus of Nola[1] and probably Nilus of Ancyra[2] articulate the didactic function of visual imagery in Christian places of worship, thus by developing an ancient idea they are the first to formulate the theory that images are *biblia pauperum*. Before this time there is no conceptualized or argumentative reflection on Christian imagery. Not even in the hostile sense. I find it curious that modern scholarship took the iconophobic passages attributed to Epiphanius of Salamis seriously; a reason could have been the authority of K. Holl.[3] However, already G. Ostrogorsky pointed out that the fitting context

---

[1] Paulinus of Nola, *Carmina* 27, 511-98; 607-47; see H.L. Kessler, 'Pictures as Scripture in the Fifth Century Churches', *Studia Artium Orientalis et Occidentalis* 2 (1985), 17-31.

[2] Nilus of Ancyra, *Ep.* IV 61 (PG 79, 577-8). The letter survives in an iconoclastic and an 'iconophile' version. Although H.G. Thümmel argued for the authenticity of the former, the latter suites better the context of the early fifth century: Hans Georg Thümmel, 'Neilos von Ankyra und die Bilder', *BZ* 71 (1978), 10-21. The choice to disregard western evidence played a major role in shaping his reconstruction of the development of Christian attitude towards sacred images in late antiquity: Hans Georg Thümmel, *Die Frühgeschichte der ostkirchlichen Bilderlehre, Texte und Untersuchungen zur Zeit vor dem Bilderstreit*, TU 139 (Berlin, 1992).

[3] Karl Holl, 'Die Schriften des Epiphanius gegen die Bilderverehrung', *Sitzungsberichte der königlich Preussischen Akademie der Wissenschaften* 11 (Berlin, 1916), 828-68; reprinted in *id.*, *Gesammelte Aufsätze zur Kirchengeschichte* (Tübingen, 1928), II, 351-87. For the modern

Studia Patristica LXXIII, 281-295.
© Peeters Publishers, 2014.

of these writings can only be that of the iconoclastic controversy,[4] while, more recently, I have argued that one of these writing exhibits a conspicuously Origenist anthropology and Christology – ideas that Epiphanius so fervently fought against up to his death.[5] The other piece, the iconoclastic letter attributed to Epiphanius presents the author as an expert on Christian iconography and assumes a rigidly fixed physiognomic uniformity of the representation of Christ – a thing we definitely do not have in the Theodosian period. Seeing that Epiphanius himself confesses in a letter that he has seen only but one representation of Christ, makes this claims of the faked letter comical. In fact, the text quite plainly reveals the sources the forger used.[6] The issue of the twentieth century carrier of the forgeries has now been critically revisited in a monograph of 2007 by St. Bigham.[7] Eusebius' alleged letter to Constantia has a similar story. The authenticity has been most recently again challenged by T.D. Barnes.[8]

What we do have in the fourth century is friendly or hostile *sentiments* in connection with Christian imagery but nothing that would amount to articulated theological considerations and arguments. These sentiments, more often than not, gain expression in some common-places repeated – not always consistently – from ancient literature on the relative value of words, images and deeds.[9]

---

reception see *e.g.* Pièrre Maraval, 'Épiphane, «docteur des iconoclastes»', in E. Bœspflug and N. Lossky (eds), *Nicée II, 787-1987: Douze siècles d'images religieuses: Actes du colloque international Nicée II tenu au Collège de France, Paris* (Latour and Marbourg, 1987), 51-62; and just one more recent example: Robin M. Jensen, *Face to Face: Portraits of the Divine in Early Christianity* (Minneapolis, 2005), 134-5; 185-6; 196.

[4] Georg Ostrogorsky, 'Die pseudo-epiphanischen Schriften gegen die Bilderverehrung als Bindeglied zwischen den ikonoklastischen Synoden von 754 und 815', in *Studien zur Geschichte des byzantinischen Bilderstreites* (Breslau, 1929), 61-113.

[5] István M. Bugár, '"Origenist Christology" and Iconoclasm: The Case of Epiphanius of Salamis', in Ysabel de Andia and Peter Leander Hofrichter (eds), *Christus bei den Vätern: Forscher aus dem Osten und Westen Europas an den Quellen des gemeinsamen Glaubens*, Wiener Patristische Tagungen 1 (Innsbruck and Wien, 2003), 96-110 (I regret that the proofs were ignored when this volume was printed).

[6] István M. Bugár, 'What Did Epiphanius Write to Emperor Theodosius?', in Basile Lourié and Alexei Muraviev (eds), *Universum Hagiographicum: Mémorial Michel van Esbroeck*, Scrinium 2 (St. Petersburg, 2006), 34-53. Besides Epiphanius' famous letter to John of Jerusalem (on which see pp. 290-1 below), Socrates, *Hist. eccl.* V 16 seems to have been used by the forger.

[7] Stéphane Bigham, *Épiphane de Salamine, docteur de l'iconoclasme? Déconstruction d'un mythe* (Montréal and Paris, 2007).

[8] Timothy D. Barnes, 'Notes on the Letter of Eusebius to Constantia (*CPG* 3503)', *SP* 46 (2010), 313-8.

[9] Günther Lange, *Bild und Wort: Die katechetischen Funktionen des Bildes in der griechischen Theologie des sechsten bis neunten Jahrhunderts*, München, theol. Diss. 66-7, Schriften zur Religionspädagogik und Kerygmatik 6 (Würzburg, 1968), 14-43; Kristoffel Demoen, 'The Theologian on Icons': Byzantine and Modern Claims and Distortions', *BZ* 91 (1998), 1-19; István M. Bugár, 'St. John Chrysostom and His Contemporaries on the Relative Power of Words and Images', in *Giovanni Crisostomo: Oriente e occidente tra IV e V secolo. XXXIII incontro di studiosi dell'antichità cristiana*, Studia Ephemeridis Augustinianum 93 (Roma, 2005), 87-100.

The issue does not seem to have been a central one for the Christian élite of the fourth century.

What comes closest to a theology of images is the *negative* theology of images by Evagrius. This, however, does not concern primarily works of art but mental images. Discouragement of art and its reception is, nevertheless, an obvious consequence of this spiritual doctrine.[10] It gains a possible expression in a fragment again attributed to Epiphanius, which, at least, seems to come from this period.[11]

Further, Augustine, who is anyhow sensitive for aesthetical considerations, makes some remarks in his early career that come close to a theology of images in bud. First, in a work written around 400, he makes sarcastic remarks at the fictitious character of visual representations powerfully expressed by the pun *pingentes-fingentes*.[12] This characteristic of art is paralleled with apocryphal literature and opposed to the trustworthiness of canonical Scripture. A few years earlier he argued that the Father, the invisible divine being, can in no way be visually represented.[13]

There is a theology of image in the fourth century in the form of considerations about Christ as *eikōn* of the Father in writings of prominent theologians of the period. This could later be exploited by theologians of icons but in the given epoch it was related only to different works of art: the imperial images. It were the depictions of the Emperor that first received theological attention, which culminated in the first decades of the fifth century in the theological justification of the veneration of images by an anonymous Latin author.[14]

So much on theology of images in the fourth century – or, more precisely, on the lack thereof.[15] Now let us look at the other possible sphere of interference between theology and art – now on the latter's home field. The existence of this interaction has been taken for granted by ages of scholarship,[16] but there is a recent tendency to question – or rather ignore – the evidence. Let me take

---

[10] See *e.g.* J.-M. Spieser, 'The Representation of Christ in the Apses of Early Christian Churches', *Gesta* 37 (1998), 63-73, 66.

[11] István M. Bugár, 'Epiphanius of Salamis as a monastic author? The so-called *Testamentum Epiphanii* in the context of fourth-century spiritual trends', *SP* 42 (2006), 73-81.

[12] Augustine, *De consensu euangelistarum* I 10,15-6, ed. F. Weihrich, CSEL 43 (1904) 15,8-16.

[13] Augustine *De fide et symbolo* 7, ed. J. Zycha, CSEL 41 (1900), 16-7.

[14] István M. Bugár, 'Zacchaeus and the Veneration of Images: Image of an Emperor Image of a Saint', *SP* 34 (2001), 11-22.

[15] See also Robin Margaret Jensen, *Understanding Early Christian Art* (London, 2000), 106.

[16] For a comprehensive overview of the relation of the two fields of cultural expression see Sister Charles Murray, 'Artistic Idiom and Doctrinal Development', in Rowan Williams (ed.), *The Making of Orthodoxy: Essays in Honour of Henry Chadwick* (Cambridge, 1989), 288-307; esp. 288-95. She however lays the emphasis on the unifying function of Christian art, focusing on the post-Chalcedonian situation. In the following I shall rather look for traces of polemics within the sphere of art.

just a single example. One of the most common scenes in Christian art in the last decades of the fourth century is the so-called *traditio legis*. It has been a subject of a vivid debate, what theological ideas lay behind this scene. What no one has questioned was that there had been such. A scholar, however, who has most recently worked extensively on the subject has asserted that there is no need to look for such ideas behind the popularity of the scene. As a triangular and symmetrical composition, it simply looks good on the central panel of a sarcophagus and is a design easily variable to meet the demands of the customer.[17]

I wonder that any student of ancient Christian texts and images will be satisfied by this argument. Let me just quote a few obvious examples that go against such an approach. It would be more than extravagant to doubt elaborate theological and exegetical considerations behind the famous sarcophagus of Junius Bassus[18] or the Dogmatic Sarcophagi of Rome and Arles.[19] Prudentius' *Dittochaeon* is a fine example how exegesis – a synonym for theology in the period – and visual art go hand in hand – no matter, whether Prudentius only envisaged or had seen the pictorial cycle that is the subject of the *stephanos* of his epigrams.[20] The typology of the Christian sacrament of initiation and Eucharist conspicuously coincide in the earliest Christian texts and visual art.[21] Sometimes the *locus* of the representation (Dura Europus) or an inscription (sarcophagus of Junius Bassus) makes the connections plain. Paulinus of Nola shows fine examples how Christian images could be deciphered, indeed read.[22] With a less theologically and more historically oriented reading, Asterius of

---

[17] B. Snelders, 'The *Traditio legis* on Early Christian Sarcophagi', *Antiquité Tardive* 13 (2005), 321-33, 333. For a considerate interpretation of the seen see Geir Hellemo, *Adventus Domini: Eschatological Thought in 4th-century Apses and Catecheses*, Supplements to Vigiliae Christianae 5 (Leiden, 1989), 65-90 and Y.M.-J. Congar, 'Le thème du «don de la Loi» dans l'art paléochrétien', *Nouvelle revue théologique* 94 (1962), 915-33.

[18] Best see Elizabeth Struthers Malbon, *The Iconography of the Sarcophagus of Junius Bassus* (Princeton, N.J., 1990).

[19] See Jean-Maurice Rouquette, 'Trois nouveaux sarcophages chrétiens de Trinquetaille (Arles), *Comptes-rendus des séances de l'Académie des Inscriptions et Belles-Lettres* 118 (1974), 254-77; and Robin M. Jensen, 'The Economy of the Trinity at the Creation of Adam and Eve', *Journal of Early Christian Studies* 7 (1999), 527-46; *ead.*, *Understanding Early Christian Art* (2000), 178-80.

[20] See Renate Pillinger, *Die 'Tituli historiarum' oder 'Das sogenannte Dittochaeo' des Prudentius: Versuch eines philologisch-archäologischen Kommentars*, Denkschriften Österreichische Akademie der Wissenschaften, Philosophisch-historische Klasse 142 (Vienna, 1980). Generally, for exegesis and art in the period see R.M. Jensen, *Understanding Early Christian Art* (2000), 64-93, esp. 77-9.

[21] Wladimir Weidlé, *The Baptism of Art* (Westminster, [1950]); see Heidl György, *Érintés Szó és kép a korai keresztény misztikában* [Touch: Word and image in early Christian mystics] Catena monográfiák 14 (Budapest, 2011), 171-210.

[22] See the texts of Paulinus above n. 1, compare also *id.*, *Ep.* 10, ed. G. Hartel, CSEL 29 (1894), 285,17-286,21 and 17, CSEL 29,291,12-24; 292,8-20.

Amasea[23] and Prudentius (in the *Peristephanon*)[24] provide earlier samples of perusing images. This is a skill that these Christian authors attribute to the simple believer – as opposed to Porphyry, who reserves the ability of deciphering images to the learned.[25]

An intimate connection between art and theology can be traced in images that reflect theological controversies of the period.[26] The finest example is certainly the mosaic in a cubiculum attached to the catacomb of Domitilla with the inscription 'QVI FILIUS DICERIS ET PATER INVENIRIS'.[27] This seemingly amounts to a modalist (or Marcellianist) defence of Nicaea. In fact, as a little extravagantly put by Th. Mathews,[28] and already suggested by A. Grabar,[29] images were a most suitable media for religious polemics. This must have been

---

[23] Asterius of Amasea, *Hom. XI: in laudem S. Euphemiae*, ed. Datema, 153-5 (PG 40, 335D-337C).

[24] Prudentius, *Peristefanon* IX: *Passio Cassiani Forocorneliensis* and XI: *Ad Valerianum episcopum de Passione Hippolyti beatissimi martyris* ll. 123-44. See Anne-Marie Palmer, *Prudentius on the Martyrs*, Oxford Classical Monographs (Oxford, 1989), 113-7; 242-3; 248-50; 273-5 (who is, however, more ready to diminish the significance of the relevant images as sources of the respective poems).

[25] Porphyry, *Peri agalmatōn* frgg. 1-3.

[26] R.M. Jensen is first very cautious either to deny or to affirm the reflection of theological debates in art: *Understanding Early Christian Art* (2000), 101-3, but then affirms the growing emphasis on the divinity of Christ in art: *ibid.* 103-12; then again, she denies that there is any difference between the orthodox and 'Arian' art of Ravenna (in the sixth century) that can be traced back to theological divergence. Her use of the concept 'Arian' here is, however, vague and appears to suggest that Arians were psilanthropists, which is certainly not true even of Arians in the strict sense, not to mention homoean Gothic Christians.

[27] See Victor Schultze, 'Qui et filius diceris et pater inveniris', *ZKG* 45 N.F. 8 (1927), 513-6; Antonino Ferrua, 'Qui filius diceris et pater inveniris: mosaico novellamente scoperto nella catacomba di S. Domitilla', *Rendiconti. Pontificia Accademia Romana di Archeologia* 33 (1960/1961), 209-24; J. Knackstedt, 'Qui filius diceris et pater inveniris', *Theologisch-praktische Quartalschrift* 110 (1962), 226-31; Luciana Cuppo Csaki, 'Qui *filius diceris et pater inveniris: il* mosaico «dello scalone» nella catacomba di S. Domitilla a Roma', in Mongi Ennaifer and Alain Rebourg (eds), *La mosaïque gréco-romaine VII: Tunis, 3-7 octobre, 1994: VIIᵉ Colloque international pour l'étude de la mosaïque antique: actes* (Tunis, 1999), II 777-94 (and pl. CCCXIV-CCCXV). See Umberto Maria Fasola, *La catacomba di S. Domitilla*, Catacombe di Roma e d'Italia 1 (Vatican, 1989); J.-M. Spieser, 'The Representation of Christ' (1998), 69 with fig. 4. on p. 68, and Thomas F. Mathews, *The Clash of Gods: A Reinterpretation of Early Christian Art* (Princeton, N.J., 1993), 117-8 with fig. 92 on p. 122. See esp. Antonio Ferrua, S.J., *La polemica antiariana nei monumenti paleocristiani*, Studi di antichità cristiana 43 (Città del Vaticano, 1991), 15-36, 24-6. The anti-Arian – and modalist – character of the inscription is, however, denied by M.-Y. Perrin, 'La paternité du Christ. À propos d' une mosaïque de la catacombe de Domitille', *Rivista di Archeologia Cristiana* 77 (2001), 481-518, 500-18. His interpretation, argued superbly, remains an alternative to consider but is not fully convincing. See also pp. 289-90 below.

[28] Th.F. Mathews, *The Clash of Gods* (1993), 10.

[29] André Grabar, *Christian Iconography: A Study of its Origins*, Bollingen Series XXXV 10 (Princeton, N.J., 1968), 28-30; see also Jaś Elsner, *Imperial Rome and Christian Triumph: The Art of the Roman Empire 100-450*, Oxford History of Art (Oxford, 1998), 140-4.

the case not in connection with Christian-Pagan relations alone, but also in the context of inter-Christian debates.

With all this in mind, let us turn to the mural at Pécs. I shall argue that the suitable context of this design can be uncovered and is not that of the technical and commercial prospects of the craftsmanship of Roman decorators.

On the secco[30] we can see two figures on either side of a Christogram surrounded by a purple wreath. The two shapes dressed in white tunic and pallium – point to the Christogram with the gesture of acclamation. The entire scene is bordered with an imitation of a curtain. If we compare the scene with similar compositions from roughly the same period, we might get the impression that a third figure is missing: Christ has been replaced by a symbol.[31] What can be the reason for that? [32]

An answer would be that there was not enough space above the recess for a figure of appropriate size. Although this state of affairs is obviously true, I doubt that it is the *raison-d'être* of the composition. Lack of space is no sufficient explanation (see Fig. 1). Neither is the fact that a Christogram in purple medallion looks good in such a central design. The painter – or better, the patron[33] – chose an existing pattern, as shown by the close parallel in Naissus/Niš.[34] Now, what does that pattern express?

---

[30] See Krisztina Hudák and Levente Nagy, *A Fine and Private Place. Discovering the Early Christian Cemetery of Sopianae/Pécs*, Heritage Booklets 6 (Pécs, rev. ed. ²2009), 40.

[31] Compare *e.g.* the stylistically and chronologically close mural on the vault in cubiculum 3 of the catacomb of SS. Pietro e Marcellino, see Johannes Georg Deckers, Hans Reinhard Seeliger and Gabriele Mietke, *Die Katakombe 'Santi Marcellino e Pietro': Repertorium der Malereien* (Città del Vaticano, 1987), no. 3 ceiling, with coloured plates 2-3; the mosaic in the Catacomb of Domitilla mentioned above (n. 25); frg. of sarcophagus in Museo Pio Cristiano, Angela Donati (ed.), *Pietro e Paolo: La storia, il culto, la memoria nei primi secoli* (Milano, 2000), cat. no. 53; Guilded Glass, Rome Catacombe of S Callisto: A. Donati (ed.), *Pietro e Paolo*, cat. no. 90; compare also the numerous 'Traditio legis' representations, for which an (incomplete) catalogue can be found in B. Snelders, 'The *Traditio legis*' (2005), 325 and the parallels to the mural in Pécs on sarcophagi adduced by Friedrich Gerke, 'Die Wandmalereien der Petrus-Paulus-Katakombe in Pécs (Südungarn)', in *Neue Beträge zur Kunstgeschichte des I. Jahrtausends*, Forschungen zur Kunstgeschichte und christlichen Archäologie I/2 (Baden-Baden, 1954), 147-99, 169; 178; see K. Hudák and L. Nagy, *Fine and Private* (²2009), 44 with n. 114.

[32] Such a tendency is observed by G. Hellemo, without commenting on it, *id.*, *Adventus Domini* (1989), 101.

[33] On views of the execution-process of the murals see K. Hudák and L. Nagy, *Fine and Private* (²2009), 57.

[34] See K. Hudák and L. Nagy, *Fine and Private* (²2009), 44[114]; representation in Zsolt Magyar, 'The World of Late Antique Sopianae: Artistic Connections and Scholarly Problems', Miša Rakocija (ed.), *Niš and Byzantium: Seventh Symposium, Niš 3-5 June 2008. The Collection of the Scientific Works VII* (Niš, 2009), 108-18, fig 4. on p. 112; see also the guilded glass in A. Donati (ed.), *Pietro e Paolo* (2000), cat. no. 92; the lunette of the arcosolium in the catacomb of Domitilla, cubiculum 18 with Peter and Paul, see Josef Wilpert, *Die Malereien der Katakomben Roms* (Freiburg im Breisgau and Rome, 1903), Taf. 154,1 where indeed there is a lack of space for the figure of Christ.

Fig. 1. Guilded glass
(after A. Donati, *Pietro e Paolo* cat. no. 86).

There is an inner tension in the composition created by the naturalistic figures surrounding a symbolic design. Such a discrepancy was later discouraged by the Quinisexta council,[35] but was common until then.[36] Can this mingling have a special reason here, since the symbolical is not paralleling but replacing the figurative? Why does the artist avoid iconic representation in the case of Christ?

A possible first guess could suspect a sort of iconophobia. Is there contemporary evidence for such? The answer is definitely yes. First, we have a canon in the collection associated with Elvira [Iliberis in Baetica]:

We have decreed that there should be no paintings in churches, lest what is worshiped and adored be depicted on walls.[37]

The canon, however, does not appear to belong to the council of Elvira around 305-306.[38] In case it is from the Visigothic period, it might be taken as a sign

---

[35] Quinisexta Council, canon 82: Mansi XI 977sqq; ed. Joannou 218-20.

[36] See for example the mural in S. Pietro e Marcellino quoted above in n. 31.

[37] Synod of Elvira, canon 36: '*Placuit picturas in ecclesia esse non debere, ne quod colitur et adoratur in parietibus depingatur*', edited in Alfred William Winterslow Dale, *The Synod of Elvira: Christian Life in The Fourth Century* (London, 1882), 326.

[38] Maurice Meigne proposed a tripartite division of the canons: Canons 1-21 were proclaimed at the council of Elvira, Canons 63-75 belong to other pre-Nicaean councils, while the rest is a collection of different synodical canons that resemble the canons of Arles, Sardika, other fourth-century councils, and the Apostolic Canons: Maurice Meigne, 'Concile ou collection d'Elvire?', *Revue d'histoire ecclésiastique* 70 (1975), 361-87, quoted in Péter Erdő, *Az ókeresztény kor egyházfegyelme (az első négy évszázadban)* [Church orders in the ancient Christian period (in the first four centuries)] (Budapest, 1983), 377[133]; see also D. Ramos-Lisson and J. Orlandis, *Die Synoden auf der Iberischen Halbinsel bis zum Einbruch des Islam* (Paderborn, 1981), 3-30, who reject all critique concerning the early date and the integrity of the collection.

of iconophobia on the side of conservative non-Nicaeanism.[39] Such an attitude has been once supposed by E. Demougeot[40] in case of Aquitania. The present author has also once attempted to trace a similar tendency in Pannonia. The arguments advanced, however, not appeared to be convincing enough.[41]

In the following, I shall point to evidence that the immediate context of our representation *is* indeed the so-called Arian controversy, but in a different sense. If we accept the current dating of the composition,[42] we are in a period after the Council of Constantinople and the imperial sanction of non-Nicaean Christianity. No matter how far from the cultural centres of the late Roman world, Pannonia was especially sensitive for the controversy over Nicaea because of the prominence therein of Valens of Mursa, Ursacius of Singidunum, and Photinus of Sirmium and because some four councils of various size were held over the issue in Sirmium,[43] the local metropolis and seat of Constantius, in the 340s and 350s. The controversy appears to be reflected in the *passiones* of Pannonian martyrs, which echo different creedal formulas.[44] The late phase of the controversy with the radical neo-Arianism of Eunomius especially explicitly focused on the divinity of Christ. Gregory of Nyssa provides a much-quoted description – albeit rhetorical – how deeply all cultural levels of the

---

[39] The collection at least is not known before the second half of the 6th century. Tarraconensis is under Visigothic control from 414, but Alans and Silings do not establish themselves for long in Baetica, which is occupied by Visigoths only after 476. If, however, the canon would prove to belong to the Synod in 305/306, then the context is the *disciplina arcani* of the Christian community under strong pressure even in the Western half of the Empire.

[40] Emilienne Demougeot, 'Y-eut-il une forme arienne de l'art paléochrétien?: Sarcophages paléochrétiens d'Aquitaine', in *Atti del VI Congresso Internazionale di archeologia cristiana: Ravenna 23-30 Settembre 1962* (Rome, 1965), 491-519; see also Sister Charles Murray, 'Art and the Early Church', *JTS* 28 (1977), 303-45.

[41] István M. Bugár, 'The Martyrdom of the Quattuor Coronati: Art and the Early Church in Pannonia', in A. Angusheva, M. Dimitrova, R. Kostova and R.R. Malcher (eds), *In stolis repromissionis: Saints and Sainthood in Central and Eastern Europe* (Sofia, 2013; preprint in 2003), 289-306. For a thorough criticism, see Levente Nagy, 'Eretnekek temetkezései a 4. századi Valeria provinciában?', in Judit D. Tóth and György Heidl (eds), *Irodalom teològia, műrészet. Studia Patrum* 5 (forthcoming); see also *id.*, *Pannóniai városok, mártírok, ereklyék: Négy szenvedéstörténet helyszínei nyomában* [Pannonian cities, martyrs, relics: tracing the context of four passions], *Thesaurus Historiae Ecclesiasticae in Universitate Qinqueecclesiensi* 1 (Pécs, 2012), 147-50 and Zsolt Magyar, 'Jelen volt-e az arianizmus Sopianaeban?' [Was Arianism present in Sopianae?], in Imre Peres and Péter Jenei (eds), *Az ókori keresztyén világ. Konferenciakötet*, Patmosz Könyvtár 1 (Debrecen, 2012), 67-79.

[42] For the dating see Krisztina Hudák, 'The chronology of the paintings in the Saint Peter and Paul burial chamber of Sophiane', in Szilvia Bíró (ed.), *Ex officina...: Studia in honorem Dénes Gabler* (Győr, 2009), 225-38.

[43] See *e.g.* J.N.D. Kelly, *Early Christian Creeds* (London, 1972³), 281-95.

[44] For the *Passio Quirini*, see Tibor Nagy, *A Pannoniai kereszténység története a római védőrendszer összeomlásáig* [Christianity in Pannonia until the collapse of the Roman defence-system], Dissertaiones Pannonicae, Ser. 2. No. 12 (Budapest, 1939), esp. 68; for the *Passio Quattuor coronati*, see I.M. Bugár, 'The Martyrdom of the Quattuor Coronati' (2003), 298-301, recapitulated in L. Nagy *Pannóniai városok* (2012), 130-2.

society were involved, even to the extent of absurdity.[45] It is obvious that Christian art of the period could not have been exempted from reflecting on the issue.[46] Indeed, it has been recently argued that reflection on Christ's divinity has been the leading issue in the development of the monumental art of the fourth and fifth centuries.[47]

Before the Christology-centred debates of the fifth century, in the late fourth century the emphasis is definitely laid on the divine nature of Christ on the side of the pro-Nicaean party. This could receive various expressions in depictive art. On some images – like on the sarcophagus of Junius Bassus and a number of contemporary Roman sarcophagi – Christ is seated above the allegorical representation of Caelus. On some sarcophagi we find two obviously distinct types of Christ simultaneously. A young, beardless or short-haired Christ in his earthly life is contrasted with a bearded and/or long-haired Christ in his eternal kingdom, or manifested after resurrection.[48] This is explained by the involvement of classical iconographic vocabulary to express divinity, as in the case of Zeus or Apollo.[49] The mosaic in the catacomb of Domitilla mentioned above exemplifies another possibility. There, Christ among Peter and Paul is surrounded by

---

[45] *Oratio de deitate Filii et Spiritus Sancti* (PG 46, 557). Although in interpreting ancient works of art we tend to refer to the ancient viewer, in fact we cannot escape being the viewer ourselves, as the ancient viewer is nothing more than a construction of our mind, a representation of our perception of the ancient viewer that necessarily reflects our own ideas. In an age when modern scholars were still interested in theology, the ancient viewer was theologically minded. When most people irrespective of their religious convictions think that theology is futile, or, just a language-game merely reflecting in fact endeavours, conditions – whether political, economical or sexual – alien to the rules of theological discourse; in such an environment the ancient viewer thinks no more of theology, or of the *regula fidei*. There are, however, still some criteria that help to decide which view of the ancient viewer is more authentic. And from the reference of Gregory of Nyssa it appears that the traditional one has a considerable advantage to the postmodern one.

[46] Besides A. Ferrua, 'Qui filius diceris' (1960/1961), see Arne Effenberger, 'Bemerkungen zum antiarianischen Programm des Mosaiks von San Michele in Affricisco', *Staatliche Museen zu Berlin: Forschungen und Berichte* 16 (1974), 245-54.

[47] See J.M. Spieser, 'The Representation of Christ' (1998), 65-9; see also R.M. Jensen, *Understanding Early Christian Art* (2000), 103-12.

[48] See I.M. Bugár, 'What did Epiphanius Write' (2006), 83-4 with notes 55 and 58, compare also the sarcophagus of Sylicho in S. Ambroggio, Milan, where the young Apollo-like Christ is seated teaching among the apostles in the back, and the bearded 'Zeus-like' Christ is standing in the same assembly – but Peter carrying his cross – in the front, while two small figures prostrate at his legs. R.M. Jensen, *Understanding Early Christian Art* (2000), 113-8 has formulated a similar interpretation in case of the two apse-mosaics in S. Constanza, Rome, but judged it a 'tantalizing thesis' without approving of it, since she observes that this way of distinction was not a general rule. I, however, see no reason why one should believe that all artists/patrons used the same vocabulary in the fourth century. Indeed, as I am arguing, there were different iconographical phrases to express the same idea.

[49] See Th. Mathews, *The Clash of Gods* (1993), 126-8; R.M. Jensen, *Understanding Early Christian Art* (2000), 119. The similarity in the case of Zeus was conspicuous for the contemporaries: see *e.g.* Theodore the Reader, *Ad annum* 462: frg. 11: 107,11-108,3 ed. Hansen (= John Damascene., *Apology* III 130) and *Epitome* 382: 107,21-24 ed. Hansen (vö. Theophanes,

a mandorla and raised above the earthly level.[50] It has been suggested that this representation, possibly from the episcopate of Damasus, belonged to a Sabellian group.[51] I wonder whether there is evidence of such a distinct community. Although the third century Roman author of the *Refutatio omnium haeresium* does mention that Callistus excommunicated Sabellius, this claim does not amount to stating that Sabellius, in his turn, established a separate school. Though one must be careful with arguments *e silentio*, I assume that the ardent heresiologist would have mentioned if Sabellius had done so. Epiphanius' statement that there are many following the doctrine of Sabellius at Rome[52] does not at all suppose such distinct communities.[53] I wonder whether it is just a general remark concerning the monarchian tendency of Roman theology criticised already by the Roman heresiologist. This explains the welcome of Marcellus of Ancyra – like that of Eustathius and Paulinus of Antioch – at Rome, whose understanding of Nicaea could at least be given a modalist reading.[54] For a patron with definite monarchian inclinations, the mosaic simply expressed the triumph of Nicaea. The terminological nuances just being advanced by the Cappadocians were not – in fact, since the confusion of terms in translations could not be – widely received in the West that was turning to be predominantly Latin-speaking.

In the very same period we have the first evidence of reflection on the possibility of representing divinity in Christian context. When in 393 Augustine speaks about the impossibility of representing the Father, he does so in connection with the creedal formula of Christ 'sitting at the right hand of the Father'.[55] In the same year Epiphanius of Salamis tears down a curtain in a church with

---

Chronogr I 112,29-32 ed. de Boor; Leon Grammaticus [Symeon Logothetes] 114,21-24 ed. Bekker; Nicephorus XV 23 [68A]).

[50] For other artistic idioms to the same effect see R.M. Jensen, *Understanding Early Christian Art* (2000), 110.

[51] V. Schultze, 'Qui et filius diceris' (1927), 514-5.

[52] Epiphanius, *haer* 62,8-9: πολλοὶ δὲ ἐν τῇ μέσῃ τῶν ποταμῶν καὶ ἐπὶ τὰ μέρη τῆς Ῥώμης τοῦ αὐτοῦ δόγματος ὑπάρχουσιν.

[53] Here I fully agree with. M.-V. Perrin, 'La paternité' (2001), 501[54]. The location of the mosaic in the new access to the catacomb built in the last third of the fourth century excludes its attribution to a schismatic group: *ibid.* 502.

[54] This was done at least by his disciple, Photinus, and his opponent, Eusebius. Epiphanius (*Haer.* 72), while quoting Marcellus' letter to pope Julius, is unable to decide on the orthodoxy of the author, although he remarks that the fact that he had to apologize is suspicious enough; see Basil of Caesarea, *Ep.* 59, 125, 239, 265 concerning Marcellus and 226, 244, 263 concerning Eustathius. On the theology of Marcellus see Klaus Seibt, *Die Theologie des Markell von Ankyra*, Arbeiten zur Kirchengeschichte 59 (Berlin, 1994) with the *Forschungsgeschichte* on pp. 15-202, esp. 199 and the introduction in Markell von Ankyra, ed., intr. Markus Vinzent, Supplements to Vigiliae Christianae 39 (Leiden, 1997), xiii; xxvi-lxxvi, who is more balanced and reluctant to make Marcellus a champion of a one-*prosōpon* Trinitology.

[55] Augustine *De fide et symbolo* 7, ed. J. Zycha, CSEL 41 (1900), 16-7.

the supposed representation of Christ.[56] Since he mentions it in his famous letter against Origenism, it was translated by Jerome very soon, who in turn interpolated some – rather obscure – comments to Epiphanius' act: 'It is contrary to the authority of the Scripture to have a human being represented in the Church of Christ.'[57] Although it is hopeless to recover the exact motives of Epiphanius, it appears that again the representation of Christ in human form is questioned. What was most important for the contemporary – as shown by the Pannonian *Passio Quirini* – is that He is 'verus Deus'.[58] And God cannot be circumscribed.

This understanding of the issue can be supported with a later parallel. A hundred years, or so, after the period concerned, Philoxenus, the bishop of Mabbug, appears to have banned representations of Christ, the angels, and the Holy Spirit.[59] Although the evidence must be taken with a pinch of salt, and further, Philoxenus was a moderate miaphysite, it is again the emphasis on the divinity of Christ that provides the context that makes such scruples meaningful: angels and divine Christ are invisible and consequently cannot be depicted.[60] In a different way though, but the emphasis on the divinity of Christ does acquire visual expression in early miaphysite art, where there is a preference to represent Christ on the cross with open eyes as opposed to Chalcedonian depictions with closed lids.

The reason why Christians before the first decades of the fifth century definitely shunned depiction of the Corpus on the cross,[61] must have been similar. For an observer less familiar with paradoxes than Melito of Sardis and other authors of a poetical language,[62] such a depiction suggested a denial of Christ's divinity. Christ's passion played a major role in Arian reasoning.[63] A replacement of the corpus with a triumphant symbol, or with other typological and historical

---

[56] Epiphanius, *Ep. ad Johannem Hierosolymitam*, frg. in H.G. Thümmel, *Frühgeschichte* (1992), §34.

[57] Jerome, *Ep.* 51, CSEL 54, 410-12.

[58] *Passio Quirini* 2,1, ASS VI1 381-3, 382.

[59] John Diakrinomenos, *Hist. Eccl.*, frg. in Mansi, XIII 180E-181B (= Thümmel, *Frühgeschichte* [1992], §56); and frg. 550b, ed. Hansen 156,1-9, where similar arguments against the representation of the Holy Spirit in the form of a dove are added.

[60] Philoxenus of Mabbug, *De trinitate*, ed. A. Vaschalde, CSCO Syr. 9, 12; see Sebastian Brock, 'Iconoclasm and the Monophysites', in Anthony Bryer and Judith Herren (eds), *Iconoclasm: Papers Given at the Ninth Spring Symposium of Byzantine Studies, University of Birmingham, March 1975* (Birmingham, 1977), 53-7; 53-4. S. Brock is sceptical about the testimony of Diakrinomenos, and interprets Philoxenus' ban on doves in the background of the cult of Atargatis in the form of a dove at Mabbug/Hierapolis.

[61] On this see R.M. Jensen, *Understanding Early Christian Art* (2000), 130-55; Paul Corby Finney, *The Invisible God: The Earliest Christians on Art* (Oxford, 1994), 141[51].

[62] See Melito, *Peri pascha* 96; Hippolytus, *Contra Haeresin Noeti* 18; see the Byzantine idiomelon for Holy Friday: Antiphon 15 of the Matins of Holy Friday, in Mother Mary and Archimandrite Kallistos Ware (trs.), *The Lenten Triodion* (London, 1977), 587.

[63] See Gregory of Nyssa, *Oratio Catechetica magna* 9; 13; 16.

Fig. 2. Sarcophag Rome, Museo Pio   Fig. 3. Sarcophag Rome, Museo Pio
Cristiano (Pietro&Paolo cat. No. 48),   Cristiano (Pietro&Paolo cat. No. 96);
photo of the author.   photo of the author.

scenes referring to the passion helped to avoid the offence. The choice of a non-similar symbol – with the terminology of Pseudo-Dionysius – appeared to be suitable for emphasising the divinity of the Son.[64] We can observe similar replacements on Passion sarcophagi.

On the sarcophagus of Fig. 2 the sign of Christ's death is transformed into that of the resurrection by the depiction of the sleeping guards and the victorious sign, the labarum in a wreath – as we find it in Pécs. The effect is enhanced by the birds and the streams of life flowing from the wreath – the latter motif is apparently present on the mural at Pécs as well. This reminds us that the context of the scene is the resurrection – as duly recognized by K. Hudák.[65] What is more appropriate for funerary art, and – we can now add – what is more appropriate for proclaiming the divinity of Christ?[66]

The resurrection, at the same time has an eschatological meaning. The streams of life and the white tunic of the acclaiming figures – reminding us of the parable of the heavenly banquet of *Matth.* 22:11-2[67]– help the viewer to decipher the message. The wreath around the labarum is also an abbreviation of the eternal reward – as seen on the different gilded glass examples shown above, and, to come closer to the design of the burial chamber in Pécs, on sarcophagi with the *aurum coronarium* scene (Figg. 4 and 5).[68] If I am right in

---

[64] For the problem of representing the Invisible God *before* the fourth century, see P.C. Finney, *The Invisible God* (1994), 275-97, esp. 289.

[65] K. Hudák and L. Nagy, *Fine and Private* (²2009), 43.

[66] See Gregory of Nyssa, *Oratio Catechetica magna* 9; 13; 16.

[67] See *Matth.* 28,3; *Rev.* 3,4-5; 18; 4,4; 6,11; 7,9; 13.

[68] Wilhelm Friedrich Deichmann, *Repertorium der christlich-antiken Sarkophage*, ed. by and revised by Giuseppe Bovini and Hugo Brandenburg (Wiesbaden, 1967) [= *Repertorium* I], 208; Jutta Dresken-Weiland, *Repertorium der christlich-antiken Sarkophage II: Italien mit einem Nachtrag Rom und Ostia, Dalmatien, Museen der Welt* (Mainz, 1998) [= *Repertorium* II], 136; 143. See also the sarcophagus in Rome, S. Sebastiano, *Repertorium* I no. 175, and Josef Wilpert, *I sarcofagi cristiani antichi*, Monumenti dellá antichità cristiana 1 (Rome, 1929-1936), II 4. For the scene see K. Wessel, 'Kranzgold und Lebenskronen', *Archaeologischer Anzeiger* (1950/1951), 103-14.

Fig. 4. Sarcophagus frgg. in Krakow, Rome, Berlin, after *Repertorium* II 136 and I 208.

Fig. 5. Sarcophagus in Palermo, after *Repertorium* II 143.

suggesting that this latter design echoes the famous *fastigium*[69] in the Lateran basilica, than here, again, we can trace a replacement of the human figure of Christ with a symbol.[70]

In the eschatological context I wonder whether contemporary learned viewers might have seen in the wreath an allusion to the spherical shape of the resurrected body, an idea popular in Origenist circles.[71] This impression is enhanced if wee look at the ceiling – obviously representing heaven – where the portraits of the dead – whether martyrs or members of the patron's kinship

---

[69] See *Liber Pontificalis* 34: *S. Sylvester* 9-10, ed. Mommsen 52,8-53,5; on the remains and later fate of the object see Sible de Blaauw, *Cultus et decor: liturgia e architettura nella Roma tardoantica e medievale: Basilica Salvatoris, Sanctae Mariae, Sancti Petri*, Studi e testi 355-6 (Vatican City, 1994), 117-27, and *id.*, 'Das Fastigium der Lateranbasilika: Schöpferische Innovation, Unikat oder Paradigma', in Beat Brenk (ed.), *Innovation in der Spätantike: Kolloquium Basel 6. und 7. Mai 1994*, Spätantike, frühes Christentum, Byzanz: Reihe B, Studien und Perspektiven 1 (Wiesbaden, 1996), 53-65.

[70] On the symbolical representation of Christ in the period see G. Hellemo, *Adventus Domini* (1989), 89; see K. Hudák and L. Nagy, *Fine and Private* (²2009), 41.

[71] Origen, *De oratione* 31,3 could be carelessly interpreted in this way: Jerome, *Contra Johannem Hierosolymitanum* 29; see the question in Methodius, *Res.* III 15 (Photius, *cod.* 234): 'Whether the resurrected body is spherical, rectangular or cubical?'

– are in tondos with a sky-blue background. Gy. Heidl at least intimated, that Jerome's commentary on Jonah meant especially for the community in Aquileia was in some form known to the designer of the Jonas-scene in the burial chamber.[72] Such an up-to-date involvement in the current debates of the far-away élite does not need to be assumed from the side of the patrons or artists at Sopianae, since we have here a repetition of existing patterns. Nonetheless, the 'Origenist' interpretation does appear to me a little far-fetched.

Be that as it may, the resurrection was appropriate to reveal Christ's divinity, since the status of human nature of Christ after the resurrection has not been fully clarified in the fourth century. Origen's influence, who warned that the human form is only a shade that must be superseded,[73] was still strong in this respect.[74]

Already Zoltán Kádár assumed that the *raison-d'être* of the chamber is celebrating the triumph of orthodoxy over Arianism.[75] This is close to our conclusion. We may add that if the identification of the two acclaiming figure as Peter and Paul is right – which seems plausible to me – we may see here a Roman connection, as indeed K. Hudák does.[76] The figure of Peter and Paul as a symbol for the Roman Church has been taken up by Damasus.[77] Augustine also in his treatise mentioned above connects this representation to Rome:

Peter and Paul occurred to them, I believe, just because in many places they chanced to see these two apostles represented in pictures as both in company with Him [*i.e.* Christ]. For Rome, in a specially honourable and solemn manner, commends the merits of Peter and of Paul, for this reason among others, namely, that they suffered [martyrdom] on the same day.[78]

---

[72] See n. 40. above.

[73] Origen, *Contra Cels.* II 9; 41; IV 15; *Com. Ioh.* I 32. A key text is *ibid.* II 6.

[74] See Gregory of Nyssa, *In Christi resurrectionem* Or. 1; GNO I 9,304,15-20 ed. Jaeger.

[75] Z. Kádár, 'Lineamenti dell'arte romana della Pannonia nell'epoca dell'antichitá tarda e paleocristiana', in *Corsi di cultura sull'arte ravennate e bizantina, ed. Università degli Studi di Bologna, Istituto di Antichità Ravennatie Bizantine, Ravenna Vol. 16, Ravenna, 16-29 Marzo 1969, 179-202* (Ravenna, 1969), 187-8; *id.*, 'Pannónia keresztény emlékeinek kapcsolatai az ókor és a középkor triumphális mûvészetéhez' [Christian antiquities in Pannonia and the triumphal art of Antiquity and the Middle Ages], in *Emlékkönyv Gerevich Tibor születésének hatvanadik fordulójára* (Budapest, 1942), 7, see *id.*, 'A triumphus eszme a pécsi ókeresztény héroon egyik freskóján' [The concept of triumph on a fresco of the ancient Christian *heroon* in Pécs], *Regnum* 4 (1940-1), 65-9.

[76] K. Hudák and L. Nagy, *Fine and Private* ([2]2009), 59-61. She gives further support to this idea by the presence of the Nicean orthodox metropolitan of Sirmium at a synod in Rome in 382. The concept of 'primacy' that she is using is, however, somewhat vague and anachronistic.

[77] See Damasus, *Epigrammata* 20: *In SS Apostolorum Catacumbas* ll. 3; 6, but see also Augustine, *De consensu euangelistarum* I 10.15-6, ed. F. Weihrich, CSEL 43 (1904), 15 quoted just below.

[78] Augustine, *De consensu euangelistarum* I 10.15-6, ed. F. Weihrich, CSEL 43 (1904), 15; translation is by S.D.F. Salmond, NPNF Augustine VI.

And the Roman see – except for Liberius' concessions[79] to Constantius – was emblematic for remaining true to the Nicaean formula.

In the 380s, Gregory of Nyssa in his manual for catechists emphasizes that there are two episodes in the history of Incarnation that especially reveal Christ's divinity: the beginning and the end; conception/birth and resurrection.[80] Thus, beside our scene, that of the adoration of the Magi appears to serve the same purpose[81] – although in a less manifest manner. Already Irenaeus uses the episode to show that Christ is God.[82]

[79] Unwillingly though, but he signed the creed of Sirmium in 351; see Hilarius of Poitiers, *Fragmenta historica* frgg. 4-6 (PL 10, 679-95); CSEL 65 (ed. Feder, 1916), 89-93; 155-7; 164-73, with Liberius' letters (esp. 169,7 with commentary on 170,3) of doubtful authenticity; see CPL 1630 and B. Studer, s.v. 'Liberius', in *Encyclopedia of the Early Church* (1992).

[80] Gregory of Nyssa, *Oratio Catechetica Magna* 12; the other marks of Christ's divinity are the miracles, so prominent in Christian art of the earlier part of the fourth century, on this see R.M. Jensen, *Understanding Early Christian Art* (2000), 95; 120-4.

[81] On the identification see K. Hudák and L. Nagy, *Fine and Private* (²2009), 60; see György Heidl, 'Remarks on the iconography in the "Peter-Paul" (No. 1) Burial Chamber of Sopianae' and Péter Csigi, 'Deliberate Ambiguities in Early Christian Wall Paintings in Sopianae' in this volume.

[82] Irenaeus, *Adv. haer.* III 9,2.

Conquest or Shared Backcloth –
On the Power of Tradition

Markus Vɪɴᴢᴇɴᴛ, King's College London

Aʙsᴛʀᴀᴄᴛ

In our assessment of early Christian art it is quite natural that our own eyes, long trained by our upbringing in a world that for centuries has been Christianised at the expense or even in the fight against its Greco-Roman past, would view art objects retrospectively in the light of the outcome of history. This article begins with the example of Thomas F. Mathews and shows with examples from Pecs and its surrounding how similar our own referencing of art objects seems to have been to the way, early Christians were approaching their own world of symbols and images. Instead of looking for what was new, they would have been informed by what they knew, most of the time subconsciously, as old. Experience, especially religious experience seems to be more traditional than apologetic preachers would like to have it.

Thomas F. Mathews begins *The Clash of Gods: A Reinterpretation of Early Christian Art* (2003) by pointing to the powerful contrast between on the one side 'the last Roman Emperor to put the image of Jupiter on his coins', a mistaken Valerius Licinius (r. 308-324), and on the other side 'a painter of the grave-diggers' union, working by lamplight in the underground cemetery of Domitilla in Rome', who 'was tracing a rival god on the plaster'.[1] This contrast of an ending era in the lamplight of imperial power propaganda and the dawning beginnings of a subversive movement summarizes the apologetic narrative of a religious clash between Rome and Jerusalem, Emperor and Pope, Paganism and Christianity.

Both figures Mathews gives the same attribute 'Enthroned', although he sees the grave-digging artist rendering 'a fragile and nervous Christ'. The victorious epithet, however, he sees derived from the further course of history, in which

of these two images, unlikely as it may seem, the crude cemetery painting was proven by events to be the more powerful. Licinius' Jupiter was unable to confer victory on him in his final contest with Constantine, whose forces carried standards surmounted with the monogram of Christ.[2]

---

[1] Th.F. Mathews, *The Clash of Gods: A Reinterpretation of Early Christian Art* (Princeton, 2003), 3-4.
[2] *Ibid.* 4.

Fig. 1. Jupiter 'Enthroned', *Solidus* of Licinius,
Antioch, 321.

Fig. 2. Christ 'Enthroned' among His Apostles,
Catacomb of Domitilla, Rome, c. 325.

Mathews reads these events 'as a contest of the gods', or, as the title of his book states, a 'clash' of them with a 'fourth century ... unparalleled war of images', determined in outcome by 'the strength and energy of the winning images'.[3]

Here, early Christian art is promoted not only to reflect Christian triumphalism, but is even given credit for the final victory in its battle with paganism.

I am skeptical of such hyperbolic reading of the past. One only needs to begin with re-visiting these two initial images.

Mathews describes the image with Christ as follows:

> ... beardless and adolescent, seated on a high-backed chair, with his apostles grouped around him on either side. An open book on his knee, Christ waves his right hand to emphasize a point in his lesson. He glances around at his companions with flashing eyes. They, like Christ, are dressed in the traditional purple-striped tunic of the roman citizen of senatorial rank, but they appear even younger than Christ, hardly more than schoolboys with short haircuts, and they look at him stiffly as if hoping they won't be called upon to recite. Who commissioned this modest work and whose tomb it protected we do not know, but even in its anonymity it attests the community's faith in the power of this new divinity and his teaching to bring salvation, even in death.[4]

Christ is, indeed, shown in senatorial tunic which not only indicates that he is the most important person in the scene, biggest in stature, his clothes also reveal that the image removes any foreign taint from the group. People of senatorial rank were citizens of Rome, not *peregrini*. Contrary to Mathews' description, Christ does not wave 'his right hand', but has both his hands open in the way of an *Orans*.[5] Christ is not emphasizing a particular point of his teaching, he is rather directing his disciples, sat on the right and on the left of him, and all the viewers in front of him – the community of those visiting the deceased's grave. Although Christ is of importance, he is not centre-stage of the image in contrast to the opened page of the book. That the centrality of the book is not an accident, can be seen from other depictions of similar scenes. The iconography of the man with the open book in funerary iconography often refers to the *traditio* or reading out of the deceased's testament to the living. This iconography we find, for example, with the philosopher in the midst of his students.

Comparing the details of these two third century images we encounter the Roman philosopher in the midst of female and male students who holds an open roll. As in our mural from the *Domitilla catacomb*, the deceased is not placed in the middle of the picture, whereas the book roll keeps centre stage.[6]

---

[3] *Ibid.*

[4] *Ibid.*

[5] As can be found in other places in the *Domitilla catacomb*, see, for example, O. Marucchi, *Roma Sotterianea Cristiana* I/2 (Roma, 1914), 216 (Figg. 101, 102), 223 (Fig. 109).

[6] See Henri-Irénée Marrou, *Mousikos Anēr. Étude sur les scènes de la vie intellectuelle figurant sur les monuments funéraires romains* (Grenoble, 1938).

Fig. 3. Details of a Philosopher and his pupils, 3rd c.,
Sarcophagus, Latern-Museum, Rome.

Fig. 4. *Brescia Lipsanotheca*; 4th c.,
Museo Civico dell'Eta Cristiana, Brescia.

Fig. 5. Detail of *Brescia Lipsanotheca*;
Christ in the midst of his disciples, an ivory.

In our Christian scene, not only Christ has the open book in front of him, but each Apostle has his own booklet.

Let us compare, how this iconography of the deceased teacher, handing over his testament develops further in contrast with Mathews' reading of it. Let us first look at the famous *Lipsanotheca* or reliquary from Brescia, dated to the 4th c.[7]

In this later depiction, 'placed directly below the lock and key',[8] the motive of the philosopher-Christ, teaching in the synagogue, has been elaborated on. Now the role of the testament has become even more important than before: the disciples are no longer able to read the text themselves, but need the hierarchically elevated master for reading and explaining it to them. The teacher is no longer sitting, but different fom his audience, he stands in the midst of them. He has become as important as the roll had been and both, roll and man, form a cross in the middle of the scene. Christ's head together with those of his disciples and the scroll form a triangle with the scroll as its basis. As already in the *Domitilla* image, there are no women present amongst the disciples.

---

[7] See Carolyn Joslin Watson, 'The Program of the Brescia Casket', *Gesta* 20 (1981), 283-98; see now Catherine Brown Tkacz, *The Key to the Brescia Casket: Typology and the Early Christian Imagination*, Collection des études augustiniennes (Paris, 2002).

[8] C. Brown Tkacz, *The Key to the Brescia Casket* (2002), 96.

The veil which formed the background in the philosopher iconography has been moved into the front and overshadows the disciples while only the master keeps a free sight. He is the revelator who unveils what until him, according to Paul, has been veiled in the Law:

3:14 But their minds were closed. For to this very day, the same veil remains when they hear the old testament read. It has not been removed because only in Christ is it taken away. 3:15 But until this very day whenever Moses is read, a veil lies over their minds, 3:16 but when one turns to the Lord, the veil is removed (see *Ex.* 34:34). (*2Cor.* 3:14-6)[9]

Yet, in the case of *Domitilla*, we are not yet in the Ambrosian hierarchical 4th century with its divide, although, in both cases, the deceased is identified with Christ. Christ is handing down his own testament as the main topic of the image.

As can be seen from both our Christian images, Christ's 'New Testament' as handed down to his disciples is core to this iconography. What may surprise us is his depiction as a deceased philosopher without any sign or indication of his Resurrection. As Mathews rightly notices in the *Domitilla* mural, Christ looks stiff, and his disciples are anxious, at best hoping and they are depicted all facing Jesus' suffering and his death on the cross.

One more element of this imagery has already been indicated by Mathews: the people's Roman, senatorial dresses. The scenery is not an assembly of a Jewish Rabbi and his students, but we are moved into the classrooms of civil Roman aristocracy where we get an insight into the interaction between a master and his disciples, all being of high rank. The iconography reflects the grown standing which sees the New Testament firmly set on Roman, no longer on Jewish grounds, within the high, not, as Mathews wants it, in one of the lower social classes. The books mark them as learned people, not as *illiterati*.

With this image, we are close to Justin's contrast between Christian philosophers and writers on the one side and craftsman and idiots on the other side.[10] The importance of both, learning and rank, can be seen from other examples of Christian catacomb paintings, as for example, the man with the book from the *Peter and Marcellinus catacomb*:

---

[9] See also Augustine, *In solemnitate martyrum Machabaeorum* (PL 38, 1377-8): '*Testamentum enim vetus velatio est novi Testamenti, et Testamentum novum revelatio est veteris Testamenti ... Hoc utique clausum erat quia nondum clavis crucis accesserat*' ('For the Old Testament is the veiling of the New Testament, and the New Testament is the unveiling of the Old Testament ... The [Old Testament] had been closed because the key of the cross had not yet come'); Paulinus of Nora, *Letter 38 to Aprus* (CSEL XXIX, 326-7): '*Christus ... qui in lege velatur, in Evangelio revelatur*' ('Christ, who was vveiled in the Law, is unveiled in the Gospel'), see on these texts C. Brown Tkacz, *The Key to the Brescia Casket* (2002), 97-9.

[10] Justin, *2Apol.* 10,8; see also Markus Vinzent, 'Die Frühchristlichen Lehrer und ihr Unterricht', *Altertum* 41 (1996), 177-87, 187[15].

Fig. 6. *The Man with the Book*, Marcellinus?,
4/5th c., Rome.

With these images we are placed into an environment where no longer oral tradition, hearsay and the living experience with Christ count, but where the dead Jesus has left his written message to his disciples to contemplate death and hope.

Let me add one further element to what Mathews has only hinted at with his description of both, Jupiter and Christ as being 'enthroned'. Christ, indeed, sits on a very similarly high-backed chair as does Jupiter. How else could a viewer who for centuries inhabited this world of Jupiter and was used to see masters and Gods sitting on such thrones decipher the code of this image other than giving Jesus the rank of Jupiter? In this sense, Mathews gives the appropriate answer: He will see Jesus as the enthroned divinity, in power and command, as Greco-Roman king and emperor, and his testament as an edict proclaimed as the new law. Edicts in Rome did only last for the turn in office of the magistrate who had created and published them. Older edicts had to be endorsed by the newly incoming magistrate to carry further weight. Or put the other way: From the very moment that artists placed Christ on divine thrones of Roman Gods and chairs of philosophical masters, the depicted himself entered the language game which existed already as a matrix, transferring meaning from frame to content, enhanced by the shared emotion associated with such power displaying imageries, while at the same time, the expectation of the viewer challenged the received message and re-read it in the light of the New Testament narratives and the exegetical readings of them. Messages themselves, as little as their underlying language with a steering grammar underneath, as Allen Brent with reference to the later Wittgenstein has shown in his article, are neither exhaustive nor unambiguous. Instead of giving exhaustive definitions artists, poets and philosophers develop and re-write invitations to re-read the known in the light of their creative innovations, or a new text or image becomes an element, the meaning of which is heavily impacted by the backcloth of its background.

Even today, standing in front of the *Domitilla* mural, we face the clear image of the renewed Divine, the powerful and wise teacher, the teaching divinity who in answering the questions of life and death opens his book in front of the mourners. What the writing of the New Testament achieved, a modeling of Christ in the given frame of Moses and the Torah, Christian iconography does with regards to the pagan and Jewish frames that the artists deploy. Despite all attempts to define Christ and Christians as the new people in a new covenant, and distance them from both the Jews and the Pagans, the chosen typology of a testament sets the Christian message within social and semiotic pointers which were meant to be left behind. In a similar way did Christian iconography receive not only, as Erwin Goodenough once thought, the value of the older symbol, in adopting its affective power, but its content and meaning was shaped by what existed before.[11] Not unquestioned, of course, not determined – as little as any grammar or rule can dictate the poet's wording. Therefore, we are not talking about a Judaization or Hellenization of Christianity, less we discover a battle or conquest, defeat or triumph. The old war-rule remains valid that battles between enemies would need to be fought on shared grounds. Instead, the more the common mythological, poetic and linguistic memory provided the creative tools that allowed for novelty of old and, conversely, the power of tradition, the more this tradition was apologetically rejected, sometimes even destroyed.

An example from Pécs is provided by the tradition of Jonah,[12] 'one of the most popular biblical cycles in Early Christian art up to the end of the fourth century',[13]

---

[11] See Erwin R. Goodenough, 'The Crown of Victory in Judaism', *The Art Bulletin* 28 (1946), 139-59, 139.

[12] Reinhart Staats, art. 'Auferstehung II/2', *TRE* 4 (1979), 513-29, 522; Guntram Koch, *Frühchristliche Sarkophage* (München, 2000), 154-6; Pierre Prigent, *L'art des premiers chrétiens* (Paris, 1995), 159-78.

[13] Krisztina Hudák and Levente Nagy, *A Fine and Private Place: Discovering the Early Christian Cemetery of Sopianae/Pécs*, Heritage Booklets 6 (Pécs, 2009), 46.

Fig. 7. Sopianae, picture 'East Wall', photo G. Heidl.

in a depiction that we find in Sopianae. Krisztina Hudák and Levente Nagy have given a detailed description of this cycle in their book *A Fine and Private Place* (2009). According to them we find the main episodes of the Jonah story compressed into one single picture: Jonah thrown into the sea, thrown up by the Ketos or sea monster, and Jonah under the plant.

Krisztina Hudák and Levente Nagy endeavour to expound the message of this image despite the fact that its precarious state of preservation makes it difficult to decifer it from this illustration:

Jonah is shown naked and upside down, his legs between the two sailors. His left leg is clearly discernible near the face of the sailor on the left. The left sailor stands at the stern of the ship, with raised (?) arms. Right below the sailor on the left, a whale with a gray head and green body opens up his mouth to swallow up Jonah. On the right, the whale appears yet again, throwing up Jonah onto the shore. In order to compress disparate events into a single picture, the prophet literally 'falls' under a plant right next to the prow of the ship. Jonah is represented as thrown up by the whale by his legs. He already rests under the plant symbolizing the Garden of Paradise in the upper right corner of the painting. The whale (*ketos*) of the Jonah-cycle is usually represented as a four-legged, dog-eared sea monster with a curly tail. The monster of the Sopianae painting belongs to a rare type: the head of the gray beast looks like a pelican with a huge beak. The whale's body is deep green from below his neck since dark colors were usually employed to illustrate the monster. The whale has sturdy forelegs and his narrowing tail – above the lower frame, near the sailor on the left – looks like a dragon's tail. The sea is symbolized by long green lines in the lower part of the picture. While the ship is of a well-known type, its white sail takes the form of a triangle turned upside down: a highly unusual representation. Only the masthead can be seen at a distance between the heads of the two sailors, near the upper frame.

The most interesting element in the Sopianae Jonah-scene is the prophet's plant. Instead of the gourd-tree (*kolokynte, cucurbita*) commonly shown in Early Christian art, Jonah is surrounded by small, heart-shaped ivy-leaves (*hedera*, in the original Hebrew version *qiqeion*) and the characteristic gourds are also missing. The appearance of ivy-leaves in the Jonah-cycle may be a reference to the new Latin translation of the Bible credited to Jerome, and perhaps the commentary on the Book of Jonah written by Jerome in AD 296-397.[14]

According to the *Book of Jonah* its protagonist had been devoured by a fish to be spat out on the third day. Nothing in this picture reminds of *Luke* 11:29-32 or *Matth.* 16:1-4 ('No other sign will be given to you than that of Jonas'[15]) nor is any link made to Jesus' death and Resurrection 'on the third day'. The depiction shares its non-canonical message with many other Jonah-imageries, although numerous interpreters give this iconography a Christian resurrection-reading,[16] all the more as *Luke* and *Matthew* locate Jesus' mention of the sign of Jonah in his discussion with Pharisees and Sadducees. The dispute, however, was not about the resurrection of the dead, but about the arrival of the end of time, the final judgement.[17] Except the dramatic circumstances, indicated by the monster, our Sopianae-mural does not provide any of the eschatological elements either. While most early Christian Jonah depictions rather aim at typological comparisons with Christ, who offers human beings so much more than what was offered to Jonah,[18] others actualise Jonah's fate 'for preaching penitence.'[19] As many Jonah-imageries show little or no references to our canonical literature, scholars have looked for other sources of inspiration than the Gospels and pointed to non-canonical stories as *Vorlage*.[20] Although the Sopianae mural is badly preserved, it is clear that the monster, the boat, Jonah and the plant are the dominating elements of it with the plant energetically and

[14] *Ibid.* 46-8.
[15] Note that *Mark* 8:11-3 asserts that no sign at all will be given.
[16] See Eduard Stommel, 'Zum Problem der frühchristlichen Jonasdarstellungen', *JAC* 1 (1958), 112-5, 112.
[17] See Jean Allenbach, 'La figure de Jonas dans les texts préconstantiniens ou l'histoire de l'exégèse au secours de l'iconographie', in A. Benoit *et al.* (eds), *La Bible et les Pères* (Paris, 1971), 97-112, 107.
[18] See *ActPaul* 8,3; Iren., *Adv. haer.* IV 19,1; IV 52,1; V 5,2.
[19] Justin, *Dial.* 107,3, so P. Prigent, *L'art des premiers chrétiens* (1995), 177; Ernst Dassmann, *Sündenvergebung durch Taufe, Buße und Martyrerfürbitte in den Zeugnissen frühchristlicher Frömmigkeit und Kunst* (Münster i. W., 1973), 231.
[20] See E. Stommel, 'Problem' (1958), 112-4.

dynamically reaching out to Jonah in a protective embedding, while the boat, rocked by the monster, left Jonah gazing to the spectators, sharing fear, anxiety, but also determination, standing against the sea monster's attack. What might look like a challenge of Allen Brent's communal reading of early Christian art – here the single fighter against the single power of evil – on reflection becomes a critical endorsement of it. No single being can stand the powers of destruction, of illness and death, no individual escapes from being devoured by the monster of the night, no boat or community can hold the person back, but the protecting heart-formed ivy-leaves of the *qiqueion* are many, stretching out not only to surround the resting Jonah, even growing further into the scenery of the struggle between life and death, overgrowing the battlefield on sea. The Sopianae tomb was created for a family, hence, the tacit knowledge that such a space with its expressive, dramatic, yet, implicit hints brought to life was nothing to be simply grasped. It is enriched from Jewish-Christian memories, dragon phantasies, sailor's experiences in bizarre distortions of empirical natural observations, but the scene would have been enlivened by the play of light and shadow of the oil lamps in the darkness that will have brought the battle and the rescuing plant to life. Such images were not dead, sterile or abstract, they were moving, disturbing and consolating. They were not meant to be dissected or described in scholarly volumes of early Christian iconography, but experienced in the cold and fright of death together with the warmth of lamps and religionists. Too often, scholars forget that the lamplight of our high quality plates disguise this shadowy nature in which these tomb-murals were painted and experienced by both artist and viewers. Ambiguity, performance and discourse were existential challenges where past memories, visual images and liturgical routine came together. And again, it was the century old entrenched experience of a gloomy grave that carried its meaning into the fresco with the iconography of a wrestling monster and a saved Jonah, where any iconographic indication of Christ's Resurrection was absent.

The Biblical Easter narratives had not yet made their way into the cemeteries of the early Christians, but it would take a few more decades until Constantine's identification of his solar religion with that of Christianity, neatly avoided his earlier allegiance to Apollo/Sol Invictus. As a result of his influence, Bible copies in his main churches caused Christian representative arts to become informed by the Resurrection scenes of canonical Scriptures. And still, despite Constantine's conscious veneration of Christ,[21] his introduction of the Sunday, he was not less informed by his cultural past than the visitors of the Christian cemeteries.[22] Christ's Resurrection did not appear on sarcophagi of his reign,

[21] See now Klaus Martin Girardet, 'Einleitung', in *Konstantin. Rede an die Versammlung der Heiligen*, Fontes Christiani 55 (Freiburg, 2013), 49-71.
[22] See, for example, now Klaus Girardet, 'Die Christianisierung der 4. Ekloge Vergils durch Kaiser Konstantin d. Gr.', *Gymnasium* 120 (2013), 549-83, 562.

but the cross-styled *labarum* stood in the centre of the iconographical display of Passion-sarcophagi that reminded – at least for a few decades – of the shared past memory.

The Sarcophagus of Domitilla, Rome, ca. 350 AD, *Museo Pio Christiano*, Rome.

The *Sarcophagus of Domitilla* shows Simon of Cyrene carrying the Cross, the crowning of Jesus with thorns, Jesus standing in front of a soldier looking at Pilate who sits, but the middle panel does not give us a depiction of the tomb or the risen Christ, but a cross with the Chi-Rho in a wreath. The sarcophagus was found in the above mentioned catacomb of Domitilla and dates from around the mid 4th c.[23] Let us look more closely at this middle panel:

The Sarcophagus of Domitilla, Rome,
Central Panel with the crowned Cross.

[23] Richard Harries, *The Passion in Art* (Aldershot, 2004), 5; Robin Margaret Jensen, *Understanding Early Christian Art* (Oxford, 2000 = 2007).

Otto Schönewolf has shown that this iconographical motif derives from the depiction of the military sign, the Constantinian *Labarum* or the older *vexillum*, sometimes guarded by two soldiers.[24]

A coin of Constantine (c. 337) showing the labarum with Chi-Rho spearing a serpent.

Hans von Campenhausen agrees with Schönewolf's interpretation, even bases his dating of Passion-sarcophagi on it (not earlier than Constantine) and, against explicit doubts in Schönewolf, links the sitting soldiers to the guards at Jesus' tomb.[25] If we followed von Campenhausen's interpretation which, in this case, follows Klauser's empiricist way of reading early Christian iconography, and take the triumphant cross signifying life over death, we should, however, acknowledge the special character of the middle panel. To Schönewolf the given iconography was ambiguous, and even von Campenhausen himself had doubts, as he wondered about the middle panel's symbolic imagery – the sole amongst a programme of representative Biblical scenes. Why was there not a scene of the Resurrection, as we find it some decades later, but the symbol of the triumphant cross in the midst of figurative scenes? Von Campenhausen concludes that symbolism was the best medium to express the deep theological meaning beyond history. If he were correct, it is hard to explain, why subsequently this triumphant cross scenary became so quickly misunderstood and the tomb guards degenerated, becoming deer, birds, or a lamb.[26] Schönewolf's scepticism is closer to our reading when we see the power of tradition in the continuation of the older Roman image of soldiers guarding the *labarum*-cross which, in other cases, were replaced by other symbols reminding rather of paradise sceneries, fitting the imagery of the wreath. Perhaps the victorious cross was read as the sign for the imperial power of preservation and salvation, expressed in the military sign of breaking the enemy's power, the power of death that has been overcome by Christ who brought victory.[27]

---

[24] See Otto Schönewolf, *Die Darstellung der Auferstehung Christi* (Leipzig, 1909), 3-22; on this type of depiction on sarcophagus see G. Koch, *Frühchristliche Sarkophage* (2000), 194-5.

[25] Hans Freiherr von Campenhausen, 'Die Passionssarkophage', *Marburger Jahrbuch für Kunstwissenschaft* 5 (1929), 39-85, 52-3, 78-9.

[26] See the examples in *ibid.* 80.

[27] H. v. Campenhausen, 'Die Passionssarkophage' (1929), 81.

How much earlier this confluence of imagery and Christian theology took place can be seen by retrospection into pre-Constantinian solar crosses, as known, for example from the Pannonian region.

Although we are not sure from where Constantine's solar cult originated,[28] the first dedication to Sol Invictus we know of dates back only to 158 AD:

To the God Sol Invictus / in accordance with the vow he had made / upon his accepted discharge / an honorable from the / equestrian guard of the emperor P[ublius] / Aelius Amandus / d[e]d[icated this] during Tertullus' and / Sacerdos' consulship.[29]

The cult became officially introduced into the wider Roman Empire by Aurelian (270-275). Zoroastrian and Mithraic elements are discernible, [in] their dualism between darkness and light, the victory of good over evil, life surrendering death, and a super-powerful solar deity that fights against and wins over any divine power below it. Thus it formed a monotheism above a Graeco Roman pantheon. This connection between Mithras and Deus Sol can be seen from depictions on monuments at Sopianae.[30] When Constantine 'entered Rome as its master on 29 October 312, the day after the Battle of the Milvian Bridge, which he fought under a Christian banner and in which he defeated Maxentius, who had ruled the city for six years', he took residence 'in Rome for the whole of the months of November and December 312 and remained in the city until at least 6 January 313 (CTh 15.4.3). During this period of little more than two months, Constantine, who had only announced that he was a devotee of the Christian God shortly before the Battle of the Milvian Bridge, began to lavish wealth on the Christian church and bestow privileges on Christian clergy.'[31] The victory in the sign of Christ – identical or at least equated with that of *Sol invictus* – was the trigger for Constantine. He not only proclaimed his Christianity, but also stamped his *Sol invictus* onto Christianity, interpreting the outcome as a mystery with which he himself identified in distinction to what he now considered as evil, alien, past or a *contagiosa superstitio*.[32] Timothy D. Barnes thinks that there are good reasons to believe that it was Constantine

---

[28] Gaston H. Halsberghe, *Études préliminaires aux religions orientales dans l'Empire Romain* (Leiden, 1972).

[29] *CIL* VI 715 : '*Soli Invicto deo / ex voto suscepto / accepta missione / honesta ex nume/ro eq(uitum) sing(ularium) Aug(usti) P(ublius) / Aelius Amandus / d(e)d(icavit) Tertullo et / Sacerdoti co(n)s(ulibus)*', see G.H. Halsberghe, *Études préliminaires* (1972), 45.

[30] See, for example, at Sopianae in Ferenc Fülep, *Sopianae: The History of Pécs during the Roman Era, and the Problem of the Continuity of the Late Roman Population*, Archaeologia Hungarica 50 (Budapest, 1984), 278.

[31] Timothy D. Barnes, 'The First Christmas in Rome, Antioch and Constantinople', *SP* (forthcoming).

[32] On 'evil' see Const., *Or. ad sanct.* 1,5 (128,18 Girardet); on 'superstition' see *ibid.* 16,1 (188,11 Girardet), *CTh* IX 16,1 (*superstitio*); on 'past' see *CTh* IX 16,2 (*praeteritae usurpationis officia*); on 'evil' see *CTh* XVI 2,5 (*ritus alienae superstitionis*); on *contigia superstitio* see also ILS 705 (inscription of Hispellum), l. 46-8: *contagios[a]e superstitionis fraudes*; see also

who 'fixed the date of Christmas by celebrating the Incarnation of his new Christian God on 25 December 312'.[33] Constantine also introduced the planetary week into the Roman calendar and with him came the alteration of the content of Christian Easter, which up to his time was a celebration of Christ's salvific death, but now became the day of the risen sun, of Christ's Resurrection. 'Constantine apparently never would or could differentiate Sol from Christ or separate the two ultimately', even if he chose to speak of Christ rather than of Sol.[34] How could he, as for centuries Romans were used to adopt and adapt foreign deities, introduced them in their own pantheon and saw these new arrivals in the light of their previous beliefs. Their own tradition provided the hermeneutical frame that gave meaning to the foreign imports, acknowledging that with every such input also a full range of new names, scriptures, symbolisms and ethical agendas were added to the existing one. Migotti thinks that 'Constantine's institutionalization of the connection between Sol and Christ was accompanied by the conscious creation of an iconography associating the Sun and the cross'. It highlights that Constantines decisions to introduce new feasts, calendar-frames and alter the content of existing Christian feasts to match what he perceived and prescribed as being Roman, heavily impacted on Christian iconography. Constantine's artists could make use of an existing range of imageries which had already associated cross and sun, like these Pendants from Sisak:

Fig. 8.1-8.3[35].

K. Girardet, 'Die Christianisierung der 4. Ekloge Vergils durch Kaiser Konstantin d. Gr.' (2013), 551, and id., 'Einleitung' (2013), 71.

[33] T. D. Barnes, 'The First Christmas in Rome, Antioch and Constantinople', *SP* (forthcoming).

[34] Branka Migotti, *Evidence for Christianity in Roman Southern Pannonia (Northern Croatia): A Catalogue of Finds and Sites*, BAR International Series 684 (Oxford, 1997), 10.

[35] Fig. 1: B. Migotti, *Evidence for Christianity* (1997), 10 S.1; fig. 2: *ibid.* 10 S.2; fig. 3: *ibid.* S.3; see also others *ibid.* S.4; *ibid.* 12 S.5; S.6; *ibid.* 13 S.7.

How important the tradition of *Sol invictus* for the interpretation of Christ's cross was, can also be seen from many altarstones, found in Christian quarters of settlements, for example, in Pécs.[36] Despite the emergence of representative Christian art in the 5th c. and onwards, the centrality of the older Roman cross never diminished.

---

[36] See F. Fülep, *Sopianae* (1984), 259 S/13 (CIL III 14038), S/14 (10284), S/15 (the two latter dated to the turn of the third and fourth centuries, so *ibid.* 257).

PRINTED ON PERMANENT PAPER • IMPRIME SUR PAPIER PERMANENT • GEDRUKT OP DUURZAAM PAPIER - ISO 9706

N.V. PEETERS S.A., WAROTSTRAAT 50, B-3020 HERENT